WRITING PLACEMENT IN TWO-YEAR COLLEGES

THE PURSUIT OF EQUITY IN POSTSECONDARY EDUCATION

Practices & Possibilities

Series Editors: Aimee McClure, Mike Palmquist, and Aleashia Walton
Series Associate Editor: Jagadish Paudel

The Practices & Possibilities Series addresses the full range of practices within the field of Writing Studies, including teaching, learning, research, and theory. From Richard E. Young's taxonomy of "small genres" to Patricia Freitag Ericsson's edited collection on sexual harassment in the academy to Jessie Borgman and Casey McArdle's considerations of teaching online, the books in this series explore issues and ideas of interest to writers, teachers, researchers, and theorists who share an interest in improving existing practices and exploring new possibilities. The series includes both original and republished books. Works in the series are organized topically.

The WAC Clearinghouse and University Press of Colorado are collaborating so that these books will be widely available through free digital distribution and low-cost print editions. The publishers and the series editors are committed to the principle that knowledge should freely circulate and have embraced the use of technology to support open access to scholarly work.

Other Books in the Series

Natalie M. Dorfeld (Ed.), *The Invisible Professor: The Precarious Lives of the New Faculty Majority* (2022)

Aimée Knight, *Community is the Way: Engaged Writing and Designing for Transformative Change* (2022)

Jennifer Clary-Lemon, Derek Mueller, and Kate Pantelides, *Try This: Research Methods for Writers* (2022)

Jessie Borgman and Casey McArdle (Eds.), *PARS in Practice: More Resources and Strategies for Online Writing Instructors* (2021)

Mary Ann Dellinger and D. Alexis Hart (Eds.), *ePortfolios@edu: What We Know, What We Don't Know, And Everything In-Between* (2020)

Jo-Anne Kerr and Ann N. Amicucci (Eds.), *Stories from First-Year Composition: Pedagogies that Foster Student Agency and Writing Identity* (2020)

Patricia Freitag Ericsson, *Sexual Harassment and Cultural Change in Writing Studies* (2020)

Ryan J. Dippre, *Talk, Tools, and Texts: A Logic-in-Use for Studying Lifespan Literate Action Development* (2019)

Jessie Borgman and Casey McArdle, *Personal, Accessible, Responsive, Strategic: Resources and Strategies for Online Writing Instructors* (2019)

Cheryl Geisler and Jason Swarts, *Coding Streams of Language: Techniques for the Systematic Coding of Text, Talk, and Other Verbal Data* (2019)

WRITING PLACEMENT IN TWO-YEAR COLLEGES
THE PURSUIT OF EQUITY IN POSTSECONDARY EDUCATION

Edited by Jessica Nastal, Mya Poe, and Christie Toth

The WAC Clearinghouse
wac.colostate.edu
Fort Collins, Colorado

University Press of Colorado
upcolorado.com
Denver, Colorado

The WAC Clearinghouse, Fort Collins, Colorado 80523

University Press of Colorado, Denver, Colorado 80027

© 2022 by Jessica Nastal, Mya Poe, and Christie Toth. This work is released under a Creative Commons Attribution-NonCommercial-NoDerivatives 4.0 International license.

ISBN 978-1-64215-156-5 (PDF) | 978-1-64215-157-2 (ePub) | 978-1-64642-379-8 (pbk.)

DOI 10.37514/PRA-B.2022.1565

Library of Congress Cataloging-in-Publication Data

Names: Nastal, Jessica, 1980– editor. | Poe, Mya, 1970– editor. | Toth, Christie, editor.
Title: Writing placement in two-year colleges : the pursuit of equity in postsecondary education / edited by Jessica Nastal, Mya Poe, and Christie Toth.
Description: Fort Collins, Colorado : The WAC Clearinghouse, [2022] | Series: Practices & possibilities | Includes bibliographical references.
Identifiers: LCCN 2022036310 (print) | LCCN 2022036311 (ebook) | ISBN 9781646423798 (paperback) | ISBN 9781642151565 (adobe pdf) | ISBN 9781642151572 (epub)
Subjects: LCSH: English language—Rhetoric—Study and teaching—United States—Evaluation—Case studies. | Universities and colleges—United States—Entrance examinations—Case studies. | College students—Rating of—United States—Case studies. | Junior colleges—United States—Case studies. | Educational equalization—United States—Case studies.
Classification: LCC PE1405.U6 W7565 2022 (print) | LCC PE1405.U6 (ebook) | DDC 808/.042076—dc23/eng/20220915
LC record available at https://lccn.loc.gov/2022036310
LC ebook record available at https://lccn.loc.gov/2022036311

Copyeditor: Meg Vezzu
Designer: Mike Palmquist
Cover Art: Pine Green (2022) by Julie C. Baer. Egg tempera and aquarelle pencil on paper. From the artist's Confluence series (https://www.juliebaer.com). Used with permission.
Series Editors: Aimee McClure, Mike Palmquist, and Aleashia Walton
Series Associate Editor: Jagadish Paudel

The WAC Clearinghouse supports teachers of writing across the disciplines. Hosted by Colorado State University, it brings together scholarly journals and book series as well as resources for teachers who use writing in their courses. This book is available in digital formats for free download at wac.colostate.edu.

Founded in 1965, the University Press of Colorado is a nonprofit cooperative publishing enterprise supported, in part, by Adams State University, Colorado State University, Fort Lewis College, Metropolitan State University of Denver, University of Alaska Fairbanks, University of Colorado, University of Denver, University of Northern Colorado, University of Wyoming, Utah State University, and Western Colorado University. For more information, visit upcolorado.com.

Land Acknowledgment. The Colorado State University Land Acknowledgment can be found at https://landacknowledgment.colostate.edu.

Contents

Acknowledgments vii

Foreword ix
    Lizbett Tinoco

Introduction 3
    Jessica Nastal, Mya Poe, and Christie Toth

PART ONE. THE LONG ROAD OF PLACEMENT REFORM

Chapter 1. No Reform Is an Island: Tracing the Influences and Consequences of Evidence-Based Placement Reform at a Two-Year Predominantly Black Institution 35
    Jessica Nastal, Jason Evans, and Jessica Gravely

Chapter 2. From ACCUPLACER to Informed Self-Placement at Whatcom Community College: Equitable Placement as an Evolving Practice 59
    Jeffrey Klausman and Signee Lynch

Chapter 3. A Path to Equity, Agency, and Access: Self-Directed Placement at the Community College of Baltimore County 85
    Kris Messer, Jamey Gallagher, and Elizabeth Hart

Chapter 4. Welcome/Not Welcome: From Discouragement to Empowerment in the Writing Placement Process at Central Oregon Community College. 107
    Jane Denison-Furness, Stacey Lee Donohue,
    Annemarie Hamlin, and Tony Russell

PART TWO. INNOVATION AND EQUITY IN PLACEMENT REFORM

Chapter 5. Narrowing the Divide in Placement at a Hispanic-Serving Institution: The Case of Yakima Valley College 131
    Carolyn Calhoon-Dillahunt and Travis Margoni

Chapter 6. Putting ACCUPLACER in Its Place: Expanding Evidence in Placement Reform at Jamestown Community College. 151
    Jessica M. Kubiak

Chapter 7. Tracking the Racial Consequences of Placement by Probability: A Case Study at Kingsborough Community College 173
    Annie Del Principe, Lesley Broder, and Lauren Levesque

Chapter 8. Mind the (Linguistic) Gap: On "Flagging" ESL Students at Queensborough Community College 191
    Charissa Che

PART THREE. PANDEMIC-PRECIPITATED PLACEMENT REFORM

Chapter 9. Pandemic Placement at Cuyahoga Community College: A Case Study 225
    Ashlee Brand and Bridget Kriner

Chapter 10. A Complement to Educational Reform: Directed Self-Placement (DSP) at Cochise College................................. 243
    Ella Melito, Erin Whittig, Cathy Sander Matthesen, and Denisse Cañez

Chapter 11. Community College Online Directed Self-Placement During the COVID-19 Pandemic 263
    Sarah Elizabeth Snyder, Sara Amani, and Kevin Kato

Afterword. Placement, Equity, and the Promise of Democratic Open-Access Education 279
    Darin L. Jensen and Joanne Baird Giordano

Contributors 287

Acknowledgments

To the contributors of this collection for their perseverance and dedication to our students, and to the students who give our work purpose. To Norbert Elliot, for his friendship and for his unending work in assessment to uphold students' dignity. To the family, friends, and colleagues who have sustained me in the midst of a global pandemic: Robert and Patti Nastal, Drew and Colleen Nastal, Ariana and Deane Pantaleo, Bridie, Jules, Ava, Rowan, James, Beau, Tom Brennan and Diane Monnich, Albert Letizia, Michael Lewis, John Raucci, Bethany Johnsen, Ashley Rowden, Hanna Auza, Christine Brooms, William Condon, Melanie Eddins-Spencer, Jason Evans, Christopher Fogarty, Jessica Gravely, Angela Hung, Andrew Schott, Dana Trunnell, Justin Vidovic. To Elise Blaise, who fills my life with joy. Thank you to Mya and Christie, too.

— J.N.

My deepest thanks to my colleagues, Jessica, Christie, and the remarkable contributors to this collection. A special thanks to my dear friend, mentor, and collaborator, Norbert Elliot who has helped me navigate many troubled waters and inspired me to reach further. Thank you to the scholarly muses who have long shaped thinking—Gloria Ladson-Billings, bell hooks, Sonia Nieto, Arnetha Ball, Geneva Smitherman, Keith Gilyard, Tukufu Zuberi, and Asa Hilliard III. I return to you often. Thank you to the kick-ass muses who push my thinking today—Ellen Cushman, Jennifer Randall, David Slomp, Maria Elena Olivera, and Tieanna Graphenreed—and to the fearless data queens—Qianqian Zhang-Wu, Cherice Escobar Jones, Cara Marta Messina, and Devon Regan. Thank you to my husband John Aloysius Cogan Jr. who shares in working to change the needlessly cruel processes of inequity while co-managing a wild household. And as always, to my children and other people's children who sent me on this journey decades ago.

— M.P.

Thank you to mentors Hildy Miller, Steve Reder, Anne Ruggles Gere, and Laura Aull, all of whom provided me with early opportunities to learn about writing placement. Special thanks to the many two-year college colleagues who have taught me so much about writing placement in open admissions settings over the last decade, with particular shout-outs to community college faculty in Washington, Arizona, and the City University of New York. Finally, thank you to my partner, Ben, and to our elders—Mom, Stuart, Faith, Off, and John—who shouldered so much childcare while I worked on this collection through the pandemic.

— C.T.

A special thanks to the team at the WAC Clearinghouse—Aimee McClure, Aleashia Walton, Jagadish Paudel, and Mike Palmquist. Your unfailing support of academic scholarship is a gift.

Thank you to the anonymous reviewers for their support of this project. We appreciate your wisdom in helping us guide this collection. And thank you to copyeditor Meg Vezzu for the care and diligence you put into this project.

A special thank you to Julie Baer for graciously allowing us to use her image as cover art for this collection. The contributors in this collection are drawn to the vibrant colors Baer chose for Pine Green and to the idea of confluence—of bringing ideas together from disparate locations. For Baer, confluence was to acknowledge the multiple forces that brought her back to painting after a 15-year hiatus as a writing teacher. The artwork reminds us that nature is foundational, beautiful, and functional, systematic and adaptive—and that assessment systems, too, are a dynamic part of larger ecologies within education.

— J.N., M.P., and C.T.

Foreword

Lizbett Tinoco
Texas A&M University–San Antonio

Beginning with a doctoral class on writing program administration and continuing throughout my doctoral coursework, I noticed the limited integration of writing scholarship about two-year colleges and produced by two-year college scholars. Having worked as an adjunct faculty at various community colleges in California and later in Texas and New Mexico, I devoted my earliest research efforts to examining the various ways writing program administrators are teacher-scholar-activists (Sullivan, 2015) constantly working to advocate for change within their departments and programs (Tinoco, forthcoming). The case studies in *Writing Placement in Two-Year Colleges: The Pursuit of Equity in Postsecondary Education* are a powerful example of this advocacy and activism as the authors in this collection ask readers to bear witness to the inequities caused by writing placement—such as systemic under-placement, cost in tuition, and persistence—and share ways two-year college writing faculty are redressing the harm inflicted on students.

Writing Placement in Two-Year Colleges: The Pursuit of Equity in Postsecondary Education both acknowledges the harm caused by placement and offers approaches to more equitable writing placement. For example, it lets readers experience moments like those described by Jessica Nastal, Jason Evans, and Jessica Gravely, who share how their department at a predominately Black two-year college did not analyze disaggregated placement data to examine racial and equity disparities caused by their placement process. In another example, Jeffrey Klausman and Signee Lynch share that prior to placement reforms, their institution's ACCUPLACER cut-off score placed only about 30 percent of students into their English 101 course. Additionally, Charissa Che demonstrates that state-mandated placement mechanisms meant to close the equity gap can still be rooted in standard English language ideologies that harm linguistically diverse students. Bringing forth and making these things visible is risky, but the authors also show how acknowledging these injustices offers possibilities for radical change.

If we want institutions to move away from commercial, automated, computer-based placement exams and adopt more equitable approaches to writing placement as a response to the recommendations of the 2016 TYCA White Paper on Placement Reform (Klausman et al., 2016) and Mya Poe and Asao B. Inoue's (2016) call for socially just writing assessment, then we must direct our attention to the possibilities offered in this collection. *Writing Placement in Two-Year Colleges: The Pursuit of Equity in Postsecondary Education* shows readers how placement reform, whether it be multiple measures, directed self-placement, or informed self-placement, has closed equity gaps, and in some cases, created almost no equity gap, as seen at one two-year college. Annie Del Principe, Lesley Broder, and Lauren Levesque share how placement reform has reduced the number of developmental writing courses at their college from more than 100 sections to seven. We also learn from Calhoon-Dillahunt and Margoni how placement reform has facilitated professional development on antiracist and equitable assessment. The authors in this collection share their intellectual experiences as they develop placement practices that meet the needs of their students, all while their work starts to create small but significant campus-wide shifts towards ongoing equity work.

Although placement reforms were in action at various institutions in this collection well before the COVID-19 pandemic, the third section of this book, "Pandemic-Precipitated Placement Reform," hones in on the opportunities created by the kairotic moment caused by the pandemic's disruptions. I write this foreword still in the midst of the pandemic, but over the last two years, we have all seen how the COVID-19 pandemic has altered higher education. For some of the authors in this collection, the pandemic created an exigency for placement reform as institutions and faculty were required to make dramatic adjustments to their placement practices, specifically how they used unproctored placement exams. Remote instruction considerably complicated the delivery of student services. Scholars, such as Brand and Kriner, in this last section of Writing Placement in *Two-Year Colleges: The Pursuit of Equity in Postsecondary Education* demonstrate how they were able to implement placement methods that met the needs of their student body amidst the pandemic. Even though the pandemic allowed for placement reform to occur, such as the online direct self-placement discussed by Sarah Elizabeth Snyder, Sara Amani, and Kevin Kato (this collection), they do caution us about the consequences of implementing such rapid, emergency placement, especially for multilingual students. This section of the book reminds us all to not sacrifice the opportunities the pandemic has presented for us to learn and improve our writing placement.

Through the case studies brought together in this book, the authors help teachers, researchers, and administrators understand the complexities in leading placement reform at two-year colleges. They show us how state laws and policies, local contexts, and resources can hinder or facilitate this work. They show us that the work of writing placement requires their disciplinary and professional knowledge, *and* it should not only be the work of English faculty but the entire institution. The writers demonstrate that this process needs institution-wide support—from institutional research to grant funding to support from faculty, administrators, advisors, IT, and information systems staff. In writing their stories, the authors illustrate the importance of placement reforms being developed by faculty who understand their institutional context and student demographics. These scholars remind us that placement also needs continual revision to fit the changing student demographics of not only two-year colleges but all institutions of higher education.

Writing Placement in Two-Year Colleges: The Pursuit of Equity in Postsecondary Education contributes to our body of disciplinary knowledge on writing assessment ecologies (Inoue, 2015), allowing us to reimagine the radical possibilities of writing assessment beyond the classroom. But more importantly, this collection reminds us that scholars at two-year colleges are at the forefront of advocating for and developing transformative and humanizing writing placement assessments that create more equitable conditions for historically minoritized students at two-year colleges.

References

Inoue, A. B. (2015). *Antiracist writing assessment ecologies: Teaching and assessing writing for a socially just future.* The WAC Clearinghouse; Parlor Press. https://doi.org/10.37514/PER-B.2015.0698.

Klausman, J., Roberts, L., Giordano, J., Griffiths, B., Sullivan, P., Swyt, W., Toth, C., Warnke, A. & Williams, A. L. (2016). TYCA white paper on placement reform. *Teaching English in the Two-Year College, 44*(2), 135–157. https://cdn.ncte.org/nctefiles/groups/tyca/placementreform_revised.pdf.

Poe, M. & Inoue, A. B. (2016). Toward writing as social justice: An idea whose time has come. *College English, 79*(2), 119–126.

Sullivan, P. (2015). The two-year college teacher-scholar-activist. *Teaching English in the Two-Year College, 42*(4), 327–350.

Tinoco, L. (forthcoming). Community college WPAs creating change through advocacy. In L. Graziano, K. Halasek, R. Hudgins, S. Miller-Cochran, F. Napolitano & N. Szymanski (Eds.), *Making administrative work visible: Data-driven advocacy for understanding the labor of writing program administration.* Utah State University Press.

WRITING PLACEMENT IN TWO-YEAR COLLEGES
THE PURSUIT OF EQUITY IN POSTSECONDARY EDUCATION

Introduction

Jessica Nastal
PRAIRIE STATE COLLEGE

Mya Poe
NORTHEASTERN UNIVERSITY

Christie Toth
UNIVERSITY OF UTAH

Since the mid-twentieth century, two-year colleges—known historically as junior colleges, technical colleges, and community colleges, depending on the specific mission and programming of the institution—have served a critical function as an open-admissions pathway to postsecondary education for a wide range of students.[1]

With more than 1,000 two-year colleges in the US, including 936 public colleges, 35 tribal colleges, and 73 independent colleges (American Association of Community Colleges [AACC], 2021), these institutions encompass a wide range of educational and geographic spaces. Two-year colleges serve an enormous number of students, annually includi ng 6.8 million credit-seeking students and 5.0 million non-credit-seeking students. During the 2018–2019 academic year alone, two-year colleges awarded 20,700 baccalaureate degrees in addition to 878,900 associate degrees and 619,711 certificates (American Association of Community Colleges, 2021).

These institutions provide local educational access, offering non-credit coursework in high school equivalency, adult basic education, English as a second or additional language, and lifelong learning for community members; developmental courses for those institutionally classified as underprepared for college coursework; vocational degrees and certificates (often with close ties to local industries); transfer-oriented general education and associate programs for those pursuing bachelor's degrees; as well as growing dual/concurrent enrollment and early college initiatives for high school students (Cohen et al., 2014).

Two-year colleges are new majority institutions. Of students enrolled in credit-earning coursework at two-year colleges, 27 percent are Hispanic/Latinx, 13 percent are Black, 44 percent are White, 6 percent are Asian or Pacific Islander, 1 percent are Native American, 4 percent identify as two or more races, 4 percent

---

1. Adapted with permission from "Introduction: Writing Assessment, Placement, and the Two-Year College" by Christie Toth, Jessica Nastal, Holly Hassel, and Joanne Baird Giordano, which appeared in the 2019 special issue on two-year college writing placement in the *Journal of Writing Assessment*.

identify as "other/unknown," and 2 percent are international students (AACC, 2021). Diversity data are even more revealing when compared to percentages of the national undergraduate population from underrepresented groups. Two-year colleges enroll 56 percent of Native American undergraduates, 52 percent of Hispanic/Latinx students, and 43 percent of Black students nationally (AACC, 2017); 29 percent of community college students are in the first generation of their family to attend college (AACC, 2021). Community college students are also more likely than students at four-year institutions to be older than age 24, returning to higher education, parents, veterans, immigrants or refugees, DACA recipients or unDACAmented, and/or students with disabilities (Cohen et al., 2014). More than one-third of Pell Grant recipients attend two-year colleges, and nearly 80 percent are working students (AACC, 2022). Two-year college students are more likely than those at four-year institutions to work full-time and be the main source of family care.

Two-year colleges provide a crucial point of entry to students who would otherwise be unable to access (or re-access) public postsecondary education. Many of these students are not making "market" choices between two- and four-year institutions, but rather between two-year colleges or no college at all, or between two-year colleges and for-profit institutions that may leave them deep in debt with unimproved employment prospects (Toth et al., 2016). To the extent that writing assessment—for placement, in the classroom, or as a requirement for exiting required course sequences—functions to support or undermine student success at two-year colleges, it plays a key role in either opening or foreclosing access to learning, credentials, and, ultimately, socioeconomic mobility for some of the least advantaged students in the U.S. postsecondary system. This reality has become all the more pressing since Spring 2020, when the COVID-19 pandemic hit hardest many of the communities most likely to enroll in two-year colleges.

The pandemic has caused massive and inequitable human suffering, both nationally and globally. It disrupted face-to-face instruction at all institution types, with the least advantaged students experiencing disproportionate harm in terms of course completion and semester-to-semester retention (U.S. Department of Education, 2021). It also disrupted the on-site, proctored placement testing used at many community colleges. For faculty, researchers, and policymakers who had been advocating for placement reform, this upheaval created a(nother) kairotic opening. Throughout the spring and summer of 2020, two-year college writing faculty queried professional listservs about placement options and shared materials from placement reforms already underway (e.g., Benton, 2020). Several of us who worked on the 2019 special issue of the *Journal of Writing Assessment* (*JWA*) on two-year college writing placement were contacted by colleagues across the country seeking advice on redesigning their placement processes. Many contributors to this collection, most of whom submitted chapter proposals prior to the pandemic, found themselves writing case studies of placement reform in the time of COVID.

Published research on this subject is only just beginning to appear, but initial studies suggest the pandemic has accelerated large-scale changes to placement. A January 2021 report from the Center for the Analysis of Postsecondary Readiness stated, "Perhaps counterintuitively, the onset of COVID-19 created opportunities for state systems to facilitate institutional adoption of multiple measures assessment" (Bickerstaff et al., 2021, p. 2). The report describes pandemic-driven moves to large-scale multiple measures assessment (MMA) for placement in Indiana, Virginia, Texas, and Washington; in Virginia and Washington community colleges, direct, informed, or "guided" self-placement (DSP/ISP/GSP) options were implemented or expanded for at least some groups of students ((Bickerstaff et al., 2021, pp. 5, 8). The authors of the report view those movements favorably, stating,

> The pandemic has . . . created opportunities for institutions to decrease their reliance on standardized assessments. This can serve to help more students enroll in college courses sooner, with the aim of reducing disparities in outcomes and improving student success. (Bickerstaff et al., 2021, p. 9)

Yet, at least in the short-term, enrollments at community colleges nationwide have declined sharply and inequitably. According to the National Student Clearinghouse Research Center (2021), "While declines in undergraduate enrollment [have been] evident across all institutional sectors, community colleges remain hardest hit [in Spring 2021] (-9.5%, 476,000 fewer students)" (p. 1). Those declines have continued into the 2021–2022 academic year (National Student Clearinghouse Research Center [NSCRC], 2021), where two-year colleges are at a 13.5 percent decline in enrollment since Fall 2019 (NSCRC, 2022). These broad dynamics are playing out in specific contexts shaped by institutional histories and structures, emplaced manifestations of political polarization, and local diversities/structures of inequality.

Writing Placement in Two-Year Colleges: The Pursuit of Equity in Postsecondary Education was born out of a history of placement innovation at two-year colleges that has been given new visibility in the pandemic. As the case studies in this volume demonstrate, some two-year college faculty have been seizing the national moment of reform as an opportunity to challenge the idea that writing placement is ideologically or consequentially neutral and to develop more equitable approaches to writing placement. Moreover, as the chapters in this collection make clear, changes to placement are only part of a much more complex, resource-intensive process of making it possible for all students—including the hundreds of thousands of expected students who did not show up for college in 2021—to pursue their interests and achieve their goals through open-admissions two-year colleges.

In this introductory chapter, which is adapted and updated from the introduction to the 2019 special issue of *JWA*, we lay out several layers of context for this moment of potential transformation we are navigating in the opening years of the 2020s. These layers include the critical interrogation of the assumptions long underpinning two-year college writing placement, the broader policy context for two-year college placement reform, ongoing effort to gain greater visibility for two-year colleges in writing assessment scholarship, and the implications of the ethical turn in writing assessment for placement reform. We then present an overview of the chapters in this collection, each of which presents a site-specific case study of two-year college placement reform at the turn of the decade. These case studies exemplify how the strands we trace here play out in local contexts while identifying complex challenges and new possibilities for placement in the wake of COVID. We close with a discussion of directions for future research and praxis.

Interrogating the Assumptions of "Placement"

Today, few would argue that traditional high-stakes, single-score purchased placement tests are accurate or fair for the purposes of placing students into writing courses. However, we often do not step back from such debates to reflect on the larger ecology in which placement testing was developed and continues to operate. Placement is a writing assessment process unique to postsecondary education in the United States (Haswell, 2004). While other countries use proficiency testing for institutional admissions, many U.S. colleges use placement assessments once students have already been admitted. In the nation's open-admissions two-year colleges, where students enter from a wide range of academic trajectories and often have not taken any kind of admissions exam, placement assessment is nearly universal. The rationale for placement hinges on the following argument:

1. Placement testing identifies students with the weakest writing abilities.
2. In order to boost those abilities, placement tests funnel students into specific classes or sections where instruction can be more manageable and students can learn better.
3. Therefore, placement testing leads to improved student learning, retention, and completion.

This rationale is predicated on the algorithmic, decision-tree approach to placement advanced by Warren W. Willingham (1974, p. 71) more than four decades ago. Willingham's model is a closed system—i.e., a system in which "mastery" of "skills" lies within the bounds of the placement test and the "post-test." The model relies on a linear progression of a preset notion of expertise labeled as skills: Students demonstrate mastery of Skill A; they are then tested on Skill A; those who succeed on test of Skill A progress to Skill B (which relies on Skill A); those who fail on test of Skill A return to the beginning of the unit. The construct of "skill" is not questioned and neither is the assumption that Skill B is dependent on Skill A. Another assumption regarding the necessity of placement into writing courses, as Michael Kane (1990) has identified, is "that performance on the placement test is relevant to readiness for the . . . course" (p. 11). Over the last several decades, however, we have learned much about the recursive nature of writing. We know, for instance, that decontextualized grammar-usage-mechanics instruction does not necessarily lead to improved writing; as a result, placement assessments that rely on outdated notions of the writing construct are often neither valid, reliable, nor fair. The traditional placement algorithm is a model in which the student has no agency beyond demonstration of skills that may not be relevant to the writing course. The assessment process has been stripped from institutional or community context, which are essential aspects of any communicative act.

Willingham's binaristic, decontextualized model has not only become the tacit theory undergirding most writing placement, it has also been a technological apparatus mapped onto discussions of standards and equity. Thirty-five years ago, Edward A. Morante (1987) argued that placement tests and their corresponding cut scores "play important roles in access, retention, and quality" (p. 63), asserting, "To dump everyone in the same level of course is significantly to increase the probability of lowering standards or of failing many students" (p. 63). A decade later, Edward White (1995) claimed placement testing "[serves] to help underprepared students succeed instead of washing them out . . . these are the students for whom required placement and the required freshman course are necessary, for they are most in need of guidance and support" (pp. 76–77).

Assumptions that map the technology of placement testing onto discourses of standards and equity have not gone unchallenged. Teacher-scholars like Richard Haswell (2004) questioned the test-retest reliability of placement exams when students have been found to change their score significantly the second time they take the test. He compellingly demonstrated how research conducted since placement testing began with the 1874 Harvard entrance exams shows both indirect and direct methods of testing do little in the way of predicting student success (Haswell, 2004). Likewise, William L. Smith (1993) analyzed the locally designed test at University of Pittsburgh, which used a robust scoring method that relied on its expert teachers, and found that 14 percent of students were under-placed. While this may seem like a "good enough" number for some, Smith (1993) argued, "For the students and for the teachers, 'very few' [underplacing] is too many" (p. 192). This limited ability for placement exam scores to predict which writing course is best suited for a student is precisely what led ACT to halt the COMPASS placement exam in 2015.

Placement testing has also been mapped onto discourses about teacher efficiency. Indeed, placement has long been viewed as necessary to increase the productivity of both instructors and students in writing classes. The perceived value of such efficiency relates directly to the material conditions of postsecondary writing instruction, especially at two-year colleges where undercompensated and not-always-well-supported adjunct faculty teach many of the writing courses. In these settings, sorting based on abilities is presumed to help ease the labor of teaching.

Because writing assessment has often been driven by such questions of efficiency (see Williamson, 1994; Yancey, 1999), this orientation treats composition courses as a necessary burden for both students and the institution. In recent decades, writing program administrators and writing studies teacher-scholars have made headway in shifting the conversation about college composition from teaching "basic skills" to engaging students around disciplinarily-informed insights that help prime them for life-long development as critical readers, writers, and community members. At many institutions, however—and particularly at two-year colleges, where writing faculty often have less disciplinary authority over assessment—placement into composition courses is still viewed *not* as a pivotal educational moment for introducing students to local pedagogical orientations and the valued construct of writing, but rather a mechanism for putting students in their "proper" seats quickly, easily, and inexpensively. This perspective has led to the proliferation of methods that leave unaddressed critical questions about what accuracy means, how it might shift depending on the stakeholder, and what messages placement conveys.

Ultimately, placement testing does more than direct students into certain courses. Placement is an introduction to the institution and how it conceives of writing (Harrington, 2005, p. 15). It communicates specific cultural values, language ideologies, and expectations to test-takers and participants: In short, it communicates power. It can replicate or trouble inequitable social structures; it can support or challenge the current era of testing/assessment despair (Gallagher, 2007). Decontextualized algorithmic approaches to placement offer little helpful information about the ways most composition teacher-scholars conceive of writing. For too long, the widespread reliance on commercially produced tests that measure a limited construct of writing has prioritized knowledge of Edited American English conventions at the expense of any other capacity, primarily because these are the skills that can be easily measured through multiple-choice tests (Huddleston, 1954; Stein, 2016; Williamson, 1994), quickly written paragraphs (Bereiter, 2003; Faigley et al., 1985), and automated writing evaluation (AWE) software (Burstein, 2012). Placement assessments with such limited construct representation might work to quickly put students into writing classes. They do little, however, to expand the narrow conceptions of writing held by much of the public, conceptions bolstered by that public's experiences with school-based writing assessment. They certainly do not prepare students for longer-term rhetorical awareness and writing knowledge transfer.

Traditional placement models communicate inaccurate and counterproductive messages about what we value in college writing; they appear to misplace students at unacceptable and often inequitable rates; they fail to assess key capacities necessary for college success; and they do not provide information about what kinds of supplementary supports might benefit students—something that contextualized, nonbinaristic measures with broader construct representation can offer (Hassel & Giordano, 2015). At two-year institutions, the consequences of poor placement practices are not simply a matter of how many credit-bearing writing courses a student will need to complete. In an unreformed two-year college curriculum, misplacement can mean taking as many as three non-credit developmental courses before entering into credit-bearing composition (see Nastal, 2019; Patthey-Chavez et al., 2005). Many students will not have the time, money, or motivation to persist through a year of additional and unnecessary writing coursework—more if they do not pass a class. Such barriers can be reduced or eliminated if we develop placement processes that prioritize fairness, antiracism, and justice.

Contextualizing Reform Efforts at Two-Year Colleges

In *Gateway to Opportunity? A History of the Community College in the United States*, J. M. Beach (2012) reviewed scholarly perspectives on the function of two-year colleges and concluded that these institutions offer "a limited opportunity and a mixed blessing" (p. 128). The early mission of the community college was to "*limit* access to higher education in the name of social efficiency" (Beach, 2012, p. xx), but students, faculty, and administrators galvanized by the democratic potential of open admissions "tried to refashion this institution into a tool for increased social mobility, community organization, and regional economic development" (Beach, 2012, p. xx). Tensions between these institutional missions, which reflect impulses of constraint and opportunity, have persisted through the demographic and economic upheavals of the twenty-first century, as two-year colleges became the focus of renewed scholarly debate, philanthropy-driven reform efforts, and state and federal policymaking aimed at increasing the percentage of Americans holding postsecondary credentials. These forces have been rapidly reshaping writing curricula and placement assessment at two-year colleges. At many institutions, however, neither English faculty nor the discipline of writing studies has traditionally been well-positioned to influence these reforms (Griffiths, 2017; Hassel et al., 2015; Toth et al., 2013).

Community college researchers and reformers often invoke low and inequitable degree completion rates as a major motivation for enacting change (e.g., Bailey et al., 2010; Barnett & Reddy, 2017; Scott-Clayton et al., 2014; Zaback et al., 2016). For example, Doug Shapiro et al. (2016) reported that only 39 percent of students who enrolled at two-year colleges earned any kind of credential within six years, and nationally, just 16 percent of entering two-year college students went on to earn a bachelor's degree. Moreover, only 33 percent of Hispanic/Latinx students and 26 percent of Black students who enrolled at two-year colleges earned a credential within six years, and just 11 percent of Hispanic/Latinx students and nine percent of Black students who began at two-year colleges eventually completed bachelor's degrees (Shapiro et al., 2016).

Few argue that there is no need for reform; rather, debates hinge on the nature, goals, and underlying ideologies of those changes. As Patrick Sullivan

(2008, 2017) has reminded us, measuring "student success" at open admissions institutions is a complex endeavor. Not all two-year college students aspire to transfer or to earn degrees: Many are pursuing two-year vocational, technical, or para-professional certifications, or simply need a few classes to update their resume or job skills. Other students may be enrolling to experience higher education and determine if it aligns with their personal, professional, community, and academic priorities. Some are dual-enrollment/early college high school students or reverse transfer students—that is, students who are already enrolled at four-year institutions and take a limited number of classes at their local two-year college to fulfill specific degree requirements, save on tuition, and attend classes with smaller student-faculty ratios and, therefore, increased opportunities for individualized instruction and collaboration. Degree-seeking students at two-year colleges may shift their aspirations throughout the course of their education, and many students find themselves facing financial pressures, life crises, or family and community responsibilities that take priority over schooling, at least temporarily (Griffiths & Toth, 2017; Sullivan, 2008, 2017). Longstanding federal measures of completion rates have penalized community colleges by not including part-time students or those who transfer to four-year-institutions before completing a degree in their success metrics; some metrics are limited to first-time, full-time students, which represents a slim margin of two-year college students. When the Department of Education revised these criteria in 2017, it found the eight-year combined graduation and transfer rate for community college students was 60 percent (Carey, 2017).

Over the last few decades, calls among both state and federal policymakers to improve students' course completion, persistence, and degree completion have increasingly been framed as a matter of institutional accountability. As Christie Toth and colleagues (2016) have observed, accountability measures often fail to acknowledge that "the academic playing field is not level. An institution's record of 'success' is largely shaped by its student demographics and resources. The performance metrics are stacked in favor of selective colleges and universities, particularly the most elite among them" (p. 401). This dynamic makes performance-based funding problematic. Such policies risk punishing under-resourced institutions that serve under-resourced students by further denying them resources.

Given that traditional measures often fail to capture the successes of two-year college students, the American Association of Community Colleges has recently launched the Voluntary Framework of Accountability (VFA), piloted in 2011 with funding from the Bill and Melinda Gates Foundation and the Lumina Foundation for Education and begun in 2018; it is now funded by membership dues (AACC, 2022). The VFA is "the first national system of accountability specifically for community colleges and by community colleges" (2022). Rather than defining student success only by conventional metrics such as graduation rates, the VFA looks at three areas:

- Student progress and outcomes (SPO), including measures on developmental education progress, one-year progress, two-year progress, and six-year outcomes
- Career & technical education
- Adult basic education (ABE) (AACC, 2022)

For example, one-year progress measures include the following:

- Credits earned: first term, by end of year one
- Completed college math in year 1, completed college English in year 1, and completed college math and English in year 1
- Persistence from term 1 to term 2
- Successful completion of credits by end of year 1 (AACC, 2022)

Career and technical education includes a number of measures, including enrollment (credit and non-credit) and completions (credit and non-credit) as well as measures such as passing rates on licensure exams. Finally, ABE measures include whether the student completed ABE, enrolled in more education post-ABE, and gained employment post-ABE. Data from each area are analyzed independently and disaggregated by race/ethnicity, part-time/full-time status, Pell status, age, gender, and pathway key performance indicators (AACC, 2022). Such innovation in evidence-based program assessment is yet another demonstration of what four-year researchers can learn from two-year colleagues: progress measures that capture student success in more fine-grained ways.

The discourse of degree completion at two-year colleges has attracted the attention of mega-philanthropies like the Lumina and Gates foundations, as well as higher education researchers who have made use of the influx of funding from such organizations. Perhaps the most influential researchers have been those associated with the Community College Research Center (CCRC) at Columbia University's Teachers College. Over the last decade, CCRC has produced a number of high-profile publications arguing that one major cause of departure prior to degree completion is the amount of time many two-year college students spend in developmental courses before they can enroll in credit-bearing college-level coursework (e.g., Bailey et al., 2010; Jaggars & Stacey, 2014): During the first decade of the twenty-first century, 68 percent of two-year college students enrolled in at least one developmental course (Chen & Simone, 2016). These researchers have found that, for many students, the costs of the time and resources spent in developmental courses seem to outweigh the benefits to learning, with particularly negative impacts on Black, Indigenous, and People of Color (BIPOC) students (Bailey & Cho, 2010; Bailey et al., 2010; Henson & Hern, 2019; Jaggars & Stacey, 2014; Nastal, 2019).

This line of research has fueled the now-robust movement for reducing enrollment in and/or accelerating developmental instruction at two-year colleges. It has spawned heated debates between CCRC researchers and advocates of developmental education, who have questioned reformers' analyses and the political endgame of their research (for an illustrative exchange, see Bailey et al., 2013; Goudas & Boylan, 2012, 2013). It has also fueled continued struggles over the implementation and perceived successes and failures of California's A.B. 705 (e.g., Gilman et al., 2019; Nazzal et al., 2020; Siegal & Gilliland, 2021). The Council of Learning Assistance and Developmental Education Associations (CLADEA, n.d.), which includes most professional developmental education organizations, has responded to policy initiatives that reduce developmental education support with a statement on college access, arguing that "elimination or underfunding of learning assistance programs inevitably restricts college access in ways that lead to blatant educational disparities, very often with patterns related to race and socioeconomic status." The Council offered their own college completion plan in a white paper, *Meaningful Access and Support: The Path to College Completion*, that the authors describe as a call to action for higher education institutions to provide access and support for all students through evidence-based practices (Casazza & Silverman, 2013).

While many two-year college English faculty have embraced—and, in some cases, have been important leaders in—efforts to reduce the time students spend in developmental coursework (Adams et al., 2009; Cho et al., 2012; Hassel et al., 2015; Hern, 2012), many also share CLADEA's concern that broad-stroke critiques of developmental education are leading policymakers to cut resources and eliminate programs that provide necessary support for the least advantaged students, ultimately foreclosing their ability to access higher education (Hassel et al., 2015; Siegal & Gilliland, 2021). Again, few of these faculty argue against the importance of enrolling students into college-level courses as quickly as possible. The debates center on what combination of reforms to curriculum, pedagogy, assessment, professional development, and resource allocation will best achieve that goal for the diverse student groups entering two-year colleges.

This broad rethinking of developmental education has drawn increased attention to the assessment practices used by two-year colleges to place incoming students into courses. CCRC researchers have released a series of studies suggesting that the common use of high-stakes, single-score purchased placement tests leads to widespread misplacement, and particularly "underplacement": that is, placing students—disproportionately, first-generation college students and BIPOC students—who are capable of succeeding in college-level coursework into developmental courses, which can negatively impact their persistence to degree completion (e.g., Bailey et al., 2010; Belfield & Crosta, 2012; Hodara et al., 2012; Scott-Clayton, 2012). Recognition of this systemic injustice and debates about how best to counter it have fueled the push for two-year college placement reform.

Bringing Visibility to Two-Year College Writing Assessment

Given the research that is being published by CCRC, Center for the Analysis of Postsecondary Readiness, and National Student Clearinghouse Research Center, the disciplinary community of writing studies should have a significant interest in assessment at two-year colleges. Yet, two-year colleges and the faculty who teach in them have long been underrepresented in writing studies, and specifically in writing assessment, scholarship (Hassel & Giordano, 2013; Lovas, 2002; Morris et al., 2015; Nist & Raines, 1995; Toth & Sullivan, 2016). While community college faculty publish in journals such as *Assessing Writing* and the *Journal of Writing Assessment* (for example, Blankenship et al., 2017), most assessment scholarship by two-year college faculty is published in *Teaching English in the Two-Year College*. Because that journal is not open-access and historically has been either disparaged or ignored by university-based scholars (Connors, 1984; see Hassel et al., 2019; Rodrigo & Miller-Cochran, 2018; Sommers, 2017), it often has been overlooked as a site for cutting-edge research.

Fortunately, there is growing recognition of the critical importance of two-year faculty voices in national conversations on writing assessment. For example, the *White Paper on Placement Reform* (Klausman et al., 2016), which was composed by a Two-Year College English Association (TYCA) research committee and approved by TYCA's executive committee, provided a synthesis of research on placement that emerged from higher education reformers—particularly researchers associated with the CCRC—as well as writing studies through the first half of the 2010s. The paper offered case studies of promising approaches to two-year college writing placement and articulated several key principles for designing, administering, and assessing placement practices. Those principles include (1) grounding in disciplinary knowledge, (2) involvement of English faculty in the development of placement processes, (3) sensitivity to the effects of placement processes on diverse groups of students, (4) ongoing local validation, and (5) integration of placement reform with other campus-wide efforts to support student success (Klausman et al., 2016, p. 126).[2]

Spurred by the 2015 demise of the widely-used COMPASS placement test and the 2016 TYCA statement, the *Journal of Writing Assessment (JWA)* released a special issue on writing placement in two-year colleges in 2019. Published before the pandemic and the murder of George Floyd, the special issue was driven by contributors' pursuit of equity for their students and influenced by the ethical turn in writing assessment as well as emerging conversations about antiracism in writing studies. The special issue led to a featured presentation on two-year college writing placement at the Council on Writing Program Administrators conference as well as a panel at National TYCA. Contributors to the special issue

---

2. Following the recommendations of CCRC and TYCA, many community colleges have adopted various forms of MMA placement that increase the range of ways that students can demonstrate readiness for college-level writing (Barnett & Reddy, 2017; Klausman et al., 2016). The idea of MMA aligns with the Conference on College Composition and Communication's (CCCC) position statement on writing assessment (CCCC Executive Committee, 2009). Holly Hassel and Joanne Giordano (2011, 2015) presented a successful two-year college model for multiple-measures placement grounded in disciplinary knowledge and values.

engaged with mounting pressures for placement reform emanating from higher education researchers, policymakers, administrators, and two-year college faculty. They addressed the racial inequities often promulgated through high-stakes single-score placement tests and explored the promise of emerging alternatives.

In the three years since the publication of the *JWA* special issue, the landscape of two-year college writing placement has continued to evolve. California's A.B. 705 legislation, which took effect in 2018, has now restructured developmental education and its associated placement systems at community colleges throughout the state (see Gilman et al., 2019). In the years since its implementation, the legislation has fueled wide-scale movements to MMA and GSP at hundreds of two-year colleges (Kretz & Newell, 2020). Amid the pandemic crisis in 2020–2021, many students could not access college testing centers, and long-standing methods for in-person placement assessment at many community colleges were impossible. Some of the changes discussed in the *JWA* special issue were pushed into mainstream practice. Suddenly, moving to MMA or forms of self-placement was not a cautious experiment: In many contexts, such moves were the only available option.

The chapters in this collection show how two-year college faculty have continued to be influenced by the ethical turn in writing assessment (Elliot, 2016; Slomp, 2016a). That movement has challenged conventional measurement approaches to validity and fairness that ignore adverse impact and minimize students' cultural and linguistic backgrounds (Hammond, 2019; Inoue & Poe, 2012a; Olivieri et al., 2022; Poe & Cogan, 2016; Randall, 2021; Saenkhum, 2016). For example, over the last decade, writing assessment scholars Mya Poe and Asao B. Inoue (2016) have argued for a "sociocultural model[s] of validity" (p. 118) that "provide[s] a useful reworking of validity theory for the purposes of social justice" (p. 118). Scholars in this turn have drawn insights from a number of transdisciplinary critical fields, including philosophical works on ethics and social justice; critical race theory, whiteness studies, and antiracism; feminist standpoint theory; translingual theory; queer theory; disability studies; psychology and cognitive studies; educational development and educational measurement. These scholars ask the field to consider how writing assessments are shaped by dominant epistemological assumptions, values, and language ideologies that are raced, classed, gendered, colonial/imperialistic, and often predicated on normativities regarding physical abilities, sensory processing, and neurotypicality.

In short, the field of writing assessment today is expansive in theoretical orientation. It is also an exciting time as scholars look for new methods that serve the goals of these theoretical horizons. New critical approaches challenge algorithmic assessment models like Willingham's (1974). They offer valuable conceptual tools for analyzing the social consequences of two-year college assessment practices and ontological options for imagining fairer alternatives. These tools include *racial validity inquiry* (Inoue, 2012b, 2015) and *disparate impact analysis* (Poe & Cogan, 2016; Poe et al., 2014), which encourage disaggregating assessment data by race and other legally protected categories. Extending these concepts,

David Slomp (2016b) has argued for "disaggregation of data so score interpretation can be clearly understood for all groups and each individual within those groups," with particular attention to determining "whether assessment practices are having an adverse impact on some student communities" (see also Elliot, 2016; Slomp, 2016a). If so, these assessment practices can and should be redesigned to achieve more equitable outcomes.

Such redesigns may require not only revising assessment processes and instruments, but a fundamental rethinking of the values, goals, and practices driving writing assessment in the context of local diversities. Both Ellen Cushman's (2016) argument for decolonizing the concept of validity and West-Puckett et al.'s (forthcoming) suggestions for queering writing assessment ask us to question the epistemological universalism and normativities built into why and how we measure writing performance. They encourage us to develop assessments that value the plurality and diversity of our students' languages, literacies, and rhetorics. Such local re-valuation is particularly pressing at two-year colleges, given their diverse students, institutional missions, and community contexts. Contributors in *Writing Placement in Two-Year Colleges: The Pursuit of Equity in Postsecondary Education* show us how such issues are being addressed in local two-year contexts.

Overview of the Book

As the chapters in this collection demonstrate, the scholarly conversation about writing assessment, social justice, and the advancement of opportunity is shifting from its historically four-year focus to an awareness of the distinctive conditions of teaching and administering writing in a variety of settings. Those conditions include the missions and student populations served, constraints on institutional resources, writing instructors' varying disciplinary backgrounds and professional identities, labor conditions, and the on-going reform-minded policy contexts in which two-year college faculty are undertaking their work.

The chapters in this book bring together established and new voices in two-year college English studies, writing studies, and writing assessment. These teacher-scholars write from institutions in the Pacific Northwest, Southwest, Midwest, Northeast, and Mid-Atlantic. They are accredited by the Northwest Commission, the Higher Learning Commission, and the Middle States Commission on Higher Education, respectively. All have worked to enact placement reform amid local manifestations of the layered challenges and opportunities we have traced in this introduction.

This book may be read in several ways: by timespan, method, geography, or accrediting commission. To navigate the case studies by timespan for placement reform, readers can use the dedicated subheadings by which the chapters are arranged. These subheadings are "The Long Road of Placement Reform," "Innovation and Equity in Placement Reform," and "Pandemic-Precipitated Placement Reform."

In Part One, "The Long Road of Placement Reform," contributors from Central Oregon Community College, Prairie State College, Whatcom Community College, and the Community College of Baltimore County document many years of adapting to local students' communities, testing hypotheses and refining practices, and advancing systematic reforms. These processes have been commended by regional accrediting bodies and by national organizations. In 2021, for example, Central Oregon Community College received the Diana Hacker TYCA Outstanding Programs in English Award for Fostering Student Success for their *Rethinking Placement as Part of Redesigning Developmental Literacy: Using Multiple Measures and Directed Self-Placement to Improve Student Success*. The Community College of Baltimore County received an honorable mention in the same category for their work on *Self-Directed Placement*. Whatcom Community College won the award in 2020 for their *Informed Self-Placement Program*.

In Chapter 1, "No Reform Is an Island: Tracing the Influences and Consequences of Placement Reform at a Two-Year Predominantly Black Institution," Jessica Nastal, Jason Evans, and Jessica Gravely report on the consequences of placement reform for students and for their composition program. Students at Prairie State College appear to be placing into the college credit-bearing class at higher rates and succeeding at higher or similar rates than with past placement methods, though arriving at these conclusions has proved to be challenging. Nastal and colleagues share how their placement ecosystem operates as they document the logistical challenges of reform, including staffing and access to accurate and timely data.

In Chapter 2, "From ACCUPLACER to Informed Self-Placement at Whatcom Community College: Equitable Placement as an Evolving Practice," Jeffrey Klausman and Signee Lynch discuss how their institution moved from ACCUPLACER to MMA and ultimately, to ISP. Doing so alongside curricular reform efforts has dramatically increased the number of students placed into the college credit-bearing class and narrowed equity disparities. Since Composition I is the gateway class to earning a credential at Whatcom and most other institutions nationwide, these results offer evidence of how practices explicitly designed to achieve equity can fulfill the two-year college goal of making "education accessible to all."

In Chapter 3, "A Path to Equity, Agency, and Access: Self-Directed Placement at the Community College of Baltimore County," Kris Messer, Jamey Gallagher, and Elizabeth Hart reflect on the fundamental questions of writing placement at two-year colleges: Who are our students? What are their educational and career goals? How are we prepared to support their achievement? Their case study offers compelling evidence regarding the value of *self-directed* placement (SDP)—their reconceptualization of DSP—for expanding "flexibility, agency, and control" in placement for students at two-year colleges. Their qualitative data is especially compelling, demonstrating how "intelligent, driven, [and] linguistically sophisticated" students are, and how they "bring a range of experiences that can serve to strengthen our classrooms and our larger culture" when offered the opportunity to do so. Messer and colleagues discuss the complexity of advancing student agency in an educational system built on maintaining the status quo, particularly as business-as-usual has excluded and penalized so many in the communities two-year colleges purport to serve. They also describe how the pandemic created opportunities to expand SDP at a previously reluctant institution but has also presented challenges for sustainability.

Finally, in Chapter 4, "Welcome/Not Welcome: From Discouragement to Empowerment in the Writing Placement Process at Central Oregon Community College," Jane Denison-Furness, Stacey Lee Donohue, Annemarie Hamlin, and Tony Russell document the systematic effort they have undertaken at Central Oregon Community College to improve student outcomes. They present a careful discussion of an MMA placement system that integrates DSP alongside redesign of developmental literacy courses, outcomes, and curricula to support first-generation and new majority college students. Denison-Furness and colleagues emphasize the importance of institutional support in undertaking these reforms. Such support includes reassigned time to attend to the design, institutional investment in the processes, and ongoing conversations and input from administrative and faculty stakeholders.

The second section, "Innovation and Equity in Placement Reform," presents contributions from faculty at Yakima Valley College, Jamestown Community College, Kingsborough Community College, and Queensborough Community College. In each case, these colleges have been responding to institutional, system, or statewide mandates to redesign placement to address issues of equity. In Chapter 5, "Narrowing the Divide in Placement at a Hispanic-Serving Institution: The Case of Yakima Valley College," Carolyn Calhoon-Dillahunt and Travis Margoni assert that writing placement is a "key everyday practice" that has the potential to influence equity work across Yakima Valley College's campus. Tracing the demographic shift from a Predominantly White Institution to a Hispanic-Serving Institution, Calhoon-Dillahunt and Margoni document how their customized version of The Write Class, an MMA instrument developed by compositionists at Boise State University, has mitigated some of the previous equity disparities in placement. They describe how seeking to cultivate an antiracist writing assessment ecology (Inoue, 2015) has further improved their course-level success outcomes.

In Chapter 6, "Putting ACCUPLACER in Its Place: Expanding Evidence in Placement Reform at Jamestown Community College," Jessica Kubiak traces Jamestown Community College's (JCC's) work toward MMA and developmental education reform, integrated within a college-wide general education framework. JCC's unified faculty, guided by quantitative data, successfully contextualized reading instruction and general education requirements to ensure more students enroll in and complete the composition sequence earlier in their academic career. Since a significant percentage of the student body is composed of non-matriculated students enrolled in early college or dual enrollment programs, Kubiak's questions about how high school GPA will factor into future placement decisions are prescient.

In Chapter 7, "Tracking the Racial Consequences of Placement by Probability: A Case Study at Kingsborough Community College," Annie Del Principe, Lesley Broder, and Lauren Levesque challenge the face validity of using a direct sample of student writing to place students into composition courses and highlight the promises of MMA, particularly for BIPOC students. Their case study of placement is situated in Brooklyn's Kingsborough Community College, part of the City University of New York (CUNY) system, which recently mandated MMA for all its colleges. Del Principe, Broder, and Levesque provide welcome evidence that, for their students, MMA results in gains for all racial/ethnic groups. As a result, Kingsborough's disaggregated rates of placement into credit-bearing composition classes more equitably represent the demographics of the student body. Del Principe, Broder, and Levesque demonstrate how placement reform is one step toward supporting "student success for a more fair and just society."

In Chapter 8, "Mind the (Linguistic) Gap: On 'Flagging' ESL Students at Queensborough Community College," Charissa Che offers nuance to the portrait of CUNY's approach to MMA, particularly as it relates to multilingual students. Through a mixed-method study at Queensborough Community College, located in Queens, Che demonstrates how a focus on racial/ethnic equity often omits the complexities of students' linguistic identities, experiences, and communities. Che argues that placement reform must account for the dynamic ways students speak English as an additional language and the linguistic strengths they bring to college campuses. To do otherwise is to continue upholding Standardized Edited American English ideologies.

Finally, Part Three, "Pandemic-Precipitated Placement Reform," shows how faculty at Cuyahoga Community College, Cochise College, and Arizona Western College seized the disruptions of the pandemic as an opportunity to implement methods of writing placement that attend to concerns about equity and ethics. In Chapter 9, "Pandemic Placement at Cuyahoga Community College: A Case Study," Ashlee Brand and Bridget Kriner discuss their on-the-fly development of MMA in response to the pandemic. Attuned to the benefits and drawbacks of contemporary placement methods, particularly for new majority college students, faculty at "Tri-C" implemented a method where students can gain entry to the college credit-bearing course via past performance or ISP. Reactions to the reform affirm the value of faculty coming together to discuss their students' placement as it humanizes the event, prepares faculty to meet students' needs, prompts curricular revision, and develops camaraderie sorely missed during the pandemic.

In Chapter 10, "A Complement to Educational Reform: Directed Self-Placement (DSP) at Cochise College," Ella Melito, Erin Whittig, Cathy Sander Matthesen, and Denisse Cañez identify the constellation of factors two-year colleges faced in the early days of the pandemic and elaborate on the effects after 18 months. Their DSP method was implemented to assuage institutional concerns about facilitating an unproctored placement exam for students whose past record did not place them into the college credit-bearing course. This emergency method quickly turned into an ongoing practice relying on the entire placement ecosystem at Cochise College, with promising early results for students.

Finally, in Chapter 11, "Community College Online Directed Self-Placement During the COVID-19 Pandemic," Sarah Elizabeth Snyder, Sara Amani, and Kevin Kato describe how a pre-pandemic effort to develop an online DSP process for multilingual students unexpectedly became their college's main placement process. Their case makes stark the challenges two-year college faculty faced during the first year of the pandemic as they sought to a) implement an unproctored method of placement, b) attend to administrator concerns about moving away from purchased exams, and c) ensure all local student communities would benefit from the method. Snyder and colleagues emphasize the importance of methods that account for the linguistic diversity of our students and provide detailed evidence of positive early results.

Readers interested in reading case studies of specific approaches to placement can navigate this book by placement method (Table 1). Many of the contributors document how they moved from one placement method to another, and it is intriguing to see how the logics and local ecologies for placement led each institution to their current placement method.

Table 1. Navigating Chapters by Placement Method

Method	Chapters
System-Mandated Multiple Measures	Ch. 1: No Reform Is an Island: Tracing the Influences and Consequences of Placement Reform at a Two-Year Predominantly Black Institution
	Ch. 7: Tracking the Racial Consequences of Placement by Probability: A Case Study at Kingsborough Community College
	Ch. 8: Mind the (Linguistic) Gap: On "Flagging" ESL Students at Queensborough Community College
Multiple Measures	Ch. 6: Putting ACCUPLACER in Its Place: Expanding Evidence in Placement Reform at Jamestown Community College
	Ch. 7: Tracking the Racial Consequences of Placement by Probability: A Case Study at Kingsborough Community College
	Ch. 8: Mind the (Linguistic) Gap: On "Flagging" ESL Students at Queensborough Community College
Multiple Measures with Self-Placement	Ch. 4: Welcome/Not Welcome: From Discouragement to Empowerment in the Writing Placement Process at Central Oregon Community College
	Ch. 5: Narrowing the Divide in Placement at an HSI: The Case of Yakima Valley College
	Ch. 9: Pandemic Placement at Cuyahoga Community College: A Case Study

Method	Chapters
Multiple Measures with Timed Impromptu Exam	Ch. 1: No Reform Is an Island: Tracing the Influences and Consequences of Placement Reform at a Two-Year Predominantly Black Institution
Self-Placement	Ch. 2: From ACCUPLACER to Informed Self-Placement at Whatcom Community College: Equitable Placement as an Evolving Practice
	Ch. 3: A Path to Equity, Agency, and Access: Self-Directed Placement at the Community College of Baltimore County
	Ch. 10: A Complement to Educational Reform: Directed Self-Placement (DSP) at Cochise College
	Ch. 11: Community College Online Directed Self-Placement During the COVID-19 Pandemic

Table 2. Navigating Chapters by Region

Region	Accrediting Body	State	College	Chapter
Pacific Northwest	Northwest Commission on Colleges and Universities	WA	Yakima Valley	Ch. 5: Narrowing the Divide in Placement at an HSI: The Case of Yakima Valley College
		OR	Central Oregon	Ch. 4: Welcome/Not Welcome: From Discouragement to Empowerment in the Writing Placement Process at Central Oregon Community College
		WA	Whatcom	Ch. 2: From ACCUPLACER to Informed Self-Placement at Whatcom Community College: Equitable Placement as an Evolving Practice
Southwest	Higher Learning Commission	AZ	Cochise	Ch. 10: A Complement to Educational Reform: Directed Self-Placement (DSP) at Cochise College
		AZ	Western Arizona	Ch. 11: Online Directed Self-Placement During the COVID-19 Pandemic: The Case of Arizona Western College
Midwest		IL	Prairie State	Ch. 1: No Reform Is an Island: Tracing the Influences and Consequences of Placement Reform at a Two-Year Predominantly Black Institution
		OH	Cuyahoga	Ch. 9: Pandemic Placement at Cuyahoga Community College: A Case Study

Region	Accrediting Body	State	College	Chapter
Mid-Atlantic	Middle States Commission on Higher Education	MD	Baltimore County	Ch. 3: A Path to Equity, Agency, and Access: Self-Directed Placement at the Community College of Baltimore County
Northeast		NY	Jamestown	Ch. 6: Putting ACCUPLACER in Its Place: Expanding Evidence in Placement Reform at Jamestown Community College
		NY	Kingsborough	Ch. 7: Tracking the Racial Consequences of Placement by Probability: A Case Study at Kingsborough Community College
		NY	Queensborough	Ch. 8: Mind the (Linguistic) Gap: On "Flagging" ESL Students at Queensborough Community College

A final way to read this book is by geography (Table 2). Placement and related reform initiatives are often precipitated by state-level policy pressures or mandates. Likewise, geographical location often shapes the demographics of particular two-year colleges. Moreover, many reforms are, in part, dictated by the influence of the accreditation commission as well as state legislatures. Too often writing studies scholars ignore how such influences can drive local assessment practices.

Research and theory published over the last decade show that the commercial exams which have long dominated two-year college writing placement have offered inadequate representations of local constructs of college writing and yielded inequitable outcomes. They have reproduced language and literacy ideologies that advantage students from White, middle-class communities. While faculty have long tolerated such constraints in the name of efficiency—or a distorted sense of equity—at often under-resourced open admissions institutions, it is now clear that those constraints have, in fact, harmed the least advantaged. Through systematic misplacement, particularly underplacement that delays enrollment in college-level courses, two-year colleges have reduced those students' likelihood of degree completion. In the process, they have also sent students destructive messages about their capacities as writers and learners and about the value of the rhetorical and literacy practices in their out-of-school communities. These disparate, adverse impacts are neither fair nor, in many cases, legal (Klausman et al., 2016; Poe & Cogan, 2016; Poe et al., 2014). Taken together, the chapters in this collection further the ongoing work of imagining and implementing possibilities toward a more fair and just future.

From Theoretical Expansion to Methodological Innovation in the Future of Writing Placement at Two-Year Colleges

We hope *Writing Placement in Two-Year Colleges: The Pursuit of Equity in Postsecondary Education* prompts readers to recognize the enormous potential of writing assessment research at two-year colleges to inform practices at all institution types.[3] This collection highlights how two-year colleges are leaders in making evidence-based decisions about placement reform within their local contexts. The contributors demonstrate how faculty agency—informed by both local data and engagement with ongoing national conversations—can be a powerful instrument for positive change in the midst of crises. Their intellectual work also raises important new questions for further research. We close this introductory chapter by identifying a few of those questions and areas.

First, many of these chapters point to the challenges many two-year college faculty face in collecting, accessing, and analyzing high-quality data—particularly disaggregated data—regarding both longstanding placement practices and new initiatives. Future research should contend with the challenges and consequences of inadequate institutional research infrastructure at many two-year colleges, as well as institutional cultures and policies that prevent faculty from gaining access to existing data and assistance with analysis. Likewise, the field needs more work on how to improve the kinds of demographic data institutions collect to enable more meaningful and relevant disaggregation based on the local communities served (Inoue & Poe, 2012b; Leonard et al., 2021; Poe & Zhang-Wu, 2020). These data could include, for example, better and more consistent information on linguistic identity, trans and nonbinary gender identities, sexual identities, a range of disabilities, documentation status, social-emotional well-being, family caretaking responsibilities, foster youth, and veteran status. Such data, especially informed by QuanCrit (Gillborn et al., 2018), could help visibilize additional disparities in placement and academic outcomes as well as offer rich intersectional analysis.

Second, the field needs more evidence that connects data from multiple points in students' academic paths: admission, placement, enrollment, course throughput, graduation and/or transfer, and beyond. We can start by examining the implementation of multiple single measures in this era of placement reform: What are the consequences of abandoning one high-stakes measure (e.g., purchased exam) for another? How can we think more expansively about connecting data sets? What do the constellation of data points we have access to tell us about our students, faculty, institutions, values? In short, we need robust forms

---

3. For example, Toth's familiarity with research on and innovations of DSP in two-year colleges—including insights gained from early versions of the chapters in this collection—directly contributed to the design of directed self-placement at the University of Utah in 2020–2021.

of validity evidence. Justice-oriented approaches to validity expand on the five traditional forms of validity evidence—construct, internal content, relation to other variables, response processes, and consequence—"to disrupt assessment practices that continue to (re)produce racism through the uncritical promotion of white supremist hegemonic practices" (Randall et al., 2022, p. 1).

Third, as the chapters in this collection demonstrate, there is not just a need to analyze data in a post hoc fashion but to connect the design of assessment with the analysis of consequence. In measurement, researchers employ theory of action (ToA) models to connect design, outcomes, and validity evidence. Suzanne Lane (2014) describes ToA as follows:

> Within a theory of action for an assessment system, the goals, purposes, and uses of an assessment system; the outcomes of the assessment system (e.g., increased rates of college and career readiness for all students); and the mediating outcomes necessary to achieve the ultimate outcomes (e.g., students will show gains on the assessment, instruction will improve) are articulated (Marion, 2010). Key components of the theory of action are then prioritized and further delineated to support the design of the assessment and the validity argument. (p. 127)

While ToA models do not necessarily explicitly attend to equity questions, they can be used for such purposes. Newer iterations of ToA models, such as the integrated design and appraisal framework (IDAF), were "designed to enable literacy educators to pay systematic attention to the broad set of consequences derived from an assessment's design and use" (Slomp & Elliot, 2021, p. 469; see also Slomp, 2016a). IDAF offers researchers and teachers a set of critical questions to ask at each stage of the design, outcome, and validity argument process regarding immediate and long-term consequences. As David Slomp and Norbert Elliot (2021) explained,

> While a ToA . . .lays out the logic that takes us from program elements to intended policy outcomes, the IDAF . . . provides a mechanism for critically examining that logic. Integrating the models provides teachers with a tool kit to draw attention of assessment stakeholders to the components and consequences of assessment implementation (p. 471).

By connecting design and consequence through frameworks such as IDAF, community college faculty can be "in-front of" future assessment revisions in that IDAF demands attention to intended and unintended consequence.

Fourth, along with innovations in model and data analysis building, we need better language to describe the plurality of approaches today to DSP and MMA. Both community college reformers and writing assessment scholars have advocated for MMA and/or DSP as alternatives to single-score placement tests.

However, as the chapters in this collection make clear, there are many different (and sometimes overlapping) approaches to both MMA and facilitated forms of self-placement. The field needs more work that clearly identifies, disambiguates, and examines the various ideological underpinnings and potential consequences of these proliferating variations. For example, how do MMA processes that produce a holistic placement based on multiple metrics differ from MMA processes that simply offer a range of single-metric options (e.g., high school GPA *or* ACCUPLACER score) to demonstrate preparedness for college-level writing classes? How do DSP/GSP processes that generate a placement recommendation based on questionnaire responses differ from ISP/SDP processes that do not?

The chapters in this collection also demonstrate the importance of iteratively designing and assessing placement practices in the context of broader reforms to developmental education, instruction and support for multilingual students, pedagogies in "gateway" college composition courses, and other campus-wide teaching and learning initiatives. Placement is always part of a broader local assessment ecology that encompasses classroom assessment practices as well as sites like supplemental instruction for accelerated learning, writing centers, exit assessments for course sequences, and assessment practices that involve writing across the curriculum. The field needs more research into how writing placement interacts with ongoing changes across these spaces, many of which are motivated by concerns regarding access and equity. Specifically, there is much to learn about how writing pedagogies can and should change in the wake of placement reform and the onset of the pandemic. Likewise, the field needs to account for the reality that placement, curriculum, and pedagogical reform alone will not address the inequities of our postsecondary system. Research must factor in the essential role that non-academic resources, services, and *policies* aimed at meeting students' basic material needs—e.g., food, housing, transportation, medical care, mental health services, family care, technology access—play in meeting the underlying goals of writing placement reform.

These chapters also hint at the under-examined role that accreditation processes can play in advancing placement reform. The pressures of upcoming accreditation reviews can provide leverage for evidence-based and equity-oriented changes to a range of institutional assessment practices, including placement. The field would benefit from more research into ways that practitioners have used the accreditation process to assert a voice in what assessment looks like at their institutions. Such research might enable writing faculty to feel empowered to participate in placement reform and to push for fairer practices without fear of being punished by accrediting bodies. Indeed, such research might help practitioners contribute to the wider field as accreditation reviewers learn about their local assessment work and carry that knowledge to other institutions.

Furthermore, the field needs more research into how colleges do and could include students and their communities in the assessment, design, and implementation of writing placement processes. Students are the most important stakeholders in these processes—they are the purported reason such processes exist—and they are the stakeholders most harmed by unfair assessments of their capacities. Yet, students are almost always excluded from direct participation as co-designers of placement reform. Likewise, the local communities that two-year colleges serve—and sometimes fail to serve—typically have no input on what writing placement processes value and measure. Future research might interrogate *who* gets to determine what the "valued local construct of writing" is, and how such values might be developed in collaboration *with* students and their communities.

While finalizing this introduction for publication, we realized we have had heartbreakingly similar conversations with two-year college students—both first-generation, one a woman of color returning to higher education; the other a traditional first-year student—who described their experiences with standardized placement exams by saying, in essence, "I thought I was smart until I took that test." Those experiences had negative consequences for these women's educational trajectories, their self-concepts and self-efficacy as students, and their relationships with writing, even years after their colleges had stopped using those tests. Recent research calls attention to the impact of students' mental health on their education; for instance, with results indicating students with depression are less likely to persist than their peers (Mamiseishvili & Koch, 2012). However equitable new placement processes might be, such reforms do not undo the harm that has already been caused, with real consequences for individual students' lives, the material circumstances of their families, and entire communities. We close, then, with a call for more scholarship focusing on how colleges and the field will begin making reparations for the harm wrought by decades of unfair and unjust writing placement.

References

Adams, P. D., Gearhart, S., Miller, R. & Roberts, A. (2009). The Accelerated Learning Program: Throwing open the gates. *Journal of Basic Writing*, 28(2), 50–69. https://doi.org/10.37514/JBW-J.2009.28.2.04.

American Association of Community Colleges. (2017). *2017 FactsSheet*. http://www.aacc.nche.edu/AboutCC/Pages/fastfactsfactsheet.aspx.

American Association of Community Colleges. (2021). *Voluntary Framework of Accountability*. https://www.aacc.nche.edu/programs/voluntary-framework-accountability/.

American Association of Community Colleges. (2022). *FAQs*. Voluntary Framework of Accountability. https://vfa.aacc.nche.edu/about/Pages/FAQs.aspx.

Association of Community College Trustees. (2022). *Pell Grants*. https://www.acct.org/page/pell-grants#:~:text=Credit%20Alignment%20Lab-,Pell%20Grants,wages%2C%20and%20a%20stronger%20economy.

Bailey, T. & Cho, S.-W. (2010). *Developmental education in community colleges* (Issue Brief Prepared for the White House Summit on Community Colleges). Teachers College, Columbia University.

Bailey, T., Jaggars, S. S. & Scott-Clayton, J. (2013). Commentary: Characterizing the effectiveness of developmental education: A response to recent criticism. *Journal of Developmental Education*, 36(3), 18–34.

Bailey, T., Jeong, D. W. & Cho, S. W. (2010). Referral, enrollment, and completion in developmental education sequences in community colleges. *Economics of Education Review*, 29(2), 255–270.

Barnett, E. A. & Reddy, V. (2017). *College placement strategies: Evolving considerations and practices* (CAPR Working Paper). Columbia University.

Beach, J. M. B. (2012). *Gateway to opportunity? A history of the community college in the United States*. Stylus Publishing, LLC.

Belfield, C. & Crosta, P. M. (2012). Predicting success in college: The importance of placement tests and high school transcripts (CCRC Working Paper No. 42). Columbia University.

Benton, E. (2020). Turning to each other: Reflections on teaching and collaborating during the pandemic of 2020. *Montgomery College Innovation Journal*. http://mcblogs.montgomerycollege.edu/innovation-journal/2020/06/21/turning-to-each-other-reflections-on-teaching-and-collaborating-during-the-pandemic-of-2020/.

Bereiter, C. (2003). Foreword. In M. D. Shermis & J. C. Burstein (Eds.), *Automated essay scoring: A cross-disciplinary perspective* (pp. vii-x). Lawrence Erlbaum.

Bickerstaff, S., Kopko, E., Lewy, E. B., Raufman, J. & Rutschow, E. R. (2021). Implementing and scaling multiple measures assessment in the context of COVID-19. https://ccrc.tc.columbia.edu/media/k2/attachments/implementing-scaling-multiple-measures-covid.pdf.

Blankenship, C., Canava, A., Jory, J., Lewis, K., Stanford, M. & Stephenson, B. (2017). Re-assessing composition at open access institutions: Using a threshold framework to reshape practice. *Journal of Writing Assessment*, 10(1). http://www.journalofwritingassessment.org/article.php?article=113.

Burstein, J. (2012). Fostering best practices in writing instruction and assessment with E-rater®. In N. Elliot & L. Perelman (Eds.), *Writing assessment in the 21st century: Essays in honor of Edward M. White* (pp. 203–217). Hampton Press.

Carey, K. (2017, October 31). Revised data shows community colleges have been underappreciated. *New York Times*. https://www.nytimes.com/2017/10/31/upshot/revised-data-shows-community-colleges-have-been-underappreciated.html.

Casazza, M. E. & Silverman, S. L. (2013). *Meaningful access and support: The path to college completion*. Council of Learning Assistance and Developmental Education Associations. http://49123941-214107090244894478.preview.editmysite.com/uploads/3/9/9/3/39938161/cladeawhitepaper_81413.pdf.

Chen, X. & Simone, S. (2016). *Remedial coursetaking at U.S. public 2- and 4-year institutions: Scope, experiences, and outcomes* (NCES 2016-405). U.S. Department of Education. National Center of Education Statistics. https://nces.ed.gov/pubs2016/2016405.pdf.

Cho, S.-W., Kopko, E., Jenkins, D. & Jaggars, S. S. (2012). *New evidence of success for community college remedial English students: Tracking the outcomes of students in the Accelerated Learning Program* (CCRC Working Paper No. 53). Community College Research Center, Columbia University.

Cohen, A. M., Brawer, F. B. & Kisker, C. B. (2014). *The American community college* (6th ed.). John Wiley & Sons.

Conference on College Composition and Communication Committee on Assessment. (2009). *Writing assessment: A position statement*. National Council of Teachers of English. http://www.ncte.org/cccc/resources/positions/writingassessment.

Connors, R. (1984). Journals in composition studies. *College English, 46*(4), 348–65.

Council of Learning Assistance and Developmental Education Assocations. (n.d.). *College access* (Policy Statement). Council of Learning Assistance and Developmental Education Associations. https://cladea.info/resources/CLADEA_policy_CA.pdf.

Cushman, E. (2016). Decolonizing validity. *Journal of Writing Assessment, 9*(1). https://escholarship.org/uc/item/0xh7v6fb.

Department of Education Office for Civil Rights. (2021). *Education in a pandemic: The disparate impacts of COVID-19 on America's students*. https://www2.ed.gov /about/offices/list/ocr/docs/20210608-impacts-of-covid19.pdf.

Elliot, N. (2016). A theory of ethics for writing assessment. *Journal of Writing Assessment, 9*(1). https://escholarship.org/uc/item/36t565mm.

Faigley, L., Cherry, R., Jolliffe, D. & Skinner, A. (1985). *Assessing writers' knowledge and processes of composing*. Ablex Publishing Corporation.

Gallagher, C. W. (2007). *Reclaiming assessment: A better alternative to the accountability agenda*. Heinemann Educational Books.

Gillborn, D., Warmington, P. & Demack, S. (2018). QuantCrit: Education, policy, "Big Data" and principles for a critical race theory of statistics. *Race, Ethnicity, and Education, 21*(2), 158–179.

Gilman, H., Giordano, J. B., Hancock, N., Hassel, H., Henson, L., Hern, K., Nastal, J. & Toth, C. (2019). Forum: Two-year college writing placement as fairness. *Journal of Writing Assessment, 12*(1). https://escholarship.org/uc/item/4zv0r9b2.

Goudas, A. M. & Boylan, H. R. (2012). Addressing flawed research in developmental education. *Journal of Developmental Education, 36*(1), 2–13.

Goudas, A. M. & Boylan, H. R. (2013). A brief response to Bailey, Jaggars, and Scott-Clayton. *Journal of Developmental Education, 36*(3), 28–32.

Griffiths, B. (2017). Professional autonomy and teacher-scholar-activists in two-year colleges: Preparing new faculty to think institutionally. *Teaching English in the Two-Year College, 45*(1), 47–68.

Griffiths, B. & Toth, C. (2017). Rethinking "class": Poverty, pedagogy, and two-year college writing programs. In W. Thelin & G. Carter (Eds.), *Class in the composition classroom: Pedagogy and the working class* (pp. 231–257). Utah State University Press.

Hammond, J. W. (2019). Making our invisible racial agendas visible: Race talk in *Assessing Writing*, 1994–2018. *Assessing Writing, 42*, 1–19.

Harrington, S. (2005). Learning to ride the waves: Making decisions about placement testing. *WPA: Writing Program Administration, 28*(3), 9–29.

Hassel, H. & Giordano, J. B. (2011). First-year composition placement at open-admission, two-year campuses: Changing campus culture, institutional practice, and student success. *Open Words: Access and English Studies, 5*(2), 29–39. https://doi.org/10.37514/OPW-J.2011.5.2.03.

Hassel, H. & Giordano, J. B. (2013). Occupy writing studies: Rethinking college composition for the needs of the teaching majority. *College Composition and Communication, 65*(1), 117–139.

Hassel, H. & Giordano, J. B. (2015). The blurry borders of college writing: Remediation and the assessment of student readiness. *College English, 78*(1), 56–80.

Hassel, H., Klausman, J., Giordano, J. B., O'Rourke, M., Roberts, L., Sullivan, P. & Toth, C. (2015). TYCA white paper on developmental education reforms. *Teaching English in the Two-Year College, 42*(3), 227–243.

Haswell, R. (2004). Post-secondary entrance writing placement: A brief synopsis of research. *CompPile.Org.* http://comppile.org/profresources/writingplacementresearch.htm.

Henson, H. & Hern, K. (2019). Let them in: Increasing access, completion, and equity in English placement policies at a two-year college in California. *Journal of Writing Assessment, 12*(1). https://escholarship.org/uc/item/3nh6v5do.

Hern, K. (2012). Acceleration across California: Shorter pathways in developmental English and math. *Change: The Magazine of Higher Learning, 44*(3), 60–68.

Hodara, M., Jaggars, S. S. & Karp, M. M. (2012). *Improving developmental education assessment and placement: Lessons from community colleges across the country* (CCRC Working Paper No. 51). Community College Research Center, Columbia University.

Huddleston, E. M. (1954). Measurement of writing ability at the college entrance level: Objective vs. subjective testing techniques. *Journal of Experimental Education, 22,* 165–213.

Inoue, A. B. (2012). Racial methodologies for composition studies: Reflecting on theories of race in writing assessment research. In L. Nickoson & M. P. Sheridan (Eds.), *Writing studies research in practice: Methods and methodologies* (pp. 125–139). Southern Illinois University Press.

Inoue, A. B. (2015). *Antiracist writing assessment ecologies: Teaching and assessing writing for a socially just future.* The WAC Clearinghouse; Parlor Press. https://doi.org/10.37514/PER-B.2015.0698.

Inoue, A. B. (2019). Classroom writing assessment as an antiracist practice: Confronting white supremacy in the judgments of language. *Pedagogy, 19*(3), 373–404.

Inoue, A. B. & Poe, M. (2012a). *Race and writing assessment.* Peter Lang.

Inoue, A. B. & Poe, M. (2012b). Racial formations in two writing assessments: Revisiting White and Thomas's findings on the English Placement Test after 30 years. In N. Elliot & L. Perelman (Eds.), *Writing assessment in the 21st century: Essays in honor of Edward M. White* (pp. 341–359). Hampton Press.

Jaggars, S. S. & Stacey, G. W. (2014). *What we know about developmental education outcomes. Research Overview.* Community College Research Center, Teachers College, Columbia University.

Kane, M. T. (1990). *An argument-based approach to validation* (ACT Research Report Series No. 90-13). American College Testing Program.

Klausman, J., Roberts, L., Giordano, J., Griffiths, B., Sullivan, P., Swyt, W., Toth, C., Warnke, A. & Williams, A. (2016). TYCA white paper on placement reform. *Teaching English in the Two-Year College, 44*(2), 135–157.

Kretz, A. & Newell, M. (2020). *AB 705 implementation survey: Spring 2020 summary of results*. RP Group. California Community Colleges Chancellor's Office.

Lane, S. (2014). Validity evidence based on testing consequences. *Psicothema, 26*(1), 127–135.

Lorimer Leonard, R., Bruce, S. & Vinyard, D. (2021). Finding complexity in language identity surveys. *Journal of Language Identity & Education*. https://doi.org/10.1080/15348458.2020.1863152.

Lovas, J. C. (2002). All good writing develops at the edge of risk. *College Composition and Communication, 54*(2), 264–288.

Mamiseishvili, K. & Koch, L. C. (2012). Students with disabilities at 2-year institutions in the United States: Factors related to success. *Community College Review, 40*(4), 320–339. https://doi.org/10.1177/0091552112456281.

Morante, E. A. (1987). A primer on placement testing. *New Directions for Community Colleges*, (59), 55–63.

Morris, W., Greve, C., Knowles, E. & Huot, B. (2015). An analysis of writing assessment books published before and after the year 2000. *Teaching English in the Two-Year College, 43*(2), 118–140.

Nastal, J. (2019). Beyond tradition: Writing placement, fairness, and success at a two-year college. *Journal of Writing Assessment, 12*(1). https://escholarship.org/uc/item/4wg8wong.

National Student Clearinghouse Research Center. (2021). *Current term enrollment estimates: Spring 2021*. https://nscresearchcenter.org/wp-content/uploads/CTEE_Report_Spring_2021.pdf.

National Student Clearinghouse Research Center. (2022). *Overview: Fall 2021 Enrollment Estimates*. https://nscresearchcenter.org/wp-content/uploads/CTEE_Report_Fall_2021.pdf.

Nazzal, J. S., Olson, C. B. & Chung, H. Q. (2020). Differences in academic writing across four levels of community college composition courses. *Teaching English in the Two-Year College, 47*(3), 263–296.

Nist, E. A. & Raines, H. H. (1995). Two-year colleges: Explaining and claiming our majority. In J. Janangelo & K. Hansen (Eds.), *Resituating writing: Constructing and administering writing programs* (pp. 59–70). Boynton/Cook.

Oliveri, M., Poe, M. & Elliot, N. (2022). Fairness. In A. A. and McCaffrey, D. (Eds.) *International Encyclopedia of Education. Quantitative Research/Educational Measurement*. (4th ed.). Elsevier.

Patthey-Chavez, G. G., Dillon, P. H. & Thomas-Spiegel, J. (2005). How far do they get? Tracking students with different academic literacies through community college remediation. *Teaching English in the Two-Year College, 32*(3), 261–277.

Poe, M. & Cogan, J. A. (2016). Civil rights and writing assessment: Using the disparate impact approach as a fairness methodology to evaluate social impact. *Journal of Writing Assessment, 9*(1). https://escholarship.org/uc/item/08f1c307.

Poe, M., Elliot, N., Cogan, J. A. & Nurudeen, T. G. (2014). The legal and the local: Using disparate impact analysis to understand the consequences of writing assessment. *College Composition and Communication, 65*(4), 588–611.

Poe, M. & Inoue, A. B. (2016). Toward writing as social justice: An idea whose time has come. *College English, 79*(2), 119–126.

Poe, M. & Zhang-Wu. (2020). Super-diversity as a framework to promote social justice: Designing program assessment for multilingual writing outcomes. *Composition Forum*, 44, https://compositionforum.com/issue/44/northeastern.php.

Randall, J. (2021). "Color-neutral" is not a thing: Redefining construct definition and representation through a justice-oriented critical antiracist lens. *Educational Measurement: Issues and Practice*, 40(4), 82–90. https://doi.org/10.1111/emip.12429.

Randall, J., Slomp, D., Poe, M. & Olivieri, M. (2022). Disrupting white supremacy in assessment: Toward a justice-oriented, antiracist validity framework. *Educational Assessment*. https://doi.org/10.1080/10627197.2022.2042682.

Rodrigo, R. & Miller-Cochran, S. (2018). Acknowledging disciplinary contributions: On the importance of community college scholarship to rhetoric and composition. In *Composition, Rhetoric, and Disciplinarity* (pp. 53–69). Utah State University Press, https://doi.org/10.7330/9781607326953.c003.

Scott-Clayton, J. (2012). *Do high-stakes placement exams predict college success?* (Working Paper No. 41). Community College Research Center: Columbia University.

Scott-Clayton, J., Crosta, P. M. & Belfield, C. R. (2014). Improving the targeting of treatment: Evidence from college remediation. *Educational Evaluation and Policy Analysis*, 36(3), 371–393.

Shapiro, D., Dundar, A., Wakhungu, P., Yuan, X., Nathan, A. & Hwang, Y. (2016). *Completing college: A national view of student attainment rates- Fall 2010 cohort* (Signature Report No. 12). National Student Clearinghouse Research Center.

Siegal, M. & Gilliland, B. (2021). Introduction: Why FYC teachers' perspectives are important. In M. Siegal & B. Gilliland (Eds.), *Empowering the community college first-year composition teacher* (pp. 1–18). University of Michigan Press.

Slomp, D. (2016a). An integrated design and appraisal framework for ethical writing assessment. *Journal of Writing Assessment*, 9(1). https://escholarship.org/uc/item/4bg9003k.

Slomp, D. (2016b). Ethical considerations and writing assessment. *Journal of Writing Assessment*, 9(1). https://escholarship.org/uc/item/2k14r1zg.

Slomp, D. & Elliot, N. (2021). What's your theory of action? Making good trouble with literacy assessment. *Journal of Adolescent & Adult Literacy*, 64(4), 468–475.

Smith, W. L. (1993). Assessing the reliability and adequacy of using holistic scoring of essays as a college composition placement technique. In M. M. Williamson & B. A. Huot (Eds.), *Validating holistic scoring for writing assessment: Theoretical and empirical foundations* (pp. 142–205). Hampton Press.

Stein, Z. (2016). *Social justice and educational measurement: John Rawls, the history of testing, and the future of education*. Routledge.

Sullivan, P. (2008). Measuring "success" at open admissions institutions: Thinking carefully about this complex question. *College English*, 70(6), 618–632.

Sullivan, P. (2017). *Economic inequality, neoliberalism, and the American community college*. Palgrave MacMillan.

Toth, C., Griffiths, B. & Thirolf, K. (2013). "Distinct and significant": Professional identities of two-year college English faculty. *College Composition and Communication*, 65(1), 90–116.

Toth, C. & Sullivan, P. (2016). Toward local teacher-scholar communities of practice: Findings from a national TYCA survey. *Teaching English in the Two-Year College, 43*(3), 247–273.

West-Puckett, S., Caswell, N. & Banks, W. (forthcoming). *Failing sideways: Queer possibilities for writing assessment.* Utah State University Press.

White, E. M. (1995). The importance of placement and basic studies: Helping students succeed under the new elitism. *Journal of Basic Writing, 14*(2), 75–84. https://doi.org/10.37514/JBW-J.1995.14.2.08.

Williamson, M. (1994). The worship of efficiency: Untangling theoretical and practical considerations in writing assessment. *Assessing Writing, 1*(2), 147–173.

Willingham, W. W. (1974). *College placement and exemption.* College Entrance Examination Board.

Yancey, K. B. (1999). Looking back as we look forward: Historicizing writing assessment. *College Composition and Communication, 50*(3), 483–503.

Zaback, K., Carlson, A., Laderman, S. & Mann, S. (2016). *Serving the equity imperative: Intentional action toward greater student success.* State Higher Education Executive Offices Association. https://sheeo.org/wp-content/uploads/2019/04/2016_SHEEO_CCA_ServingEquityImperative.pdf.

Part One. The Long Road of Placement Reform

Chapter 1. No Reform Is an Island: Tracing the Influences and Consequences of Evidence-Based Placement Reform at a Two-Year Predominantly Black Institution

Jessica Nastal, Jason Evans, and Jessica Gravely
PRAIRIE STATE COLLEGE

Abstract: This chapter surveys more than ten years of institutional history about writing placement at a predominantly Black two-year college, including data about placement rates and course success. Even as a community college that did not rely on standardized tests for placement, our experiences in many ways reflect the broader trends and concerns in writing placement, demonstrating that even well-intentioned homegrown placement tools also reproduce the flaws and betray the influences of the larger system.

Placement at Prairie State College (PSC) has always existed in a kind of institutional desert. The faculty determine the standards, the administration runs the day-to-day processes, but no one, it seems, is in charge. The state law governing community colleges in Illinois delegates placement authority broadly to colleges and invokes vague principles of ability, competence, and similarity to state university programs:

> After entry, the college shall counsel and distribute the students among its programs according to their interests and abilities. Students allowed entry in college transfer programs must have ability and competence similar to that possessed by students admitted to state universities for similar programs. Entry level competence to such college transfer programs may be achieved through successful completion of other preparatory courses offered by the college. (Public Community College Act, 1961/2015)

Yet the state offered community colleges little guidance about what constitutes "entry level competence" before 2018, when a statewide placement framework was released, so individual colleges have interpreted these guidelines by themselves. For our English faculty, this has largely meant interpreting course descriptions and learning outcomes mandated in our statewide course articulation agreements. But here is the institutional desert: With the day-to-day administration of placement in the hands of a non-faculty manager, the result for PSC has been that, every few years, the English faculty talk about the placement process and make small changes—but not through a regularized institutional process. There was also a division between "Reading" and "English" that, although not housed in separate divisions, meant faculty members saw themselves as somewhat institutionally separate; as primarily teachers of their respective classes, not as stewards of the larger processes and policies affecting students' placement. As there was no pressure from the state system to actively attend to placement, the English faculty focused instead on revisions to course offerings, curricula, course and program assessment, course learning outcomes, and alignment—all aspects of the institution clearly within our control.

When we did think about the placement process, which used a direct writing sample, we felt no special urgency to revisit or revolutionize what was already, in our minds, on the better end of what seemed possible or necessary. We knew, for instance, that we were in the minority of community colleges that didn't rely only on a standardized test for placement. While we recognized the limitations of both high-stakes exams and dropped-from-the-sky timed writing placement practices, we still tended to "re-place" very few students after re-assessing them at the beginning of developmental classes (that is, "bump them up" via use of a form that made it easy for our department to track these cases; cf. Poe et al., 2019). There has long been a pervasive sense that the obstacles to student success seemed to emerge from external circumstances, material conditions, and systemic racism and classism, not as a result of being over- or under-placed.

With the benefits of hindsight, this chapter traces some of our department's thinking about placement over the past ten years or more. We have not arrived at any easy answers about writing placement, but rather a deeper appreciation for the ways in which examining any institutional practice reveals an ecology of people, processes, intentions, pathways, and gateways and barriers. If reforms and revolutions are to have any success, we will need nuanced accounts of our pasts and present, the better to question both our received ways of doing things and our reasons for wanting different.

Institutional and Departmental Context

Prairie State College is a medium-sized, suburban public two-year college outside of Chicago, Illinois. The college offers certificates, associate degrees, and applied associate degrees; it fulfills its mission (Figure 1.1) by offering non-credit, career technology education (CTE), and transfer classes and programs to community members. Courses are offered in different modalities (in-person, online, and hybrid) and in different term lengths (16-, 14-, 12-, and 8-week terms during fall and spring; 8- and 5-week terms in summer).

> **Mission Statement**
>
> Prairie State College fosters collaborative relationships that empower students to achieve their education and career goals. The college embraces its diversity, nurtures life-long learning, and supports community and economic development.
>
> **Values:** **L**earning   **E**xcellence   **A**ccessibility   **R**espect   I**N**tegrity
>
> **Visions Statement**
>
> Prairie State College will offer rigorous academic programs, meet the needs of the local workforce, cultivate the values of sustainability, and demonstrate an awareness of its responsibilities in a global society.

Figure 1.1. Prairie State College mission, values, and vision from college website: https://prairiestate.edu/about-us/mission.aspx.

PSC is accredited by the Higher Learning Commission, and some programs are individually accredited: automotive technology by National Automotive Technical Education Foundation, dental hygiene by American Dental Association Commission on Dental Accreditation, nursing by Accreditation Commission for Education in Nursing, and surgical technology by Commission on Accreditation of Allied Health Education Programs. We participate in the Illinois Articulation Initiative (IAI), a statewide initiative that ensures transferability of courses among more than 100 public and private colleges and universities. PSC also has entered into individual transfer articulation agreements with local universities; for example, in pharmacy with the University of Illinois at Chicago. Prairie State College is governed by an elected Board of Trustees and guided by four labor federations: full-time faculty, adjunct faculty, support staff, and police.

Our district has been called the most geographically, socioeconomically, and racially diverse of all Illinois community colleges. We're a Predominantly Black Institution and an Emerging Hispanic Serving Institution. In Fall 2018, we enrolled 3,946 students, 55 percent of whom identified as Black, 19 percent Hispanic/Latinx, and 18 percent White (Integrated Postsecondary Education System [IPEDS], 2020). Like our community college counterparts nationwide, most of our students are part-time and women, about two-thirds each. We have a significant number of adult students as well as Early College Initiative students. The average student age is 24, and 57 percent of students are 24 and under. PSC students' program enrollment also mirrors national trends. In 2017–2018, PSC conferred 832 credentials: 35 percent of those were in the health professions, 32 percent in liberal arts and sciences, 8 percent in computer information systems, 8 percent in mechanic and repair technologies, and 5 percent in biological and physical sciences (IPEDS, 2020).

PSC's Office of Institutional Research uses IPEDS cohort definitions to determine its degree completion and transfer rates; these cohorts are constrained to first-time, full-time students, an admittedly limited definition not reflective of two-year college enrollment. PSC's 2015 cohort graduation rate was 20 percent, and its transfer-out rate was 29 percent (Prairie State College, 2018). Its overall graduation rate was recently listed as 17 percent (IPEDS, 2020). These definitions and differing numbers point to a persistent tension within higher education (cf. Sullivan, 2008): How can we effectively report on student success measures, particularly a) in two-year colleges and b) for writing placement in two-year colleges?

As of January 2018, PSC employed 83 full-time faculty and 234 adjunct faculty (Table 1.1 and Table 1.2). About 60 percent (n=49) of full-time faculty were female. White faculty (and staff) were overrepresented at the college, at 63 percent of adjunct faculty and 78 percent of full-time faculty (including the three of us). In this overrepresentation, PSC is like many institutions nationwide (cf. Inoue, 2019); the college is working to address this imbalance and its consequences through hiring practices, institutional efforts, and professional development within departments and through the Office of Equity and Inclusion as well as the Center for Teaching and Learning, both created in 2020.

The English department currently has nine full-time faculty members. Our numbers of adjunct faculty vary depending on enrollment, and a core group of eight to ten adjunct faculty members regularly teach, work as writing center consultants, and read writing placement exams. Like our counterparts across many other departments, ours is a predominantly White faculty. Members of the department are involved in national writing studies organizations and regularly attend and present at conferences, including the Conference on College Composition and Communication and the Writing Program Administration Conference.

Table 1.1. Sex Demographics of Full- and Part-Time Faculty, 2018

Role	Female	Female %	Male	Male %	Total
Adjunct faculty	117	50%	117	50%	234
Full-time faculty	49	59%	34	41%	83

Table 1.2. Race and Ethnicity Demographics of Full- and Part-Time Faculty, 2018

Role	African American/ Black	AA/BL%	Hispanic/ Latinx	H/L%	White	W%	Total
Adjunct faculty	72	31%	11	5%	147	63%	234
Full-time faculty	12	14%	3	4%	65	78%	83

In recent years, Jessica Nastal and Jason Evans have both additionally served on statewide bodies, created by the Illinois Community College Board, on writing placement and developmental education reform.

Full-time faculty at the college have a base load of 15 credit hours per semester, typically five classes (Prairie State College, 2017). If full-time English faculty teach at least two composition courses, the course load is reduced to 12 hours in recognition of the time and attention students need in a writing-intensive course. The full-time faculty contract further articulates course caps of 30 for most general education classes, 22 for credit-bearing Composition I and II, and 18 for all developmental courses (English, Reading, and Math). Many full-time faculty also receive reassigned time for administrative duties, such as department chair—who sets meeting agendas, collaborates on professional development, and serves as liaison to the administration—or program coordinator—who hires and supports adjunct faculty, staffs sections, conducts annual assessment projects, and fulfills state-required program reviews.

Jason Evans served as department chair and coordinator from 2006–2012, as chair from 2014–2015, and as Developmental Reading/English coordinator since 2017. Jessica Gravely has served as English coordinator since 2014. Jessica Nastal served as department chair from 2019–2020 and has received reassigned time for work on accreditation, assessment, and a Student Success Pilot, applying Achieving the Dream's programs at Odessa College and Oakton Community College (Barnett, 2018) to PSC.

History of Our Placement Process and Courses

Before the changes to the PSC placement process that we describe here, the most recent major changes to the process had happened in the 1990s, before any of our current faculty members were teaching at PSC. Starting in the 1990s, students wrote an essay in response to one of a few locally developed prompts, and they took the COMPASS English and Reading exams. Faculty readers would look at all three pieces of information when determining placement, though a strong writing sample would always outweigh a lower score on either COMPASS exam. Starting in about 2007, we realized we weren't relying enough on the COMPASS English score to justify the time and cost, so we asked students to complete just the in-house essay and COMPASS Reading exam (Figure 1.2).

The death of COMPASS in 2015 (cf. Nastal, 2019) had the galvanizing effect of forcing a change to a major piece of the placement puzzle. Its disappearance meant that we would lose one way to identify students who may need additional assistance with college reading. Our desire to revise writing placement at PSC was further kindled by the recent arrival of two new faculty members, one with expertise in literacy studies and one with expertise in writing placement.

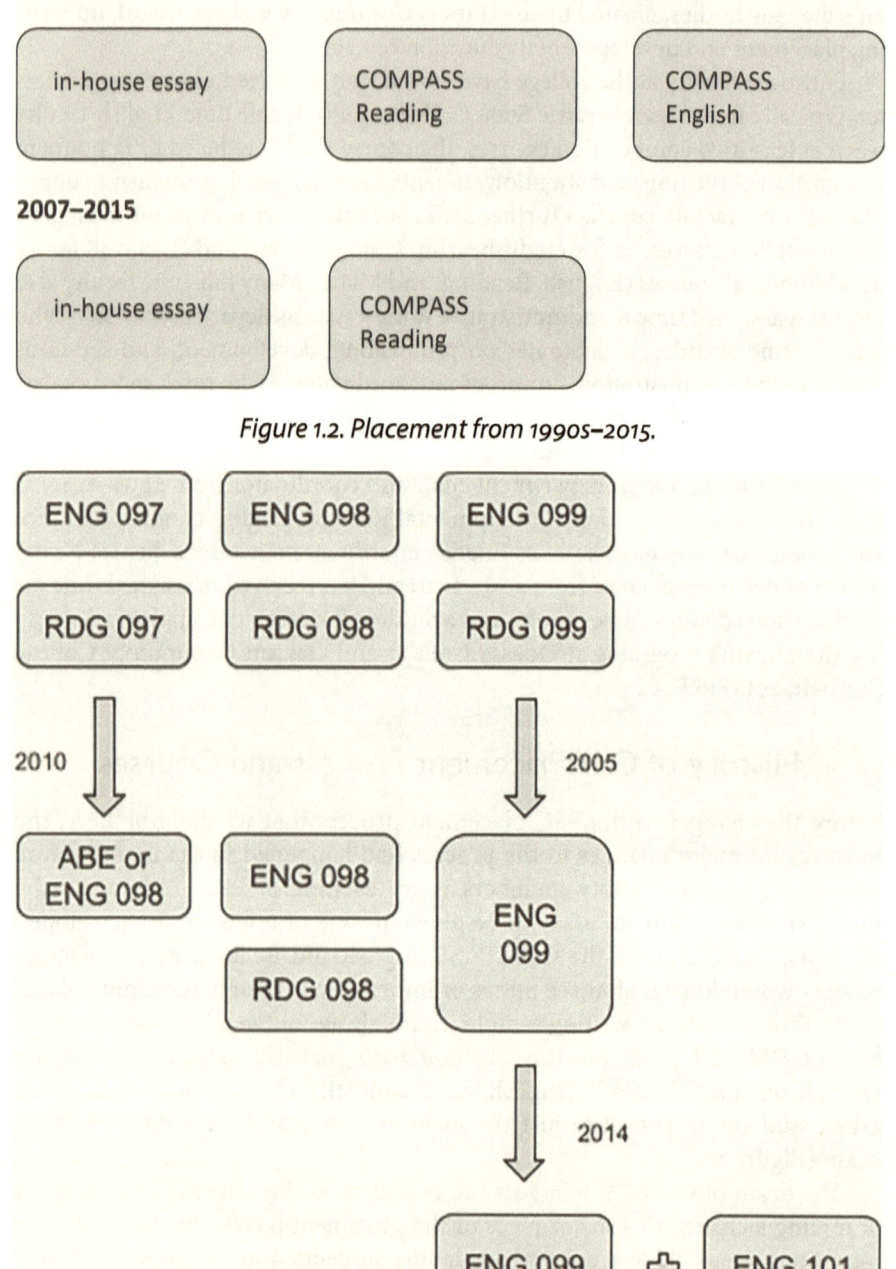

Figure 1.2. Placement from 1990s–2015.

Figure 1.3. Course offerings, 1980s–present.

Furthermore, our courses themselves had changed over the years, as represented in Figure 1.3 (see Evans, 2018). Since the 1980s, students might be placed into one of three levels of developmental English and/or reading—ENG 097, ENG 098, and ENG 099. But in 2010, after years of observing dismal success and persistence rates in students who began in ENG 097, the faculty and administration agreed to stop offering it. Students who had previously placed into ENG 097 would now either be encouraged to join literacy programs in adult basic education or take ENG 098. English 099 and Reading 099 had been separate courses until 2005, when they were combined as integrated reading and writing learning communities in a single six-credit-hour course, ENG 099. From 2012 to 2014, we piloted courses modeled on the Accelerated Learning Program (ALP; Adams et al., 2009). Around the same time, changes to Pell Grants led to sharper restrictions on the total number of credit hours considered Pell-eligible—a significant concern for many of our students, 41 percent of whom receive Pell Grants (IPEDS, 2020). As a result of the pilot and the changes to Pell, all ENG 099s were changed to three-credit-hour courses. In short, even if our placement processes had remained relatively stable, the developmental courses into which we placed students had shifted—a topic to which we return in the "Lessons" section.

Evidence for Placement Reform

Our placement process relied on a timed, impromptu writing sample, for which students selected one of three to five prompts that did not require additional preparation or knowledge. As a result, students wrote personal essays or decontextualized arguments about relatively staid topics, such as supporting school uniforms (cf. Perelman, 2012). When we revised our placement process, we wanted to provide students with an opportunity to demonstrate their integrated reading and writing processes. A department-wide portfolio assessment process in ENG 101 had taught us that entering composition students frequently struggled to summarize the viewpoints of others, and we believed that our placement process should assess students' ability to read, summarize, and respond to various viewpoints. Doing so would provide students with a better opportunity to understand the curriculum they were about to enter (Harrington, 2005) and provide readers with more information about students' familiarity with the kinds of reading and writing tasks they would encounter in ENG 101.

Looking back on a 2015 memo to the administration regarding this placement redesign, we see a concern for trying to place more students into ENG 101 while still ethically placing students overall. These desires probably grew from three experiences: our integrated reading and writing ENG 099, ALP, and concerns about justice and equity that grew from our ENG 101/102 English Program Review (2011–2016) and Jessica Nastal's survival analysis of placement data and success rates (2019).

Evidence From Integrated Reading and Writing

In our six-credit-hour ENG 099 (2005–2014), we offered students a challenging mix of reading assignments (Hern & Snell, 2013), and students made connections across a variety of course readings. We held end-of-semester faculty meetings to discuss grading standards and together considered representative examples of student work. Several years of seeing what students could do with these challenging materials contributed to a feeling that many students would be able to handle a higher placement with adequate support. Piloting ALP (2012–2014) also contributed to this feeling that students could handle a higher placement if provided this additional support. Seeing students succeed in transfer composition has a way of informing attitudes about placement!

Evidence From Illinois Community College Board Program Review

In 2016, the Illinois Community College Board (ICCB) modified its program review to more explicitly focus on equity issues. Previously, the ICCB program review process involved a general evaluation of different aspects of the programming, without much attention to data that might reveal equity gaps in success rates. Prior to 2016, program coordinators had not been asked to scrutinize disaggregated data or make specific plans to address those equity disparities (and no internal processes within the college existed yet either, nor have been developed since then). Although the English department had long been aware that our composition courses had low pass rates, we had not yet reckoned with the racial disparities in our success rates. In 2017, in her work as English coordinator, Jessica Gravely shared with the department disaggregated data about student course-level success; we learned that, across the composition sequence during the 2011–2016 period, African American students had passed ENG 101 and 102 at substantially lower rates than White students.

Evidence From Survival Analysis of Placement Data and Success Rates

Archival research and survival analysis of placement data and success rates across the composition sequence from 2012–2016, conducted by Jessica Nastal (2019), further showed just how rare it was for a student—most especially a Black male student—to be placed into ENG 098 or ENG 099 and persist and succeed in ENG 101 and ENG 102. Initial results were shared with the department in 2017 and showed that 82 percent of the students enrolled in ENG 098 from 2012–2016 were African American and Black, and only nine percent of those students ultimately passed ENG 101 at PSC. While Hispanic/Latinx students overall succeeded at higher rates than their African American and Black peers, White students were most successful throughout the courses. The data also revealed significant moments of loss throughout the writing sequence across all communities of students (cf. Zaback et al., 2016). For example, about half of the students who began ENG 098 did not pass it; then, of the students who did pass, two-thirds continued to the next course in the sequence; for ENG 099 before ALP, "about 75% of the students who began English 099 never passed English 101" (Evans, 2018).

The data alarmed our department and administration alike; they seemed to show that, despite our intentions to create on-ramps to college education, our developmental courses could be seen as a form of "apartheid," to use Ira Shor's (1997) famous indictment of basic writing programs. It appeared the courses could be reproducing the very educational and thus social inequity they aimed to combat with their opportunities to help students develop foundational literacy skills needed to navigate college-level coursework.

Together, we had substantial evidence of how different student communities performed in the classes, and an increased sense of urgency to act in ways to achieve justice or to address equity disparities. In the semesters that followed, we offered more robust professional development on a variety of topics—in reading strategies for composition students; writing assessment and research-based approaches to feedback; assignment design that encouraged metacognitive reflection; as well as the history, grammar, and rhetorics of African American English. Along with many faculty across the college, our department discussed texts such as Kathleen A. Ross's (2016) *Breakthrough Strategies: Classroom Based Practices to Support New Majority College Students*. Additionally, we rewrote our ENG 101 department-wide course agreements to work toward parity across the 30 or more sections among courses being taught.

Locating the Right Placement, Post-COMPASS

With COMPASS about to expire and substantial data to show where inequities existed in our program, we knew that we needed something more institutionally responsive and equitable than a purchased test like ACCUPLACER. We also knew that we wanted to continue using a direct writing sample, in which we have had a fair amount of confidence. We already had in place the institutional pathways—a placement testing center, funds and processes for organizing readers, an understanding from Enrollment Services that placement results would not be instantaneous—and so our faculty could focus on the form and content of a new placement tool. These pathways, we might add, exert constraints on the kinds of options we were considering: Funding for readers, for instance, also means one income stream for our adjunct faculty members.

The department explored a few different options for our post-COMPASS world. We considered using a standardized reading assessment. Several department members took the TABE and COMPASS exams to see what the experience might be like for students. While standardized reading assessments offered some benefits that we would not be able to realize by ourselves—development under the guidance of psychometricians and large sample groups, for starters—they also have been shown, broadly, to perpetuate inequitable educational outcomes (Scott-Clayton, 2012), which is particularly alarming at our Minority-Serving Institution. Plus, they're kind of a drag to take. We weren't sure their potential benefits were worth the potential costs.

We also considered the possibility of using directed self-placement (DSP), which was something we'd discussed since at least 2005. We recognize that, particularly in the wake of the COMPASS exam ending and in the move toward equity and justice, leaders in the field have called on practitioners to implement more agency-affirming methods of writing placement. The TYCA White Paper placement reform (Klausman et al., 2016), for example, recommends using multiple measures or directed self-placement, and the state of Illinois has moved toward a multiple *single* measures approach. Over the years, however, faculty members have expressed a number of concerns with the DSP process: the potential for students—especially women and people of color—to under-place themselves (Cornell & Newton, 2003; see also Ketai, 2012; Inoue & Poe, 2012), a disconnect between how students perceive their writing abilities and how their instructors perceive them (DasBender, 2012; Lewiecki-Wilson et al., 2000), the challenge of requiring students to apply past experiences to new writing situations (Bedore & Rossen-Knill, 2004; Gere et al., 2010), the difficulty of encouraging self-awareness for students who may have internalized a negative educational gaze (Schendel & O'Neill, 1999), and the complex skills of encouraging metacognition and transfer of knowledge to new situations. Here, Mike Rose's (e.g., 2012) scholarship resonated with many of our faculty who were raised in working-class families and have intentionally chosen to teach at a two-year college where most students are eligible for Pell Grants.

Of special concern to us, based on interactions with students in and out of class, is that DSP requires students to self-identify whether they would benefit from additional support—and we know that this is an admission not readily made. In our courses, students express hesitancy in using office hours, for instance, because they don't want to burden their instructors and because they believe they should just know how college works; if they have questions, they think it's up to them to figure out the answers or else it's more evidence they don't belong (cf. Villanueva, 1993). Thus, while we saw value in DSP encouraging students to assert their agency—and our composition sequence seeks to instill this agency—we were not yet convinced DSP was the best method of placement for PSC. Furthermore, the already-ambiguous institutional location of placement at the college made us question whether the college would support the labor involved in implementing DSP—from creating a procedure to working closely with all stakeholders on the process (Blakesley et al., 2003; Saenkhum, 2016). We are interested to learn more about how DSP affirms student dignity and contributes toward their success in the course (cf. Toth, 2019). We will continue to take a cautious approach to implementing DSP as we wait for more information on how the practice affects new majority college student communities; here, we echo Laura Aull's (2021) call regarding "the critical need to investigate student group differences, because fairness and justice are crucial for evaluation of assessment efficacy" (p. 11).

Our department also considered implementing a capabilities-based approach (Poe et al., 2019)—that is, not having placement at all—especially in light of the state moving toward reduced developmental education course offerings. States like Florida had fully eliminated developmental education courses, and in Illinois, new initiatives were on the horizon, such as high school transitional English and math classes that would guarantee successful students direct placement into college-level English courses.

Eliminating the placement process entirely would require the college to route students to the free adult basic education courses for literacy instruction or to enroll them in the college credit-bearing course ENG 101. This would require a radical revision, and expansion of, existing student support structures not only within our department but in other areas of the college. Placement into ENG 099 or higher is a prerequisite for many general education courses and certificate programs; the placement score has long been used as a proxy for students' literacy skills across the college. Without a clear way to fund a robust expansion of student support structures, not to mention professional development for faculty across the college, our department felt that this no-placement option would pose significant challenges. Particularly because the college's funding model is tied to student enrollment in credit hours, it seemed risky to nix ENG 098 and ENG 099 credit hours at the very moment when students enrolled in ENG 101 and other college-level courses might be in need of more reading and writing support than ever. This is another one of those instances where our limited resources inhibit us—as well as the institutional leadership we would need to make this work across the college.

Those alternatives outlined, what did we adopt? In the new placement process (Figure 1.4), students read and annotate a short nonfiction article, write a summary of the article, and then write an essay in response to the article. The annotated article, summary, and essay are reviewed by at least two trained adjunct faculty member readers, who are paid an hourly wage (currently $24–$25 per hour) for this labor.

We reviewed potential articles using Microsoft Word's Flesch-Kincaid measurements of grade level and reading difficulty, then analyzed them further using a rubric for qualitatively assessing texts (Fischer & Frey, 2013). Finally, we developed several writing prompts in which students would respond or engage in some way with the reading. Our placement rubric, which relies on analytic scoring, is shown in Figure 1.5. In using this rubric, we have had some discussion of a "Meat Loaf Rule"—i.e., two out of three ain't bad. In other words, the rubric's layout makes it seem like the annotation and essay might always carry the same weight, while we recognize that some students may not annotate *because* they understood the reading well. Likewise, students who annotate and summarize well but struggle with the essay may have some foundational literacy skills that will serve them well in ENG 101.

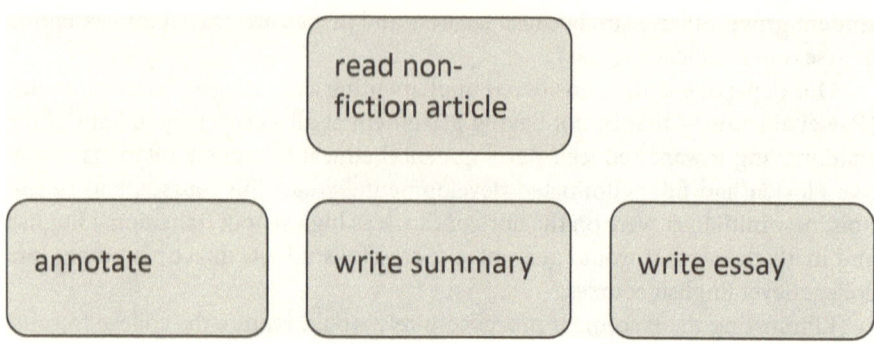

Figure 1.4. Placement process, 2016–present.

Time used to complete test ________
Article ____________________

READING/ENGLISH PLACEMENT ASSESSMENT

STUDENT ____________ SEMESTER/YEAR: ____________ OVERALL PLACEMENT ________

	AEDE 099		English 099		English 101
ANNOTATION	Sparse underlining with no written comments; Whole paragraphs highlighted with no indication of important ideas or questions ; marks limited to a single type of interaction, such as underlining unfamiliar words	☐	Some limited marking on the text showing some strategy use; Some comments in the margin, mostly general and not strategic such as, "wow" or "I think that, too"	☐	A variety of marks for a variety of strategic purposes; Strategic marking of main ideas and text signals; purposeful comments that clarify, ask and answer questions, make connections, summarize	☐
SUMMARY	Summary misses the main ideas and does not show an understanding of the article; Summary is not written in student's own words	☐	Summary indicates some understanding of the article and its main idea; summary contains main ideas, but some important details may be missing; summary is written in student's own words	☐	Clear understanding of the article and its main idea; Important details included; Summary written in student's own words	☐
ESSAY	Has some awareness of paragraphing—ideas are grouped by sentences; has some awareness of end punctuation—sentences begin and end, even if the application of punctuation is sometimes uneven; makes some kind of sense—the ideas could be clearer, but there is some sense of writing to answer a question or prove a point	☐	Has a sense of overall organization and shows some paragraphing skills; has understandable ideas in spite of some *persistent* and *varied* grammar problems; has general and unsupported claims, and the ideas in the essay need support; sometimes shows simplistic reasoning; has *persistent*, illogical word choices or sentence structures that make the essay difficult to follow	☐	Shows paragraphing and organization skills; develops ideas with detailed support; shows a sense of beginning, middle and end, even if there is no formal conclusion; may not have a thesis statement, but makes a point; has logical word choices and sentence structures that make the essay easy to read; may have some grammar problems, but essay is generally easy to read and understand	☐

Figure 1.5. Placement rubric.

We also relished the chance to introduce some subtle messages into the process. Whereas for the COMPASS Reading exam, students would read passages on several random topics, we selected articles for the new placement process with an eye towards messages that we thought would be helpful for students beginning their college studies. As David S. Yeager and colleagues (2016) demonstrated, small interventions as a student begins college can equip them with perspective on the challenges of college studies. Reading and writing about "growth mindset" in their placement exam, for instance, may make a small but important difference in how students approach studying. We have even tried, with mixed success, to avoid calling this instrument an exam or test, instead using words like "assessment" or simply "process."

After we felt the design of the new placement process captured our goals, we piloted three initial versions. To quell concerns of some faculty members, we wanted to make sure that each version tracked with the established measure. This points to a tension within the department—how do we increase the number of students, particularly BIPOC students, experiencing the college-credit-bearing class first, while attending to concerns about supporting individual students' success?

During a pilot period in the summer of 2016, we asked students to take both the COMPASS Reading exam and our new three-part placement tool as a measure of reliability, to compare our placement with the broad bands of placement that COMPASS Reading would have predicted. We analyzed a sample of 100 students who took both the new placement tool and the COMPASS Reading exam, and found that the new placement tool produced results roughly equal to what COMPASS Reading would have predicted. The two agreed 86 percent of the time; COMPASS would have resulted in higher placement six percent of the time, and our placement test eight percent of the time. Looking at some of the discrepancies more carefully, our literacy expert, Megan Hughes, noted the new version seemed to place higher those students who would have scored in the developmental range on COMPASS, but may place lower students who would have scored in the ENG 101 category based on the COMPASS Reading scores.

The pilot data showed our revised placement tool resulted in increased placement into college-level composition, which meant students were getting access to credit-bearing courses more quickly and, presumably, would be better positioned to succeed not only in English coursework but also in their longer-term plans to seek a degree, transfer, or obtain a certificate. Our administration viewed these results as an indication that the new placement methods better reflected the college's mission of access and equity.

Understanding the Effects of Placement Reform

As proud as we were to have produced a homegrown writing placement assessment—honoring the recommendations of TYCA White Paper on Placement Reform (Klausman et al., 2016)—we knew that the stakes of writing placement were very high for students, that there were no psychometricians among us, and that our pilot had been limited in some ways. Within our department, we were cautiously optimistic about the increased numbers of students placing into ENG 101, knowing that we could not really assess our new placement exam without also looking at how success rates might be affected. Many email exchanges and departmental meetings closed with the reaffirmation of our need to see the success rate data. Were we placing some students into ENG 101 and doing too little to support them? If there were equity disparities that needed to be addressed, how could we best work to support the opportunity to learn for all students? We asked, and asked again and again, but the college would not or could not provide numbers to answer our questions. In this matter, as in many faculty initiatives, our work was appreciated by the administration but neither supported nor expected.

Without having success rate data in hand, we were ill-equipped to navigate decisions about departmental policies and professional development. We needed that information to understand whether we were over- or under-placing students, whether our practice was supporting all students' success. In the wake of the new method, department members have raised questions about students' reading abilities. Could these shifts be an indirect result of less prepared students entering ENG 101? Or were other factors coming into play, such as new ENG 101 outcomes, or the dismantling of our department-wide ENG 101 end-of-semester portfolio, which had previously placed great emphasis on student ability to integrate sources into their writing?

Our inability to access data on student experiences with placement also meant that we could not validate our new process. As department chair, Nastal sought validity evidence (Kane, 2006; White et al., 2015) to begin to address our concerns. If we could understand patterns of student course completion, repeated courses in the composition sequence, or placement into the sequence, for instance, we would be better able to understand how our placement process, portfolio elimination, outcomes revision, or curricular choices affected students' success. If we could examine these data disaggregated by various communities at PSC—for example, Black/African American males or Pell-eligible students—we could better understand which student communities appear to be the most or least advantaged by our processes—an essential consideration in the pursuit of fairness (Elliot, 2016). Without the data, we were making decisions based on our personal beliefs and experiences. Nastal's concern was that our fears about under-placement were not born out in the data.

The 2017–2019 years were also marked by many other changes that shaped, and complicated, our department's understanding of how students and faculty were impacted by the new placement tool. Our pilot had suggested that the placement rates into developmental and college-level English would closely reflect the rates produced by COMPASS. How, then, could we fully account for the dramatic bumps in ENG 101 placements in Fall 2017, Fall 2018, and again in Fall 2019 (80%), and the relative drop-off in placement rates into developmental English (Table 1.3)?

Table 1.3. Student Placement Results From 2015–2019 (N=7,413)

Year	n=	NP		ENG 098		ENG 099		ENG 101		Honors	
		n=	%	n=	%	n=	%	n=	%	n=	%
2015	1,179	8	0.7%	112	9.5%	358	30.4%	696	59.0%	n/a	n/a
2016	1,726	16	0.9%	170	9.8%	502	29.1%	1,026	59.4%	n/a	n/a
2017	1,669	15	0.9%	100	6.0%	406	24.3%	1,147	68.7%	259	15.5%
2018	1,489	14	0.9%	38	2.6%	219	14.7%	1,164	78.2%	441	29.6%
2019	1,443	6	0.4%	40	2.8%	215	14.9%	1,161	80.5%	469	32.5%

A number of factors, beyond the placement test itself, were often floated in these discussions—could it be that we were seeing the impact of the Common Core State Standards, with its emphasis on mastery of nonfiction texts? In recent years, the college has experienced a demographic shift that has resulted in more students enrolling in the 18–22-year-old age range—students who are presumably closer to the writing assessment demands of their high school coursework. Additionally, during this same time period, the college has increased its numbers of high school students who are enrolling in PSC classes through our Early College Initiative program. To what extent did these demographic shifts affect our changing placement rates? Beginning in 2017–2018, our department also began collaborating with area high schools through a High School Partnerships initiative. Along with increased communication about our respective curricula, expectations, and general resources for students, our department shared our revised placement methods with area high school faculty and administrators.

Additionally, professional development for placement readers began to emphasize ways to assess placement essays without penalizing students for writing that demonstrated diverse linguistic features and grammatical patterns. Our revised placement training materials note that "Valuable ideas come in every variety of English, so readers should be careful to place students according to whether they get their messages across—to place based on writers' organization and development of their ideas, not according to whether they demonstrate a mastery of SAE [Standardized American English]."

Then there are the sea-change kinds of turns in our profession: attention to new majority college students (Ross, 2016) and their needs (and shifting understandings of our roles/responsibilities in responding to those needs), the ethical turn in writing assessment (e.g., Elliot, 2016; Inoue & Poe, 2012; Poe et al., 2014; Slomp, 2016; Toth, 2018), discussions about "stereotype threat" in our department (Steele, 2010). All these things were also having some impact on placement.

While we could not access course- or program-level institutional data, we have been able to review data from the testing center. These show the number of students earning each type of placement possible: No Placement (NP; this directs students to adult basic education classes), ENG 098, ENG 099, and ENG 101. Placement readers also indicate whether a student is eligible for an Honors section of ENG 101. Table 1.3 shows the number and percentage of students' placement results from 2015–2019. Figure 1.6 visually represents this information.

The rate students earned a No Placement remained below one percent during this four-year period. The rate at which students earned placement into ENG 098 and ENG 099, the developmental writing courses, decreased at noticeable levels. Students placed into ENG 098 at the highest rate, 9.8 percent, in 2016 and the lowest rate, 2.6 percent, in 2018. ENG 099 saw the highest rate, 30.4 percent, in 2015 and the lowest rate, 14.7 percent, in 2018. During this period, students' placement into ENG 101 increased at the highest rate, from a low of 59 percent in 2015 to a high of 80.5 percent in 2019—a 21.5 percentage point increase.

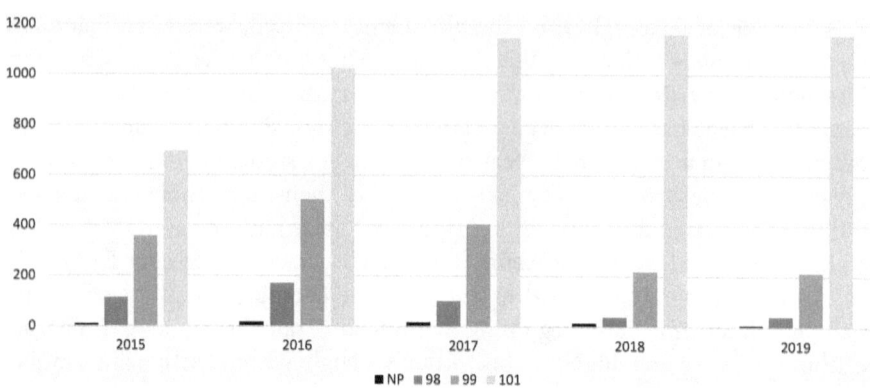

Figure 1.6. Student placement results from 2015–2019 (N=7,413).

We looked closely at students' course level success rates within all composition courses in the time since we implemented the new placement procedure, and found they remain around 60 percent (Table 1.4), consistent with what Nastal (2019) found in the archival data from 2012–2016. It appears that no one is failing because of the higher placements, but also that no one is passing more.

Table 1.4. Course-Level Success from Fall 2017–Summer 2019 (N=7,506)

Course	Pass		Not Pass		Total
	n=	%	n=	%	n=
ENG 098	33	60.0%	22	40.0%	55
ENG 099	253	62.3%	153	37.7%	406
ENG 101	1,512	58.3%	1,082	41.7%	2,594
ENG 102	954	58.5%	677	41.5%	1,631

Additionally, we reviewed pass rates in ENG 101 from 2011–2019. Students have passed the course at increasing levels, as represented in Table 1.5.

Table 1.5. Pass Rates in ENG 101 From 2011–2012 Through 2018–2019

Academic Year	Pass Rate
2011–2012	49.8%
2012–2013	48.8%
2013–2014	53.4%
2014–2015	n/a
2015–2016	56.3%
2016–2017	n/a
2017–2018	59.6%
2018–2019	59%

When we reviewed ENG 101 pass rates from the first few years of the new placement procedure, we found the general trend of students performing at higher rates in fall and summer, and lower rates in spring, maintained. Pass rates continued to stay around 60 percent, with a low of 51.2 percent in Spring 2018 and high of 67.2 percent in Summer 2019, shown in Table 1.6 and visually represented in Figure 1.7.

Table 1.6. Pass Rates for ENG 101 by Semester, Fall 2017–Summer 2019

ENG 101	Pass		Not Pass		Total
	n=	%	n=	%	n=
FA17	438	63.5%	252	36.5%	690
SP18	261	51.2%	249	48.8%	510
SU18	69	65.7%	36	34.3%	105
FA18	418	59.8%	281	40.2%	699
SP19	236	51.8%	220	48.2%	456
SU19	90	67.2%	44	32.8%	134

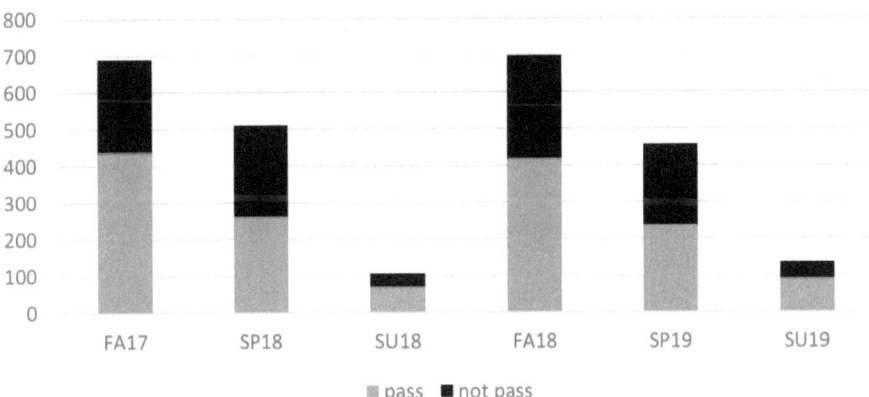

Figure 1.7. Pass rates for ENG 101 by semester, Fall 2017–Summer 2019.

Overall, students are placing into the college credit-bearing class at noticeably higher levels than they did previously with the COMPASS placement exam, and it appears students are succeeding in these classes at similar rates.

Consequences

The increasing numbers of students placed directly into ENG 101 has, over several semesters, increased our uncertainty about how to adjust the numbers of sections of ENG 098, ENG 099, and ENG 101. We want to offer enough sections to meet the enrollment needs of students without over-scheduling and running the risk of canceling sections. Data showing a general trend of diminishing enrollment across the college since 2017 also complicated our ability to make accurate projections for how many sections our department would need to offer.

Even prior to the new placement exam, we had been canceling sections of developmental English due to low enrollment, and that trend continued after 2017. Our department offers roughly 10–15 percent the number of developmental sections that we once did. Course cancellations have left some faculty members hesitant to opt for teaching developmental English; frequently faculty members who plan to teach developmental sections will request to be tentatively slated for an alternate section as a back-up plan, typically a college-level course that is likely to run without enrollment issues.

Across the college, we also began to see more students who register after the semester officially begins, and so we now make a more conscious effort to offer developmental and college-level courses in a wider variety of terms: 16-, 14-, 12-week. The new placement test also led to a renewed emphasis on diagnostic essay assessments, to confirm a student's placement in the early weeks of a developmental course. Although it remains rare for a faculty member to "bump up" students from ENG 098 to ENG 099, or from ENG 099 to ENG 101, based on early diagnostic assessment, we've realized the importance of having various course formats. We want to avoid the problem of, say, a student being told their work suggests they are in fact ready for a higher course level, only to realize that no spots remain in those sections. Along the same lines, it's far preferable for a student to transfer to a new course which has not yet begun, rather than transfer into a course that may have begun two to three weeks earlier, where they need to exchange their textbooks and quickly catch up on work they have missed.

The reduced need for ENG 099, in particular, has shaped our offerings. As of 2015, students placed into ENG 099 faced two options—to enter our ALP and co-enroll in ENG 099 and ENG 101, or to take ENG 099 in the first semester by itself, followed by ENG 101 the next semester. With fewer students placing into ENG 099 in recent semesters, we have all but phased out the latter option in favor of the ALP option. Whereas previously some developmental faculty did not teach ENG 101, it is now the case that developmental English faculty teach across the composition sequence.

Yet, despite these positive changes, it has been consistently difficult to access data. For example, Jessica Gravely has been challenged when she has requested additional information about closing equity gaps—a requirement for our regular ICCB program reviews. In spite of persistent requests at multiple levels, Jessica Nastal has waited for two years for information that would allow the department to understand and analyze the impact of the significant changes discussed throughout this chapter (an issue our colleagues in the math department also face). Without this information, it remains difficult for us to determine the efficacy and impact of our revisions. The college has discussed creating a data dashboard since at least 2010, but a more recent initiative to do so has been delayed.

These problems point to a serious consideration about our field's work in placement reform: Our institutions and systems may not have the resources, means, or desire to provide stakeholders with timely access to data, let alone the disaggregated data required to do equity work. At PSC, administrators urge all of us—including faculty—to make data-informed decisions. Our Strategic Enrollment Management plan, for instance, charges the college with addressing student persistence from developmental to college-level coursework, offering additional support to students enrolled in developmental classes, determining how to support African American students in gateway classes, improving success rates in gateway classes, creating awareness of success rates in gateway classes, identifying additional academic support services, and supporting professional development. How can we improve success rates in gateway classes without knowing what those rates are? How can we address student persistence from developmental to college-level coursework without real-time access to data, so we can see how our significant changes in a short time frame are affecting our students (Nastal, 2020)? Our discussion above of the many moving parts of the placement and composition ecosystem points to the importance of nuanced investigations of institutional context, and yet numerical data also have to be part of the conversation, particularly since the numbers exist in the college's data system and have only to be accessed.

Lessons

There remains a lot of energy around reform of developmental education at the national and state level. We have a kairotic opportunity to lead on how we want to change the placement ecosystem—placement, curricula, professional development, student support, opportunity structures, faculty and tutor support, communication with stakeholders. Any changes have to take into account the practical realities of instructors and tutors who have been prepared to work with students who come to college with different skills, competencies, and dispositions.

As an example of this tension, at a state-level meeting about developmental education reforms, one of us asked what support the state or colleges might offer for professional development for instructors and tutors to adjust to what might be a wider range of student preparedness in college-level courses. An administrator in attendance, who is now the president at an Illinois community college, dismissed the suggestion, saying that it is the faculty's obligation to do this, not the college's or the state's. We couldn't help but see this response as short-sighted, as these tectonic changes affect everyone whose classes require an English placement prerequisite, and not everyone in every discipline has access to the knowledge about language and literacy that many English faculty enjoy. This response also demonstrates how our society's responsibility to educate the citizenry, rather than being a matter of institutional or systemic priority and pride, devolves to individual instructors who can then be blamed for students' failure.

Reform doesn't happen in isolation and has significant implications for a number of stakeholders, especially students and instructors. In our case, placement reform affects staffing (cf., Blankenship et al., 2017), student reading in the credit-bearing courses, instructor grading policies, departmental curricular development, and collaborations with advisors. It points to professional development needs, reflected in our recent discussions about what "college-level" reading means; labor-based grading policies; social action research projects; linguistic variety; and genre variety. Our experiences throughout this process have underscored that writing placement reform reaches every part of our local ecosystem.

Our experience also raises questions about the potential change to our community college mission: What happens when all students enter the credit-bearing course (Poe et al., 2019)? How do we create opportunity structures (Elliot, 2016) for all students? Are we denying access to education for some—perhaps even by giving students access to the credit-bearing transfer course while denying access to educational and other supports intended to promote success? For students whose K-12 education has not given them access to rigorous literacy instruction, is the demise of developmental education—aided by our good-faith efforts to place students more accurately and avoid inequitable outcomes in placement—one more way our society says that your social destiny depends on where you were born (Evans, 2012)?

As we navigate the wake of our institutional reforms, we continue to look back at the Open Admissions movement to learn from those leaders' lessons. John Brereton explained in *Talking Back*,

> Coming from this highly literary first-year course at Rutgers, my entry to full-time teaching was a serious shock. In the City University of New York's Open Admissions program in its first year, 1970, my students were much more diverse; many were what my colleague Mina Shaughnessy would later call "basic writers," shockingly *un*literary—unacquainted with key discursive conventions and values of higher education. Their lives and their high schools offered them little preparation for the college composition course I was prepared to teach, one emphasizing careful reading and highly polished writing, assuming a specific cultural and literary background. But soon, with some of my CUNY colleagues, *I recognized that it was we, not just the students, who needed to change. And we had just fifteen weeks—one semester—to improve their writing or the students would be dismissed from college, the open door turning into a revolving door.* [emphasis added] (Gannett & Brereton, 2020, p. 142)

The English department at PSC, along with our colleagues state- and nationwide, are dedicated to making sure our open door doesn't become a "revolving door." This moment—with COMPASS's demise, the ethical turn, the explicit goal to counteract decades of systemic racism—makes it clear that we must continue to change. We must continue to learn how to meet our students' needs and help them understand the needs of their new writing contexts.

Acknowledgments

Thank you to the students, colleagues, family, and friends who support and sustain us. Thank you to the English department, Adult Basic Education and Literacy department, Student Success and Testing Center, and Advising Center at Prairie State College. Special thanks to the many dedicated stewards of community college student success.

References

Adams, P., Gearhart, S., Miller, R. & Roberts, A. (2009). The Accelerated Learning Program: Throwing open the gates. *Journal of Basic Writing, 28*(2), 50–69. https://doi.org/10.37514/JBW-J.2009.28.2.04.

Aull, L. (2021). Directed Self-Placement: Subconstructs and group differences at a U.S. university. *Assessing Writing, 48*. https://doi.org/10.1016/j.asw.2021.100522.

Barnett, E. (2018, March 9). Faculty leadership and student persistence–A story from Oakton Community College. *Community College Resource Center: The Mixed Methods Blog*. https://ccrc.tc.columbia.edu/easyblog/faculty-leadership-student-persistence-oakton-community-college.html.

Bedore, P. & Rossen-Knill, D. F. (2004). Informed self-placement: Is a choice offered a choice received? *WPA: Writing Program Administration, 28*(1–2), 55–78.

Blakesley, D., Harvey, E. J. & Reynolds, E. J. (2003). Southern Illinois University Carbondale as an institutional model: The English 100/101 stretch and directed self-placement program. In D. Royer & R. Gilles (Eds.), *Directed self-placement: Principles and practices* (pp. 207–241). Hampton Press.

Blankenship, C., Canava, A., Jory, J., Lewis, K., Stanford, M. & Stephenson, B. (2017). Re-assessing composition at open access institutions: Using a threshold framework to reshape practice. *Journal of Writing Assessment, 10*(1). http://www.journalofwritingassessment.org/article.php?article=113.

Cornell, C. E. & Newton, R. D. (2003). The case of a small liberal arts university: Directed self-placement at DePauw. In D. Royer & R. Gilles (Eds.), *Directed self-placement: Principles and practices* (pp. 149–178). Hampton Press.

Council of Writing Program Administrators (CWPA). (2014). *WPA outcomes statement for first-year composition*. https://wpacouncil.org/aws/CWPA/asset_manager/get_file/350909?ver=3890.

DasBender, G. (2011). Assessing generation 1.5 learners: The revelations of directed self-placement. In N. Elliot & L. Perelman (Eds.), *Writing assessment in the 21st century: Essays in honor of Edward M. White* (pp. 371–384). Hampton Press.

Elliot, N. (2016). A theory of ethics for writing assessment. *Journal of Writing Assessment*, 9(1). http://journalofwritingassessment.org/article.php?article=98.

Evans, J. (2012). Structuring the color line through composition. *Open Words*, 6. https://doi.org/10.37514/OPW-J.2012.6.1.02.

Evans, J. (2018). To live with it: Assessing an accelerated basic writing program from the perspective of teachers. *The Basic Writing e-Journal*, 14(1). https://bwe.ccny.cuny.edu/Evans.htm.

Fischer, D. & Frey, N. (2013). Growing your garden of complex texts. *Educational Leadership*, 70(9). https://www.ascd.org/el/articles/growing-your-garden-of-complex-texts.

Gannett, C. & Brereton, J. C. (2020). Framing and facing histories of Rhetoric and Composition: Composition-Rhetoric in the time of the Dartmouth Conference. In N. Elliot & A. S. Horning (Eds.), *Talking back: Senior scholars and their colleagues deliberate the past, present, and future of writing studies* (pp. 139–152). Utah State University Press.

Gere, A. R., Aull, L., Green, T. & Porter, A. (2010). Assessing the validity of directed self-placement at a large university. *Assessing Writing*, 15(3), 154–176.

Harrington, S. (2005). Learning to ride the waves: Making decisions about placement testing. *WPA: Journal of the Council of Writing Program Administrators*, 28(3), 9–29.

Hern, K. & Snell, M. (2013). *Toward a vision of accelerated curriculum & pedagogy: High challenge, high support classrooms for under-prepared students.* LearningWorks.

Inoue, A. B. (2019). Chair's address: How do we language so people stop killing each other, or what do we do about white language supremacy? *College Composition and Communication*, 71(2), 352–369.

Inoue, A. B. & Poe, M. (2012). Race and writing assessment. *Studies in composition and rhetoric.* Peter Lang.

Integrated Postsecondary Education System (IPEDS). (2020). *Prairie State College.* National Center for Educational Statistics. https://nces.ed.gov/collegenavigator/?q=prairie+state+college&s=all&id=148007.

Kane, M. (2006). Content-related validity evidence in test development. In S. M. Downing & T. M. Haladyna (Eds.), *Handbook of test development* (pp. 131–153). Lawrence Erlbaum Associates Publishers.

Ketai, R. L. (2012). Race, remediation, and readiness: Reassessing the "self" in directed self-placement. In A. B. Inoue & M. Poe (Eds.), *Race and Writing Assessment* (pp. 141–154). Peter Lang.

Klausman, J., Roberts, L., Giordano, J., Griffiths, B., Sullivan, P., Swyt, W., Toth, C., Warnke, A., Williams, A. (2016). TYCA white paper on placement reform. *Teaching English in the Two-Year College*, 44(2), 135–157. https://cdn.ncte.org/nctefiles/groups/tyca/placementreform_revised.pdf.

Lewiecki-Wilson, C., Sommers, J. & Tassoni, J. P. (2000). Rhetoric and the writer's profile: Problematizing directed self-placement. *Assessing Writing*, 7(2), 165–183.

Nastal, J. (2019). Beyond tradition: Writing placement, fairness, and success at a two-year college. *Journal of Writing Assessment*, 12(1). http://journalofwritingassessment.org/article.php?article=136 .

Nastal, J. (2020, February 6). *Writing analytics and two-year college pedagogy* [Keynote address]. The 9th International Conference on Writing Analytics, St. Petersburg, FL, United States.

Perelman, L. (2012). Mass-market writing assessments as bullshit. In N. Elliot & L. Perelman (Eds.), *Writing assessment in the 21st century: Essays in honor of Edward M. White* (pp. 425–437). Hampton Press.

Poe, M., Elliot, N., Cogan, J. & Nurudeen, T. (2014). The legal and the local: Using disparate impact analysis to understand the consequences of writing assessment. *College Composition and Communication, 65*(5), 588–611.

Poe, M., Nastal, J. & Elliot, N. (2019). Reflection. An admitted student is a qualified student: A roadmap for writing placement in the two-year college. *Journal of Writing Assessment, 12*(1). http://journalofwritingassessment.org/article.php?article=140.

Prairie State College. (n.d.) *Mission.* https://prairiestate.edu/about-us/mission.aspx.

Prairie State College. (2017). *2017–2020 Agreement: Board of Trustees of Community College District no. 515 and Prairie State College Federation Of Teachers, Local 3816, AFT, AFL-CIO.* https://prairiestate.edu/faculty-and-staff/union-contact-information.aspx.

Prairie State College. (2018). *Key performance indicators.* https://prairiestate.edu/about-us/operational-departments/institutional-research/key-performance-indicators/index.aspx.

Public Community College Act, Ill. Comp. Stat. ¶ 3–17 (1961 & rev. 2015). https://www.ilga.gov/legislation/ilcs/ilcs5.asp?ActID=1150&ChapterID=18.

Rose, M. (2012). *Back to school: Why everyone deserves a second chance at education.* The New Press.

Ross, K. A. (2016). *Breakthrough strategies: Classroom-based practices to support New Majority college students.* Harvard University Press.

Saenkhum, T. (2016). *Decisions, agency, and advising: Key issues in the placement of multilingual writers into first-year composition courses.* Utah State University Press.

Schendel, E. & O'Neill, P. (1999). Exploring the theories and consequences of self-assessment through ethical inquiry. *Assessing Writing, 6*(2), 199–227.

Scott-Clayton, J. (2012). *Do high stakes placement exams predict college success?* (CCRC Working Paper No. 40). Community College Research Center

Shor, I. (1997). Our apartheid: Writing instruction & inequality. *Journal of Basic Writing, 16*(1), 91–104. https://doi.org/10.37514/JBW-J.1997.16.1.08.

Slomp, D. (2016). Ethical considerations and writing assessment. *Journal of Writing Assessment, 9*(1). http://journalofwritingassessment.org/article.php?article=94.

Steele, C. (2010). *Whistling Vivaldi: How stereotypes affect us and what we can do.* WW Norton.

Sullivan, P. (2008). Measuring "success" at open admissions institutions: Thinking carefully about this complex question. *College English, 70*(6), 618–632. https://doi.org/10.1007/978-3-319-44284-6_29.

Toth, C. (2018). Directed self-placement at "democracy's open door": Writing placement and social justice in community colleges. In A. B. Inoue, M. Poe & N. Elliot (Eds.), *Writing assessment, social justice, and the advancement of opportunity* (pp. 139–172). The WAC Clearinghouse; University Press of Colorado. https://doi.org/10.37514/PER-B.2018.0155.2.04.

Toth, C. (2019). Directed Self-Placement at two-year colleges: A kairotic moment. *Journal of Writing Assessment*, 12(1). http://www.journalofwritingassessment.org/article.php?article=134.

Villanueva Jr, V. (1993). *Bootstraps: From an American academic of color*. National Council of Teachers of English.

White, E. M., Elliot, N. & Peckham, I. (2015). *Very like a whale: The assessment of writing programs*. Utah State University Press.

Yeager, D. S., Walton, G. M., Brady, S. T., Akcinar, E. N., Paunseku, D., Keane, L., Kamentz, D., Ritter, G., , Duckworth, A.L., Urstein, R., Gomez, E.M., Markus, H.R., Cohen, G.L. & Dweck, C.S. (2016). Teaching a lay theory before college narrows achievement gaps at scale. *Proceedings of the National Academy of Sciences of the United States of America*, 113(24), E3341–E3348. https://doi.org/10.1073/pnas.1524360113.

Zaback, K., Carlson, A., Laderman, S. & Mann, S. (2016). Serving the equity imperative: Intentional action toward greater student success (Research report). Complete College America. https://completecollege.org.

Chapter 2. From ACCUPLACER to Informed Self-Placement at Whatcom Community College: Equitable Placement as an Evolving Practice

Jeffrey Klausman and Signee Lynch
WHATCOM COMMUNITY COLLEGE

Abstract: This article traces the development of Whatcom Community College's placement reform efforts. From relying solely on the ACCUPLACER sentence-skills test, Whatcom developed a modified multiple-measures process on the way to the full implementation of an adapted and fully online directed self-placement process, what we call informed self-placement (ISP). Data on student placement and success in first-year writing, disaggregated by race and ethnicity, is offered for each placement process and innovation. The data show that Whatcom's placement process progressed from being among the most restrictive in the state of Washington, with only approximately one-third of all students and fewer Black, Indigenous, and People of Color (BIPOC) students placing directly into first-year writing, to among the most open in the state, with over 95 percent of all new students placing directly into first-year writing with close to no equity gap among BIPOC students in this data set. At the same time, and likely reflecting results of pedagogical and curricular efforts of departmental faculty, the data show that success rates in first-year writing rose for all but Latinx/Hispanic students, and equity gaps for Black/African American and Native American students were closed. The theoretical and research bases for each of the reform efforts are provided, as is an explanation of the larger equity issues that framed the entire effort.

Prologue

For nearly two decades, Whatcom Community College used ACCUPLACER to place students into a long sequence of developmental English courses leading to first-year writing, English 101. The sequence began in Adult Basic Education (ABE) (Figure 2.1[1]), moved through three levels of developmental English, then into a

---

1. Included in Adult Basic Education courses are courses in the English Language Learner (ELL) program that serves students who are learning English as a second language at a relatively basic level; these students are often recent immigrants. ELL is distinct from the academic ESL program that serves international students preparing for full

"bridge" course (English 100), and finally into English 101. As a consequence, a student placed into the lowest level of Developmental English, ENGL92, would be required to take three to four English classes before reaching English 101.

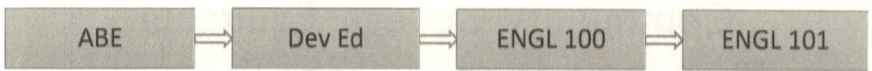

Figure 2.1. Pipeline for students placed into pre-college English.

Peter Adams and his colleagues (2009) coined the term "pipeline" to refer to this kind of course sequence to evoke the image of a "leaky" pipeline system. From the beginning to the end of any course, some students would "leak away"; thus, we'd have at best a 20 percent failure or attrition rate and often worse. In between courses, more students would "leak away," roughly another 20 percent. And with each additional course in the sequence, we'd lose more students.

So of 100 students placed into English 92: Developmental Reading, only about 78 would finish the course; of those 78, only about 62 would start the next class, English 95; of those, only about 48 would finish that class . . . etc. Ultimately, only around 22 percent of students who began in English 92 completed English 101 within three years (and likely forever). For students placed below that into Adult Basic Education (ABE) courses, their fate was worse, the equivalent of an academic death sentence. In the ten or so years we collected data prior to changing our placement process, no student from ABE ever completed first-year writing, a zero-percent success rate.

But as is sometimes said, nothing is as bad as it could be. So let's add race to the mix of placement and course sequencing. Research we conducted internally as part of our Achieving the Dream grant showed that prior to placement reform, students of color were twice as likely to be placed into developmental English or ABE than White students, a finding in keeping with Mya Poe and colleagues' (2014) disparate impact analysis. In essence, the pipeline phenomenon was heightened due to equity gaps in placement rates.

And if we really wish to make matters worse—and why not?—prior to Washington state community and technical colleges establishing placement reciprocity agreements in 2016, placement standards were developed in isolation, and our college had settled on the highest ACCUPLACER cut-off score in the state for placement into first-year writing. We suspect this decision was informed by a belief in the importance of "college-readiness" without consideration (awareness?) of the punitive and inequitable consequences such "standards" actually engendered. In fact, only around 30 percent of all incoming students entered English 101 directly in 2011; the rest (and disproportionately students of color) found themselves somewhere down the pipeline with no recourse but to swim or leak away.

---

enrollment in Whatcom's academic programs.

It's not hard to see that our placement process contributed to, and was emblematic of, the kind of systemic racism that many of us are committed to ending (see Klausman et al., 2016). But until around 2012, we were unaware even of placement as a problem nationally; instead, we were focused on updating curriculum and improving our classroom assessment of writing. But the research coming out of the Community College Research Center (CCRC; see Scott-Clayton, 2012) and the popularization of the Accelerated Learning Program (ALP) (Adams et al., 2009) awakened us to the harm a placement process can do, and we set about changing things, first through adjusting cut-off scores, and then revamping the placement process and sequence of courses.

Whatcom Community College

Institutional Context

Whatcom Community College (WCC) is a mid-sized community college serving 11,000 students annually (around 4,000 full-time equivalents [FTEs]), located in Bellingham, Washington, a city with a population of approximately 90,000. WCC offers Associate in Arts and Science and Associate in Arts (AAS and AA) degrees, numerous professional certificates, and two BAS degrees. Because Bellingham is also home to Bellingham Technical College, which offers many of the vocational programs associated with two-year colleges, WCC students are predominantly transfer-degree seeking (79%); of those pursuing a professional or technical degree or certificate, many graduate from the highly successful RN program or other health-science related programs or the nationally recognized cybersecurity program (Whatcom Community College, 2021).

WCC students are relatively young, with 68 percent between the ages of 16 and 34; about half attend full-time (53%); and roughly 10% are current high school students taking classes at WCC's campus in Washington state's dual-credit Running Start program.[2] International students account for roughly eight percent of the FTE. WCC students are also majority White and first generation (63% for both figures); 37 percent are students of color, with the largest demographic groups being Asian at six percent and Latinx/Hispanic at three percent, while 20 percent identify as "two or more groups" (Whatcom 2020–21 WCC Student Headcount and FTE, n.d.).

---

2. In Washington, Running Start is a very successful program in which high school juniors and seniors attend classes at local community colleges earning dual-credit; about half of Running Start students at Whatcom attend full-time and take few if any high school courses, seeking to earn both an associate's degree and high school diploma simultaneously. The rest of the Running Start students take one or two classes per quarter at Whatcom while taking classes at their high school. Running Start accounts for about 10–14 percent of our FTE annually; because state funds transfer with them from the high school to the college, Running Start enrollment is an important revenue source.

Like college students everywhere, a significant number of WCC students face personal challenges. During the fall of 2019, 42 percent experienced food insecurity in the prior 30 days (compared to 42 percent statewide for two-year colleges); 53 percent experienced housing insecurity in the previous year (compared to 51 percent statewide for two-year colleges); 22 percent experienced homelessness in the previous year (compared to 19 percent statewide for two-year colleges) (2019 #RealCollege Survey Results, 2020; Washington State Community and Technical Colleges #RealCollege Survey, 2020). Overall, Whatcom students are as vulnerable—if not more so—to the kind of life issues that negatively affect success for other two-year college students.

Curricular Context

The writing program at Whatcom is housed in the English department and offers two levels of college-level composition: first-year writing (English 101), which nearly every student in every program has to complete, and a second composition course required of nearly all of the associate's degrees. Prior to 2016, we offered a second composition course for transfer students, English 102, which was replaced with an offering of three courses: English 201: Advanced Composition, which faculty are free to design as they wish to meet the learning outcomes; English 202: Writing about Literature, which is probably exactly what you think it is; and English 230–235: Technical Writing (three-credit or five-credit version). All the composition courses are coordinated through parallel learning outcomes and a shared, though not mandated, recommended "learning for transfer" curriculum (see Yancey et al., 2014). A dedicated writing program administrator, with one course of reassign time and a small budget, facilitates program development, which includes facilitating our placement process.[3]

We have 11 full-time, tenure-line faculty, all of whom teach composition regularly, and 20 to 25 contingent faculty, nearly all of whom have been teaching with us for years, sometimes for more than 20. We're an active writing program, with recent tenure-track hires (three) trained mainly in composition rather than literature or creative writing. Many of us are active in the Two-Year College English Association of the Pacific Northwest (TYCA-PNW) and the Conference on College Composition and Communication (CCCC). At the 2017 CCCC in Portland, for example, we had nine faculty attend; at the CCCC the following year in Kansas City, six of our faculty attended, including two contingent faculty.

---

3. Historically, placement has been overseen by the English department in collaboration with Developmental Education and ABE faculty, but the placement process took place in the Testing and Placement Office, which administered the ACCUPLACER test; later, when multiple measures were implemented using the "Placement Scorecard," the placement decisions were made at various offices around campus. Also, Signee worked hard to coordinate all the different stakeholders, from faculty to advisors.

Our current administration is committed to equity and social justice and tends to be very supportive of writing program reform. Our department has requested three new faculty of color for our English department since currently only one faculty member identifies as a person of color (and she's a new contingent faculty member) and one (Jeff) identifies as mixed race. This faculty racial and ethnicity mix does not match the student body, which is over one-third students of color as noted previously.

Finally, one notable factor of our writing program is what we call "comp rate," which is used to calculate our annual workload. A five-credit composition course, with an enrollment of 19 or higher, is calculated as 6.25 credits toward a full-time quarterly load of 15 credit hours. This means a full-time faculty member can teach seven five-credit composition courses in a year as an equivalent to the nine five-credit non-composition courses of a full-time load. Since we're on a quarter system, a full-time composition load, then, could consist of a 3-2-2 course schedule. This workload allows faculty at Whatcom to work with students and respond to their writing in ways promoted by the discipline and avoid the burnout that is common to the field. Moreover, the more manageable workload allows for the professional development that faculty at other colleges regret having little time for (see Klausman, Roberts & Snyder, 2020; Suh, Tinoco, Toth & Edgel, 2020).

ACCUPLACER

As mentioned previously, around 2012, when CCRC studies appeared showing the inadequacy of standardized tests as placement tools (Scott-Clayton, 2012) and suggesting the disparate impact of such practices (Poe et al., 2014), we looked closely at our use of ACCUPLACER and quickly saw the unfairness—almost meanness—of the practice.

In addition to having the highest cut-off score in the state, we also tested students in both reading and sentence skills but used only the score on the sentence-skill test for placement. This practice resulted in less than one-third of all new students placing into English 101 (30%), a bit more than a third placing into English 100 (35%), and about a quarter placing into Developmental English, ABE, or one of our English language learner programs (25%).

Because our reliance on the ACCUPLACER sentence-skills test created "disparate impact" in almost a classic way (see Poe et al., 2014), students of color disproportionately placed into lower-level or pre-college classes compared to White students. Consequently, students of color completed college-level English (101 or higher) in their first year at disproportionately lower rates. For the 2011–2012 academic year, 47 percent of all students completed college-level English in their first year, but this number was far smaller for students of color (Figure 2.2).

While these numbers are stark, we'd like to consider an extended scenario to make clear the exigence we felt when we first became aware of the impact of our placement process.

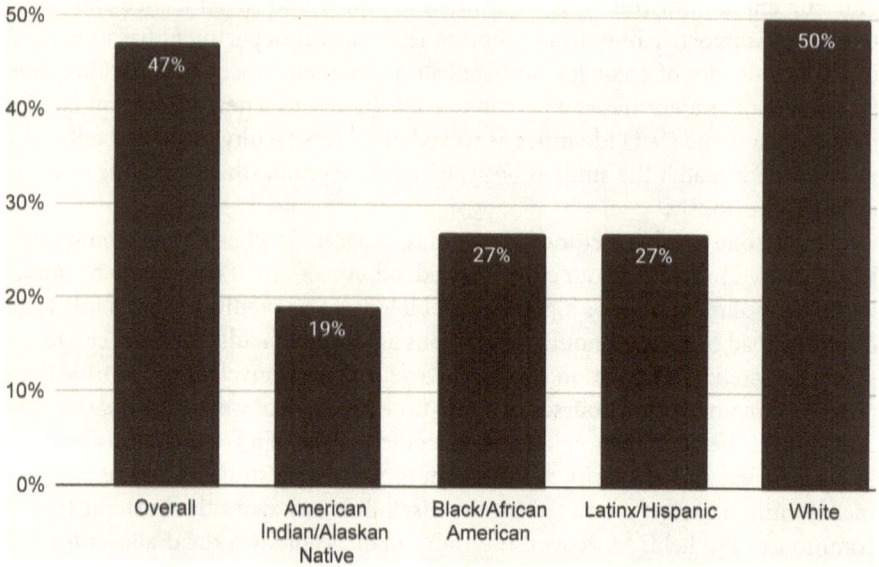

Figure 2.2. English 101 completion in first year (2011–2012)

Because Whatcom is a relatively small college, and because Latinx/Hispanic students account for only approximately three percent of new students, the *n* for Latinx/Hispanic students excluded from success in first-year writing in any given year is relatively small. But what if we multiply those numbers over ten years? This would give us a better picture of the impact of our placement process over time and on our community: In our view, this impact is part of how generational poverty persists, if we grant that higher education improves income and quality of life (American Association of Community Colleges, 2016).

If we take 2011–2012 as an average year (which it is, compared with the next three), we know that only 29 percent of Latinx/Hispanic students were successful in college-level English within one year, and only 35 percent were successful in college-level English within two years. (The comparable figures for White students are 54 percent and 63 percent.) Over ten years, then, we can see that out of approximately 14,500 total students placed using ACCUPLACER, 435 would likely have identified as Latinx/Hispanic. Of those 435, only 152 (35%) would have been successful in college-level English in two years. This means that 283 people who identified as Latinx/Hispanic would have left Whatcom without credit in college-level English. By contrast, over that same time period, 63 percent of White students were successful in college-level English within two years. For a similar *n*, this means that of 435 White students, 274 students earned college-level English credits while 161 White students left Whatcom without such credits earned (Figure 2.3).

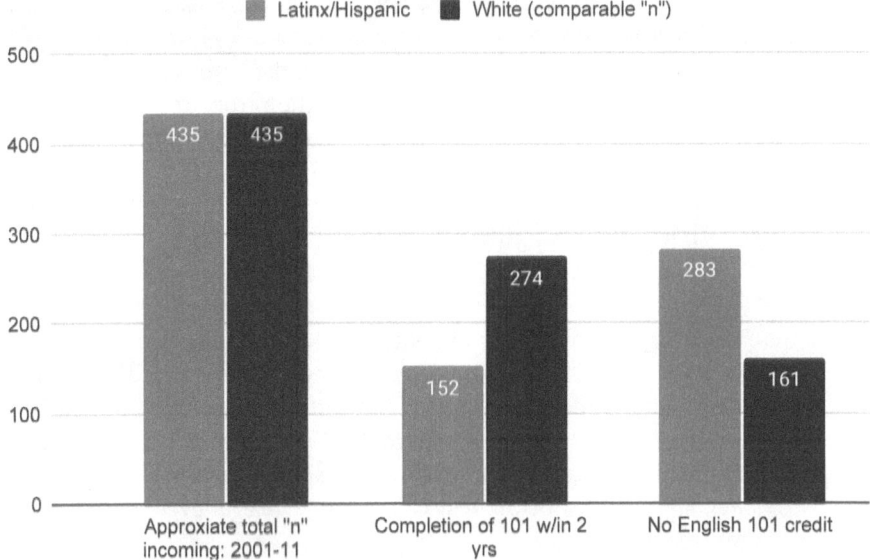

Figure 2.3. Effect of disparate impact: Latinx/Hispanic v. White students extrapolated over 10 years.

We have no way of knowing if the Latinx/Hispanic students transferred to another college or returned later; we do know that a student who does not complete English 101 at Whatcom does not complete a certificate or degree at Whatcom. The results of ACCUPLACER seem to indicate that Whatcom's placement process disproportionately and unfairly (for reasons we discuss below and suggest above) barred historically marginalized students, such as Latinx/Hispanic, from higher education and, to some degree, the better life that such an education promises.

Once we saw the problem with ACCUPLACER, Jeff related the system to the then recent CCRC study on standardized test scores and placement. He contrasted the scores on the sentence-skills test with scores on the reading-skills test (which students completed but which was not considered in placement, for unknown reasons) and found no correlation whatsoever. For example, Jeff found that students with a sentence-skills score of 88, which was the cut-off for English 100, our bridge course, had reading-skills test scores that ranked from the 3rd percentile to the 97th percentile.

There was no explanation for that huge variation, whether the reading scores actually said something about some or all of the test-takers' reading abilities or whether some or all of the test-takers knew the score didn't count and so expended effort as they wished. However, considering that the CCRC provided some evidence supporting the validity of the reading-skills test, and that there existed models in our state for using the reading-skills test only for placement (Bellevue College had instituted such a policy a few years before), we shifted our placement to using reading skills only and lowering the cut-off scores. We aimed for more students placed directly in English 101 and so simply lowered the cut-off score to achieve the number we wanted: Everyone in the 60th percentile and up got into English 101. Simple. The placement distribution from 2013–2015 reflects that change: More students entered English 101; however, those placed along the pipeline, though fewer, faced the same potential leakage points.

Moving to Multiple Measures via the "Placement Scorecard"

As we were wrestling with our unfair placement system, we were also facing pressure from the state of Washington to change our course offerings. The transfer agreement we operate under between two- and four-year colleges is managed through the Inter-Collegiate Relations Council (ICRC). The ICRC determined long ago that the first college-level English composition course must be English 101. No composition course below that could carry college-level credit and so must be numbered below 100.

At Whatcom, English 100 was offered as a bridge course to English 101. In fact, we were proud of our "modified stretch program," designed after Arizona State University's (ASU) stretch-model, which gave students a slower and more in-depth introduction to college-level writing. Its quarterly all-department assessment meeting was central to our writing program as it served both to norm our teaching and to develop ourselves professionally. Also, it reflected our "more writing is better" belief. Many of us saw it as our most valuable and important class because it gave students yet one more class to improve as writers and offered a safer introduction to college writing venues since it was only offered pass-fail. At one point, almost 40 percent of all new students placed into English 100, which in the fall quarter had the most sections of any English class; this naturally meant employment for many contingent faculty.

When the ICRC insisted, finally, that we renumber English 100 to below 100, we faced a conundrum. If we numbered the course below 100, we would be making it a Developmental English (DE) course. At Whatcom, DE courses are housed in a different department and even in a different division; they are taught by DE faculty. Our English faculty could not teach those classes. People's jobs were on the line.

After lengthy and at times heated discussion, we eliminated English 100 and, via a separate conversation about integrating reading and writing in DE, we helped DE collapse their sequence to essentially one class: English 95. At the same time, the DE faculty revised their college-level study skills class (English 174), and we in English recommended introductory literature classes as "bridge" courses into English 101 for students who felt they needed a softer landing into college-level writing instruction, under the assumption that lit classes required less writing but were still taught by English faculty who could shepherd wary students through a college-level writing process at least once. We had other plans as well, which included the creation of Accelerated Learning Program (ALP) courses[4] and a new, fairer placement process (Figure 2.7.)

To facilitate these changes, our administration secured an Achieving the Dream grant to support faculty to create an ALP English 101 course, team-taught by DE and English composition faculty. Based on CCRC research that found that high school GPA was the best predictor of success in first-year writing (Bailey, 2012), Jeff created a "Placement Scorecard" in the spring of 2014 which allowed students to use any one of a number of measures for placement: cumulative high school GPA, AP English grade or test score, SAT/ACT, college GPA, or—barring access to any of those—ACCUPLACER reading-skills score.[5]

Even here, however, we see evidence of our gate-keeping mentality. While we opened the door to multiple options for placement, we limited the scope. The high school GPA had to be from within two years (later extended to five) and required an official transcript—two limitations that very likely (and based on anecdotal evidence) disproportionately affected older and non-traditional students, including veterans, but which did not affect younger White students, those still in high school, or new graduates. Also, the GPA requirement discriminated against students who had not done well in high school but came to the college more motivated. Similarly, the other test scores—SAT, ACT,

---

4. The ALP model we developed deviates from the traditional model developed at the Community College of Baltimore County. Due to various constraints—employment of Developmental Education faculty, for instance—along with the prevalent belief at the time that "Developmental Education students" were a distinct population with unique needs—that is, we still were under the impression that our former placement methods and other markers actually identified a difference in students who in the past were placed into developmental courses—and so needed special curriculum and pedagogy which our English faculty were not trained in, we created a ten-credit team-taught linked course of English 101 and English 95; students were placed into the ten-credit class, team taught by an English department faculty member and a Developmental Education faculty member. The faculty were compensated for both classes, thus making the arrangement highly costly for the college. When the Achieving the Dream funding ran out, and the college could no longer afford the team-taught compensation model, Developmental Education faculty resisted the un-coupling of the compensation from the linked course model (in essence, Developmental Education faculty were unwilling to team teach and be paid only for one five-credit class). The ALP model was disbanded and a hodge-podge of options has since replaced it; creating "support" courses remains on the college's agenda, with a recent introduction of IBest courses—again, linked and team taught but funded by a Washington state program; however, the deficit-model thinking that grounds many of these initiatives is troubling to us (Jeff and Signee), and we have not been invited to participate in their development.

5. Note that we distinguish between "multiple options" for placement, which allows students to use any one of multiple options for placement, and "multiple measures" for placement, as is traditionally understood to use a combination of two or more measurements to determine placement.

AP—discriminated in favor of traditional, White students. The result was that the ACCUPLACER option very likely (again, based on anecdotal evidence from advisors) was utilized disproportionately by non-traditional students, many of whom were students of color.

Nonetheless, the shift to the Placement Scorecard and to using the lower ACCUPLACER reading-skills cut-off score (equal to the average cut-off score of colleges in the state, which Jeff researched) resulted in immediate increase in placement into first-year writing. In the 2015–2016 academic year, the results were dramatic (Figure 2.4).

As Figure 2.4 shows, 79 percent of new students placed into English 101. This means that far more students were placed directly into and therefore completing English 101 rather than courses lower in the sequence. College-level placement for key demographic groups showed significant improvement as well. Students of color benefited greatly, with 66 percent of Latinx/Hispanic students placing into English 101 as opposed to 29 percent before, and 73 percent of Black/African American students placing into English 101, up from 27 percent during the worst of the ACCUPLACER days.

As a consequence of students being placed into first-year writing at a higher rate, the completion rates—the percentage of students completing English 101 or higher within one year of enrolling—increased significantly. This milestone is used to measure the college's success, since completion of first-year writing in the first year correlates positively with retention and graduation (Washington State Board for Community and Technical Colleges, 2020). Our local data show that our retention rates into the fourth quarter after enrolling rose only slightly (from 57% in 2015–2016 to 62% in 2018–2019); however, retention and graduation rates, no doubt, are affected by many factors.

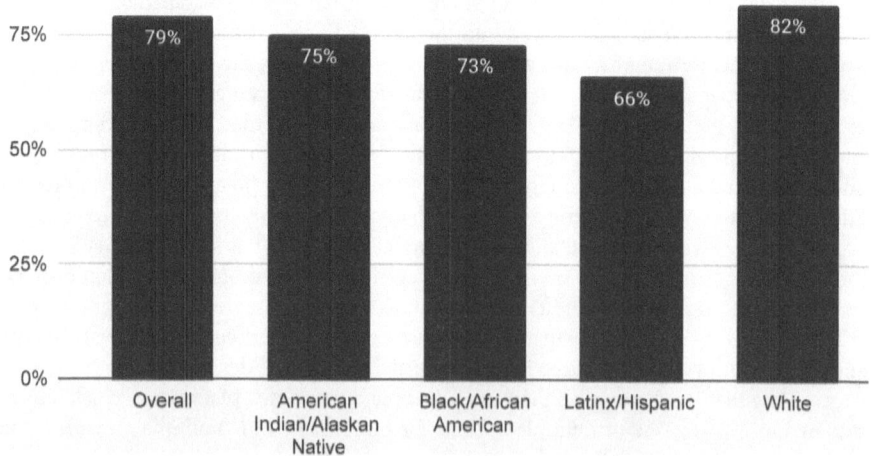

Figure 2.4. Placement into English 101: Multiple measures, 2015–2016.

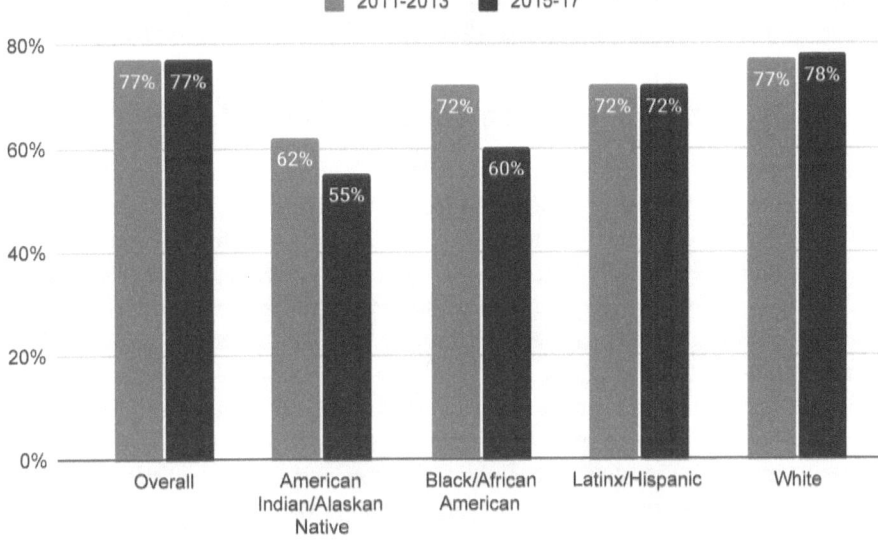

Figure 2.5. English 101 success rates: 2011–2012 v. 2015–2017.

Though the numbers of students placed directly into English 101 increased dramatically, thus side-stepping the preparatory "pipeline courses," the success rates in English 101 remained essentially the same, at around 77 percent. For most students of color, the success rates decreased somewhat, as Figure 2.5 shows, with the exception of Latinx/Hispanic students, who were successful at the same 72 percent. However, since more of all students of color placed directly into English 101, rather than further down the pipeline, a significantly greater aggregate number were successful in English 101 than before (e.g., since 73% of all Black/African American students placed directly into English 101 using multiple measures rather than 73% placing *below* English 101 using ACCUPLACER, as shown in Figure 2.1, 60% of the 73% were successful as opposed to 72% of a much smaller number).[6]

Overall, the move to the Placement Scorecard, offering students multiple options to demonstrate readiness for first-year writing, had a positive effect as did the truncating of the pipeline of developmental courses. But the reliance upon standardized-test scores and high school GPA, especially as we delimited those scores, still acted as a gatekeeper for many students. We had adopted the Placement Scorecard and program redesign out of necessity and efficiency: The sequence revision required a tremendous amount of collaboration across campus, but the move to multiple measures was a relatively easy adjustment to make, requiring relatively little structural changes to the entry-and-advising process that students followed. But we recognized the move as a temporary stop-gap measure, not one designed

---

6. Figure 2.3 uses data from two academic years for each data point in order to ensure a large enough n for each population group.

with fairness in mind, which Mya Poe and John Aloysius Cogan Jr. (2016), in "Civil Rights and Writing Assessment," cited as "the central tenet" of placement.

Reframing Placement as an Equity Issue

Shortly after we enacted our reforms, statewide developments provided additional context for more authentically addressing equity issues in placement. ACT's COMPASS, the purported writing skills test still widely used for placement across the state, had recently been discontinued due to questionable validity (Fain, 2015), providing an incentive for colleges to reassess their placement approaches. With support from our State Board for Community and Technical Colleges (SBCTC), administrators and faculty from many of the 34 two-year colleges met at Highline College, south of Seattle, for a series of workshops on directed self-placement (DSP), featuring keynote speakers Christie Toth and Asao Inoue and opportunities to share DSP models that Highline College and other early adopters were developing. Thanks to a convergence of these statewide conversations, our own federal grant funding, and the access to data afforded us by our office of Assessment and Institutional Research, we were able to hit the ground running in planning our next iteration of placement design around data-informed principles and a deliberate effort to promote equity.

Attempts to reframe placement as an equity issue, rather than within its traditional function of providing a mechanism for "ensuring success," were not without initial controversy at our campus. Efforts to question the predictive reliability and gatekeeping function of placement were met with a degree of skepticism. Traditional placement measures had long been viewed as measures of student readiness, preventing students who "needed help" from failing in first year writing, gateway courses, and the many courses in which placement in English 101 is a prerequisite. Despite the research challenging the validity and efficacy of traditional placement measures, the long-held assumption that placement "worked" (or should) was hard to abandon: Students took placement exams or earned certain GPAs, and the numbers meant something, went the rationale; the process was benign, if not beneficent, designed to support students in their success. These were all assumptions faculty and staff had to work through and abandon.

At the same time, English and DE faculty were grappling with existing and anticipated losses, including the retirement of English 100 and potential further decline in enrollments in pre-college courses. Putting aside these threats to personal lost income and programmatic identity, a belief that "more writing is better" had long been a shared core value, as mentioned above. Moreover, the DE faculty expressed concern that self-placement was simply the newest iteration of the "right to fail" paradigm and that students (and faculty) deserved better. And better meant opportunities for more support and more preparation for the rigors of college writing.

In hindsight, a possible explanation for this resistance was that we were still grappling with an assimilationist mindset—a belief that students need help doing what we think is important. We were only beginning to deliberately apply an equity framework to decision-making, with the larger systemically racist implications of our placement practices and curriculum still barely on our radar.

Ultimately, the research and the statewide conversation offered legitimacy to directed self-placement, and our own internal course success data revealed the capricious gatekeeping role of traditional placement measures. Faculty either supported or no longer openly opposed our reform efforts, and student services staff lent their support to make the many changes to the onboarding processes our college had in place.

Moving to Informed Self-Placement

In 2016–2017, while conducting our initial literature review and attending statewide meetings of colleges interested in DSP, we did not realize we would ultimately reject many of the traditional DSP practices. In fact, we originally set out to replicate early DSP efforts, for the benefit of traditionally marginalized groups of students, relying on surveys to provide us with the information necessary to direct students to the best English course for them. We considered reading and writing prompts as sources of information, and a possible reliance on English faculty advisors to guide students in need of additional direction (Blakesley, 2002; Reynolds, 2003; Royer & Gilles, 1998).

Because we set out with an ambitious aim—a fully online placement tool to be used by nearly all students[7]—we quickly realized traditional DSP methods would likely not permit us to meet our local goals. We were intrigued by the shift in perspective and practice that an *informed self-placement* (ISP) model might afford (Bedore & Rossen-Knill, 2004). We realized placement in its most equitable form might offer up a "teachable moment," in which students would rely entirely on information about course options and success strategies in order to make independent placement decisions. This was the only justification we could offer for having a placement process at all (see Nastal, 2019, who proposed the idea that "an admitted student is an already-qualified student," even at an open-door institution). As we considered each traditional element—surveys, reading samples, writing prompts, course recommendations—we asked, "Why? Is there any empirical evidence or compelling rationale to argue for inclusion?" If not, we did not include them, believing they would act only as unnecessary barriers, especially to historically disadvantaged groups (Elliot, 2016).

Granted, we did not come to these decisions lightly or quickly. We pored over survey question options. We spent a number of weeks considering various types of reading prompts and writing samples as potential sources of useful information about classes students might take. In the end, we realized that student lives

---

7. At WCC, English as a Second Language Academic (ESLA) students are admitted and placed through a separate process, with oversight by a different department.

and experiences were difficult to capture even with the most thoughtful of surveys. And because reading and writing samples would be alienated from a supportive classroom environment, we determined such mechanisms would actually risk misinforming students who could successfully navigate those same passages and prompts within the interactive environment of a well-taught college course.

Without entirely discounting concerns about student preparation or a "right to fail" paradigm, we decided to hold first to a commitment to removing barriers and fostering agency as the primary informing principles of our ISP design. The information we now share with students focuses on the importance of student agency and the value of their lived experiences, like military service or graduating from high school, and contextualizes "readiness" in everyday reading and communication experiences and "success" in the workload expectations and the support systems within and outside of the college.

Students self-select the placement information they wish to explore and choose from categories of course options rather than a single either-or choice between English 101 and something "less than" that. Figure 2.6 presents a diagram of the four possible paths a new student may follow. Following any of the paths, such as "College Writing" or "Alternate Paths," takes them to an introductory video and some written text describing what happens in each pathway, with details about the courses housed on our college website. Students then return to the main page and view another selection or move on. In this way, students inform themselves rather than being shunted through a predetermined sequence of activities.

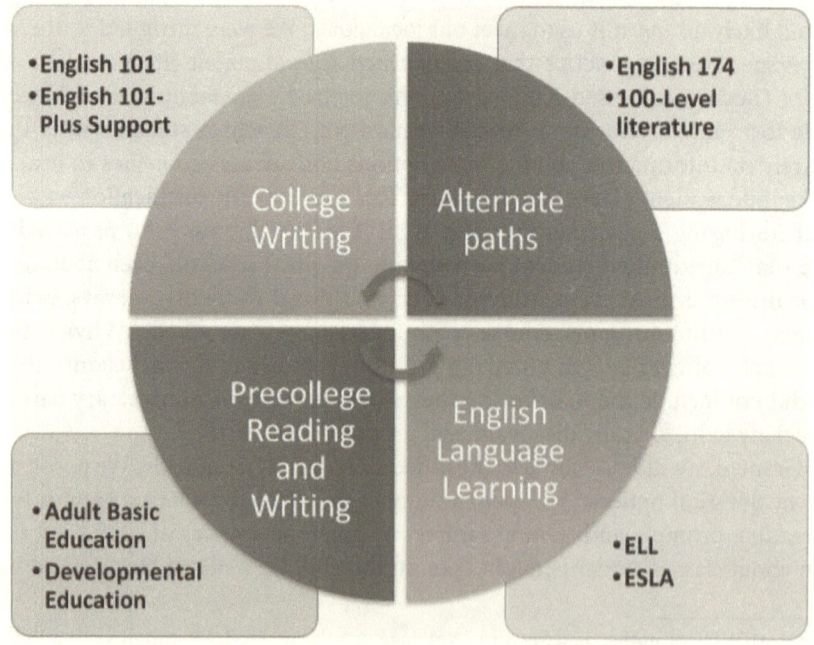

Figure 2.6. Placement options visual.

A perennial problem for budget-strapped colleges considering self-placement is the actual placement platform. We considered a variety of options, including instruments designed at Boise State, Portland State, Highline Community College, and Lower Columbia College. Lower Columbia, at one of our state DSP meetings, presented an online platform created with an iPhone camera and Google Forms—a compellingly simple combination of technologies we regrettably could not convince our IT department to approve. Eventually, we settled on Canvas, the learning management system for Washington State colleges—a familiar platform which we knew we would have control over, allowing for easy editing and updates.

Over the nearly yearlong process of researching and designing our ISP, we enlisted the help of a team of stakeholders, including advisors, faculty, and administrators. In addition, in our roles as writing program administrator and department chair, with decades of combined teaching and administrative experience, we also had a good bit of autonomy and ethos in designing the ISP instrument.

To communicate information within Canvas, we rely on a few short informational videos—to avoid a heavily text-based experience—about the ISP process and course options. Students then take two very short "quizzes" (ungraded surveys) to record their self-placement decision, and Advising and Registration have access to student decisions to reference during advising sessions and to manually input for registration access. The entire process for students takes approximately 20 minutes, meeting another of our goals.

Using student feedback, we revised our placement materials about a year after implementation, prior to the fall of 2019, this time including student voices in the informational videos and applying Transparency in Learning and Teaching (TILT) principles to make content more accessible, as well as Universal Design for Learning (UDL) elements. This revised version of ISP is in use today (though again being revised). Students complete the self-placement process independently from anywhere in the world; plus, the ISP course is fully accessible as measured by a built-in Canvas accessibility tool.

In large part due to early and frequent communication with all stakeholders, our initial ISP rollout received a largely positive reception. Approximately 1,200 students participated initially, with nearly all those who offered feedback expressing satisfaction. For example, one student wrote, "You guys did a great job explaining and helping me out. Thank you very much." Another wrote, "Thanks for keeping it simple and easy while saving me time and money. Yay!" We believe student satisfaction with the process, such as expressed here, is important, as a placement process that is welcoming throughout is key to assuaging fears and preconceptions that historically marginalized students—students for whom the educational system in general has repulsed (see Zaretta Hammond's (2015) *Culturally Responsive Pedagogy and the Brain*)—likely bring to their first encounter with our college. Granted, the satisfaction assessment may not be empirically valid, but combined with focus group feedback, along with disaggregated placement data, we feel we at least have no reason to be alarmed.

Any residual resistance from English 101 faculty regarding student readiness and/or misplacement seemed to evaporate other than the occasional anecdotal complaint about "one student who...." We encountered a short-lived "second wave" of mild pushback from DE faculty in the form of renewed questioning about methodology and grumbling about declining enrollments attributed to the placement process, likely a result of the very real threat to DE faculty teaching loads. Because we offer our first-year writing courses with several support options, including an ALP model, which we discuss below (and in note 4 and Figure 2.7), we continue to navigate the inevitable tension of working across two departments in coming up with ways to serve and communicate information to students.

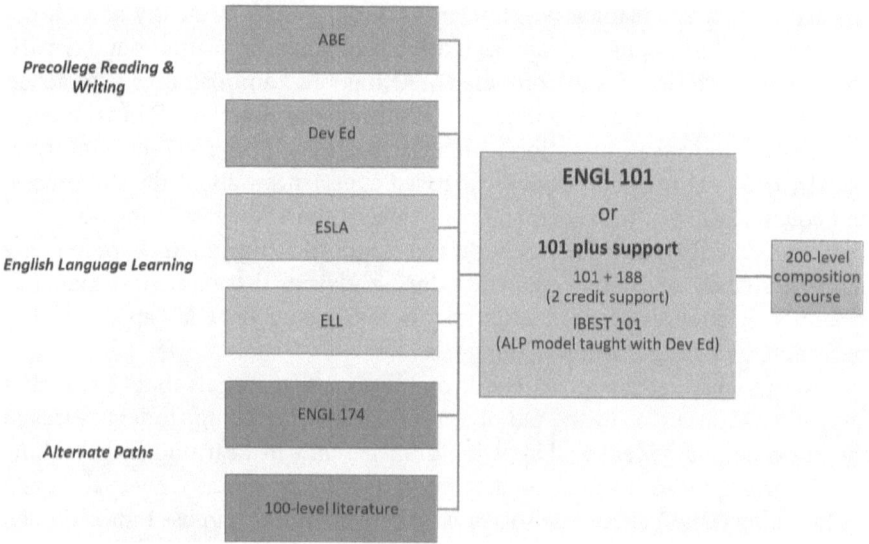

Figure 2.7. Current placement/Course progression options.

In training sessions with advisors, we learned they needed assurances that the move from gatekeeping to agency was, in fact, a priority. We originally envisioned ISP as a tool advisors would use in their conversations but have since learned Canvas is difficult for advisors to locate, possibly due to our college's byzantine website and the layers of administration that must be penetrated to revise it. Moreover, ISP is only one of many checkpoints advisors share in their conversations with incoming students; and, of course, many of our advisors are hired part-time and seasonally to respond to the largest new enrollment periods, and these temporary and sometimes new advisors have a lot to keep in mind. Similarly, data entry of the students' placement decisions has been burdensome—Canvas does not interact to our severely outmoded administrative software—and the task of downloading data in an Excel spreadsheet and then entering the placement code by hand has bounced around different student services departments, sometimes from intern to intern.

Consequences of ISP

Placement reform is only one part of Whatcom's concerted effort to improve assessment of student learning. In 2008, a dedicated institutional researcher was hired, and the Assessment and Institutional Research (AIR) office was established. Thanks to the director there, and the research analyst hired in 2012, we now have access to Tableau dashboards that give us real-time access to placement data and course success data, which we can analyze in many different ways, disaggregating along demographic lines as well as delivery modes, etc. We can compare placement, success, retention, and graduation rates for all students and for any number of combinations. For example, we can determine the success rate in English 101 within one year for part-time students who identify as low income (Pell Grant receiving). We can identify success rates for Running Start students who identify as Latinx/Hispanic—in full or part. These dashboards are publicly available.[8]

Our ISP has been far more successful than we had anticipated. When we launched the ISP in the spring of 2018, for use by incoming students that fall, we had no idea how it would work, beyond what limited reassurance positive but very small student focus groups offered us. Moreover, we were uncertain of the effect on the makeup of the English classes. Would faculty notice a shift in student ability? Would there be other effects?

Even before the start of the 2018 Fall quarter, we recognized that about 95 percent of all incoming students who completed the ISP chose first-year college English as their placement, meaning English 101, a 100-level literature course, or the college-level study skills course. We surmised correctly that the vast majority of these students would enter English 101. We were scheduled to receive our first set of data on success rates in January of 2019, after the fall quarter ended, but even before then, as classes began in September, we received informal feedback from faculty on the makeup of their classes—feedback largely in the form of silence. We heard no complaints about radical differences to perceived readiness for English 101 among students sitting in classes across campus. We breathed a sigh of relief. Apparently, the wheels had not fallen off.

Then in January, the Tableau dashboards were updated and the data was available. We learned 96 percent of all students placed themselves into college-level English. For the year, students of color also placed themselves into college-level English at high rates. As Figure 2.8 shows, 94 percent of Black/African American students placed themselves into college-level English, compared with only

---

8. While the Tableau dashboards offer real-time data on placement, success, retention, and graduation rates disaggregated in any number of ways, individual populations are not so easily defined. For example, a student may identify as Latinx/Hispanic as well as White and be included in both of those categories. Because of this, all data disaggregated along racial and ethnic identities are approximate. Links to Whatcom Community College's public Tableau dashboards can be found on this page: http://faculty.whatcom.ctc.edu/InstResearch/IR/InstitutionalDataCollegeData/datatools/index.html

73 percent using multiple measures and 32 percent using ACCUPLACER; for Latinx/Hispanic students, the numbers were higher but not as high: 87 percent self-placed into college-level English compared with 66 percent using multiple measures and 34 percent using ACCUPLACER.

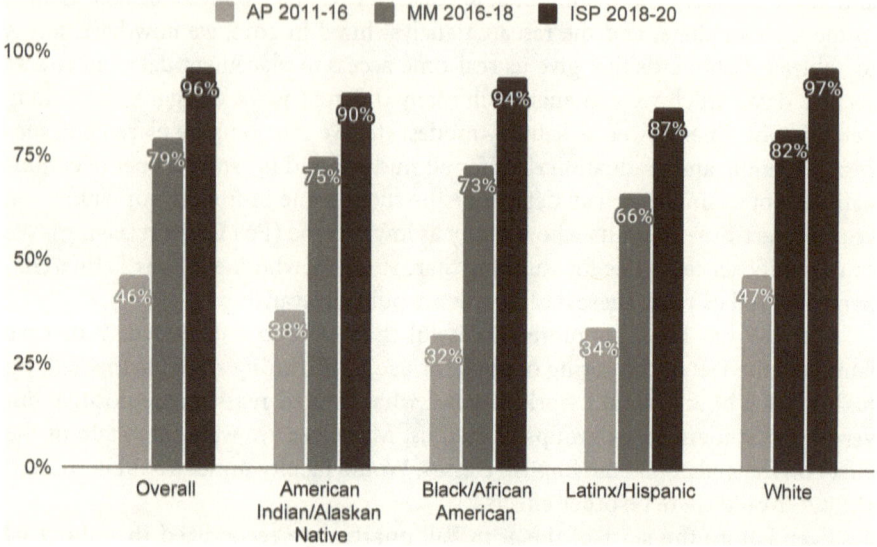

Figure 2.8. Placement in English 101: ACCUPLACER (AP) v. multiple measures (MM) v. informed self-placement (ISP).

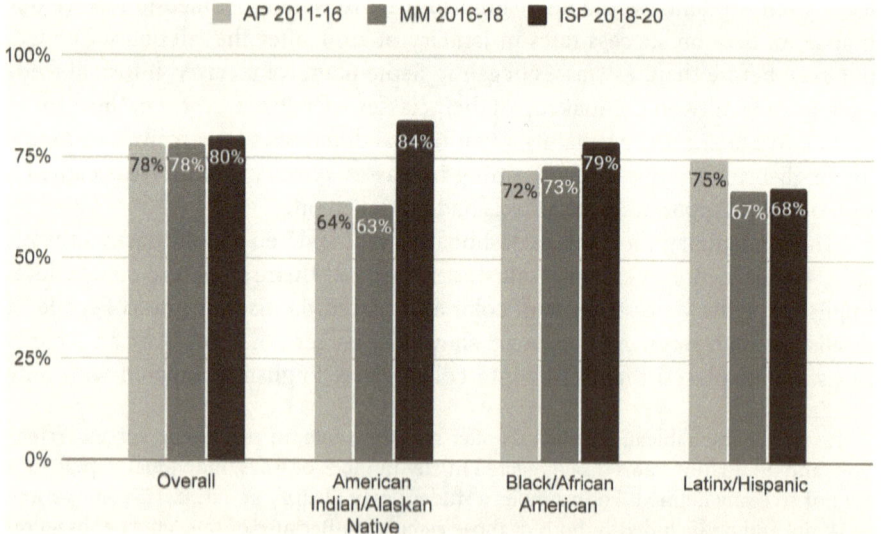

Figure 2.9. English 101: Success rates: ACCUPLACER (AP), multiple measures (MM), informed self-placement (ISP).

But were these students successful? If not, did that mean that the old placement process had some validity in identifying those students who were ready for college-level work and those who were not? The data allowed us to dismiss that worry. As Figure 2.9 shows, the success rates, for the most part, actually increased, with the exception of Latinx/Hispanic students.[9]

There are at least two ways to interpret this data. First, we can assume that nothing changed in the receptive environment—in other words, we were teaching the "same old English 101," and the students prior to ISP simply had been barred from their chance to demonstrate what they could do, either directly by being denied access to the class or indirectly via the environment of exclusion they felt they had to fight through (i.e., the stigma that comes from being placed into a lower-level English class). Second, we can recognize that the entire college was working on equity issues and that the placement revision was just one part, albeit a major one, of the innovations we were implementing. Faculty were aware that they were likely to face a different kind of student in the fall of 2018. Whether they actually did or not, we have no way of knowing except anecdotally: We both taught English 101 that year and can attest that the student makeup was largely the same. We suspect that other faculty also did not notice a significant difference since we received no complaints about student readiness. In our estimation, both factors probably played a part. The students entering our English 101 classes in the fall of 2018 were likely of no discernible difference from the students placed into Developmental English in the fall of 2011, which means that our old gatekeeping placement processes were without warrant. At the same time, our faculty were made conscious of their need to modify their pedagogical and curricular practices, and many embraced the opportunity for such revision, changes which continue today with Whatcom's equity efforts that touch every part of our campus.

The one exception to this is the decrease in success rates for Latinx/Hispanic students, from a high of 75 percent under the old ACCUPLACER placement method to 68 percent using ISP. As mentioned previously, the aggregate number of Latinx/Hispanic students successfully completing English 101 increased dramatically—simply because more students in this demographic had immediate access to the class. Nonetheless, the success rate dropped, and while the argument could be made that these students were "misplaced" or "underprepared," we are not ready to accept that conclusion but instead want to focus our attention on

---

9. Christie Toth (2018) reported in "Directed Self-Placement at 'Democracy's Open Door': Writing Placement and Social Justice in Community Colleges" that completion rates at colleges that had implemented some form of DSP "remained the same or improved," and that is certainly the case for us. Toth also stated that as of 2018, "no community colleges disaggregated DSP outcomes data to examine the consequences of DSP for different groups" (p. 139); our disaggregated data was just becoming available at the time Toth was publishing her chapter.

our readiness, as a writing program and as writing teachers, for all students, as we discuss in "next steps."

As mentioned above, our ISP process has had a great benefit for incoming students of all races and ethnicities, as well as students with disabilities, low-income students, and other demographics.[10] Over 95 percent of new students self-place into college-level English, and most of them choose English 101 as their first course. Success rates have actually risen to 80 percent and continue to rise as faculty have embraced equity-minded pedagogical practices, such as "the 4 Connections," first developed at Odessa College and adapted by Lake Washington Technical (Ames & Heilstedt, 2019). Far fewer students enroll in DE courses, while the number of students who enroll in ABE and ELL courses remains about the same, with students finding their ways to these programs through the various student-support services.

Most importantly, the course sequence which saw a majority of students placed into classes below English 101 "leak away" has largely been eliminated. Our DE faculty, our ESL-Academic faculty, and our ABE faculty all have developed short-cuts from their programs directly into English 101 for some of their students. No longer are students disempowered by a standardized test, placed at the beginning of a long sequence of often disconnected courses, and then left with no recourse to opt out. The system we have now is not perfect—the gap between different demographic groups in self-placement in college-level English gives us pause—but it is far, far better than what we had. Most importantly, it recognizes and supports student agency.

An unexpected positive development we found is that as the placement process evolved from ACCUPLACER through multiple measures to ISP, more students ended up enrolling in classes. As Table 2.1 shows, 77 percent of students using the old ACCUPLACER model enrolled at WCC within four quarters; that number moved up to 84 percent with multiple measures and went up again with ISP to 87 percent. Of course, correlation does not mean causation, and class enrollment is affected by many factors. But we believe it is safe to say that the revision of the placement process did not prove to be a deterrent and likely helped.

A less data-driven consequence is the shift that is occurring in our faculty attitudes and beliefs about readiness and about what English composition itself means. This shift is not the consequence of ISP solely; ISP is part of a larger shift toward an emphasis on social justice—a central concept in the college's strategic

---

10. Forty-four percent of students with disabilities completed English 101 in their first year under the ACCUPLACER placement process, 53 percent using multiple measures, and 60 percent using ISP. Forty-one percent of low-income students (Pell Grant awarded) completed English 101 in their first year using ACCUPLACER, 63 percent using multiple measures, and 65 percent using ISP. Some of this data seems to respond to Toth's (2018) call for "more research that examines the consequences of various approaches to DSP for different groups" (p. 138).

plan revised and adopted in 2019—and a burgeoning movement to revamp our program as an antiracist writing program, which is being fostered on multiple fronts—through campuswide Equity Project initiatives, for example, and a statewide Antiracist Writing Assessment Ecology Initiative, in which Whatcom faculty are currently participating, led partly by Asao Inoue and based on his scholarship (Inoue, 2015).

Table 2.1. Percentage of Students who Completed English Placement Processes and Ultimately Enrolled at WCC

Method/Period	Enrolled Within 4 Quarters of Placement	Enrolled Any Time After Placement
ACCUPLACER Summer 2011–Spring 2015	77%	84%
Multiple measures Summer 2015–Spring 2018	84%	88%
ISP Summer 2018–Spring 2020	87%	88%

Nonetheless, when ISP was first implemented and faculty saw that students were essentially the same, they were forced to question their assumptions about readiness. At the same time, given the growing awareness of inequity in the system of higher education and the growing diversity of our students, faculty have doubled down on training to prepare themselves for these more diverse students. And finally, faculty have begun to question traditional notions of writing, moving toward multiple Englishes, for example. We believe the move from ACCUPLACER to multiple measures and to ISP has helped faculty be more open to question and modify their traditional practices.

Another positive consequence is the greater involvement of our DE faculty as co-developers and co-teachers in our ALP model English 101 course, which has been replaced recently by a modified IBest version. And even further, with all the revisions, faculty from the different programs—ESL-Academic, ELL, ABE, DE, and English composition—have been in better communication, collaboratively designing new courses and curriculum, including pathways directly from their programs into English 101.

However, there have been some drawbacks from these rapid shifts. The departmental divide between "lit people" and "comp people," which had been growing for some years, may have deepened. With ALP and ISP and new ideas about what constitutes writing, including culturally responsive teaching, the demands on faculty to participate in professional development dedicated to teaching composition have increased and have not been universally welcome. Remnants of highly traditional views of writing persist, lingering perhaps just under the surface, but arising in deficit-minded comments about student readiness or student writing: "They don't know what a sentence is."[11] We sense that the undoubted success of ISP and other reforms mitigates many concerns of equity-minded faculty though they leave untouched a perhaps nostalgic fondness for traditional, belletristic writing and "traditional" (read: White, middle-class) students. It's evident that a shift in something as simple as a placement process can have repercussions that are far reaching, touching even the sense of identity that writing faculty hold for themselves.

Lessons From ISP and Next Steps

We've come a long way in just under six years, from living with a grossly discriminatory placement process and the highest ACCUPLACER cut-off scores in the state, to revising an already successful but far from perfect informed self-placement process. Along the way, from the very early stages of moving through a multiple-measures approach, through the wave of revitalized DSP implementation, to assessing our own ISP results, we've learned a lot about how such self-placement instruments can be designed and implemented to enhance student agency and success. These are some of the key takeaways:

- Ensure institutional commitment to equity and antiracist efforts, and tie these movements to state and national movements.
- Obtain and anticipate both initial and ongoing funding.
- Recruit key stakeholders.
- Use data to inform planning and decision making.
- Map out placement "mechanics" (platform, data management, advisor training, etc.).
- Deliberately (re)design courses into which students place themselves.

Ideally, the last two recommendations inform placement design from the outset. An effective ISP process relies on the English department's (and institution's) ability to (re)envision and communicate what students encounter and benefit from in specific courses. Equitable placement is conditioned by the classes into which students place. To this end, developing a shared vision among faculty is essential. At WCC, placement has been informed by the principle that first-year writing courses can and should be ready for all students who determine for themselves that they have "good enough" language and reading proficiency and time management skills. However, we are now questioning the potential deficit mindset and white supremacist views implicit in even this language.

Locally, our faculty are coming to terms with the nuanced and multilayered ways in which higher education is, in fact, systemically racist, and in conversations about curriculum redesign, many have been questioning their own expertise as

---

11. See Allia Abdullah-Matta (2020) for a discussion of faculty exercising autonomy contrary to programmatic intents or legislative injunctions.

educators (Inoue, 2015). This is a good problem to have and one that has implications for placement. Contextualizing placement within conversations about equitable/antiracist curriculum allows one to inform the other. By resisting the temptation to use placement as an early "filter," used to identify "unprepared" students, and instead focusing on what students will encounter and what they need—not on what we have traditionally thought we need to tell them—we improve our chances of becoming what T.B. McNair et al. (2016) called a "student-ready" campus.

Our ISP program was awarded the Diana Hacker Outstanding Program in English Awards for Two-Year Colleges from TYCA for 2020. Nonetheless, four years on and with more self-placement examples to draw upon, we've come to recognize that our program is still informed by assimilationist ideas that may prime students to adopt a conditioned deficit mindset, especially students from historically marginalized groups.

Fortunately, we obtained grant funding to revise our ISP this year (2021). Our goal will be to integrate what we've learned from antiracist writing assessment work to create an antiracist placement experience for all incoming students, which we feel is a step beyond the open gateway experience we were aiming for originally and which, we feel, better expresses the original intent of community colleges to make education accessible to all (Strohl, 2015).

Acknowledgments

We'd like to thank all those who have been involved in the complex and at times challenging transitions we describe in this article, especially Anne Marie Karlberg and Peter Horne of the Assessment and Institutional Research office at Whatcom Community College, who have worked so hard to bring us and the rest of the college easily accessible, comprehensible, and reliable data. We'd like to thank Ed Harri, Vice President for Instruction, who secured the Achieving the Dream grant while dean and has supported our reform efforts throughout; all the members of the English department and Developmental Education for their willingness to let us try out new things when even we didn't know what was going to happen; and all those in advising, placement, and other student services offices as they worked to tie together the thousand loose ends that a change to placement processes creates, especially Carla Gelwicks and Amy Anderson. Finally, thanks to our college administration for promoting the shift of culture to make Whatcom Community College a student-ready campus.

References

2019 #RealCollege survey results: Institution report for Whatcom Community College. (2020, May). Hope Center for College, Community, and Justice at Temple University. http://faculty.whatcom.ctc.edu/InstResearch/IR/IndirectIndicatorsCollegeSurveys/2019-RealCollegeSurvey-WCC.pdf.

2020-21 WCC student headcount and FTE. (n.d.). WCC Assessment and Institutional Research Office. Retrieved February 26, 2021, from https://tableau.sbctc.edu/#/site/WHATCOM/views/Enrollment/HeadcountandFTE.

Abdullah-Matta, Allia, Jones, J., Meyer, N. & Zino, D. (2020, Summer). Departmental democracy and invention in two-year college writing programs. *Writing Program Administration, 43*(3), 38–53.

Adams, P., Gearhart, S., Miller, R. & Roberts, A. (2009). The accelerated learning program: Throwing open the Gates. *Journal of Basic Writing, 28*(2), 50–69. https://doi.org/10.37514/JBW-J.2009.28.2.04.

American Association of Community Colleges. (2016). *2016 Fact sheet*. https://www.napicaacc.com/docs/AACC_Fact_Sheet_2016.pdf.

Ames, S. & Heilstedt, S. (2019, October). The 4 Connections: Moving from intuitive to intentional relationship-building to improve success and reduce equity gaps. *Instructional Leadership Abstracts, 11*(2), 1–3. https://cehs.unl.edu/documents/edadmin/ncia/4%20Connections%20October%202019.pdf.

Bailey, T. (2012, April). Improving community college assessment and placement. *CCRC Currents*. Teachers College, Columbia University, Community College Research Center. https://ccrc.tc.columbia.edu/publications/ccrc-currents-2012.html.

Bedore, P. & Rossen-Knill, D. (2004). Informed self-placement: Is a choice offered a choice received? *WPA: Writing Program Administration, 28*(1–2), 55–78.

Blakesley, D. (2002). Directed self-placement in the university. *WPA: Writing Program Administration, 25*(3), 9–39.

Elliot, N. (2016). A theory of ethics for writing assessment. *Journal of Writing Assessment, 9*(1). http://journalofwritingassessment.org/article.php?article=98.

Fain, P. (2015, June 18). Finding a new compass. *Inside Higher Ed*. https://www.insidehighered.com/news/2015/06/18/act-drops-popular-compass-placement-test-acknowledging-its-predictive-limits/.

Hammond, Z. (2015). *Culturally responsive pedagogy and the brain: Promoting authentic engagement and rigor among culturally and linguistically diverse students*. Corwin.

Inoue, A. B. (2015). *Antiracist writing assessment ecologies: Teaching and assessing writing for a socially just future*. The WAC Clearinghouse; Parlor Press. https://doi.org/10.37514/PER-B.2015.0698.

Klausman, J., Roberts, L., Giordano, J., Griffiths, B., Sullivan, P., Swyt, W., Toth, C., Warnke, A., Williams, A. L. (2016). TYCA white paper on placement reform. *Teaching English in the Two-Year College, 44*(2), 135–157. https://cdn.ncte.org/ncte files/groups/tyca/placementreform_revised.pdf.

Klausman, J., Roberts, L. & Snyder, S. E. (2020, November). *TYCA working paper #1: Two-year college English faculty teaching workload*. National Council of Teachers of English. https://ncte.org/groups/tyca/tyca-position-statements/.

McNair, T. B., Albertine, S. L., Cooper, M. A., McDonald, N. L. & Major, T. (2016). *Becoming a student-ready college: A new culture of leadership for student success*. Wiley.

Nastal, J. (2019). Beyond tradition: Writing placement, fairness, and success at a two-year college. *Journal of Writing Assessment, 12*(1). http://www.journalofwritingassessment.org/article.php?article=136.

Poe, M. & Cogan, J. A., Jr. (2016). Civil rights and writing assessment: Using the disparate impact approach as a fairness methodology to evaluate social impact. *The Journal of Writing Assessment*, 9(1). http://journalofwritingassessment.org/article.php?article=97.

Poe, M., Elliot, N., Cogan, J. A., Jr., Nurudeen, Jr., T. G. (2014). The legal and the local: Using disparate impact analysis to understand the consequences of writing assessment. *College Composition and Communication*, 65(4), 588–611. www.jstor.org/stable/43490874.

Reynolds, E. (2003). The role of self-efficacy in writing and directed self-placement. In D. J. Royer & R. Gilles (Eds.), *Directed self-placement: Principles and practices* (pp. 73–102). Hampton Press.

Royer, D. J. & Gilles, R. (1998). Directed self-placement: An attitude of orientation. *College Composition and Communication*, 50(1), 54–70.

Scott-Clayton, J. (2012, February). *Do high-stakes placement exams predict college success?* (CCFC Working Paper No. 41). Teachers College, Columbia University, Community College Research Center. https://ccrc.tc.columbia.edu/publications/high-stakes-placement-exams-predict.html.

Strohl, N. (2015, February 19). A good idea, not a new one. *Inside Higher Ed*. https://www.insidehighered.com/views/2015/02/19/essay-historic-context-behind-president-obamas-proposal-free-community-college.

Suh, E. K., Tinoco, L., Toth, C. & Edgel, P. A.. (2020, November). *TYCA working paper #5: Two-year college English faculty professional development workload*. Two-Year College English Association Workload Task Force. https://ncte.org/groups/tyca/tyca-position-statements/.

Toth, C. (2018). Directed self-placement at "democracy's open door": Writing placement and social justice in community colleges. In A. B. Inoue, M. Poe & N. Elliot (Eds.), *Writing assessment, social justice, and the advancement of opportunity* (pp. 139–172). The WAC Clearinghouse; University Press of Colorado. https://doi.org/10.37514/PER-B.2018.0155.2.04.

U.S. Department of Education. (2016, September 16). *Fact sheet: A college degree: Surest pathway to expanded opportunity, success for American students*. https://www.proquest.com/docview/1820285785/719B1BE396FA4D11PQ/1?accountid=2906.

Washington State Board for Community and Technical Colleges. (2020, September 9). *Accountability metrics*. State Board for Community and Technical Colleges Strategic Plan Accountability. https://www.sbctc.edu/about/agency/initiatives-projects/strategic-plan/strategic-plan-accountability.aspx .

Washington State Community and Technical Colleges #RealCollege Survey. (2020, February). Hope Center for College, Community, and Justice at Temple University. https://hope4college.com/wp-content/uploads/2020/02/2019_WashingtonState_Report.pdf

Whatcom Community College. (2021). *About Whatcom*. https://www.whatcom.edu/about-the-college/about-whatcom.

Yancey, K. B., Robertson, L. & Taczak, K. (2014). *Writing across contexts: Transfer, composition, and sites of writing*. Utah State University Press.

Chapter 3. A Path to Equity, Agency, and Access: Self-Directed Placement at the Community College of Baltimore County

Kris Messer, Jamey Gallagher, and Elizabeth Hart
COMMUNITY COLLEGE OF BALTIMORE COUNTY

Abstract: This case study looks back over three years of research, struggles to pilot self-directed placement, hurdles to jump through, and deeply important lessons that were hard learned. Placement hits nerves all around by directly addressing who is "prepared" for college, what it means to be "prepared" for college, what linguistic standards and practices determine that and why, what students desire out of their education, and what we feel we should give them, as well as beliefs about who students are and what they need. This case study details the use of a truly self-directed model of placement and shows promising trends on which we hope to be able to continue building.

Where We Started

Over several years, English faculty teaching in the Accelerated Learning Program (ALP) at the Community College of Baltimore County (CCBC) noticed a disturbing trend: Students of color were a majority of the population in the developmental sections of our courses.[1] Despite being a majority minority institution, we noticed that a disproportionate number of students in our credit sections were White and the students in our smaller "developmental" sections were largely non-White.[2]

While these observations were anecdotal, a small group of faculty members decided to examine the data in more detail. We discovered that, in 2016, more than two thirds of all African American students who registered at the Community College of Baltimore County were required to take at least one developmental class, while fewer than half of the White students who registered were. That stark inequity presented by that data was the impetus for change.

---

1. ALP is a nationally recognized corequisite model in which students who have been deemed "developmental" can take a credit class along with a smaller support class in the same semester (see Adams et al., 2009).

2. CCBC is a large, multi-campus community college in Baltimore County, Maryland. We are a majority minority institution. Forty-five percent of our students are White; 35 percent are Black; seven percent are Hispanic or Latino; six percent are Asian; three percent are multi-racial; and five percent are unknown.

We identified placement as the first volley in what we hope will be a progressive pattern of change. Placement exists at a pivotal point in the relationship between students and the institution. We see placement as an opportunity to truly open the door. Once intelligent, complex, and confident members of our community are entering classrooms by their choice, it is our belief that deficit mindsets will be ameliorated and pedagogical practices will shift in profound ways. We are starting to see these shifts—as discussions around self-direction, curriculum, and systematic barriers have started to occur regularly at CCBC. While many mindsets remain static, the dust that our placement shifts have kicked up is forcing greater reflection on our systems and practices.

In 2017, English and Academic Literacy faculty from CCBC who attended the Conference on Acceleration in Developmental Education (CADE) were struck by Myra Snell's contention, during her keynote, that "placement is destiny." Snell made a powerful argument that students are systemically underserved by placement. She noted that "A study of three California community colleges estimates that 50–60% of racial inequities in degree completion and transfer-readiness is explained by initial placement." The major takeaway from Snell's presentation was

> A test with very weak predictive validity is being used to place the majority of our Black and Brown students into remedial pipelines where it is guaranteed (due to inevitable attrition in the pipeline) that they will not achieve early milestones to transfer.[3]

Inspired by studies published by the Community College Research Center showing that GPA was more predictive of success than standardized tests, CCBC had already started working toward using multiple options for placement, mostly by relying on the GPA of incoming students. Initially, our college accepted a high school GPA for English placement from students who had graduated within the previous two years, and an official transcript was needed to corroborate the placement.[4] Data from the initial GPA pilot was positive, and the college successively reshaped GPA placement bands, lowering our credit-level GPA placement cutoff from 3.0 into credit level to 2.75 and then to 2.5.

Following CADE 2017, a faculty committee was formed to talk about placement reform generally. We became committed to following through with the multiple measures reforms already underway, but also became interested in

---

3. National data about placement trends into development education bear this out. A 2016 report from the National Center for Education Statistics, for instance, found that "At public 2-year institutions, 78 percent of Black students and 75 percent of Hispanic students (vs. 64 percent of White students) and 76 percent of students who were in the lowest income group (vs. 59 percent of those in the highest) took remedial courses" (Chen & Simone, 2016).

4. We eventually expanded GPA placement for students who had graduated within a five-year timeframe.

self-placement as a practice that had promise for our student population and was well-matched to our curriculum, which focuses on issues of relevance to students' lives and leveraging student experience in the classroom. Informed by the *TYCA White Paper on Placement Reform* (Klaussman et al., 2016), we wanted to enhance our multiple measures.

Struck by how our college's moment of first contact with students is "an inflection point" (Stroman, 2019), we worked to use the language of belonging throughout our processes to leverage student success. As research from the Mindset Scholars Network indicates,

> Students are particularly sensitive to these signals at certain points, such as moments of transition, difficulty, or setbacks. The cues students receive in these moments, if they do not affirm students' sense of belonging, can set in motion negative, self-reinforcing cycles that can adversely affect long-term outcomes. (Stroman, 2019)

Recent research published in the field of educational psychology suggests that there are important connections between a student's sense of belonging and their success in higher education. As Mickaël Jury et al. (2017) recognized, "Higher education is far from being a culturally neutral environment for low SES students, notably because the system is 'built and organized according to taken for granted, middle- and upper-class cultural norms, unwritten codes, or 'rules of the game'" (p. 18).

As the average age of our students is 29, we needed to identify alternative forms of placement that would serve older, first-generation, or returning college students. Our returning student population is routinely overlooked—regardless of race. Given the history of Baltimore as a highly segregated city and the county as a nexus of outmigration, the neighborhoods that surround our campuses range from highly affluent to resource-deprived, immigrant communities to White and Black working-class areas—race was a pivot point, but class and age needed to also shape our practices.

We were encouraged by the white paper's extended discussion on directed self-placement (DSP), and we believed it could be a useful complement to our existing placement options, which could help us first make strides in access. In 2018, part-time African American and White students were more than twice as likely to be placed into developmental English as their full-time counterparts; Asian students were four times more likely to be placed into developmental English if they were part-time. Returning and part-time students of all races have routinely been treated as if their substantial life experiences do not matter, and their critical thinking has been veiled by the misconception that a lack of knowledge about the college's terminology and systems equates to lack of commitment to school or a lack of intelligence.

The model we developed was informed by how our college's onboarding protocol reinforces the status quo and, by holding onto White norms of linguistic standards and social performativity, ultimately contributes to the discrepancies regarding African American and first-generation students being disproportionately placed into developmental coursework. We wanted to create an initial interaction between students and the institution that was built on actualizing the experiences and strengths of returning students and students with culturally and linguistically diverse backgrounds to let them know those strengths were needed here—a move that would offer them confidence and allow them to leverage their strengths. When access increases it is our hope that these students—full of experiences and ideas—will transform these spaces, fostering curricular and pedagogical adjustments that will erode paternalistic attitudes and help to close the racialized achievement gap we see across our institutions' highly enrolled general education classes.[5]

Theorizing and Designing Self-Placement

Flexibility, agency, and control over content are too often the domain of privileged educational settings; they are given to students who can "handle" them. While it is argued that the students in our classrooms need to be taught behaviors to guarantee career or "college readiness," students in other economically or socially privileged settings are offered exploratory vistas. If we see the idea of choice and agency as endangering a student's ability to progress in a program of study and slow their time to completion, instead of creating systems that strive to accelerate people into career patterns, we should reflect on (and change) a culture that has placed so many people into a precarious relationship with upward mobility and survival.

As we designed our instrument and processes, we were struck by the idea that—for the students being most underserved by our current placement policies—leveraging self-reflection and experience was central to how they saw themselves in relation to our curriculum and the institutional setting. We developed a way of articulating our approach through pairing the components of DSP articulated by Dan Royer and Roger Gilles (1998) with work on agency and self-efficacy, as "extensive research has shown an integral relationship between self-efficacy and student success in college.... Self-efficacy refers to one's confidence in their ability to control their emotions, behaviors, and actions in order to actualize desired objectives (Bandura, 1977, 1986)" (Wood et al., 2015, p. 3). For ease of conveyance to colleagues across the college, we termed the intertwining of these ideas an "agency-information-reflection" cycle, or AIR. Through our process, we sought to foreground the idea of the self as the deciding factor, believing that, in the end, agency is the cornerstone

---

5. Our local data shows that from Fall 2018 to Fall 2020 there is a 10 to 16 percentage point difference in pass rates between White and African American students in College Composition I and II (ENGL 101, ENGL 102).

of any *self*-placement practice; therefore, we chose to call our particular process *self*-directed placement (SDP). Wanting to focus on the *self* in self-directed placement, we were adamant on not including any kind of weighting system or "score" that would be artificially and arbitrarily created.

As self-agency was the theoretical heart of the practice, offering adults the opportunity to reflect and make their own decisions cannot be followed by a score that might undercut what they believe about themselves and their abilities. Given many students' individual histories with educational settings, generating a score would not foster agency and might not leverage the kind of self-reflexivity we believe is the core of self-placement. Scores can be based on factors that may be deeply racialized or biased. Without extensive research— and even with it—these recommendations can work to cast doubt on students' choices for themselves.[6] A score does not leverage real choice and is often generated by an institutional and societal set of standards that can be arbitrary at best and supremacist at worst. This is still placement determined by a system, not actualized by a person. These recommendations could easily reinscribe negative interactions with educational spaces and undermine belonging and confidence—two things students making an often difficult decision in returning to school need. Additionally, such recommendations can easily serve as a default mechanism for advisors, faculty, and others to encourage students to register for lower levels based on their own opinions and biases. Our design was largely influenced by Mya Poe and Asao B. Inoue's (2016) features of socially just writing assessment: "creation of opportunity structures, avoidance of value dualisms, and self-evaluation" (p. 123).

It is in taking back the active role in one's educational choices that the practice of self-placement has promise and finds power. It is our contention that placement shifts should call us to examine what we are asking of whom and why. Who gets to shape the space? Who gets freedom? Who gets the choice? Instead of asking *if* students are capable of moving through our programs, maybe, as a system, we could ask what we are doing to promote equitable choices in careers and intellectual exploration? What are we doing to provide every member of our society the right to exercise their critical consciousness?

Toward a Pilot

A long process of pilot design and support-seeking for our self-directed placement pilot began in late 2017. That work grew out of a committee charged with tackling placement reform broadly. Two faculty members, Kris Messer and Liz Hart, took on the bulk of the work researching self-placement. We looked to

---

6. Many institutions have transitioned to self-placement during the COVID-19 pandemic without significant study or the proper data analysis to generate meaningful recommendations that do not simply reinforce normative and paternalistic approaches.

other two-year colleges, as well as the extensive history of self-placement at four-year schools, in addition to disciplinary precedents. Our goal was to create an instrument and process based on educational psychology, so as to "align with DSP's theoretical underpinnings . . . to address important equity concerns" (Toth, 2019). Beyond studying the broader disciplinary context, we conducted extensive research into what had been implemented at other two-year colleges across the country. Messer and Hart reached out to nine institutions.[7] After that research, we began the design process. We modeled our tool on what we saw elsewhere, especially at Highline Community College. The design of the tool includes the following:[8]

- reading and writing experiences,
- reading passages modeled on our curriculum with reflective questions that aim to get at what the individual feels when they are performing tasks that would be performed in all of our classes,
- a writing prompt asking students to discuss how their life experiences have prepared them to be successful at CCBC,
- an image breaking down students' course choices,
- and two videos—one that details our three course options and one that seeks to leverage current students' excitement and advice.

We tried to keep the tone of the tool positive and let those taking it see that we value their experiences and perspectives, and know that they have much to offer CCBC.

We worked to develop content and built the tool in multiple iterations over the course of this process. Eventually, the placement tool was built in Microsoft Forms Pro (now Customer Voice).

One of the most important and intensive parts of the process was working on the videos that feature student discussion around course choices. We interviewed over 30 former and current students about their course experiences and worked with students and faculty in our digital media program to film and edit the material. At first, we planned to create three different videos, one for each level that students can place into. In the end, we opted to produce one video explaining all three options and one motivational video that offers thoughts from students about success, asking questions, and confronting obstacles, which students watch just prior to making their final selection. This video grew out of comments from the students we interviewed. We asked them what they would want to see in the videos and tools, and several offered that they would want advice and to see how

---

7. Highline, Moorpark, Whatcom, Salt Lake City, Shoreline College, Ozarks Technical College, Renton Technical College, Lower Columbia, Rhodes State College

8. PracticeSDPtool(asof9/1/21)https://customervoice.microsoft.com/Pages/ResponsePage.aspx?id=ACD6KiZ3IEmpVwOXwoD8PX801wCnorxIimby4erFrgpURDN-JWUM1SoJVVjdVSUNVMzNIODhIWEYyQi4u.

others succeeded. Denise Parker, a faculty member who had been instrumental in the work leading up to the pilot, acted as the faculty voice connecting the three course options. We met with Professor Parker for one long day in a classroom, during which we hammered out the differences between the three options and how to explain each option in the clearest, most student friendly way—a process that helped us better understand how we think about the differences ourselves. The main differences between the three options seemed to be the amount of support a student would receive, and we designed the language in the videos and description within the SDP mechanism to reflect that idea. Although a lot of the concern we heard about the process from fellow faculty, administration, and enrollment staff was related to students over-placing themselves, we knew from the research that under-placement was a more common issue, and we worked hard to counteract that in the videos and other material.

Currently, our levels include English 101, in which students receive the support of the instructor, the other students in the class, and other institutional support such as the writing center and academic coaches; the Accelerated Learning Program, in which students have considerably more support from instructors through a three-credit corequisite developmental offering; and ACLT 052, a standalone five-credit[9] developmental class, designed for students who need the most support—this class focuses on preparing students for college. While some of us on the committee creating self-directed placement argued against including ACLT 052 as an option, since it has been shown how important it is for students to receive credit early, we could not make a large curricular change through the placement process. We had to include the course because it is an offering at our institution.[10]

Gaining the support of stakeholders was not an easy or simple process. We had multiple meetings with various members of the student services branch of our institution. We met separately with advisors, in small groups with Admissions and Advising, and with different combinations of Planning Research and Evaluation, Information Technology, Disability Services, and Administration. We invited Shannon Waits from Highline to visit and talk to deans, faculty, and staff members in March 2018. Following that, we had focus groups for all members of the school in fall of 2019, in which people could go through the SDP tool and give us feedback. We also presented on self-directed placement for the entire Enrollment and Student Services[11] staff in October of 2019 and had multiple meetings with various stakeholders from the testing, admissions, and advising

---

9. Two of the five hours are dedicated to time in a "lab" in a computer-mediated classroom with an instructor to provide dedicated assistance.

10. As a result of placement changes, the CCBC will be revisiting whether the class will remain an offering and making recommendations for changes in 2022.

11. During the development and implementation of SDP, our Enrollment and Student Services moved under Instruction and is now called Student Development.

departments, as well as the department of Planning, Research, and Evaluation (PRE). During those meetings, we worked to develop "frequently asked questions" and advisor training materials.

Resistance existed among the Enrollment and Student Services staff about all the many placement-related changes that had been made in the recent past. There was a sense that another big change might be a burden on staff already keeping up. There were logistical concerns as well. Because our school's student information system is Banner, the SDP tool was not able to communicate directly with Banner, so the placement had to be done manually. Staff was concerned that this would be a time-consuming and difficult process, but they agreed to do this work for the pilot. The hope was that, in the meantime, our IT department would be able to develop a "crosswalk" that would automate the data and thus make manual entry unnecessary.[12] The manual entry component, however, has proven to run smoothly throughout remote placement.

There was concern among some of our academic literacy faculty that students would place themselves into classes they wouldn't be ready for and would not have the reading skills necessary to succeed or to flourish in future classes. The academic literacy department grew out of what was originally the reading department at the college. Over a series of years, the department shifted from being strictly focused on reading and developmental classes, to being focused on integrated reading, writing, and critical thinking. There is overlap between the two departments, but they exist separately as of this writing. Many of the students' responses to the reading passages in the tool have helped to allay these fears about the reading skills that students bring with them into our classes after the first pilot responses came in.

During this time, we were presenting at various national conferences and every in-house professional development day. These presentations included the Council of Writing Program Administrators, Conference on College Composition and Communication, The Two Year College Association, and the Culturally Responsive Teaching and Learning Conference. The process of preparing for and presenting at those conferences helped us to refine our thinking. At most conferences we received thoughtful feedback that helped us develop how the course options were presented, as well as to come up with technological solutions to some of our issues with Microsoft Forms. It was gratifying to see that the work we were doing locally was being done by other institutions.

Notably, the group that received the change most favorably was our then current classes. We shared drafts of the tool with our students, some of whom were the same students who participated in filming the SDP videos. Students were enthusiastic and supportive of the tool, and many shared negative stories about their experiences with standardized testing. Students understand self-placement

---

12. As we progressed, we learned that figuring out the IT on our own was crucial, as we were told IT could provide no work for our project before it was at full implementation.

perfectly: "We're the ones who know what we can do," one student said. In fact, students seemed to understand the process much more easily, and looked at it more favorably, than many administrators.

Finally, after many delays, in January of 2020, we ran a 20-day pilot in which 79 (as compared to a hoped-for 250) students placed themselves using self-directed placement. This was meant to be phase one of a two phase piloting process. Phase one was to be focused mostly on logistics—making sure that the process was as effective as it could be—while, in phase two, which was planned to run for placement into Fall 2020 classes, we hoped to get more data that could be disaggregated in meaningful ways.

Before we could finalize plans for or implement phase two of the piloting process, COVID-19 struck, necessitating a change in our plans. Before we had even received quantitative data or success rates from our pilot, we were asked to retool our process for "remote placement" and take the process—conducted previously in the testing center—completely remote, in a global pandemic in a matter of weeks. Subsequently, we have received data for students in the first cohort of remote placement.

Outcomes for Phase One Pilot

Phase One Pilot Data

Since the pilot was so small, including only 54 students who registered for classes out of 79 who took SDP, there is not much of significance we can say about the original data. We can say that students were placing themselves into credit classes at a higher rate than they have been placed into credit classes in the past through ACCUPLACER (Table 3.1).

Table 3.1. Student Placement Rates

Placement January 2021	English 101	ALP	ACLT 052
ACCUPLACER	66 (15%)	75 (17%)	46 (10%)
Self-Directed Placement	30 (38%)	16 (20%)	3 (4%)

Out of those students who took SDP, 69 percent were passing their classes at midterm, compared to 66 percent of students who placed via ACCUPLACER. At the end of the semester, after a very difficult transition to remote learning, the pass rates were about equal between the two groups. Considering the fact that more students were earning credit in their first semester by enrolling in ALP or English 101 (which also gave them the ability to enroll in other general education courses that are corequisite to English 101), if these numbers held true subsequently, we knew we would be having a significant impact on access and equity at our institution.

Remote Placement

In spring of 2020, once the pandemic had hit and ACCUPLACER was no longer available for placement, due to cost and prohibitive technological issues, there was less concern about over-placement. Something had to be done, and SDP was the only game in town. We were fortunate, unlike many colleagues at other institutions, that we had done two and a half years of research and had run a pilot, albeit a small one. We quickly revamped a process that had been used in testing centers for 20 days into a system-wide remote placement measure, working during the height of the pandemic.

Starting in May of 2020, the testing center began sending the link for the SDP tool to prospective students. Initially, only students without another measure were meant to receive the SDP tool, but as an increasing number of students had a difficult time finding their information or systems had a difficult time sending information to CCBC, an increasing number of students went through the SDP process. (For fall of 2020, 24 percent placed via SDP, while 21 percent placed via GPA; for spring of 2021, 26 percent placed via SDP and seven percent placed via GPA). From May until October 21, 2,140 students completed the SDP tool. Currently, more than 5,100 students have completed the tool.

Over the summer and to this date, we were responsible for any student questions in relation to SDP, as our colleagues in advising during the initial pilot process felt uncomfortable working with students who wanted to change their placement to a higher level after taking the SDP tool; therefore, those students who had questions about their placement were referred to our team via phone or email. This student-to-faculty contact proved to be a time-consuming endeavor, but an extremely beneficial experience that has framed our ongoing support work with students. We continue this practice to this day, and, as a result, we have been able to see and learn firsthand about students' struggles with our intake systems, as well as to discuss what students see as barriers in pursuing their education. We carried on these conversations in the broad support work we did with SDP in Fall 2020 and Spring 2021.

During this time, we shared our tool with three other community colleges, one of which developed their own institutional version of the tool for remote placement (we have shared our tool and processes many times since then). To this date, we continue to work on and advocate for *informed* revisions to these systems and to help students in the placement process while our reassigned time has been cut and the practice itself remains on insecure intuitional footing. We cannot get a commitment for any duration of time to support our work or to continue SDP and to enact needed revisions based on student responses, implementation, changing curriculum, or a radically reformed educational landscape. We are seeing some desire to reframe our work to a less agency-centered process and write faculty out of that change, allowing our Student Development colleagues to shape the process and the shape of the placement instrument with limited faculty access or input. In fact, despite the positive data shown in the next section, as of September 2021, SDP has been "paused" for spring of 2022, with a promise of support from our vice president for fall of 2022. We have no word on how students who do not have a recent GPA or any other measure will be placed for the coming spring.

Data for Remote Placement

The first thing that was clear from the data we received from Fall 2020 and Spring 2021 was that students were struggling due to the pandemic. Many more students were either withdrawing and/or receiving an FX[13] than had historically been true at our institution. It will be hard to tease out the impact of COVID-19 from the outcomes of our move to self-directed placement. However because all students, regardless of placement measure—aside from those who are currently in high school and have a high GPA—were withdrawing at high rates, it seems clear that the issue was pandemic-related. Pass rates were down across the board, and fully 11 percent more first-time students at our institution withdrew or had an FX by midterm. This is a disturbing number that will require all of us to work to meet the needs of our most vulnerable students.

We are finding that our predictions about this method of placement have been borne out. There are many positives we can see in the data. These include:

- A ten percent increase in the number of students who register after taking SDP, as compared to ACCUPLACER. Fifty-five percent of students taking ACCUPLACER registered for a class, whereas 65 percent are registering after SDP.
- A huge rise in the number of African American students who place into stand-alone-credit English classes. Via ACCUPLACER, only 18 percent of African American students placed into credit-level English in 2019, whereas with SDP, that number has increased to 58 percent in 2020. Clearly, we are having a significant impact on access, which we believe is pivotal to shifting the dial on equity at our institution.

While we do see some positives in equity and access, it is clear that many of our students are struggling to stay in school. Our Fall 2020 midterm data shows the following:

- Twenty-five percent of SDP students in general withdrew or FXed. Twenty-nine percent of SDP students placing into ALP either withdrew or FXed. Twenty-eight percent of GPA students placing into ALP withdrew or FXed.
- In general, students in ALP are struggling. There was a 43 percent GPA pass rate/50 percent SDP pass rate. For both GPA and SDP rates, the

---

13. An FX is a failure for non-attendance.

percentages are similar for African American students, with a 50 percent GPA pass rate/48 percent SDP pass rate.
- While students who placed by GPA have a higher success rate at midterm, which is more consonant with pre-COVID semester rates, over 80 percent of those students are 17 and under and likely taking these courses for high school credit, while doing remote learning.

Importantly, in the Fall 2020 final data (Table 3.2), we found that older students were outperforming younger students, sometimes performing at close to pre-pandemic numbers.

Table 3.2. Fall 2020 Placement Results

Age	ALP			ENGL101			Total		
	Attempt	Pass	Pass Rate	Attempt	Pass	Pass Rate	Attempt	Pass	Pass Rate
18 or Younger	88	30	34%	318	108	34%	406	138	34%
19–20	30	9	30%	104	43	41%	134	52	39%
21–25	45	18	40%	124	64	52%	169	82	49%
26–30	31	19	61%	70	39	56%	101	58	57%
31 or Older	22	13	59%	97	57	59%	119	70	59%

These data hold true for Spring 2021 (Table 3.3).

Table 3.3. Spring 2021 Placement Results

Age	ALP			ENGL101		
	Attempt	Pass	Pass Rate	Attempt	Pass	Pass Rate
18 or Younger	11	6	55%	40	10	25%
19–20	16	3	19%	60	18	30%
21–25	19	6	32%	61	35	57%
26–30	19	9	47%	42	25	60%
31 or Older	40	20	50%	72	28	39%

The fact that the tool was designed specifically with those older students in mind suggests that it is successful for those students. Yet, despite our requests and inquiries, our systems for taking GPA seem to still route younger students through the SDP process.

Self-directed placement has shifted placement trends in general. In fall of 2019, students placed into classes via ACCUPLACER at the following rates: 24 percent into credit-level; 30 percent into ALP; 26 percent into ACLT 052. In fall of 2020, students placed into classes via SDP at the following rates: 58 percent into credit-level; 20 percent into ALP; three percent into ACLT 052 (Table 3.4). That means that there was a 34 percent increase in the number of students placed into stand-alone credit-level classes, and a 23 percent increase in the number of students placed into credit-level and corequisite classes.

Table 3.4. Placement Method Comparison

	English 101	**ALP**	**ACLT 052**
Fall 2019 (ACCUPLACER)	247 (24%)	308 (26%)	266 (26%)
Fall 2020 (Self-Directed Placement)	774 (58%)	255 (20%)	43 (3%)

We tracked how students felt about the self-directed placement process, asking them to share any feedback they might have in the tool itself. Of those students who responded (66%), 90 percent (1,272 out of 1,421) of them responded favorably, often in glowing terms. Seven percent (102 out of 1,421) responded in neutral ways. Of the neutral responses, some of them offered advice to future students or personal affirmations about how the student believed in themself; some gave us advice for how to revise the tool slightly; and some were simply neutral responses like "thanks." A small number of students (.08%) offered mixed reviews, offering some praise along with some constructive criticism. Only two percent (35 out of 1,421) responded negatively. Though we cannot say with certainty, we suspect these results are infinitely more positive than a similar rating of the old ACCUPLACER test, as students commonly reply to the feedback section with responses that affirm that they appreciate being given agency, being respected by the institution, and being offered an opportunity to reflect on their own skills and abilities.

We could share hundreds of positive responses students wrote, responses that suggest that students truly understand what we are trying to do with this shift in placement. For instance, one student wrote,

> This experience has made me feel more comfortable in choosing which class I think I would fit best in, hearing other people's experiences in the videos made me think of my own and where I would fit right in with. After watching the videos I now know that there is no judgement and it's a great place to grow.

Clearly this student had a sense of belonging and understood placement as a source of positive connection to the institution.

We see evidence of real engagement with the reading passages that students were asked to write about. One of the reading passages and student responses can be referenced in Appendices A and B. All responses are presented here and in the Appendices as students wrote them when they took the SDP instrument. These responses did allay some of our Academic Literacy colleagues' concerns about the reading and critical thinking skills students are bringing with them into the classroom. We also saw student excitement as they prepared to return to school, sometimes after significant spans of time. We saw comments like "My experiences have led me to grow into a better person and have helped me discover who I am. I am ready for a fresh start and I am excited to attend CCBC" and "So here I am now making my last attempt to complete at least one degree. I am ready. I am focused. I read better, I write better; with passion and maturity. I'm ready to be a successful student." These students are reflecting on their own level of readiness and their willingness to put in the necessary work. We saw responses like this over and over again.

Additionally, we were fortunate to be able to teach some of the students who placed themselves via SDP. We all teach both stand-alone English 101 classes and ALP classes. In the spring of 2020, we were able to informally discuss the placement experience with students in our classrooms. One student was able to explain and introduce the concept of corequisite remediation to the rest of the class because he had taken the SDP tool. This SDP experience allowed him to understand the expectations of the course and communicate them to his peers. We suspect that this type of engagement would not have occurred had this student taken ACCUPLACER; it is unlikely that a high-stakes placement test would connect to specific curricular circumstances and provide relevant information and the opportunity to perform the cognitive tasks associated with our curriculum. Being given a say in one's education inherently places one in a different relationship to their education. Those going through this process say it best: "Giving students the option to choose which would be best for them, gives them a chance to take control of starting their education, without making them feel less for how they may have placed otherwise." In other words, "I enjoy this because it did not feel like a 'test', it was more to understand where I am in life and what I am hoping to get out of my education. . . . This is a great tool to use because nobody wants to feel like they don't belong."

Consequences

There were a couple of unexpected outcomes/consequences of moving to self-directed placement. We have strengthened our ties with other General Education colleagues and Student Development, and, at the same time, we have recognized the existence of a significant barrier to our students. Currently, students who place into

ALP are not eligible for many of the classes that other students in English 101 are eligible for, due to a block with their prerequisites. Although they are in a credit-level English class, their placement is still considered "developmental." During the initial pilot, we came up with a place-up procedure for students who were unhappy with their placement. That procedure requires students who want to move out of their chosen placement to contact our team lead (Messer) to have a conversation about what their best options actually are. Many of these place-up conversations related to this prerequisite barrier. This issue has become so extreme that many students have difficulty filling a full-time schedule. Placement has pushed us to examine and work towards alleviating this problem for our students. We are working to remove this barrier through many institutional channels.

The second consequence is more positive. As part of the move to remote placement, senior staff stipulated that we provide supports for students who placed themselves into English 101 and other general education classes. We helped students contact their professors and find their syllabi, figure out which "modality" their class was held in, and connect SDP students to Success Navigators for computing and housing issues, as well as to access the process of hardship withdrawals, so they could have refunds when COVID impacted their lives. This was particularly important in a semester as unusual as Fall 2020. Through these supports, we have developed collaborations with General Education and Student Support colleagues that we hope to build on moving forward, making SDP a process that engages students in support structures beyond the moment of placement.

Discussion

The excitement and energy students bring to the responses they are writing are impressive and can be transformational. We have worked to wrap these responses into presentations on student potential at many in-house professional development days, as well as in SDP presentations at national conferences. These responses show a clear determination, drive, and desire that many faculty don't always perceive in their students when they enter the classroom. For instance,

> As I began to grow into a young woman, I, like most young adults, began to question everything about life and everything about myself. Questioning led me to journaling, journaling lead me to poetry and both modalities became a mental, and spiritual release of many layers of trauma and emotion gathered throughout my life.

This kind of writing is something that we might not have expected to be solicited from a simple question like "How have your life experiences prepared you to be successful at CCBC?"

The responses have made this crystalline: Our students are intelligent, driven, and linguistically sophisticated, and they bring a range of experiences that can serve to strengthen our classrooms and our larger culture, if they are valued, recognized, and used to construct the parameters of our learning spaces. If flattened, homogenized, and standardized, that energy will dissipate. These responses have helped us show this drive and intellect to our colleagues and have changed some minds and practices. It is our hope that sharing responses will do more to shift the dial in favor of equity and access, as well as to force institutional reflection on words like "college-ready" or "developmental," creating a space for more direct conversations about our institutional and curricular assumptions. Because of this, we have come to see the need for training on anti-deficit work at all levels. We believe staff, faculty, and our administration could do more work to foster belonging and increase retention. In our top 25 most highly enrolled general education courses, only six have an equity gap of less than ten percent. Many have gaps of up to 20+ percent. This clearly shows that there is a need for training and development to shift our practices and perceptions.

We also recognize how SDP has the potential to be a catalyst for a shift in not just our pedagogy but our curriculum. The smaller course section in the Accelerated Learning Program (which we call ACLT 053) was originally conceived as a support class for those students who were not deemed "college ready" by standardized tests, but we are finding that what students really need is more confidence and a familiarity with the academic space. It is more a matter of confidence than competence. Since students are placing themselves into ALP, asking for more support, we think it's important to think about what that space looks like and modify our curriculum accordingly. We propose a move toward doing away with the standalone developmental class and replacing it with a model of ALP that we are thinking of as "1.5."[14]

Conclusion

On an institutional level, what we have learned from embarking on the long process of bringing self-directed placement to CCBC is that a change at this scale requires time, patience, doggedness, persistence, and institutional buy-in (which we are still in the process of securing). Institutional awareness and support is critical, and we spent a great deal of time meeting with other departments at the college, but it's important to note that waiting for institutional support is not going to get the job done. We were able to get where we are now by continuing to push for self-directed placement even when it did not receive institutional support.

---

14. In this model, the support class would be geared toward advising students. The authors each spend a lot of time in their ALP sections helping students register, discussing educational goals, and connecting students to a community at the institution. We realize that once students have this, they are often confident enough to excel in the 101 classroom, and we would like to formalize this approach.

We believed in our students and believed that this was a more equitable means of placement. We are committed to continuing to collaborate across the college to make sure that SDP is given a chance to be studied, shaped, and institutionalized, but it is not an easy process. It is necessary for someone—beyond the faculty who developed it and the students who are impacted by it—to truly believe in self-directed placement to move it forward.

At this point, despite the "pause" in our work, we believe that SDP will be institutionalized, though it is already slipping out of the hands of faculty. We remain hopeful that the volume of *pro bono* work we have done will speak for itself and that we will be permitted to apply the data from remote placement to planning and revising SDP, in a manner consistent with its intention of offering agency. In practical terms, we need to know that SDP will continue, so that we can work to adapt the tool and processes in accordance with the registration timeline which runs a year out. We hope we will be able to have the opportunity to refine and strengthen our practices. To make change, we believe, you make a bold move like trusting students, and you back up that move with supported change at all levels. We hope to one day see that support.

As we look back over the last three years of research, struggles to pilot, hurdles to jump through, and deeply important lessons that were hard learned, it is important to note—especially in our setting, a community college surrounding a major city fraught with poverty and an intensely racialized history—that placement cuts to the core of things. It hits nerves all around by directly addressing: who is prepared for college, what it means to be prepared for college, what linguistic standards and practices determine that and why, what students desire out of their education, and what we feel we should give them, as well as beliefs about who students are and what they need. It sparks fear about change. It brings on worry about the stereotypes that will be perpetuated if students are let in and don't succeed. It opens doors to curricular and institutional blind spots. It shines a light into all corners of the institution—instructional spaces, classroom practices, and the beliefs of faculty and staff. If you try to change placement, you are going to see some stuff that you can't unsee or ignore, but, in the end, bringing all of it to the table and addressing what we find in ourselves is what we need to do to change not only access but success.

References

Accelerated Learning. [@ALPdeved]. (2017, June 16). "*Placement is destiny . . . and inequitable placement drives inequitable completion*" — Myra Snell #CADEC-CBC2017 [Tweet]. Twitter. https://twitter.com/ALPdeved/status/875741993422409729.

Adams, P., Gearhart, S., Miller, R. & Roberts, A. (2009). The accelerated learning program: Throwing open the Gates. *Journal of Basic Writing*, 28(2), 50–69. https://doi.org/10.37514/JBW-J.2009.28.2.04.

Bandura, A. (1977). Self-efficacy: Toward a unifying theory of behavioral change. *Psychology Review, 84*(2), 191–215.

Bandura, A. (1986). *Social foundations of thought and action: A social cognitive theory*. Prentice Hall.

Chen, X. & Simone, S. (2016). *Remedial coursetaking at U.S. public 2- and 4-year institutions: Scope, experiences, and outcomes* (NCES 2016-405). U.S. Department of Education. National Center for Education Statistics. https://nces.ed.gov/pubs2016/2016405.pdf.

Hassel, H., Klausman, J., Giordano, J., O'Rourke, M., Roberts, L., Sullivan, P. & Toth, C. (2015). TYCA white paper on developmental education reforms. *Teaching English in the Two-Year College, 42*(3), 227–243.

Jury, M., Smeding, A., Stephens, N. M., Nelson, J. E., Aelenei, C. & Darnon, C. (2017). The experience of low-SES students in higher education: Psychological barriers to success and interventions to reduce social-class inequality. *Journal of Social Issues, 73*(1), 16–34. https://doi.org/10.1111/josi.12202.

Poe, M. & Inoue, A. B. (2016). Toward writing as social justice: An idea whose time has come. *College English, 79*(2), 119–126. http://www.jstor.org/stable/44805913.

Royer, D. & Gilles, R. (1998). Directed self-placement: An attitude of orientation. *College Composition and Communication, 50*(1), 54–70.

Stephens, N., Fryberg, S., Markus, H., Johnson, C. & Covarrubias, R. (2012). Unseen disadvantage: How American universities' focus on independence undermines the academic performance of first-generation college students. *Journal of Personality and Social Psychology, 102*, 1178–1197. https://doi.org/10.1037/a0027143.

Stroman, C. (2019, May 16). Strategies to support belonging in education (part 2 of 4): Anticipating key moments of belonging uncertainty. *Student Experience Research Network Blog*. https://studentexperiencenetwork.org/strategies-support-belonging-schools-part-2-4-anticipating-key-moments-belonging-uncertainty/#.

Toth, C. (2019). Directed self-placement at two-year colleges: A kairotic moment. *Journal of Writing Assessment, 12*(1). http://www.journalofwritingassessment.org/article.php?article=134.

Wood, J. L., Newman, C. B. & Harris, F., I., II. (2015). Self-efficacy as a determinant of academic integration: An examination of first-year Black males in the community college. *Western Journal of Black Studies, 39*(1), 3–17.

Appendix A: Reading Passages from CCBC Self-Directed Placement Tool

The following figures show screen captures from selected pages on CCBC Self-Directed Placement website.

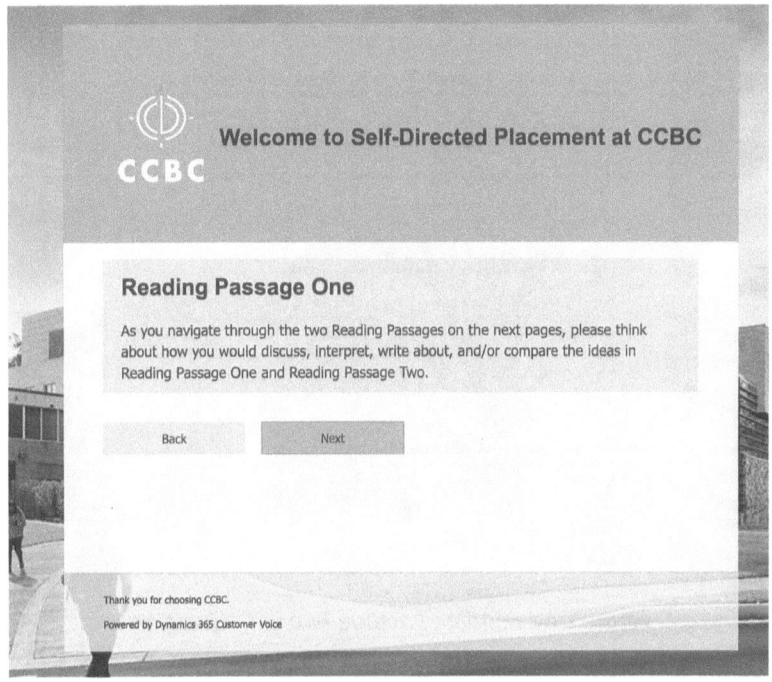

Figure 3.A1. Introductory Screen for Reading Passages.

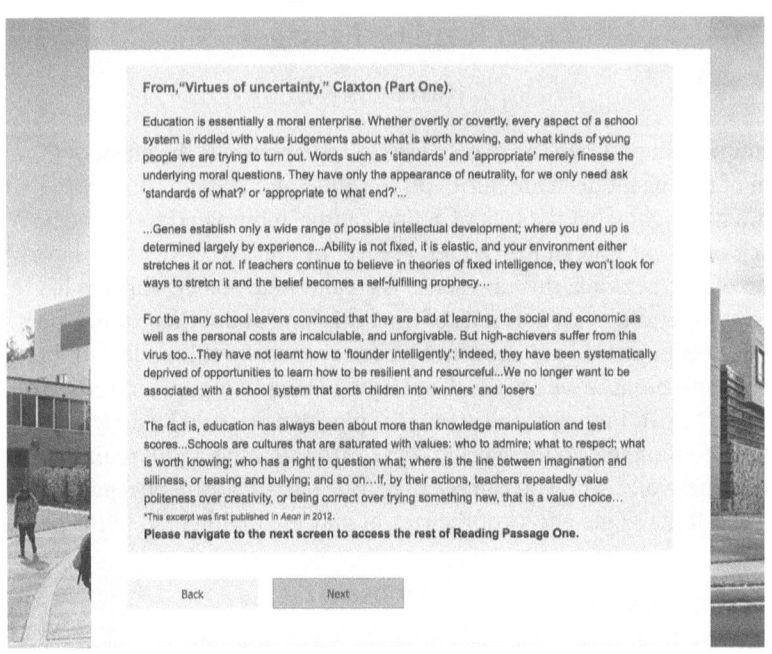

Figure 3.A2. Reading Passage One.

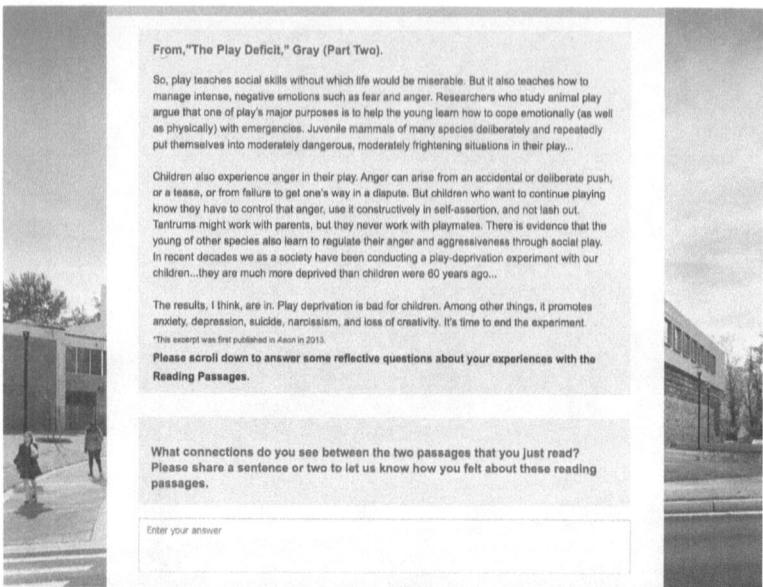

Figure 3.A3. Reading Passage Two with Question.

Appendix B: Sample Student Responses to Reading Passages

Response #1

The connection between the two articles in my opinion is the effect of the culmination of all our modern amenities on the child and student. Both articles in my opinion highlight what the lack of action causes in human development. When I say lack of action I mean it in a literal sense. In the last 20 years we have all created an online persona, this in essence is an alternate reality. This has led to most off society spending vast amounts of time thinking about their online persona in the now. It is impossible to be in two places at once. So this reality suffers from a lack of action because we are paralized trying to act in our own minds in a reality that doesn't exist. In the second article the play deficit could be directly tied to the monkey see monkey do theory. Little eyes are watching and learning the wrong processes basically. And you can see that cycle has already happened in the previous generations as the effects of the lack of play are highlighted in the first

Response #2

After reading passage one "Virtues of Uncertainty" and passage two "The Play Deficit" I have come to realize that in my perspective they are both correct about the school systems and children's experiences. The passage that I mostly agree with though is passage one. The reason behind this is because the topic it discussed in paragraph #5 about teachers valuing politeness over creativity, or even trying a new method of learning the correct information, I have witnessed plenty of times in my days of high school. The student had discovered a new technique to solve the equation that was given correctly, as the teacher proceeded to telling the student that it was incorrect which lead the student to stop participating in class discussions due to the fact the individual thought they were incapable to answer any other problems. In the last paragraph is states "when students are helped to become more confident . . . they do better, not worse, on the test," I personally agree with this because Ive had a teacher spend extra time to help me understand a topic I needed for a state test which lead me to pass with a good grade.

Response #3

The two passages are very interesting and talks on things that I can relate to. I don't feel that it hits deep enough though. I think we should talk on why we have these mental issues? Why do we struggle on test or feel like we are not smart enough? When will school cater to people that have different learning styles. Yes, I believe we have the basics we need in life like math, how to read and spell but not everyone learns the same. Shouldn't play be educational too, learning strategies, having fun and not having to worry about who beats who or if there's a prize in the end because in reality life don't come with prizes. The only prizes you get in life are the things you work towards and the things you value most in life . . .

Response #4

There's a huge gap between today's youth and the youth 50 years ago regarding how social skills are (were) developed. Due to societal differences in the way children spend their time (i.e. outside socializing vs. the over-usage of technology while isolated indoors), today's youth struggle in comparison to their elders with regard to developing social interaction and coping skills, and building psychological resilience to life's normal (common) challenges.

Response #5

In modern times, there is an unrealistic expectation for children to function essentially as adults, without adequate guidance or nurturing from their adult support systems. Individuality is often discouraged in order to fulfill rigid educational standards, while individualism is preached over community. These conflicting ideals serve to isolate, and stunt mental and emotional growth among children.

Chapter 4. Welcome/Not Welcome: From Discouragement to Empowerment in the Writing Placement Process at Central Oregon Community College

Jane Denison-Furness, Stacey Lee Donohue,
Annemarie Hamlin, and Tony Russell
CENTRAL OREGON COMMUNITY COLLEGE

Abstract: At Central Oregon Community College, we have redesigned placement and our developmental literacy curriculum to enable students of diverse backgrounds to achieve their college and career goals. Our purpose was to help students achieve success in college writing while reducing time and money spent on coursework that did not count toward a degree. To achieve that, we focused on placing students at the highest level at which they could succeed and providing the curriculum and support they need to progress quickly yet effectively through first-year composition (FYC). Our target population was students placing below college-level writing—a group of mostly first-generation students who were "welcomed" to college with a high-stakes placement exam. We shifted to a multiple-measures placement tool, redesigned developmental literacy course outcomes and curriculum to better align with FYC, and created a corequisite support course for FYC for students whose placement information indicated they were likely to be successful in FYC with additional help and resources. The changes required significant funding and support from stakeholders across campus. This chapter explores the process, challenges, and successes of our redesign, and offers advice for those programs who are at the start of their redesign phase.

Until recently, like most community colleges in Oregon, Central Oregon Community College (COCC) relied on a standardized, multiple-choice grammar and reading comprehension test in order to place students into an initial writing course. After submitting their application to college, this was a student's first encounter with the campus: a test that effectively told up to 60 percent of new—often first-generation—college students, *Welcome to COCC; however, you are not "college material."* This welcome/not welcome messaging was a key factor in motivating the change in our writing (and math) placement process from single measure ACCUPLACER to what we are calling multiple measures directed self-placement.

Central Oregon Community College, whose main campus is in Bend, Oregon, serves a 10,000 square mile district that is mostly rural and covers all or portions of six counties. Our mission statement focuses our work on promoting student success in transfer and career and technical education (CTE) and providing community enrichment opportunities through our credit and non-credit programs (Figure 4.1). Fifty-nine percent of COCC students enroll in transfer coursework, and just under half of our graduates in 2020 earned a transfer degree.

OUR MISSION

Central Oregon Community College promotes student success and community enrichment by providing quality, accessible, lifelong educational opportunities.

OUR VISION

To achieve student success and community enrichment, COCC fosters student completion of academic goals, prepares students for employment, assists regional employers and promotes equitable achievement for the diverse students and communities we serve.

Figure 4.1. Central Oregon Community College mission and vision.

While transfer coursework garners the majority of our enrollment, CTE and developmental education are critical components of our mission. Regional industry needs drive much of our work in CTE, which comprises about 28 percent of our enrollment. Health care, natural and industrial resources, and hospitality services are the broad areas that employ many of our CTE graduates. Adult basic education at COCC served approximately three percent of our students in 2019–2020 in the areas of English language learning, essentials of math, and essentials of communication. Developmental education (math and integrated reading/writing) comprised 11 percent of our course offerings in 2019.

Central Oregon Community College went from a small rural college to a multicampus, medium-sized college as a result of the 2008 economic downturn, and while a stronger economy and the COVID-19 pandemic have flattened growth in enrollment, we are still the most affordable college choice for local residents. Based on data from 2019–2020, we have over 7700 credit students, average age 25.1, with a slight majority of female students (52%). Sixty-five percent identify as White; however, enrollment among students of color is growing. Latinx students comprise the largest group to self-identify by ethnicity, at 11.7 percent. Almost four percent identify as Native American or Alaska Natives; 4.5 percent as Asian, Native Hawaiian, or Pacific Islander; and 1.6 percent as Black or African American. Students self-identifying as "other" comprise 13.5 percent of students.

Our faculty, both in writing and collegewide, do not reflect the diversity of our students, and, as at most community colleges, the majority of our faculty are part-time, with only 52 percent of our credit courses taught by full-time faculty.[1] In the humanities department (where developmental literacy, composition, literature, creative writing, and film are housed), we have 12 full-time faculty members (a number that has remained consistent for decades) and 12 part-time faculty members (a number that continues to decrease since enrollment is trending downward). The majority hold M.A. or Ph.D. degrees in English (including M.F.A.s). Of the faculty with Ph.D.s, only two have degrees specific to writing and developmental education. One faculty member holds an M.A.T. Currently, our colleague with the degree in developmental literacy oversees, supports, and facilitates instruction of developmental literacy courses taught by a mix of full- and part-time faculty. As to ethnicity, among writing faculty, the majority of whom are women, one identifies as Black and one identifies as Latinx; all others are White. Among all faculty at COCC, less than ten percent self-identify as Latinx, Asian, Native Hawaiian and Pacific Islander, or Black/African American.[2] These numbers are consistent with classified staff and administrators as well, but among temporary workers, up to 15 percent self-identify as Latinx, Asian, Native Hawaiian and Pacific Islander, or Black/African American.[3]

Placement and Developmental Literacy Redesign

The first assessment most community college students encounter is a single-measure instrument designed to assess reading, writing, and math skills. Because the majority of community college students have not taken the ACT or SAT, these "placement tests" (as they have come to be called) compare student scores "to a normative group of students representing a random sample of potential test takers" (Boylan & Saxon, 2012, p. 32). A number of reports and articles have questioned community colleges' historic reliance on standardized tests, pointing out their limitations (Barnet et al., 2018; Barnett & Reddy, 2017; Belfield & Crosta, 2012; Hughes & Scott-Clayton, 2011). When addressing the impact of relying on standardized tests for placement, Christie Toth (2018) pointed out that the "high-stakes standardized tests used for placement at most community colleges were 'under-placing' large numbers of students into developmental courses" (p. 138). Additionally, concerns with cultural bias have pushed many colleges—especially those involved in developmental redesign—to consider alternatives to relying primarily on standardized tests for placement. Jeffrey Klausman et al. (2016) even raisee the question of legal implications which may be linked to issues such as racism, white supremacy, and sexism.

COCC had similar concerns and began exploring alternatives and learned that the change would not be simple or quick. As noted by Ashley Stich (2019),

---

1. Note that by Winter 2021, with a drop in enrollment expected to exceed 13 percent, this number will go down as more sections are taught by full-time faculty.
2. The authors of this chapter all self-identify as White.
3. Respondents were able to choose multiple categories when reporting ethnicity.

replacing one single measure (ACCUPLACER) with another (high school GPA) is no more successful at accurately placing students. Although the case can be made that high school GPA is in itself a type of multiple measure because it is an accumulation of assessed assignments, combining multiple measures by *including* high school GPA (HSGPA) produces a "rich predictive placement algorithm" that is more predictive of future success in college coursework (Scott-Clayton, 2012b, p. 33). HSGPA has been shown to be a much better predictive measure than standardized tests, which a visit to Highline Community College in Washington confirmed. However, we wanted to create an assessment that provided the best possible measure for placement for our students, which continued to point to multiple measures that included but were not limited to HSGPA.

Even what researchers call multiple single-measure placement, or privileging certain single measures, puts expediency over a more holistic and accurate assessment, focusing again on an indirect rather than a direct measure of writing ability (Toth, 2018). Research points to a number of other problems with standardized tests used for single-measure placement, such as construct validity (whether a test measures what it claims to be testing) and consequential validity (the social consequences of a test), which makes them a poor predictor of student success in a course (Toth, 2018; Poe & Inoue, 2016). Finally, concerns about revising assessment as a form of social justice, as discussed by Mya Poe and Asao B. Inoue (2016), and Toth (2018), pushed us to consider how we might attempt to "undertake validation for social justice" through the creation of our own writing assessment (Toth, 2018, p. 145). Wary of replacing one flawed system with another, we looked to research but also knew that change would require large-scale effort and energy on behalf of multiple areas of the college. Alexandros Goudas (2019) discussed current trends in redesign, pointing out that a "thoughtful, well-supported and holistic system for admissions and placement" requires "a significant investment of time, staffing, software, and money" ("Goal of Multiple measures"). Although we did not yet have sufficient funding in 2016, (a state grant for redesigning developmental education allowed us to pilot a small placement redesign, but not to scale up), we began to discuss how to use multiple measures for placement as our first step.

Our work on placement took place alongside our work on developmental redesign, so it is worth a brief segue to address that work and its larger context. The need to bridge the gap between high school and college is not a recent phenomenon. Ellen Brier (1984) provided an overview of the history of developmental education in the United States, noting that access to higher education for underprepared students "has been an integral part of the development of higher education" for hundreds of years (p. 2). Hunter R. Boylan and W. G. White (1987) also pointed out that from its inception in 1636, Harvard has provided tutoring that "may rightly be regarded" as the "earliest antecedent of developmental education in American higher education" (p. 4). The belief that developmental coursework appeared as a byproduct of the 1944 Servicemen's Readjustment Act, the

Civil Rights movement, or the advent of the open-door policy at community colleges in the 1960s is an apocryphal myth that persists today, especially in regard to developmental redesign. Colleges like the University of Wisconsin, Cornell, and Vassar have a long history of helping underprepared, admitted students gain the knowledge and skills needed to succeed in college-level coursework (Brier, 1984).

Efforts to improve developmental coursework have become a hot topic in the last ten years, with critics characterizing it as a "trap" and a "bridge to nowhere" (Barshay, 2018; Complete College America, 2012). While critique of developmental education is sporadic and often insufficiently supported, it is important to note that the debate over the legitimacy of stand-alone developmental coursework and accelerated and/or compressed models is ongoing (Goudas & Boylan, 2012; Goudas, 2020a). An important part of this work has been culturally responsive teaching, which views the "underprepared student" and their rich life experiences as an asset, rather than a deficit. We have seen how social inequality and unequal access have allowed some of our students to be better prepared for college than others. Students from more rural areas often struggle with reliable access to high-speed internet, while some first-generation students do not have the same access to institutional knowledge and family support as their peers. In 2019, The Hope Center's #RealCollege Survey found that among community college students in Oregon, 41 percent of respondents were food insecure in the past 30 days, 52 percent were housing insecure, and 20 percent were unhoused in the previous year (Goldrick-Rab et al., 2019, p. 2). Other factors like employment, childcare, and transportation also create significant obstacles for many of our students. Finally, anxiety about writing and writing trauma, or negative writing experiences from the past, can interfere with some students' ability to achieve their writing goals. In order to meet these needs, we offer both stand-alone developmental coursework and, most recently, accelerated course models.

Fifteen years ago, we offered six developmental classes (three for reading, three for writing) at COCC. Over time, this has been reduced to two courses of integrated reading and writing. Within the past five years, we became eager to engage in redesign but did not want to completely eliminate developmental education as some states have done because we know that not all of our students are prepared for first-year composition. Calls for redesigning (or eliminating) developmental education are cyclical and often ebb and flow in response to poor persistence and retention rates, especially at community colleges. Paco Martorrell and Isaac McFarlin's (2007) report for the Rand Corporation drew erroneous conclusions that developmental education has failed because students completing developmental coursework seemed to do no better than students who did not take these classes (Calcagno & Long, 2008; Pretlow & Wathington, 2012). Complete College America's (2012) *Remediation: Higher Education's Bridge to Nowhere* introduced the idea of "exit ramps," or opportunities for failure, which they said increased when students began in developmental coursework. As low-hanging fruit, developmental coursework is often characterized as the only thing standing between students and success. This is a charge that oversimplifies a complex problem much more symptomatic of social inequality, educational hegemony (or linguistic and cultural privileging that rewards students in possession of behaviors and knowledge that are institutionally legitimized), a lack of professionalization of the field, or institutional greed (Boylan, 1995; Goudas & Boylan, 2012; Lundell & Higbee, 2002). Our own experience in developmental classrooms told us that some students benefited from these courses and persisted into college-level coursework, so we set our sights on redesigning placement so that the students who would benefit the most from these classes were enrolling. Then we redesigned the developmental literacy curriculum to align better with first-year composition and to follow the current best practices in the field (Figure 4.2).

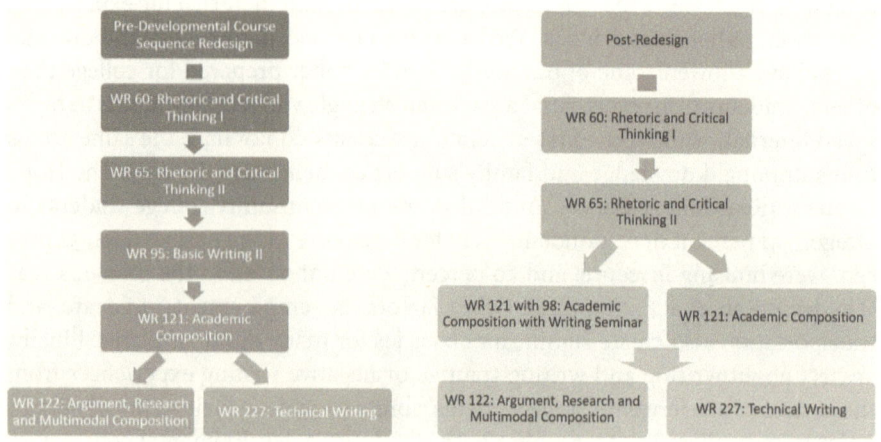

Figure 4.2. Pre-developmental course sequence redesign (left) and post redesign (right) course sequences.

Two alternatives that we considered for placement were multiple measures and guided self-placement (GSP) or one of the many forms of directed self-placement (DSP). Research demonstrates that multiple measures (which include but are not limited to considerations such as non-cognitive factors, high school GPA, and high school transcripts) are more effective than single measures for placement (Klausman et al., 2016; Scott-Clayton et al., 2015 Stitch, 2019; Toth, 2019). Supported by this research, community colleges continue to move away from single-measure placement to better identify students who can succeed in credit-bearing coursework with targeted support (Belfield & Crosta, 2012; Scott-Clayton, 2012b). Often, directed self-placement utilizes a combination of tools for assessment (e.g., survey, writing prompts, reflective questions). This more holistic assessment guides placement by using a matrix determined by what is known about the particular student population at an institution. Ultimately, the result of DSP—or in our case an adaptation of DSP—is a course recommendation used to place students into a first-year writing course. In our case, this resulted in "placement zones" instead of cut scores—a compromise reached between administration, placement, and writing faculty.[4]

While it could be argued that providing agency trumps all else, we do not agree with the conclusion that students who overplace themselves and fail will learn the hard way that "college education is a serious endeavor" or that students *should* be able to accurately estimate their own abilities (Royer & Gilles, 1998, p. 70). This seems to speak from a point of privilege which fails to take into account the impact a lack of institutional knowledge can have on first-generation and marginalized students. Instead, we hope to mitigate this by avoiding mistakes made at other institutions/initiatives, believing that "equality and efficiency need not always be opposing goals" (Nix et al., 2020). For more on this, see research by Rebecka Sare (2017); Holly Larson (2020); Amanda Nix, Tamara Bertrand Jones, Rebecca Brower, Shouping Hu (2020); and Elizabeth Rutschow and Emily Schneider (2012). Toth (2019) pointed out that "DSP is not a single procedure, product or algorithm, but rather a set of principles grounded in student choice that can be implemented in a variety of ways" (p. 2). We agree and believe that it is essential that institutions adapt and implement placement and curriculum redesign that takes into account equity, diversity, students, and resources. In short, no two programs should look alike. At COCC, although students are free to select a lower course placement, they cannot self-select to enroll in a course above the level into which they place through a multiple-measures assessment; however, they can challenge their placement by taking the ACCUPLACER test in reading. This decision was influenced by preliminary research from states like Florida that have instituted self-placement policies (S.B. 1720) that have made developmental coursework optional, and the restraints of compromising with administration, who were already skeptical about DSP (Park et al., 2016).

Collectively, multiple measures and DSP allow colleges to look more closely at direct evidence of student learning in order to more accurately place students at levels where they can be successful but also feel challenged as they move toward first-year composition. DSP also provides students a greater degree of agency in their placement into writing and math coursework, "a recognition of students' right to make an informed choice about their own education"—or what Royer and Gilles (1998) refer to as a matter of 'rightness'" (Toth, 2018). Emerging research demonstrates that students who are engaged in the placement process are more invested and satisfied with their placement overall (Kuh et al., 2006; Toth, 2018). For the most part, we have found this to be true with the students who have been placed using multiple measures and DSP during the past two years of our redesign. Additionally, data from our first few years (detailed in the

---

4. Please email writingplacement@cocc.edu for questions or information on our original placement questionnaire or placement process.

Data section) of using multiple measures and DSP demonstrate the success of this type of placement at our institution, where we've experienced improved rates of course completion and overall persistence (term to term), and higher rates of overall student satisfaction in developmental coursework.

Scaling up Directed Self-Placement

Our journey to redesign placement has taken many years, has been supported by state and federal grants, and has required a significant time investment by many faculty and staff members. Beginning in 2013–2014, a statewide team of educators representing Oregon's 17 (independently governed) community colleges began meeting regularly to consider recommendations for improving developmental education practices and to address growing critique about the efficacy of developmental math and writing coursework. For over a year, the Developmental Education Redesign Workgroup, under the enthusiastic facilitation of Elizabeth Cox Brand, who is currently the executive director of the Oregon Student Success Center—a subgroup of the Oregon Community College Association—met with national educational leaders to begin to address problems with success and persistence. A $30,000 grant from Oregon Community College Association (OCCA) helped COCC develop a pilot program to rethink placement (math and writing) and move from strict cut scores to placement zones that also considered other measures for placement.

The timing for this change in placement seemed ideal. In 2015, ACT phased out COMPASS, and in 2016, the College Board introduced ACCUPLACER Next Gen. No longer were we tasked with defending the need for change, since change was now inevitable. Instead, the conversation quickly switched away from the decades-long reliance on test scores for placement to multiple measures and directed self-placement.

Prior to that, in 2012, the Community College Research Center (CCRC) released two studies that described the failure of standardized placement exams, taking aim at the tests' most notable claim: predictive validity, or a correlation between test scores and subsequent course grades (Belfield & Crosta, 2012; Scott-Clayton, 2012b). As Goudas (2019) pointed out, in addition to poking holes in this long-standing claim, the studies also discovered that combining a placement exam with high school GPA (HSGPA) was much more successful in predicting success in college-level coursework. As a result, in 2015–2016, the humanities department participated in two distinct placement pilots, designed to determine which measures might better predict student success:

- using Smarter Balanced (a statewide competency exam) scores of 3 or higher, or college-ready level ACT score of 18 in English taken in a student's junior year, to count as automatic placement into first-year composition, and/or

- using multiple measures, such as high school GPA, grade in last English class, and student self-reporting on reading and writing skills, to adjust placement after students took ACCUPLACER.

Ultimately, the second pilot proved more effective, since some faculty and advising staff were still wedded to the requirement for students to take ACCUPLACER before registering for classes. Additionally, our online registration system was structured to require a placement score; thus, the tail was wagging the proverbial dog. Our earliest attempt at using multiple measures was based on information gathered from statewide meetings about using multiple measures like high school GPA, last grade in a composition or English course, and familiarity with conventions like MLA format and academic essays. Supported with course load release and a summer stipend from the state grant, writing faculty members interviewed those students whose ACCUPLACER scores indicated a high achievement in reading (an 81 cut score, or college ready) and slightly lower achievement in sentence skills (at 85–94, where 95 was the college-ready score) to discuss whether they might qualify for placement into WR 121 (our first-year composition course). We asked students about their high school GPA, their most recent writing classes and assignments, as well as their reading habits and comfort level with academic writing. Based on their responses, the faculty member and student decided together whether the student should enroll in WR 95 (an upper-level developmental "review" course) or WR 121. We tracked students who opted for WR 121 throughout the term and collected data to see whether those students were successful.

While this was time- and labor-intensive, we were pleased enough with the results of our initial attempt at placement redesign to continue. In Fall 2016, 33 students were eligible to bypass developmental coursework and take WR 121. Of this group, 29 passed WR 121 (two others dropped, only one failed), meaning that in this initial pilot, 88 percent of the students who bypassed developmental coursework were successful. Over the two previous years, the rate of success for students passing WR 121—all of whom would have placed via ACCUPLACER[5]— was 74 percent. From Fall 2016 through Fall 2017, 55 students successfully completed a regular section of WR 121 (most with As and Bs) without having to take WR 65 or WR95 first. Of that group, only 15 were not successful, meaning that 79 percent of the students who bypassed developmental coursework in this pilot year were successful, and while in previous years they would have had to complete developmental coursework in order to be "successful" in WR 121, five percent

---

5. One way to have further tested our results would have been to have compared our pilot students to students who placed with ACCUPLACER and whose scores were high in reading but low in sentence skills. While we have been given access to a lot of data, we were unable and are still unable to drill down into reading and sentence-level scores for comparison.

more of them passed than students that ACCUPLACER had placed into WR 121. The two senior writing faculty members who designed this pilot program had ultimate authority to bypass ACCUPLACER's placement, although they relied on our placement office to make the change in our registration system (Banner) allowing students to register for WR 121. This was, effectively, our initial attempt at testing directed self-placement on a small group of students.

Our data analysis shows that, with some exceptions, students who had earned a 3.0 high school GPA, no matter how many years in the past, tended to succeed in WR 121 even though ACCUPLACER had placed them into WR 95 (then, our highest-level developmental writing course). Analysis of both pilots also showed that Hispanic last names dominated the list of students placed into developmental coursework, which indicated something about the inequity of relying solely on ACCUPLACER. The "writing" portion of ACCUPLACER is a multiple-choice grammar test, one that penalizes students who may not know the prescribed rules of grammar determined by the creators of the assessment. In June 2021, the Conference on College Composition and Communication (CCCC) issued the *CCCC Statement on White Language Supremacy*, noting higher education's lack of recognition of linguistic diversity, which limits academic discourse by "shap[ing] aesthetics, epistemologies, attitudes, [and] ideologies . . . that reinforce white power structures to the detriment of BIPOC [Black, Indigenous, and People of Color] and minoritized people." Again, our experience highlighted and punctuated problems with relying on standardized tests for placement, which often deny students' right to their own language, especially for linguistically oppressed groups.

The process of individually interviewing students to determine placement was time-consuming and unsustainable. In addition, students were still required to take ACCUPLACER in order to register for any writing course, thus limiting our pool of students to those who scored in a higher reading range. However, these interviews gave us enough information to begin choosing measures for consideration in our revised placement process. We knew from consultation with other colleges, and the research told us, that we should scale up quickly in order to mitigate challenges such as logistical problems (having too many different types of developmental pathways), instructional buy-in (we think this might work, but we're not ready to commit), and coordinating with other departments (labor-intensive practices like different types of placement, hand-scoring placement, assessing efficacy), and on and on. We also needed to look at other areas that can affect student persistence and success, such as professional development of faculty, course redesign, and acceleration (Edgecombe et al., 2013).

We consulted with five other community colleges involved in placement and developmental course redesign (in Oregon and Washington) and followed another recommendation by the statewide Developmental Redesign group: allowing some students who placed into developmental reading/writing to take college composition with a support course (the corequisite model). Findings suggest that corequisite students tend to continue their college education at a higher rate than students who start in developmental coursework (Daugherty et al., 2018; Hassel et al., 2015). We developed the curriculum for what we called WR 98 Writing Seminar, a two-credit co-enrolled course with our first-year composition course, WR 121. We started with one or two sections of this course per term, and by Fall 2020, we were offering seven sections of corequisite first-year composition, all fully enrolled with waiting lists. As you can see, from the start, we followed the recommendation we received from our tour of colleges who were already ahead of us in developmental redesign: that redesigning curriculum and course structure should coincide with redesigning placement.

Challenges

Our path to developing the new placement measures included several challenges and opportunities. Originally not successful in our bid for a federal Strengthening Institutions Title III grant,[6] we began a small-scale redesign in developmental literacy and math on our own. One year later, the college learned we were awarded a $2.5 million grant, which focused on three areas: developmental literacy, developmental math, and first-year experience. The delay meant that our redesign efforts were beginning at different places rather than happening within a coordinated effort across the college. While this issue is perhaps unique to COCC and the circumstances of the grant, we would argue that having a clear timeline of activities early in the process would have led to fewer frustrations.

Another challenge involved the number of departments and areas involved in implementing the projects needed to accomplish the goals of the grant—a challenge that cannot be overstated. The three areas of the grant are housed in two different branches within the college organizational structure: Student/Enrollment Services and Instruction. Each of these branches are led by different administrators: the Vice President for Instruction and the Vice President of Student Affairs. Also, the redesign of developmental math and developmental literacy required assistance from other departments housed in these two branches. Unfortunately, not all of these departments were included in the original language of the grant, which limited the compensation that could be provided for the extra work needed to accomplish stated goals, most notably placement. We were able to secure release time or stipends for writing and math faculty working on the changes under the terms of the grant, and we also were able to expand our placement testing coordinator's position to full time.

Where we ran into constraints was with support staff who did not receive release time or shifted assignments in order to complete the technological changes needed to create a fully online directed self-placement system (including the instrument and the system to record placement levels on student accounts). Administrators and staff in these areas had to complete their part of the work

---

6. For more on Title III, visit https://www2.ed.gov/programs/iduestitle3a/index.html

without the ability to shift their ongoing responsibilities to others, resulting in a heavier workload and creating an inequity in relation to faculty. Our advice here would be to clearly request much more support for staff members at the grant application stage.

The difficulty of bringing together the departments and personnel required for implementation of the grant cannot be overstated. For example, Developmental Literacy cannot redesign its course sequence (adding a corequisite, accelerated learning course) until there is more accurate placement; however, Placement Services (which consists of a single staff person at COCC) did not know how to implement multiple measures of placement, and due to personnel and software problems, the staff member was not compensated under the grant to make these changes. Additionally, once the Title III grant was awarded, Developmental Literacy and Developmental Math were more than a year ahead of everyone else involved in the redesign, and because of this, the faculty in these departments were often frustrated by how long it took to build buy-in. Math and writing faculty spent many hours in meetings trying to convince colleagues in other departments of the changes needed to support their work under the grant (e.g., collecting data on persistence and retention or entering corequisite classes in Banner, which is the school's student information system).

Related to our student information system is the issue of making changes to our directed self-placement tool, changes we feel are necessary as we continue to tweak our placement process to meet other challenges (such as students who forgot their GPA,[7] or have earned a modified high school diploma,[8] or current high school students). Making changes to the directed self-placement tool is cumbersome as it is controlled by instructional technology staff who are the most familiar with creating an effective Qualtrics survey. We have been told that any edits/changes can only be made once a year because such changes are time-consuming. Since the college has chosen to go with Qualtrics, we are committed to staying with that system for our survey tool despite the difficulty in easily editing the survey.

A related challenge is a communication issue with faculty outside of our department: with so many advisors (a mixture of full-time advisors and full-time faculty serving as advisors), and despite our best efforts, many faculty continue to be unclear about parameters of our directed self-placement, so we are often

---

7. Like many community colleges, we do not require newly admitted students to submit a high school transcript, and we do not have the staff to collect and evaluate them, thus we do not have their high school GPA or course grades in our system.

8. An Oregon modified high school diploma is designed for students with a disability who cannot pass regular high school coursework with support. Thus, students can earn a modified high school diploma, allowing them to bypass some coursework. Their cumulative GPAs, however, do not reflect the modification, thus they can have a 3.8 GPA based on coursework that did not prepare them for college-level work, so their placement on the DSP is inaccurate.

sent students (via our dedicated email, writingplacement@cocc.edu) who do not meet our minimum qualifications and are thus disappointed when they are not permitted to take WR 121, that is unless they score high enough on the challenge reading test in ACCUPLACER. While the majority of new students take the DSP, they do have agency in the process, namely that they may elect to place into a writing course via ACCUPLACER or they may challenge their DSP placement by taking ACCUPLACER. Because our college employs so many advisors, we have invested time in training faculty advisors and meeting with our advising director to minimize confusion. This training will need to continue as part of our annual advising training day.

Another challenge that must be anticipated with any long-term redesign is faculty burnout: Three full-time faculty members have been the primary figures researching and implementing placement redesign since 2014. Our department of 12 full-time faculty is small enough that there are not many who can relieve us. Placement redesign must be continuously assessed and tweaked, especially in these initial years of our DSP, and as we continue to assess whether the tool is accurately recommending the highest possible placement for all students, or if we need different placement tools for certain populations of students (e.g., students who have been out of school for over a decade, or who are still in high school and have yet to take junior or senior language arts classes). Yet our grant funding is spent, as are faculty who have been working on this process for six years.

Data

Despite the resistance we encountered—and we sometimes still encounter it—the data reflect the success of our changes while revealing other challenges. Nevertheless, the results of this switch from ACCUPLACER to the DSP were immediately apparent: More students were placing higher than with ACCUPLACER. Whereas 40 percent of students taking the standardized exam had placed into a first-year writing course, 84 percent of students taking the DSP placed into a first-year composition course. This group includes students who take first-year composition (WR 121) with a corequisite course (WR 98). Even when students who elected to place via ACCUPLACER are factored in, the overall percentage of those who place into college-level writing is 42 percent higher than in the 2014–2015 academic year (Figure 4.3).[9]

---

9. When gathering data, noticing the timing of students' choices has been important. For instance, we can track the time taken between writing courses and how successful students are when they take these courses in a shorter time frame, particularly developmental literacy courses. One thing we would have liked to have had access to was data on how long a student takes to enroll in a writing course once the DSP or ACCUPLACER has been taken; however, because this data exists on different technological platforms across various operational areas at the college, we have not been able to access it.

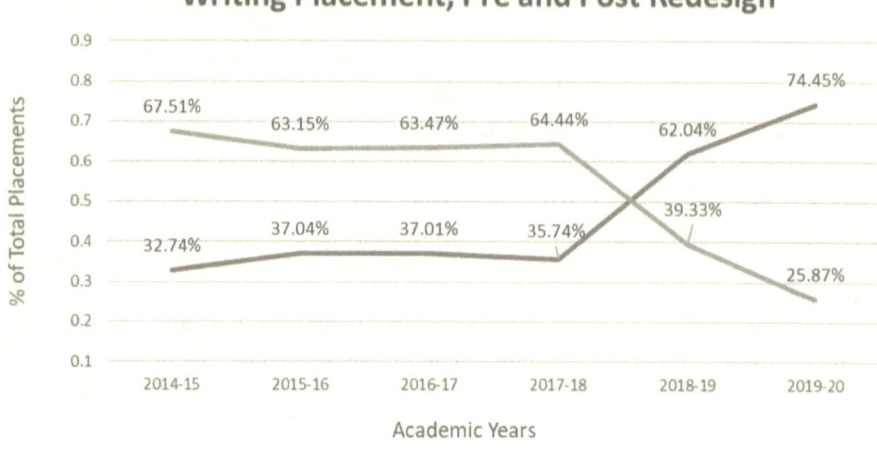

Figure 4.3. Writing placement (all methods), 2014–2020.[10]

Tracking students via the DSP has helped us gain a clearer picture of who our students are as writers. While the majority report having taken a writing course within the last year, the next most significant number of students report having taken a writing course five or more years ago. We have also found that while many students report earning As and Bs during high school, several respondents do not answer the question or claim that they do not remember. Students who were on a modified track in high school—for example, an Individualized Education Program designed for students with special needs and with fewer strict course and graduation requirements—may have As and Bs that are not equivalent to what we would traditionally associate with academic success; however, we are unable to ask that question on the DSP, and thus some students are, indeed, placed too high, as we have determined anecdotally from students who withdraw from our accelerated course WR 121 plus WR 98.

We expected that more students would place into college-level writing courses, and we expected that more of them would be successful in those courses. Indeed, we did observe higher pass rates and lower drop rates in the switch from the standardized exam to the DSP. For example, 2.6 percent fewer students drop their first writing class when they place via the DSP rather than ACCUPLACER. More significantly, 8.9 percent more of them complete that first course. Beyond the DSP, our Title III grant allowed us to make substantial improvements to our developmental literacy courses and classrooms.[11] Since

---

10. Orange represents students placing via test (e.g. ACCUPLACER) while blue represents revised and directed self-placement.

11. Full- and part-time faculty have received training in hybrid and online instruction, andragogy, universal design, Quality Matters, and English language learners (ELL),

that redesign and the launching of the DSP, six percent more of our students are successful in their developmental coursework (Table 4.1). Since the creation of our accelerated course WR 121 plus WR 98, 81.83 percent have completed the course with a C grade or above. This rate is 3.65 percent higher than students who take WR 121 alone.

Table 4.1. Course Success for Developmental Literacy Courses Pre- and Post-DSP

Course	Before Fall 2018	Since Fall 2018	Variance
WR 60	62.58%	69.17%	+6.59%
WR 65	63.63%	69.70%	+6.08%

Note. Course success is defined here by registered students who complete the course with an A, B, C, or P grade.

Before the introduction of the DSP and accelerated writing course, attrition rates for our developmental writing courses, WR 60 and WR 65, averaged 25.02 percent and 23.5 percent respectively. Since 2018–2019, the attrition rates for WR 60 have dropped 2.97 percent, while the rates for WR 65 have dropped 7.61 percent (Table 4.2). While these results are favorable, the COVID-19 pandemic has surely had a profound effect upon them, just as it has had on the lives of our students.[12] After eight terms of offering our accelerated course, the average attrition rate is 10.59 percent, but this rate has steadily fallen. After two terms of 2020–2021 (we have three terms per academic year, not including summers), only 5.1 percent of registered students have dropped the course.

Table 4.2. Attrition Rates for Developmental Literacy Courses Pre- and Post-DSP

Course	Before Fall 2018	Since Fall 2018	Variance
WR 60	25.02%	22.05%	-2.98%
WR 65	23.50%	15.89%	-7.60%

Note. Attrition rate is defined here as the percentage of students registered for a course who drop (before Week 7 of a 10-week course) or withdraw (drop with instructor permission after Week 7) from a course.

---

and 98 percent of our developmental and accelerated courses are taught in a computer classroom.

12. Our WR 60 courses often include our most vulnerable students. In the wake of the COVID-19 pandemic, they were the students most likely to report a lack in access to technology and instability in housing, child care, and employment. This was likely a major contributing factor to the fact that 30 percent of these students dropped or withdrew from WR 60 in 2019–2020.

What has produced the most impressive gains has been what happens after students are recommended placement using our new placement process. Revising our placement tool allows students some self-determination in choosing their initial writing course. We believe that that choice contributes to persistence, but we have also noticed a tendency among a small group of students to question their placement and take a lower-numbered course when given a choice.[13] More often than not, when a student disagrees with their placement after taking the DSP, they self-select a *lower*, not *higher*, placement. In these instances, we ask advisors to encourage students to enroll in the higher-level course while simultaneously taking advantage of support services (e.g., tutoring, disability services). Here, the difference between the two systems of placement was remarkable. When students took the DSP and elected to take a lower-numbered course than the one they placed into, only about seven percent of these students did not pass the course. Failure rates with the standardized exam were much higher, with some faculty reporting almost a third of the students not passing the course into which they were placed. In other words, students who self-selected to take a lower-level developmental course because of writing anxiety were generally accurate in doing so. The slower pace of the developmental course and the enhanced support tended to benefit these students, resulting in higher pass rates.

Overall, the results of these changes are positive; many more students are beginning their college careers enrolled in college-level writing and math classes, skipping the developmental courses that do not count toward their degrees or certificates. From 2018 to 2020, more than 2,000 students placed into accelerated writing courses rather than developmental literacy ones, saving them close to $90,000 in tuition and fees. Student success in first-year courses has increased, partially due to curriculum and advising changes implemented along with the placement reform. While COCC faculty and staff are still assessing the results of the placement changes, refining the criteria used, and tracking the progress of students as they move through their college pathways, the data show that this has been a major success for students, saving them both time and money, which makes administration and students happier, and starting off their college careers on surer footing, which we argue is the key goal and our original intent.

Conclusion

We recognize that the necessary ingredients for any college attempting this overhaul include a grant that allows faculty release time to make the placement and curriculum changes, ongoing institutional investment, and the time to meet with faculty and staff for continuous discussion of goals, changes, and needs. We

---

13. This has been a perplexing phenomenon that we have attributed to writing anxiety and writing trauma due to comments students have made that signal a lack of self-efficacy.

also recommend that faculty argue for flexibility for the first few years to make changes annually in response to emerging information. Replacing one placement tool with another reveals that we need to consider different placement options for different populations of students.

Because of the two grants we received, we were able to address, at the same time, other necessary changes to boost student success. We revised the curriculum for our remaining developmental literacy courses, requesting that all instructors follow the same model (though they could select from a group of readings and assignment topics). This addressed one concern we had that different instructors were placing too much emphasis on research and citing sources, rather than in working with students on integrated reading and writing. We began offering a first-year composition class with a support course: This required specific workshops and mentoring for instructors wishing to teach the combined courses. We also, often in collaboration with developmental math faculty, held ongoing in-house professional development workshops for faculty, focusing on ways we can support student success and address non-cognitive concerns. For over a year, we held joint meetings with instructors (one per term), focusing on issues like technology in developmental classrooms (Winter 2019), social justice and the syllabus (Spring 2018), first-generation students and success (Spring 2018), and the art and science of teaching and learning (Winter 2018). We invited colleagues from other disciplines (human development, sociology) and areas of expertise (e.g., e-learning and disability services) to share knowledge that would enhance our instruction.[14] Finally, we made ACCUPLACER a challenge tool instead of the initial placement tool for students, and we now only require the reading section: Research shows that the multiple-choice writing section did not assess students' ability to write. Ultimately, maintaining this test as a challenge option was another compromise we made with administration, who reluctantly agreed to placement redesign from the start, and our future plans call for reevaluating this challenge option once we get enough data (most students do not choose to challenge, currently). We strongly believe that it was the combination of all of these initiatives that has led to student successes: Changing placement alone would not have worked.

A recent article by Erik Armstrong et al. (2020) reminds us all to anticipate the inevitable backlash that will happen to changes in placement and the addition of the corequisite options, whether based on fiscal concerns, the mistaken belief that such changes are watering down standards and the ineffable "rigor" of composition courses, or conversely, the mistaken belief that all students should simply bypass developmental courses and be placed in the supported WR 121 course. The article details how California colleges used multiple measures for placement

---

14. See the "Developmental Education Workshops" page on COCCs Dev Ed Digital Library for links to info from these sessions: https://sites.google.com/view/coccdigitallibrary2017/home.

in the early 1990s, only to return to high-stakes testing for placement by the early 2000s. Today, California Assembly Bill 705 requires colleges to return to multiple-measures placement, as did a 1988 lawsuit.[15] The authors argued that we must continually tell stories of our students' successes with a fairer placement model and a more appropriate support system, to our colleagues, our administrators, and to the general public.

Another consideration that Armstrong et al. (2020) proposed is working statewide to develop a shared version of multiple-measures placement, as Idaho has done successfully, among community colleges and universities.[16] While Oregon chose to encourage local options, the fact that our students regularly move among colleges requires either an expectation that placement at one college will be accepted at another college, or that colleges share similar placement instruments.

Acknowledgments

We would like to thank the following for supporting our work on redesigning placement: the Title III Strengthening Institutions Program grant by the U.S. Department of Education; the Oregon Student Success Center grant; Elizabeth Cox Brand; and our colleagues at Central Oregon Community College, including Eleanor Sumpter-Latham; Jennifer Newby; Betsy Julian; Alicia Moore, Beth Wright, Brian Gutierrez, Delia Go, Sharon Bellusci, Chris Mills, Brynn Pierce, Chris Egertson, Kathy Smith, Doug Nelson.

References

Armstrong, E., Geist, M. B. & Geist, J. (2020). Withstanding the backlash: Conceptualizing and preparing for coercive reactions to placement reform and corequisite support models in California. *Composition Studies, 48*(2), 74–92.

Barnett, E. A., Bergman, P., Kopko, E., Reddy, V., Belfield, C. & Roy, S. (2018). *Multiple measures placement using data analytics: An implementation and early impacts report*. The Center for the Analysis of Postsecondary Readiness and MDRC. https://ccrc.tc.columbia.edu/publications/multiple-measures-placement-using-data-analytics.html.

Barnett, E. A. & Reddy, V. (2017). *College placement strategies: Evolving considerations and practices* (A CAPR Working Paper). Center for the Analysis of Post-Secondary Readiness. Community College Research Center. https://ccrc.tc.columbia.edu/publications/college-placement-strategies-evolving-considerations.html.

---

15. Assembly Bill 705 also requires colleges to show evidence that their standalone developmental courses improve outcomes for students, thus diminishing the very real need for a standalone preparatory option for students before first-year composition. We disagree with that component of the bill. For more on this, see Gilman et al. (2019).

16. See Estrem et al. (2014)

Barshay, J. (2018). How to help students avoid the remedial ed trap. *Hechinger Report*. https://hechingerreport.org/help-students-avoid-remedial-ed-trap/.

Belfield, C. & Crosta, P. (2012). *Predicting success in college: The importance of placement tests and high school transcripts* (CCRC Working Paper No. 42). Community College Research Center. https://ccrc.tc.columbia.edu/publications/predicting-success-placement-tests-transcripts.htm.

Boylan, H. R. (1995). Making the case for developmental education. *Research in Developmental Education, 12*(2), 1–4.

Boylan, H. R. & Saxon, D. P. (2012). *Attaining excellence in developmental education: Research-based recommendations for administrators*. National Center for Developmental Education.

Boylan, H. R. & White, W. G. (1987). Educating all the nation's people: The historical roots of developmental education, part I. *Research in Developmental Education, 4*(4). 3–6.

Brier, E. (1984). Bridging the academic preparation gap: A historical view. *Journal of Developmental Education, 8*(1), 2–5.

Calcagno, J. C. & Long, B. T. (2008). *The impact of postsecondary remediation using a regression discontinuity approach: Addressing endogenous sorting and noncompliance* (No. w14194). National Bureau of Economic Research. https://www.nber.org/papers/w14194.

Complete College America. (2012). *Remediation: Higher education's bridge to nowhere*. ERIC Clearinghouse. https://completecollege.org/wp-content/uploads/2017/11/CCA-Remediation-final.pdf.

Conference on College Composition and Communication. (2021, June). *CCCC statement on white language supremacy*. https://cccc.ncte.org/cccc/white-language-supremacy.

Daugherty, L., Gomez, C. J., Carew, D., Mendoza-Graf, A. & Miller, T. (2018). *Designing and implementing corequisite models of developmental education: Findings from Texas community colleges*. Rand Corporation. https://www.rand.org/pubs/research_reports/RR2337.html.

Edgecombe, N., Cormier, M., Bickerstaff, S. & Barragan, M. (2013). *Strengthening developmental education evidence on implementation efforts from the scaling innovation project* (CCRC Working Paper No. 61). Columbia University, Teachers College, Community College Research Center. https://ccrc.tc.columbia.edu/publications/strengthening-developmental-education-reforms.html.

Estrem, H., Shepherd, D. & Duman, L. (2014). Relentless engagement with state educational policy reform: Collaborating to change the writing placement conversation. *WPA: Writing Program Administration, 38*(1), 88–128.

Gilman, H., Baird-Giordano, J., Hancock, N., Hassel, H., Henson, L., Hern, K., Nastal, J. & Toth, C. (2019). Forum: Two-year college writing placement as fairness. *The Journal of Writing Assessment, 12*(1). http://journalofwritingassessment.org/article.php?article=139.

Goldrick-Rab, S. (2015). *Hungry to learn: Addressing food and housing insecurities among undergraduates*. Wisconsin Hope Lab. https://hope4college.com/wp-content/uploads/2018/09/Wisconsin_HOPE_Lab_Hungry_To_Learn.pdf.

Goldrick-Rab, S., Baker-Smith, C., Coca, V. & Looker, E. (2019). *Oregon community colleges #realcollege survey*. The Hope Center. https://hope4college.com/wp-content/uploads/2020/02/2019_OregonCC_Report_v2.pdf

Goudas, A. (2017a). *Multiple measures for college placement: Good theory, poor implementation*. Community College Data. http://communitycollegedata.com/articles/multiple-measures-for-college-placement/.

Goudas, A. (2017b). *Return of the right to fail*. Community College Data. http://communitycollegedata.com/articles/return-of-the-right-to-fail/.

Goudas, A. (2019). *Multiple measures for college placement: Good theory, poor implementation*. Community College Data. http://communitycollegedata.com/articles/multiple-measures-for-college-placement/.

Goudas, A. (2020). *The corequisite reform movement: A higher education bait and switch*. Community College Data. http://communitycollegedata.com/articles/the-corequisite-reform-movement/.

Hughes, K. L. & Scott-Clayton, J. (2011). Assessing developmental assessment in community colleges. *Community College Review, 39*(4), 327–351. https://ccrc.tc.columbia.edu/media/k2/attachments/assessing-developmental-assessment.pdf.

Klausman, J., Toth, C., Swyt, W., Griffiths, B., Sullivan, P., Warnke, A. & Roberts, L. (2016). TYCA white paper on placement reform. *Teaching English in the Two-Year College, 44*(2), 135–157.

Kuh, G. D., Kinzie, J. L., Buckley, J. A., Bridges, B. K. & Hayek, J. C. (2006). *What matters to student success: A review of the literature* (Vol. 8). National Postsecondary Education Cooperative.

Larson, H. (2020). The rhetorical machinations of SB 1720: Defunding developmental courses. *Voices of Reform: Educational Research to Inform and Reform, 3*(1), 77–90.

Lundell, D. B. & Higbee, J. L. (2002). *Histories of developmental education*. University of Minnesota. https://conservancy.umn.edu/bitstream/handle/11299/5366/mono2.1.pdf?sequence=3.

Martorell, P. & McFarlin, I. (2007). *Help or hindrance: The effects of college remediation on academic and labor market outcomes*. Rand Corporation. https://direct.mit.edu/rest/article-abstract/93/2/436/58605/Help-or-Hindrance-The-Effects-of-College?redirectedFrom=fulltext.

Nix, A. N., Jones, T. B., Brower, R. L. & Hu, S. (2020). Equality, efficiency, and developmental education reform: The impact of SB 1720 on the mission of the Florida college system. *Community College Review, 48*(1), 55–76.

Nix, A. N., Jones, T. B. & Hu, S. (2020). The panhandle is different than the peninsula: How rural colleges in Florida implemented education reform. *Rural Sociology, 85*(3), 658–682.

Park, T., Woods, C. S., Richard, K., Tandberg, D., Hu, S. & Jones, T. B. (2016). When developmental education is optional, what will students do? A preliminary analysis of survey data on student course enrollment decisions in an environment of increased choice. *Innovative Higher Education, 41*(3), 221–236.

Poe, M. & Inoue, A. (2016). Toward writing as social justice: An idea whose time has come. *College English, 79*(2), 119–126.

Pretlow, J., III & Wathington, H. D. (2012). Cost of developmental education: An update of Breneman and Haarlow. *Journal of Developmental Education*, 36(2), 3-44.

Royer, D. & Gilles, R. (1998). Directed self-placement: An attitude of orientation. *College Composition and Communication*, 50(1), 54-70.

Rutschow, E. Z. & Schneider, E. (2012). *Unlocking the gate: What we know about improving developmental education*. MDRC. https://www.mdrc.org/sites/default/files/full_595.pdf.

Sare, R. J. (2017). *Students' decision-making after Florida Senate Bill 1720: Guiding students through math placement* [Doctoral dissertation, Walden University]. Walden Dissertations and Doctoral Studies. https://scholarworks.waldenu.edu/dissertations/3471.

Scott-Clayton, J. (2012a, April 20). Are college entrants overdiagnosed as underprepared? *The New York Times*. https://economix.blogs.nytimes.com/2012/04/20/are-college-entrants-overdiagnosed-as-underprepared/.

Scott-Clayton, J. (2012b). *Do high-stakes placement exams predict college success?* (CCRC Working Paper No. 41). Community College Research Center, Teachers College, Columbia University. http://ccrc.tc.columbia.edu/media/k2/attachments/high-stakes-predict-success.pdf.

Stich, A. N. (2019). *The use of high school GPA for community college placement through a social justice lens* (Order No. 27805413). ProQuest Dissertations & Theses Global. (2350122039).

Toth, C. (2018). Directed self-placement at "democracy's open door": Writing placement and social justice in community colleges. In A. B. Inoue, M. Poe & N. Elliot (Eds.), *Writing assessment, social justice, and the advancement of opportunity* (pp. 137-171). The WAC Clearinghouse; University Press of Colorado. https://doi.org/10.37514/PER-B.2018.0155.2.04.

Toth, C. (2019). Directed self-placement at two-year colleges: A kairotic moment. *Journal of Writing Assessment*, 12(1). https://escholarship.org/uc/item/6g81k736.

Toth, C., Nastal, J., Hassel, H. & Giordano, J. B. (2019). Writing assessment, placement, and the two-year college. *Journal of Writing Assessment*, 12(1). https://escholarship.org/uc/item/8393560s.

Part Two. Innovation and Equity in Placement Reform

Chapter 5. Narrowing the Divide in Placement at a Hispanic-Serving Institution: The Case of Yakima Valley College

Carolyn Calhoon-Dillahunt and Travis Margoni
YAKIMA VALLEY COLLEGE

Abstract: This chapter's case study demonstrates how writing placement that arises from and responds to local contexts increases equitable student outcomes and supports programmatic and institutional change. In the past decade, Yakima Valley College (YVC), a Hispanic-Serving Institution (HSI) located in Central Washington, has shifted from a predominantly White institution to a majority Latinx institution. Local demographic shifts, coupled with increased intervention in developmental education reform by policymakers and funding entities, propelled YVC to adopt an "equity agenda." YVC's English department collaboratively developed innovations to ameliorate placement issues and to improve the efficacy of our developmental writing sequences, into which the majority of students and the vast majority of students of color placed prior to 2017. After COMPASS's discontinuation (2016), English faculty seized upon the moment to develop a new placement methodology that combined alternative means of demonstrating first-year writing-readiness with a customized version of Boise State's The Write Class. Since the change in placement procedures (effective Fall 2017), the majority of students place directly into first-year writing while maintaining high success rates. The authors argue that YVC's placement reform plays an important role in the college's mission as an HSI and serves as a foundation for reforms across campus toward more equitable and antiracist practices.

A College in Transition

A recent *New York Times* article, entitled "The Divide in Yakima Is the Divide in America," examines the nation's changing demographics and the social, economic, and political implications of these changes through the lens of the Yakima Valley, situated on the traditional homelands of the Yakama Nation:

> The changes in this farming valley, known as the nation's fruit basket, mirror demographic trends in numerous U.S. cities where the population is becoming increasingly less White. . . . In Yakima, young adults are nearly twice as likely to be Latino as older adults. (Searcey & Gebeloff, 2019)

The student body at the largest local high school, Eisenhower High School, for example, consisted of 23 percent Latinx and 70 percent White students in 1999; a decade later, Latinx students were in the demographic majority at the high school (Searcey & Gebeloff, 2019). In many ways, Yakima Valley College (YVC) also represents the changing landscape in higher education. In the past decade, YVC has transitioned from a predominantly White institution (though identified as a Hispanic-Serving Institution [HSI] since 2001) to a majority Latinx institution, a shift that has surfaced tensions and created opportunities as we try to embrace the "serving" component of our federal designation.

Across its adult basic education, workforce education, transfer, and, now, applied baccalaureate programs, YVC enrolls roughly 8,000 students—nearly 4,000 full time equivalents (FTEs)—with an average age of 27. Hispanic/Latinx students make up 60 percent of the total student population, and YVC serves the largest number of college-level DACAmented and unDACAmented students in the state. About 11 percent of YVC's student body is composed of high school juniors and seniors taking college courses tuition-free through Washington State's 27-year-old dual credit program, Running Start. The majority of YVC students are employed in the community, and 73 percent are identified as "low income." Eighty-four percent of YVC students are first-generation college students, and 70 percent identify as female (*2020–21 Quick Facts*, 2021). According to the U.S. Department of Education's *College Scorecard* (n.d.), YVC's eight-year graduation rate is 44 percent; its three-year graduation rate (150% time) is approximately 30 percent (National Center for Education Statistics, n.d.).

YVC faculty and staff demographics, however, have not aligned with the changes seen in the student body. According to YVC's Office of Institutional Effectiveness data, the percentage of YVC's total workforce that identifies as people of color currently stands at 29.7 percent, the highest percentage in the Washington state two-year and technical college system. However, only 15 percent of YVC full-time faculty identify as people of color, and that percentage is even lower in the English department, which has only two BIPOC (Black, Indigenous, and People of Color) faculty members, both recent hires, among its 17 full-time faculty members. Due in part to its rural location and the lack of advanced degree-granting universities in the area, YVC is unique in that it maintains a high proportion of full-time faculty; more than 75 percent of YVC's English department members teach full time, and that ratio is similar in other departments across the college.

YVC's governance is also unique from many peer institutions. It has few administrative layers—a president and two vice presidents, to whom five deans of the various instructional and support divisions and the directors and supervisors of the other administrative areas report. YVC does not have a faculty senate, but faculty are unionized and collectively bargain contracts. At the department level, YVC has department heads, but these positions are minimally compensated and have limited authority. As a result, YVC's English department is accustomed to a distributed leadership model, in which faculty members regularly rotate in and out of various positions of responsibility, including department head, and engage in collective and informed decision-making. This model, which Carolyn Calhoon-Dillahunt (2011) describes as a "decentered" writing program, "enables our faculty to collaborate to create a coherent writing program while allowing space for faculty autonomy" (p. 125). This "team approach" (Taylor, 2009), enhanced by YVC's high ratio of full-time faculty, has resulted in high levels of engagement in department work and strong faculty buy-in with department initiatives, processes, and policies.

Placement Reform: Converging Forces and a *Kairotic* Moment

Much like Jessica Nastal (2019) and others have described, the announcement of the COMPASS placement test's discontinuation in 2016 marked the *kairotic* moment for YVC's placement system—an opportunity "to disrupt the current systems of higher education and take responsibility for those aspects of inequality that are under our control" (Withem et al., 2015, p. 9). However, the beginnings of our placement and developmental education reform journey can be traced back to the early 2000s, around the time YVC was first recognized as an HSI. Like other colleges nationwide, YVC was grappling with its shifting demographics as well as increased intervention in higher education reform by policymakers and what Linda Adler-Kassner (2017) refers to as the Educational Industrial Complex: non-governmental organizations (NGOs), granting agencies, policy institutes, and corporations. State higher education funding formulas and legislation, competitive grant funding from Title V and Achieving the Dream, and accreditation processes propelled YVC's articulation of a college "equity agenda" at the same time that the Washington State Board of Community and Technical Colleges (SBCTC), the body that coordinates Washington state's system of 34 community and technical colleges, adopted a vision centering its work on "leading with racial equity" (2020). Thus, YVC's placement system change was, ultimately, the result of parallel forces, internal and external, converging after years of groundwork. Disciplinary scholarship laid the foundation upon which we could build something new once the opportunity presented itself.

Like most other two-year colleges (Fields & Parsad, 2012), for decades, YVC relied on a single measure—in our case, the COMPASS test—to determine students' need for developmental coursework. The COMPASS test was long viewed as an inexpensive and efficient way of determining college "readiness"; its convenience met YVC's need for year-round, on-demand testing and supported its self-sustaining placement model, one in which placement fees fully cover testing and related administrative costs. Over time, COMPASS placements in math and English were being used for purposes beyond their intent or capacity to measure, adopted as course and program prerequisites in many departments across the college. In other words, the COMPASS placement test was high-stakes testing, determining student access and associated educational costs and time to degree. However, most incoming students were unaware of the significance and consequences of placement testing (Hughes & Scott-Clayton, 2011). Moreover, the process of paying for and completing YVC placement tests involved multiple steps and offices on campus, some of which were only accessible during regular business hours.

English department members had long been troubled by using placement tests focused on conventional grammar, usage, and punctuation for placement into writing courses which, for a time, included up to three levels of developmental courses prior to first-year writing. Well before department members fully understood the concept of "disparate impact," we recognized that our editing-focused multiple-choice test did not fit well with our learning outcomes and curriculum, nor did it provide a very good rough sort of students into the writing courses they needed. Anecdotally, we noticed that Hispanic surnames dominated the rosters of our developmental writing courses. Department members often observed the wide range of abilities of students placed into the same course or noted that students placed into our lowest level of developmental writing courses may, in fact, be stronger writers than those in the higher-level courses they were teaching at the same time. Our observations were corroborated by Peter Crosta and Clive Belfield (2012), who found that COMPASS misplaced about one in three students in writing, often "severely." A growing body of evidence, both local and national, also revealed some of the serious ramifications of misplacement. For instance, Thomas Bailey et al. (2009) found that the lower students place in a developmental sequence, the less likely they are to complete college-level coursework—results that mirrored findings by YVC's Office of Institutional Effectiveness: YVC students who placed into developmental coursework (math and/or English), which was the majority of students—and the vast majority of students of color—were unlikely to be retained into the following academic year, let alone complete a certificate or degree. Still, despite the growing emphasis on data-driven decision-making and increasing engagement with equity at YVC, placement was not yet the focus of growing reform efforts within the college.

To ameliorate some of the problems English department members observed with COMPASS misplacement over the years, the department adopted a "jump" process, based on students' revised writing (often a portfolio), which enabled faculty members to move students who had been under-placed or who had excelled and "accelerated" in their developmental coursework directly into college-level writing courses the following quarter. However, we didn't have an easy way to intervene early in the quarter if a student in a course appeared to be misplaced. As per YVC policy, students were allowed to retake the COMPASS placement test once per quarter prior to enrolling in a math or English course, but doing so cost students additional money and time, and retakes rarely resulted in a higher placement. Even when students did earn higher scores, by the time the student completed the retake, it was often too late in our short ten-week academic quarter for students to find an appropriate writing course with open seats or too difficult for students to rearrange their entire schedules to add a different writing course than the one for which they had originally registered.

At the same time, the English department also examined other possibilities for improving placement validity within the constraints of our self-sustaining, on-demand placement system. At one point, inspired by a peer college in our system (Highline Community College), we pushed for combining reading and writing COMPASS scores, but local data did not show that combined cut scores were more predictive of success than writing cut scores alone. YVC's math department had found a correlation between writing placement and math success and used English placement to determine whether the lowest placing math students should begin math in our adult basic education program (non-credit bearing) or in our credit-bearing developmental math sequence. However, the English department did not find the reverse to be true: math placement was not a predictive indicator of success in English courses at any level. In 2006, we even investigated the COMPASS eWrite Essay Writing Test, an automated writing evaluation, only to discover in our in-house pilot of it that our own "placements" based on the students' eWrite writing samples correlated more strongly with students' original COMPASS writing skills test scores (see *TYCA White Paper on Placement Reform* [Klausman et al., 2016] for a list of sources critiquing machine-scored writing exams). Although we longed for a more authentic and valid alternative, no one was ready to give up placement entirely, so we were "stuck" with COMPASS.

Without a better placement alternative, the English department focused its attention on making its developmental writing sequence a productive one for students, given that about 60 percent of enrolled students—and two-thirds of enrolled Latinx students—placed into developmental writing courses. Our efforts were facilitated by department members' engagement with disciplinary scholarship and professional organizations, such as the Two-Year College English Association of the Pacific Northwest (TYCA-PNW), as well as YVC's participation in the national Achieving the Dream initiative from 2006 to 2013. More than 15 years ago, the department removed traditional letter grades from courses below college level, replacing letter grades with a variation of a pass/fail system, to focus attention on learning and to reduce the negative effects letter grades can have on students' motivation, self-esteem, GPA, and financial aid (see, among others, Kohn, 2011). Developmental writing courses were (and are) taught almost exclusively by full-time faculty. When the department engaged in end-of-program assessment, we used what we learned from student performance at the end of the first-year writing series to align course outcomes at all levels so that all courses in the writing sequence reinforced and built on prior learning and emphasized the development of academic writing and reading strategies.

In addition to improving our developmental courses themselves, we also shortened the developmental sequence, eliminating the lowest developmental writing course (Bailey et al., 2013), and we worked closely with our adult basic education program, now named College and Career Readiness (CCR), to develop pathways from GED, ESL, and other skill-development programs into college writing classes (Table 5.1).

Table 5.1. YVC Writing Sequence

Course/Title	Brief Description
ENGL 90T, English Essentials I	Students use a recursive process to develop short focused and organized compositions; students also engage in reading processes and are introduced to MLA documentation. Students can expect direct instruction in grammar, editing, and proofreading strategies.
ENGL 95, English Essentials II	Students use a recursive process to write focused, organized, and developed essays that incorporate cited evidence; students engage in active reading and practice with editing and proofreading strategies, and they reflect on their learning and writing processes.
ENGL& 101, English Composition I	In the first of two college-level writing courses, students use a recursive process to write focused, organized, and developed essays of increasing complexity; students learn to integrate and analyze cited evidence in support of their ideas, and they reflect on their rhetorical choices.

After learning about the Accelerated Learning Program (ALP) at the Community College of Baltimore County (CCBC; "What is ALP?," n.d.) and a couple of variations of ALP adopted by peer colleges in our state, we developed accelerated options for both of our remaining developmental offerings. In 2013–2014, we piloted an integrated reading and writing learning community for students who placed into the lowest level of our developmental sequence, ENGL 90T, and a corequisite ALP course (based on CCBC's "mainstreaming" model) combining ENGL 95 and ENGL& 101 (first-year writing). Both ALP courses have had strong success rates and have increased the numbers of students completing first-year writing. Additionally, borrowing from one of our peer colleges in the state system, Whatcom Community College, with whom we had a strong connection through our shared engagement in the Two-Year College English Association of the Pacific Northwest (TYCA-PNW), we developed a writing-intensive Introduction to Literature course (ENGL 135) as a college-level alternative to developmental writing coursework (see *TYCA White Paper on Placement Reform*). This humanities course is open to students who placed into ENGL 95 or higher; earning a C or higher in this course provided students another means of demonstrating eligibility for ENGL& 101. Still, all this work to improve our developmental writing program was essentially a work-around for the problems with COMPASS placement.

Serendipitously, several YVC English department members attending the 2015 Conference on College Composition and Communication (CCCC) Convention in Tampa Bay were introduced to Boise State University's "evidence-based" placement process ("The Write Class")—and Asao B. Inoue's labor contracts—at the Council on Basic Writing Preconvention Workshop, "Risky Relationships in Placement, Teaching, and the Professional Organization," just months before the June 2015 announcement of COMPASS's discontinuation. After years of engagement with department and college-wide initiatives and attention to disciplinary innovations, the time was finally ripe for a systemic change at YVC; the English department seized the moment, immediately contacting key administrators to express our interest in placement reform and to offer research-based alternatives that may help YVC advance its equity agenda.

Creating Change in Context: Opportunities and Constraints

Although the college's initial impulse was to replace the COMPASS test with a similar commercial product—and we did briefly adopt ACCUPLACER as our interim placement tool—YVC created a placement taskforce in Fall 2015 with key stakeholders, including math and English department representatives, to think through options, with the caveat that whatever placement methodology we chose would have to remain self-supporting and easily administered year-round. The COMPASS test would be available through November 2016, so our time frame to develop a replacement tool was limited.

Because the majority of two-year colleges in the state system were in the same situation as YVC, needing to quickly adopt new placement methods, the Washington State Board of Community for Technical Colleges (SBCTC) held a placement workshop in Fall 2015 with invited speakers, both folks doing innovative work within our state system, including directed self-placement (DSP), and assessment experts from the field of writing studies, including Christie Toth (two-year college writing assessment) and Asao Inoue (antiracist assessment). Several YVC placement task force members, including our arts and sciences division dean. Disciplinary scholarship laid the foundation upon which we could build something new once the opportunity presented itself. The take-aways from this SBCTC workshop reinforced the English department's message: that placement reform was essential to improving student outcomes and reducing equity gaps at YVC. According to SBCTC data dashboards, from 2010–2016, all racial/ethnic groups except Asian lagged behind White students in three-year completion rates.

Given our initiative, professional engagement, and in-house expertise, the YVC English department was granted latitude by administration to select its new placement methodology. We sought a placement process that would reduce student over-placement into developmental writing courses, particularly for Latinx students. We wanted a tool that utilized multiple measures to determine a student's placement, both because Washington State Senate Bill 5712 (Wash. 2013) encouraged its use in community college placement and because a growing body of research demonstrated that multiple measures assessment was more effective and ethical (see Klausman et al., 2016). Since students had long been successful in our composition courses (generally upwards of 75% success rates at all levels), we wanted to ensure success rates remained high under our new placement methodology, and we wanted to ensure equitable student success rates in English. We also needed a placement tool that didn't require much time or labor—for students or for faculty and staff—and that was affordable. Interestingly, although the English department had long been dissatisfied with our placement tool, campus student satisfaction surveys consistently found a large majority of students, around 80 percent, were generally happy with their placement, which may be an expression of the relative ease of placement testing for students or of students' subsequent satisfaction with their writing courses.

In a series of meetings, starting in the fall of 2015, the English department reviewed a range of placement tools and methods that we felt reflected our curriculum and learning outcomes and better matched writing courses to students' learning needs. Several department members favored a directed self-placement (DSP) model (see Royer & Gilles, 1998). There was a growing body of evidence about its efficacy (see Toth, 2019), and we valued the student self-reflection at the heart of DSP. However, the two-year college examples we had at the time were fairly labor intensive, both in creating some sort of self-assessment questionnaire from scratch that would enable students to make informed decisions about course selection and in administering the questionnaire and accompanying advising conversations. Our college had just begun a process of implementing "pathway advising" (advising duties are part of the regular faculty contract), a process that was met with some early resistance, and we were concerned that these advising-intensive initiatives may compete with rather than complement each other. The peer colleges that were beginning to implement DSP in our state were doing so in limited ways, often targeting specific student groups, and, without a writing program administrator (WPA) to advocate for and direct changes or the promise of long-term support for this placement reform work, we needed a full replacement tool within a year if we hoped to truly transform our placement system.

We were familiar with—and chose to adopt immediately (starting Spring 2016)—multiple means of demonstrating ENGL& 101-readiness, all borrowed from Whatcom Community College, which included high school Smarter Balanced scores (part of a system-wide SBCTC agreement), high school GPA, AP test scores, SAT/ACT scores, and, for the time being, ACCUPLACER scores. Later, we added other forms of evidence to demonstrate ENGL& 101-readiness, including "Bridge to College" grades (high school courses designed to develop college-readiness) and GED Reasoning through Language Arts test scores. This placement method reduced barriers to accessing first-year writing and honored students' high school work, and it worked especially well for our growing dual credit student population. In fact, for English, the placement method most predictive of success is high school GPA (93% success rate, overall and for Latinx students specifically). Nearly 39 percent of all students—and approximately 38 percent of Latinx students—use high school GPA for placement into ENGL& 101. However, we recognized that these alternative means of demonstrating college-level readiness also did not break us from standardized testing, as a larger portion of students, those who were more than two years out of high school and those who did not have evidence suggesting college-readiness, were still reliant on ACCUPLACER scores.

A customized version of The Write Class (TWC) seemed particularly promising and is ultimately the method we selected, accompanied by allowing students other means of demonstrating college-level writing course readiness. Heidi Estrem, Dawn Shepherd, and Samantha Sturman (2018) describe the TWC placement process as "one of reflection and projection" (p. 66). The Write Class's evidence-based "course matching" incorporated multiple measures, including student self-reflection on prior reading and writing experiences and confidence, to determine placement, and TWC also communicated course information and expectations for college students and asked students to reflect on their own situations and needs before selecting their writing course (Estrem et al., 2018). We were drawn to the fact that the components of TWC's placement process were derived from current research in the field and that the tool had already been tested and implemented in various contexts, including a customized version for an Idaho community college. At Boise State University, TWC placement had increased the number of college-level placements, increased success rates (over single measures), and improved student retention (Estrem, 2015), all goals the YVC English department had for its new placement tool. More importantly, this tool could be developed and maintained at a similar cost to other single-measure commercial placement products and could be administered fully online (though our current method of collecting payment prior to enabling students access required that students continued to take their placement on site, at least until the pandemic moved us online).

For the English department, we felt TWC could serve as sort of a hybrid version of DSP. Students responded to questions similar to many DSP protocols, and the students essentially "chose" their placement through their responses, and then were able to select from courses within that placement category. Our placement categories aligned with our pre-existing levels of placement, two developmental levels and one college level, and each category below college level offered students three course options to choose from, including an accelerated option (Table 5.2).

Table 5.2. Placement Levels

Developmental	Transitional	College-Ready
CCR: College and Career Readiness (non-credit and non-tuition bearing) ENGL 90T (5 credits) ENGL 90T/ENGL 81T: Integrated Writing and Reading (10 credits, ALP)	ENGL 95 (5 credits) ENGL& 101/95 ALP (10 credits) ENGL 135: Introduction to Literature (5 credits, writing-intensive humanities course)	ENGL& 101 (5 credits)

The "developmental" cluster offered students the choice of non-credit-bearing coursework in our CCR (adult basic education) division (which doesn't charge for tuition or books), a stand-alone ENGL 90T course, or the ten-credit intensive reading and writing acceleration option. The "transitional" cluster offered students the choice of stand-alone ENGL 95, the writing-intensive "Introduction to Literature" course (for college-level humanities credits), or our corequisite ENGL& 101/95 ALP course.

Offering developmental students course options from already established courses enabled us to create our placement tool without having to quickly revise or create new courses first; it enabled us to preserve—and promote—the innovative courses that we had recently developed and that were demonstrating success but were not in as high of demand as stand-alone versions of developmental courses. Importantly, having multiple developmental writing course options enabled us to maximize flexibility for students to select a course that served their particular needs and preferences, which is essential for students who attend part-time or have to schedule around work and other commitments as well as those who are preparing for workforce programs that may not require a first-year writing transfer course.

We began our work developing a customized TWC for YVC in Spring 2016, under the guidance of Samantha Sturman, Heidi Estrem, and Dawn Shepherd. The process of development provided the department as a whole an opportunity to reflect on our curriculum and expectations for each course in our writing sequences and also to include local considerations that our collective experience taught us were important to student success and retention. For example, we agreed that students' ability to keyboard and perform basic computer functions is essential to their success in college-level coursework—and this ability, or even access to technology and Wi-Fi, is not universal among our student population—so we requested that a question about students' confidence with word processing be included, and we also articulated these expectations in our course information. Additionally, in reviewing the version of TWC adopted by College of Western Idaho, a two-year college, we were attracted to its inclusion of a reading comprehension and reflection section, as we felt reading ability better correlated with student success than editing skills. Plus, all of our writing courses included at least one reading-related learning outcome. We knew that YVC's student population was predominantly first generation, and recognizing that few students likely arrived having had access to "college prep" work—at 73 percent, local high school graduation rates for 18–25-year-olds lag behind the state averages (Retka, 2019)—we also chose to include a satisfactory college-level student sample essay for students to reflect on, to show students what type of writing they can expect to do in their college writing courses. Although, anecdotally, we are aware that we have a significant number of English language learners and Gen 1.5 writers at YVC, YVC doesn't, at present, collect information on students' linguistic backgrounds, and the department no longer offers any credit-bearing ESL writing courses. Without a significant international student population, the courses were persistently under-enrolled, and COMPASS typically placed ELL students directly into developmental writing. Therefore, we did not opt to include questions about multilingualism in the placement tool.

In Fall 2016, about half of the department engaged in piloting YVC's customized TWC in their ENGL 90T, ENGL 95, and ENGL& 101 classes, approximately three or four sections (75–100 students) per course level. Department members noted how long the process took and reported any issues that arose when they administered the TWC in their classes. Additionally, post-placement, students were asked to reflect anonymously on their experiences with TWC. On the whole, the pilot went smoothly. Faculty reported that few students needed more than 30 minutes to complete the entire questionnaire. Overall, students responded positively to YVC's The Write Class. Most participants found TWC "easy," and some explicitly indicated they preferred it to the COMPASS test. Many observed, often with surprise, that they were basically "evaluating themselves" and "placing themselves." Although some students resisted the idea of self-placement, explicitly wishing that they would be evaluated "objectively" on their "skills," most enjoyed the self-reflection and appreciated the ease of the TWC questionnaire. While the students' placements on the TWC pilot did not always correspond to the class in which they were enrolled (based on COMPASS placement scores), more often than not, students placed at or above their current course level. When students did place lower, there was often an explanation. For instance, in almost every pilot class section, a few students admitted they rushed through or skipped elements of the TWC. Several instructors also noted that some of the students who placed below their current course level lacked confidence or had been struggling in their course, which likely affected the students' self-assessments on the TWC.

Rollout and Reactions

In 2017–2018, the year of our new placement system rollout, a YVC team, including one of the authors, participated in the SBCTC's Placement360 program, which provided workshops and coaching to ensure a smooth transition into our new placement systems in math and English. Placement reform was generally accepted across campus, with administrators supportive of evidence-based reforms that lead to more equitable student outcomes. For our information technology department, The Write Class was both inexpensive and relatively easy to implement, and, for the testing center, the English department's combination of TWC and multiple pathways into ENGL& 101 was easy to administer on both campuses and to use with high school students applying for the Running Start program. The testing center director commented that students seemed satisfied, which is corroborated by YVC fall student satisfaction surveys. Rates of satisfaction with English placement increased from about 80 percent to 86.5 percent after implementing our new placement methodology. And, as an added benefit, students only completed the placement process once: no retesting.

Anecdotally, some English department faculty expressed occasional concern about a perceived lack of preparedness of some students in their classes, especially English language learners, though these concerns were not widely or consistently shared, seemingly attributable to the usual variations in groups of students rather than an actual placement problem. Some faculty members outside of the department, particularly those whose classes list ENGL& 101 as a prerequisite, initially grumbled that the new placement system did not provide the traditional gatekeeping function to which they had become accustomed; they preferred to teach students who "already knew how to write."

Increasing College-Level Access and Closing Equity Gaps

Currently, among over 3,200 placements since Fall 2017, 42.2 percent of all students who enroll after taking the placement exam identify as Latinx, 29.9 percent identify as White, and 20.7 percent identify as multiracial (a recently added classification category, which likely includes many students who formerly may have identified as Latinx); the remaining 7.5 percent reflects all other ethnic groups—African American, Asian, Native American, Pacific Islander—and "other" (which includes "prefer not to answer"). Because of the small numbers in racial/ethnic groups besides Latinx, White, and multiracial, data for those groups are not included below. Although some groups of BIPOC students appear to be overrepresented in developmental placement, college level represents the majority placement for all racial/ethnic groups, and success rates in English also appear fairly comparable across all groups.

One significant and unanticipated outcome of our change from COMPASS placement to TWC and alternate means of demonstrating ENGL& 101-readiness is an increased number of students who enroll in college after completing their placement (Table 5.3).

Table 5.3. Placement vs. Enrollment: Pre-/Post-Placement Intervention

Placement	2012–2013 Academic Year $n=1,560$	2018–2019 Academic Year $n=1,546$
ENGL 90T	50.1% enrolled (of 461 placed)	63.9% enrolled (of 180 placed)
ENGL 95	51% enrolled (of 431 placed)	63.4% enrolled (of 331 placed)
ENGL& 101	56.9% enrolled (of 668 placed)	65.5% enrolled (of 1,035 placed)

Latinx students, who make up the largest proportion of placements and enrollees, further increased their enrollment percentages post-placement shift, from 67.6 percent (343/509 overall) in 2012–2013 to 70.9 percent (390/550 overall) in 2018–2019.

Perhaps the most important outcome of our new placement methodology has been the increased number of college-ready placements among enrollees. In a placement snapshot of the 2012–2013 enrollees (prior to any changes in placement or implementation of ALP), more than half of all students (54.4%), including close to two-thirds of our majority Latinx population (65.3%), placed below college level (Table 5.4). Among those who placed into developmental writing using the COMPASS test, 27.8 percent of all students—and 37.6 percent of Latinx students—placed two or more levels below college level.

Table 5.4. Placement Level Snapshots: Pre-/Post-Placement Intervention

Placement	2012–2013 (COMPASS)	2018–2019 (TWC+)
ENGL 90T	231/832 (27.8%)/37.6% Latinx	115/1,001 (11.5%)/16.4% Latinx
ENGL 95	221/832 (26.6%)/27.7% Latinx	210/1,001 (21%)/28.1% Latinx
ENGL& 101	380/832 (45.7%)/24.7% Latinx	676/1,001 (67.5%)/60.5% Latinx

After full implementation of TWC and multiple methods of demonstrating college-level readiness, a snapshot of the 2018–2019 academic year reveals that 67.5 percent of all enrolled students, including 60.5 percent of students who identify as Latinx and 66 percent of students who identify as multiracial, placed directly into college-level writing. While Latinx and multiracial students are still overrepresented in developmental writing courses and underrepresented in college-level writing, the placement gaps have closed considerably under our new placement methodology.

When considering this same snapshot looking at age demographics, a similar trend can be seen, as shown in Table 5.5.

Table 5.5. Placement Level Snapshots by Age: Pre-/Post-Placement Intervention

	2012–2013 (COMPASS)			2018–2019 (TWC+)		
Course Placement	Under 20 $n=542$	20–29 $n=140$	30+ $n=60$	Under 20 $n=681$	20–29 $n=148$	30+ $n=57$
ENGL 90T	26%	36.4%	33.3%	9%	17.6%	19.3%
ENGL 95	22.5%	23.6%	30%	16.3%	35.8%	45.6%
ENGL& 101	51.5%	40.7%	36.7%	74.7%	46.6%	35.1%

Students under 20, which includes a growing Running Start (dual credit) population, make up the largest proportion of placements, and in that group, students had almost 50 percent fewer developmental placements and significantly increased college-ready placements, which is likely attributable to our adoption of multiple means of demonstrating ENGL& 101-readiness, most based on high school GPA or other high school assessments and coursework. Students in the 20–29 age bracket also decreased their developmental placements significantly (by more than half in the lowest developmental placement category) and increased their college-ready placements using TWC placement. Although those over 30 years old did not increase their college-level placements, fewer placed at the lowest level of developmental writing, which suggests that the tool is working to match students to courses that fit their needs. Those who have been out of school for more than a decade often do benefit from developmental coursework to help them brush up their skills, re-establish academic routines, and build confidence.

Historically, English courses have enjoyed high success rates at YVC, and our goal was to maintain high success rates while ensuring equitable success rates. Since the new placement methods were fully implemented three years ago, students continue to succeed in the courses into which they place, even as more students place into college-level writing courses. See Table 5.6 for success rates across demographic categories.

Table 5.6. Success Rates (C or Higher) in Placement Writing Course, Fall 2017–Fall 2020

Placement Category	Overall n=3,262	White n=976	Latinx n=1,366	Multiracial n=244	Female n=2,009	Male n=1,214
Developmental	76%	73%	76.1%	85%	80.4%	67.5%
Transitional	71%	68.3%	71.5%	74.5%	74%	67.1%
College-level	84.2%	85.4%	85.5%	81.7%	86.8%	80%

Our majority-Latinx student population performs slightly better than the overall success averages in all placement levels, and our majority-female population significantly outperforms their male counterparts as well as the overall success averages. While still mostly successful in their English coursework, male students have the lowest success rates at YVC, which corresponds to national data about male student academic perform\ance: male students complete at lower rates than female students (National Center for Education Statistics, 2020). Our transitional English courses (ENGL 95, ENGL& 101/95 ALP, and ENGL 135), which serve the largest number of pre-college-level-placing students, have the lowest success rates overall and across demographic groups.

While Latinx students remain proportionally overrepresented in developmental coursework (approximately 38% place below college level as compared to the 33.3% overall average), they outperform their White peers in those developmental courses. Latinx students also perform slightly above the overall average in their first-year writing course, suggesting that success rates are generally equitable. Additionally, according to the Washington SBCTC, on statewide developmental education outcomes, YVC surpasses peer colleges in measurements of the rate at which students complete developmental writing sequences and gateway college-level English courses. Since reforming our placement system, 66–67 percent of students now complete this milestone within their first year, which is more than 11 points higher than the state system average. This may in part be due to the fact that few colleges in Washington have implemented a tool such as TWC to allow for self-guided or self-directed English placement; most departments in the system currently use multiple measures to place students into the first-year composition (FYC) sequence.

Despite the positive outcomes of writing placement reform, there is still work to be done, both at the course level and institutional level. Increasing the number of students who place at college level and maintaining equitable success rates in writing courses is important, but it's not sufficient. Ultimately, placement is only one assessment, one piece of our writing ecology. Changing student outcomes requires examining and transforming all department and college policies, processes, and practices so that they enact "servingness."

Stepping Toward Equity, Collaboratively

As development of The Write Class has both paralleled and helped initiate campus-wide racial equity initiatives and awareness, English department faculty have come to serve key roles in equity initiatives at YVC. English faculty members are participating in statewide first-year writing outcomes working groups ("(De)Composing ENGL& 101"), developing a writing across the curriculum program, leading institutional assessment work (with an equity focus), and instituting Guided Pathways. Recognizing that our next steps in closing equity gaps involve curriculum, pedagogy, and assessment, nearly all English department faculty members have completed certifications for teaching at an HSI from Escala Education, LLC, a national program grounded in culturally responsive pedagogy that has been woven into professional development at YVC, and several, including the authors, serve in peer coaching and other leadership roles in the program.

Moreover, in Fall 2020, YVC's English department was awarded College Spark funding via the Washington SBCTC to begin working alongside six other departments as state leaders build an antiracist writing assessment ecology (AWAE) for first-year composition with the support of Asao Inoue and other antiracist educators. YVC's work on placement reform was noted by AWAE grant directors as the type of systemic reform needed across Washington state, serving as the foundation or entryway to a future antiracist ecology for students in YVC English courses. Building on what they are learning through their AWAE work, YVC's AWAE team is developing a reflective tool designed to help department members self-assess their use of culturally responsive pedagogy and antiracist assessment practices in their own classrooms, with a longer-term goal of collaboratively revising course outcomes throughout the writing sequence to minimize outcomes that privilege what Inoue (2015) described as a "White racial habitus" in writing and assessing writing.

At the same time that YVC engages in the statewide AWAE project, writing across the curriculum (WAC) development is taking place as new assessment measures and innovative teaching are being promoted across departments and academic divisions. Antiracist assessment and curriculum development is informing WAC in new ways at YVC and elsewhere. To date, seeds of a more traditional WAC program have been planted, and the vision is evolving. In the past two years, faculty across the curriculum have participated in workshops on a range of WAC strategies from developing writing assignments to using low-stakes writing-to-learn exercises in their classrooms. Additional professional development around equitable assessment is planned for the coming year. A campus-wide cultural shift toward equity, antiracist assessment, and culturally responsive pedagogy may be a long journey, but these goals are worthy of deep investment and pursuit.

Educators often face systemic challenges that seem—and sometimes are—insurmountable from the positions into which they are hired. For example, an English instructor alone might not find support in a meeting for a policy or curriculum change, even one grounded in convincing evidence. However, reflecting on the implementation of TWC is a reminder that change does not and typically cannot happen in isolation at YVC or at any college or university, for that matter, and improvements toward equitable outcomes and antiracist education require coalitions and collaboration. Jeffrey Klausman and others have argued that two-year college writing programs are and must be "collaborative, needs based, and decentered" (qtd. in Spiegel et al., 2020, p. 10).

To be needs-based requires continual review of disaggregated data. Where data reveals inequitable outcomes, racism is embedded, and we have focused on one stop in students' academic paths. As Tia Brown McNair and colleagues (2020) explained, "the most pernicious form of racism is routinely created and reinforced through everyday practices such as hiring, program review, what gets included in strategic plans, what data gets reported, tenure and promotion reviews, syllabi and curriculum, the agendas of boards of trustees," and more (p. 40). YVC faculty and staff include placement as a key everyday practice.

If two-year colleges are indeed "access intensive institution[s] meant to serve communities" (Spiegel et al., 2020), their critical placement tools and practices help guide students into the courses where they are most likely to succeed. Christine Busser (2020) recently argued that "Offering students' greater agency through transparency, finally, calls on WPAs to examine programmatic and institutional initiatives that presume students' needs, goals, and lived experiences," and that doing so may call for "a reexamination of placement procedures (Brunk-Chavez & Fredericksen), an adoption of antiracist assessment practices (Inoue), and greater scrutiny of initiatives that promote a single college lifestyle: inflexible class scheduling, credit limits, and out-of-class requirements" (p. 105). We believe The Write Class is an example of examination and collaboration that leads to more equitable student outcomes, and it serves as a key foundation for ongoing antiracist and racial equity work at Yakima Valley College, where the institution must continue striving to learn from and respond to the oft divided community in which it is located.

Acknowledgments

We gratefully acknowledge our Yakima Valley College English department colleagues who have collaborated on this and all other department initiatives and who work tirelessly on behalf of YVC students.

References

2020–21 Quick facts. (2021). Yakima Valley College. https://www.yvcc.edu/oie/quick-facts//

Adler-Kassner, L. (2017). 2017 CCCC chair's address: Because writing is never just writing. *College Composition and Communication, 69*(2), 317–340.

Bailey, T., Jaggars, S. S. & Scott-Clayton, J. (2013, February). *Characterizing the effectiveness of developmental education: A response to recent criticism.* Community College Research Center. https://ccrc.tc.columbia.edu/publications/characterizing-effectiveness-of-developmental-education.html.

Bailey, T., Jeong, D. W. & Cho, S-W. (2009, November). *Referral, enrollment, and completion in developmental education sequences in community colleges* (CCRC Working Paper No. 15). Community College Research Center. https://ccrc.tc.columbia.edu/publications/referral-enrollment-completion-developmental-education.html.

Busser, C. (2020). Challenging the efficiency model: Supporting inclusive pathways toward student success. *WPA: Writing Program Administration, 43*(2), 89–108.

Calhoon-Dillahunt, C. (2011). Writing programs without administrators: Frameworks for successful writing programs in two-year colleges. *WPA: Writing Program Administration, 35*(1), 118–134.

Crosta, C. & Belfield, P. M. (2012). *Predicting success in college: The importance of placement tests and high school transcripts* (CCRC Working Paper No. 42). Community College Research Center. https://ccrc.tc.columbia.edu/publications/predicting-success-placement-tests-transcripts.html.

Estrem, H. (2015, March 18). *Situated placement: The rewards of developing placement processes* [Conference workshop presentation]. 2015 Conference on College Composition and Communication (CCCC) Convention, Tampa Bay, FL, United States.

Estrem, H., Shepherd, D. & Sturman, S. (2018). Reclaiming writing placement. *WPA: Writing Program Administration, 42*(1), 56–71.

Fields, R. & Parsad, B. (2012). *Tests and cut scores used for student placement in postsecondary education: Fall 2011.* National Assessment Governing Board. https://files.eric.ed.gov/fulltext/ED539918.pdf.

Hughes, K. L. & Scott-Clayton, J. (2011, February). *Assessing developmental assessment in community colleges* (CCRC Working Paper no. 19). Community College

Research Center. https://ccrc.tc.columbia.edu/publications/assessing-develop mental-assessment.html.

Inoue, A. B. (2015). *Antiracist writing assessment ecologies: Teaching and assessing writing for a socially just future.* The WAC Clearinghouse; Parlor Press. https:// doi.org/10.37514/PER-B.2015.0698

Kezar, A., Maxey, D. & Eaton, J. (2014, January). *An examination of the changing faculty: Ensuring institutional quality and achieving desired student learning outcomes* [CHEA Occasional Paper]. Council for Higher Education Accreditation. https://www.chea.org/examination-changing-faculty-ensuring-institutional -quality-and-achieving-desired-student-learning

Klausman, J., Roberts, L., Giordano, J., Griffiths, B., Sullivan, P., Swyt, W., Toth, C., Warnke, A. & Williams, A. L. (2016). TYCA white paper on placement reform. *Teaching English in the Two-Year College, 44*(2), 135–157. https://cdn.ncte.org/ncte files/groups/tyca/placementreform_revised.pdf.

Kohn, A. (2011, November). The case against grades. *Educational Leadership.* https:// www.alfiekohn.org/article/case-grades/.

McNair, T. B., Bensimon, E. M. & Malcom-Piqueux, L. (2020). *From equity talk to equity walk. Expanding practitioner knowledge for racial justice in higher education.* John Wiley & Sons.

Nastal, J. (2019, February). Beyond tradition: Writing placement, fairness, and success at a two-year college. *The Journal of Writing Assessment, 12*(1). http:// journalofwritingassessment.org/article.php?article=136.

National Center for Education Statistics. (n.d.). *College navigator: Yakima Valley College.* Retrieved September 25, 2020, from https://nces.ed.gov/collegenavi gator/?id=237109#retgrad.

National Center for Education Statistics. (2020). *Fast facts: Graduation rates.* https:// nces.ed.gov/fastfacts/display.asp?id=40.

Retka, J. (2019, August 20). More of the story: What's happening with Yakima County graduation rates? *Yakima Herald-Republic.* https://www.yakimaher ald.com/news/education/more-of-the-story-whats-happening-with-yakima -county-graduation-rates/article_3b3e233e-f8bd-5923-a117-5d676c862fd8 .html.

Royer, D. & Gilles, R. (1998). Directed self-placement: An attitude of orientation. *College Composition and Communication, 50*(1), 54–70.

Searcey, D. & Gebeloff, R. (2019, November 19). The divide in Yakima is the divide in America. *The New York Times.* https://www.nytimes.com/2019/11/19/us /politics/yakima-washington-racial-differences-2020-elections.html.

Spiegel, C. L., Jensen, D. & Johnson, S. Z. (2020). Don't call it a comeback: Two-year college WPA, tactics, collaboration, flexibility, sustainability. *WPA: Writing Program Administration, 43*(3), 7–18.

SB 5712, 63rd Legislature, 2013 Reg. Sess. (Wash. 2013). https://app.leg.wa.gov/bill summary?BillNumber=5712&Year=2013.

Taylor, T. (2009). Writing program administration at the two-year college: Ghosts in the machine. *WPA: Writing Program Administration, 32*(3), 120–139.

Toth, C. (2019, February). Directed self-placement at two-year colleges: A kairotic moment. *The Journal of Writing Assessment*, 12(1). http://journalofwritingassessment.org/article.php?article=134.

U.S. Department of Education. (n.d.). *College scorecard: Yakima Valley College*. Retrieved September 25, 2020, from https://collegescorecard.ed.gov/school/?237109-Yakima-Valley-College.

Washington State Board for Community and Technical Colleges. (2020). *Our history*. https://www.sbctc.edu/about/history.aspx.

Withem, K., Malcolm-Piqueux, L. E., Dowd, A. C. & Bensimon, E. M. (2015). *America's unmet promise*. Association of American Colleges and Universities.

What is ALP? (n.d.). Accelerated Learning Program. Retrieved December 18, 2020 from https://alp-deved.org/what-is-alp-exactly/.

Chapter 6. Putting ACCUPLACER in Its Place: Expanding Evidence in Placement Reform at Jamestown Community College

Jessica M. Kubiak
JAMESTOWN COMMUNITY COLLEGE

Abstract: This study of a small (2,500 student) community college in the State University of New York system describes concurrent placement reform and developmental English curriculum reform. Highlighting the affordances of an English department that includes not only literature but developmental composition and reading instructors, the chapter charts the efforts of this unified English faculty as it responded to various demands and desires relative to placement, especially during the 2018–2019 academic year. Of particular note are the impacts of dual-enrollment programs, which both influence the composition of campus-based first-year composition (FYC) classrooms and disrupt attempts at multiple measures placement implementation. Indeed, unique to this study is consideration of how academic programs serving non-matriculated students impact placement reforms. Additionally, the interdependence of the humanities program and FYC, and the college-wide reliance upon English placement for determining content area course requisites, are explored. This study contributes to ongoing conversations about writing placement, especially in the context of access-oriented colleges and universities seeking to update not only placement but writing curricula to better enact equity-oriented pedagogies. It also maps relationships among institutional stakeholders and curricular practices, echoing common concerns regarding equity and illustrating challenges unique to an institution with a large full-time and transfer-oriented student population and a system of tightly woven course requisites.

At Jamestown Community College (JCC), the first locally sponsored community college in the State University of New York (SUNY) system, 25.1 percent of all first-time full-time students placed into developmental coursework in Fall 2018 (Jamestown Community College [JCC], 2018),[1] and nearly every student sat for placement tests in math and English as part of their orientation to the college. A long-standing institutional insistence that learners must demonstrate "basic"

---

1. Most references affiliated with Jamestown Community College (2019b, 2019a, 2018, 2017, 2014) are unpublished internal reports on student performance in developmental coursework. These are housed on the college's intranet.

competencies prior to enrolling in college-level courses came from a view of literacy as a singular, objective, linear measure of textual ability. Ascribing to what Shannon Carter (2008) called an autonomous view of literacy, the faculty at large believed reading and writing instruction could and should be done outside of the context of the college's credit-bearing curriculum. As such, JCC's sole placement procedure—administration of computer-based ACCUPLACER placement tests—was seen as supportive of its overarching pedagogical structures.

While internal data on reading and writing placement in the developmental English curriculum seemed to support continued use of both standard single-measure placements and prerequisite developmental literacy course sequences, several factors led to significant changes during the 2018–2019 academic year. These factors compelled English faculty to analyze data in new ways, specifically through the lens of throughput, which challenged us to explore the efficacy of placement procedures and the existing developmental English curriculum. This ultimately led to an expansion of placement measures that coincided with the elimination of all prerequisite developmental reading and writing. After a few semesters of gradually de-emphasizing the ACCUPLACER reading comprehension and writing tests, the college shifted to a placement scheme that now uses high school grade point average (HSGPA) as the sole placement factor for most students and considers various success indicators for others, reserving administration of the ACCUPLACER reading test for students wishing to challenge their multiple measures placement. By using HSGPA for automatic placement out of or into newly developed corequisite support courses, and by using multiple measures to determine placement for students in the middle, the college effectively expanded the range of evidence used for writing placement.

This Study in Context

Like the other case studies in this collection, this chapter contributes to ongoing conversations about writing placement, especially in the context of access-oriented colleges and universities seeking to update writing placement and curricula to better enact equity-oriented pedagogies. Longstanding concern about assessment validity has been reframed in recent decades by movement away from high-stakes testing and toward portfolio assessment (Huot & Williamson, 2009; Reynolds & Rice, 2006; Walvoord, 2014). The extent to which the portfolio movement has shaped assessment for the sake of *placement* is not evident; practice and research suggest early attempts at portfolio-based writing placement (e.g., Elbow & Belanoff, 1986) have not taken hold. At the same time, writing placement reform has focused on increasing student agency and enrollment in college-level coursework (Klausman et al., 2016; Phillips & Giordano, 2016; Toth et al., 2019).

This chapter also maps relationships among stakeholders, curricular practices, and college placement. New York State has not legislated placement in community colleges and state-operated institutions, but such mandates loom large elsewhere (Fain, 2013; Miller et al., 2017; Minnesota Rev. Code Ann. § 120B.13, 2021). Though legislated mandates do not play a role in this case, they do highlight the influence of underlying institutional structures, both departmental and curricular. For the two-year college in particular, administration of developmental writing and composition sequences often falls to English program directors or chairs (Janangelo & Klausman, 2012; Klausman, 2018; Taylor, 2009), whose expertise may or may not be in composition and rhetoric. Thanks to a core of full-time English faculty and several creative and risk-taking part-time faculty at JCC, various decision-makers quickly coalesced around data-informed research from entities such as Columbia University's Community College Research Center (CCRC) and the Association of American Colleges & Universities (AAC&U).

During placement reform, JCC's faculty were moved by two kinds of research about writing assessment broadly and writing placement in particular. First, theory on linguistic justice speaking to the urgency of placement reform struck a chord. Asao B. Inoue's (2015) work on minimizing the damaging effects of feedback alerted us to problems inherent in using a "single standard" (p. 116) for evaluation. Pushing against strategies promoted by Brian Huot in particular, Inoue claims writing assessment scholars have avoided racism's impact on our processes and practices (2015, p. 21). Likewise, Jamila Lyiscott (2017), a literacy educator who led a professional development residency at JCC in 2016, and April Baker-Bell (2020) interrogated the White supremacy of teaching and learning standard written English, advocating for mechanisms that allow students to use their own language(s). Acknowledging these ideas in light of the fact that placement is the college's first engagement with student writing moved us toward a recognition that our use of ACCUPLACER as a single standard for writing assessment and placement was a racist act.

Quantitative studies that provided new ways of working with data also gave us faith in our decision-making. SUNY had initiated a CCRC study involving seven system institutions, and initial progress (Barnett et al., 2018) suggested the importance of using multiple measures, which recent updates (Barnett et al., 2020) confirm. Because such gathering of system-specific data was in its relative infancy, JCC relied on research from California's state system to inform local decisions. The California Acceleration Project (CAP) was driven by the Multiple Measures Assessment Project Team's (2018) tightly controlled analysis of state community college students. Their study suggests HSGPA is a more useful and valid predictor of preparedness for college-level English than ACCUPLACER, and it promotes use of additional measures (e.g., SAT) for students with subpar GPAs. At a 2018 conference, CAP researchers posited that HSGPA was a better predictor because it reflected learners' abilities not at a single moment of testing, but over time. This reference to student persistence spoke to JCC's desire to consider "non-cognitive" skills and attitudes in placement, and it issued confidence that removing what we had perceived as the safety net of placement into prerequisite developmental writing was unlikely to result in additional harm to learners.

As I hope is the case for all institutions differentiating learners at entry, JCC sought to craft mechanisms to support learners without disenfranchising them. Despite lack of departmental awareness of two-year writing placement scholarship, a full- and part-time English faculty increasingly well-versed in composition pedagogy allowed progressive movement in service of our placement goal. Faculty exposure to the texts and ideas introduced above led to a series of decisions made between fall of 2015 and June of 2019 that shifted placement systems, as well as the content and structure of developmental and first-year writing, in a way that followed several national and statewide trends. At the same time, given the cross-training of some English faculty in both writing and reading instruction, and given the roles played by the remaining developmental reading course in the curriculum, JCC's updated systems and structures also made space for contextualized reading instruction.

Jamestown Community College

Jamestown Community College was established in 1950 as "the first locally sponsored community college accepted into the State University of New York" (JCC, 2021). An open-access, public two-year community college accredited by the Middle States Commission on Higher Education, it boasts almost 400 articulation agreements with transfer programs. The two campuses, one on the outskirts of Jamestown, NY, and the other in Olean, NY, sit on either side of the Seneca Nation of Indians' Allegany Territory.

JCC's learners are largely from western New York State and northwestern Pennsylvania; as such, the student population reflects the region's racial, ethnic, and economic demographics. In Fall 2019, 79 percent of students identified as White, seven percent as Hispanic or Latinx, three percent as Black, and two percent as American Indian or Alaska Native. Ninety-one percent of newly matriculated students in 2018–2019 received financial aid, with 63 percent receiving Pell Grants averaging $4,498 per grant for tuition and fees of $5,850.[2]

Many of JCC's students fit the profile of a "traditional" student. Most (56%) in 2018–2019 attended full-time, enrolled in at least 12 credit hours per 15-week semester. Of first-time, full-time students, 60 percent were retained from year to year. Most (59%) identified as female, and 62.4 percent of matriculated students were under 23 years old.

Of the 4,467 students enrolled in coursework in 2018–2019, only 2,515 were matriculated students. The balance constitutes concurrent enrollment learners from regional high schools who take courses for both high school and college credit from secondary teachers approved and trained to teach JCC's curriculum.

---

2. Demographic information on all learners comes from the National Center for Education Statistics (2020), while matriculated-student-specific information comes from the college's office of institutional research (JCC, 2019b).

The program provides extensive support for high school teachers, including discipline-specific liaisons employed by the college to offer professional development. Among the most popular courses taught via concurrent enrollment are those in JCC's first-year composition sequence: English Composition I (ENG 1510) and English Composition II (ENG 1530). Because so many concurrent enrollment sections of English courses are taught across partner schools, English-specific professional development responsibilities require a dedicated liaison who is not otherwise employed by the college.

JCC faculty who teach composition and other first-year reading and writing courses to matriculated students are part of the English department, a subset of the humanities (now language, literature, and writing) program. The humanities program, offering an associate of arts degree, included eight full-time faculty in 2018–2019, seven of whom taught primarily "English" and aligned courses including developmental writing and reading. All full-time program faculty at the time identified as White, and the majority identified as male; this demographic breakdown held for part-time faculty as well. They varied in terms of their disciplinary preparation—with degrees in creative writing, literature-focused English, adult education, composition and rhetoric, and language and literacy—yet all full-time English faculty had recently started teaching regularly in the first-year composition sequence, with many also teaching developmental courses, as well as literary and writing studies courses.

Developmental English Placement

In Fall 2018, 25.1 percent of all matriculated, first-time full-time students placed into developmental coursework (JCC, 2018). Up to this point, and for at least the previous two decades, placement into developmental coursework had been determined by student performance on ACCUPLACER's computerized, largely standardized set of placement measures, assessing learner abilities in math, reading, and writing. Significant efforts on the part of the faculty, as well as student development and continuing education staff, were undertaken to ensure test-takers' performance accurately reflected their abilities relative to readiness for college-level courses. Continuing education courses in pre-collegiate English and math prepared students to place out of developmental coursework. English faculty members provided planning and preparation guides on the college website. And reading courses were modified to allow learners to retest after several weeks in the hopes they'd "knocked off the rust."

More than determining which developmental writing course a learner might be placed into, English placement also influenced students' access to content-area courses and thus program progress. Most courses in the curriculum featured either explicit or implied English requisites, such as the common requisite limiting enrollment to students who had scored an 80 or above on the ACCUPLACER reading measure. English placement therefore determined not only whether a student would enroll in developmental writing (ENG 0430), first-semester composition (ENG 1510), or second-semester composition (ENG 1530) during their first semester, but what content-area coursework they would be eligible to enroll in. In 2018, learners who placed into developmental English courses were restricted from the majority of the college's introductory-level courses.

Since at least January 2013, when I joined JCC's English faculty, we had been told that developmental education needed an overhaul and that placement needed to change (Table 6.1). The message we heard about developmental education was, "The more developmental courses students take, the higher their likelihood of failure." About placement, we were hearing, "High school GPA is the best indicator of success in college."

Table 6.1. Timeline of JCC Revisions and Reforms: Placement and Developmental English

Fall 2015	JCC English faculty pilot of contextualized developmental reading courses
January 2016	Jamila Lyiscott residency on language and race at JCC
Spring 2016	JCC curriculum committee redefinition of terms related to course requisites; redefined terms would be approved in Spring 2017
June 2017	Rockland CC hosted workshop on the Accelerated Learning Program (ALP); deemed SUNY's first meeting on developmental English
Spring 2018	JCC receives planning grant from SUNY Developmental English Community
January–February 2018	Approval of JCC's corequisite writing support course, ENG 0500
May 2018	JCC full faculty approval of motion to eliminate required writing placement, defaulting to reading placement performance as primary measure of preparedness for college-level reading and writing
June 2018	Conference on Acceleration in Developmental Education (CADE) in Washington, DC, with keynote speakers Hearn and Inoue
July 2018	JCC humanities program external review team visit
August 2018	JCC placement committee approval of additional placement revisions
September 2018	Presentation to full JCC faculty on pending English placement and corequisite plans
October 2018	JCC full faculty approval of motion to implement English placement revisions and to remove ENG 0190, Essential Reading Skills, and ENG 0430, Essential Writing Skills, from curriculum
Spring 2019	JCC receipt of two-year implementation grant from SUNY Developmental English Learning Community to scale corequisite efforts
January–May 2019	Updates to JCC course requisites: approximately 300 course requisites are revised and refined
June 2019	SUNY-wide discussion on multiple measures in Albany, NY, includes updates from seven system institutions taking part in Center for the Analysis of Postsecondary Readiness (CAPR) (Barnett et al., 2018 & 2020) studies

Because of how these messages were framed by media reports on state legislation across the country, we reacted defensively: *Of course* HSGPA predicts how the same privileged students who do well in high school will perform in college, but we were interested in breaking such cycles and sought to level the placement playing field. And *of course* students who place into developmental coursework are less likely to be successful, but it's not *because* of the courses themselves (which was the national narrative we were hearing). In fact, examining our own data, we confirmed that students who completed developmental writing often had better success in ENG 1510 than those who didn't "need" ENG 0430, which we were proud of: Pass rates in ENG 1510 after successful completion of developmental writing (ENG 0430) ranged from 55 percent to 74 percent between 2014 and 2017. In some semesters, these results even outpaced those of students who had not been placed into developmental writing coursework. For example, of the students who placed directly into first-semester composition (ENG 1510) in Fall 2013, only 65 percent passed the course. Conversely, of the students who first placed into and completed ENG 0430 and then went on to take ENG 1510 in Fall 2013, 83 percent passed ENG 1510 (JCC, 2014, p. 8). Such reading of data, however, ignored a bigger picture that required us to look beyond the students who completed developmental coursework.

Indeed, in spite of such perceived successes, JCC wasn't entirely ignoring calls for reform. English faculty knew anecdotally that ACCUPLACER wasn't providing accurate information about learners' skills, and discontent with the placement mechanism grew as faculty with updated training in literacy and composition were hired. I had been hired to teach three developmental reading and writing courses (ENG 0190, 0410, and 0430), and I learned quickly that students' placement in these courses also excluded them from enrolling in classes they wished to take, including introductory courses in their majors. Those of us who regularly taught developmental coursework surmised the one-two punch of placing into "reading" courses and being ineligible to progress toward intended degrees negatively impacted affect and the positive identity required for success. To rectify this, a pilot corequisite writing support course for ENG 1510 was developed in 2015 by full-time faculty who had taught developmental writing. Concurrently, thanks to faculty involvement with the College Reading and Learning Association, efforts were made to contextualize developmental reading instruction: English faculty worked with content-area faculty who taught introductory courses in sociology, human services, psychology, and anthropology to waive registration restrictions for those placing into Develop Reading Versatility (ENG 0410), provided students also enrolled in specified "co-req" 0410 sections. The pilot immediately suggested success.[3] A new English faculty hire with expertise in composition and rhetoric in 2016 moved the

---

3. In Fall 2015, 52 percent of those co-enrolled in ENG 0410 and a content-area course passed their content course with a C or better, whereas 50 percent of those who passed ENG 0410 in a previous semester passed their content course with a C or better.

faculty and curriculum toward process-oriented writing pedagogies in composition courses, and portfolio assessment was finally underway. JCC was moving in directions touted by the CCRC but in ways that worked for our local contexts.

In June 2017, what was deemed the first ever SUNY-wide meeting on developmental English took place at Rockland Community College (SUNY). There, a JCC administrator and I learned more about the movement we were already engaging in. Peter Adams' pleas to not only pilot an accelerated learning program (ALP) but scale it quickly were convincing and reflective of the work initiated by JCC's English department. Beyond pilots of integrated reading and writing (IRW) courses, corequisite support courses, and contextualized reading, placement at JCC was also being scrutinized. Initial placement reform plans had included not eliminating placement tests, but rather layering additional measures on top of ACCUPLACER for some students. Specifically, we'd planned to assess the non-cognitive skills of those placed into developmental coursework to determine learner persistence, time management abilities, and even affective stances toward learning (Adams, 2020). This vision for placement was abandoned: because of unwieldiness, because of budgets, and because JCC had engaged with SUNY's learning community on developmental English reform and aligned concerns. So instead of adding layers to placement, we began stripping them away, streamlining students into ENG 1510 by eliminating the writing placement test and instead using the reading test as the indicator of readiness for college-level writing.

Initial Placement Revisions

Movement away from ACCUPLACER-dependent placement initially resulted from several realizations about learner experience, and revisions were undertaken to align the developmental curriculum. Members of the cross-disciplinary, cross-divisional developmental studies (DS) committee—with representation from English, math, the counseling and advisement center, academic administration, and placement staff—sought to determine where learners encountered various challenges during their first year so appropriate supports might be better built into the program. However, the design of the college's placement scheme (Table 6.2) allowed for too many variables in terms of course placement, thus making it difficult for the DS committee to make any assumptions about developmental learners' instructional experiences.

In mapping out learners' various potential developmental pathways, as illustrated in Figure 6.1, major placement-related gaps emerged. Specifically, while many learners who placed into developmental reading coursework also placed into writing coursework, this was not the case for all. For example, learners scoring in the lowest range on the reading test (0–56), regardless of their placement out of developmental writing (ENG 0430), were required to complete first-level developmental reading (ENG 0190) their first semester before enrolling in Comp I (ENG 1510) and second-level reading (ENG 0410) their second semester (Figure 6.1).

Table 6.2. ACCUPLACER-Dependent Placement

Reading Score	Writing Score	First Semester Course Placement
80+	7+	ENG 1530 (second-semester composition, no dev. reading)
80+	4–6	ENG 1510 (first-semester composition, no dev. reading)
70–79	4+	ENG 0410 and ENG 1510 (second-level reading, first-semester composition)
57–69	4	ENG 0410 (second-level reading, no composition) Scenario A in Figure 6.1)
0–56	4+	ENG 0190 (first-level reading, no composition) Scenario B in Figure 6.1
0–56	1–3	ENG 0190 and ENG 0430 (first-level reading, dev. composition) Scenario C in Figure 6.1
57+	1–3	ENG 0430, ENG 0410 (second-level reading, dev. composition) Scenario D in Figure 6.1

Note. *Placement into two or more developmental courses (including math) also requires enrollment in Human Development 1310.*

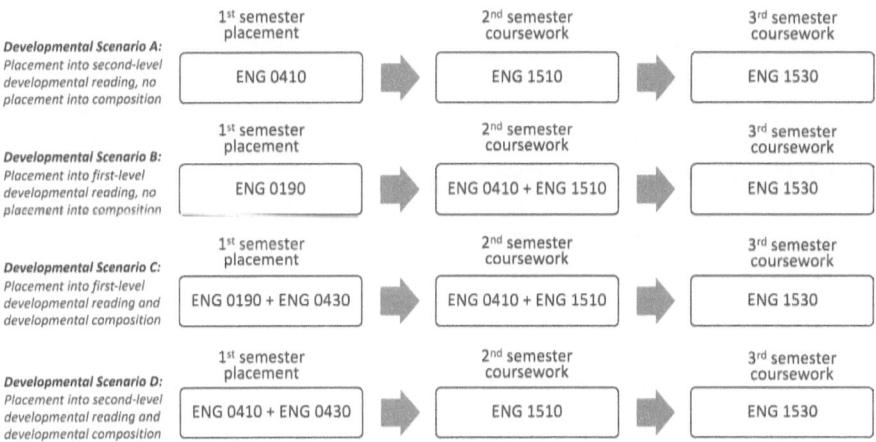

Figure 6.1. Developmental English course sequence scenarios.

Similarly, learners scoring in the mid-range on reading (57–69) and writing (4) were deemed ready in terms of writing skills for Comp I (ENG 1510) but in need of reading instruction. Students in this placement category were required to enroll in second-level developmental reading (ENG 0410) during their first semester but were restricted from enrolling in Comp I until after successful completion of ENG 0410 (Figure 6.1). In both cases, learners were not being placed into a writing course during their first semester. In fact, in 2015, 45 percent of students who placed into a developmental reading course were not also placed into a writing course (JCC OIR, 2017). By engaging in this mapping process, the DS committee recognized that no first-semester writing instruction was required *or even recommended* for roughly half of the students deemed by placement tests as most in need of literacy instruction, not only likely impeding learner progress toward credit-bearing coursework but divorcing reading and writing learning experiences, making it impossible to develop a mutually informed developmental curriculum. Faculty were eager to streamline the developmental English curriculum and placement into associated courses. And while ACCUPLACER itself was less the culprit than the college's overarching placement design, the move toward revision afforded us an occasion to review its usefulness.

Varied reading and writing placement options led to uneven experiences of literacy instruction not only during the first semester, but also as students progressed through their next semesters. Note that students enrolled in any developmental English coursework (course numbers beginning with "0," such as 0410) were typically excluded from enrolling in most introductory-level content-area courses.

Recognition of these unintended consequences of existing placement mechanisms prompted immediate placement revisions. Data were reviewed to determine the extent to which both reading and writing ACCUPLACER tests were, in fact, useful for placement. We found that, historically, over 70 percent of students taking the writing test scored a 4 or higher, placing them into college-level writing for their first composition course. Review of Fall 2016 placement data in particular suggested some correlation between student performance on reading and writing tests (Figure 6.2). Reading scores correlated positively with writing scores for the students tested, suggesting college-level reading scores indicate comparable learner preparedness for college-level writing coursework. Though we continued to ascribe some validity to the tests, we began to view ACCUPLACER writing testing as redundant and unnecessary for the majority of our matriculated students.

Therefore, in spite of limited data on those few learners who scored both 80+ on the reading test and 1–3 on writing, the English faculty proposed any student with a reading score of 80+ should be placed into first-semester credit-bearing composition (ENG 1510). A sample of student grades and reading scores were then compared to determine the lowest possible reading score (45) that might be predictive of success in ENG 1510. For those earning writing scores of 4–6, learners who also scored under 45 on reading (who were therefore among those not enrolling in any writing their first semester anyway) would be automatically placed in the DS suite of courses: ENG 0190, ENG 0430, and HUM 1310. This initial revision to reading and writing placement was still ACCUPLACER-dependent (Table 6.3), but it shifted that dependency, eliminating writing-specific measures from the placement equation while also streamlining placement options and ensuring all learners would enroll in a writing course their first semester.

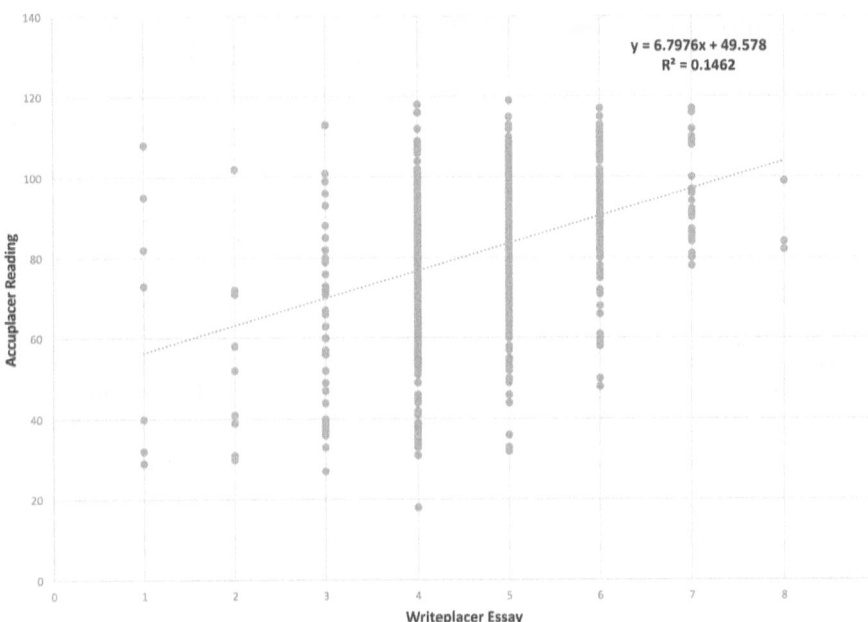

Figure 6.2. Reading and writing correlation.[4]

Table 6.3. Initial Revisions to ACCUPLACER-Dependent Placement (Removal of Writing Measure)

Reading Score	First Semester Course Placement
80+	ENG 1510 (first-semester composition, no dev. reading); with option to take writing placement test for placement into ENG 1530
46–79	ENG 0410 and ENG 1510 (second-level reading, first-semester composition)
0–45	ENG 0190, ENG 0430, and HUM 1310 (first-level reading, dev. composition, and dev. human development course)

Recognition of the mismatch between our writing pedagogy and our writing assessment provided the last element of our rationale for eliminating the writing placement test. At-entry writing testing such as that required by ACCUPLACER involved timed, inauthentic, auto-scored, decontextualized essays. As indicated in the English faculty's proposal to the full faculty in May 2018, this process did not reflect the construct of writing that JCC wished to assess. In the two years previous, blue book final exit exams had been eliminated in composition courses, and portfolio assessment had been instituted in alignment with revised course

---

4. ACCUPLACER reading test scores correlated with writing placement test scores (for 765 first-time students in Fall 2016). Data and graph provided by JCC's Office of Institutional Research (B. Russell, personal communication, 13 Dec. 2016).

learning outcomes focusing on rhetorical awareness and collaborative writing process. Furthermore, while ACCUPLACER had pushed back their rollout for new writing test implementation, we worried the new test, consistent with SAT's move to multiple-choice testing emphasizing copyediting skills, was imminent. While the faculty found the "Classic" ACCUPLACER test in writing problematic to begin with, it at least invited test-takers to compose. A shift to the multiple-choice writing test would mean an increased emphasis on single standards for grammatical "correctness." We feared the consequences for adopting the new writing placement test not only for our incoming college students, but for the high school students in our service region. As Christie Toth et al. (2019) pointed out, high school curricula are likely to focus on preparation for success in local placement measures, and JCC's faculty did not want to provide any additional incentive for our regional high school teachers to "de-emphasize the difficult and often messy practice of teaching writing within purposeful rhetorical contexts."

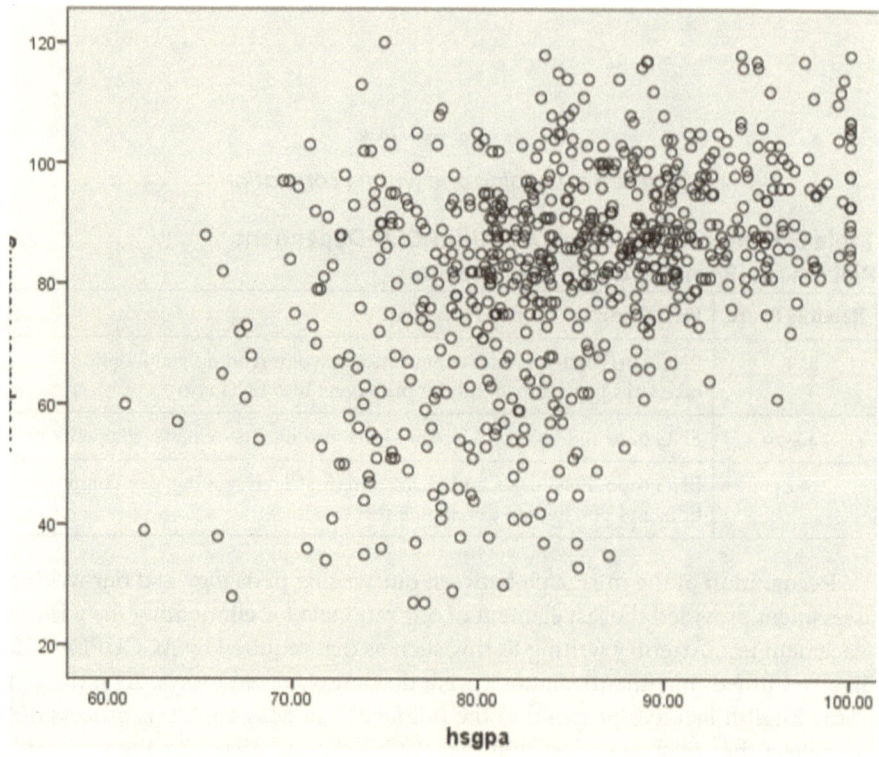

Figure 6.3. ACCUPLACER reading test scores correlated with HSGPA (for 831 first-time students in Fall 2017).[5]

---

5. Though analysis shows statistical significance, it is a weak correlation. Data and graph provided by JCC's Office of Institutional Research (B. Russell, personal communication, Aug. 15, 2018).

With one major placement-related hurdle cleared after initial revision, English faculty and the DS committee sought to explore HSGPA as a potential alternative to the remaining high-stakes ACCUPLACER reading test. Because we found an insufficient correlation between ACCUPLACER reading test results and HSGPA (Figure 6.3), we did not initially pursue HSGPA as a placement option. Of course, the assumption that we might find a correlation revealed our rather baseless reliance on ACCUPLACER scores as indicative of learner aptitude or readiness. The lack of clear relationship or correlation between ACCUPLACER reading score and HSGPA suggests a disconnect that we ultimately recognized. That is, to the extent that HSGPA actually does function as a better indicator of learner readiness to engage with college-level texts, and to the extent that the ACCUPLACER reading measure does not, we should not expect to see a strong correlation between the data compared.

Summer of Growth

The summer of 2018 saw concerted efforts by faculty to further challenge assumptions about reading and writing curriculum and placement. In June, all full-time English faculty and a college administrator attended the Conference on Acceleration in Developmental Education (CADE) in Washington, D.C. There, we heard keynote speeches by Katie Hern and Asao Inoue, and attended sessions by researchers from California who shared compelling evidence for using HSGPA as the primary placement measure in a multiple measures framework. Thanks to the initial placement revisions and curriculum realignment of the previous few months, faculty were primed to have our perspectives shifted, and CADE's focus on equity-driven, data-supported reforms in placement spoke to our current mindset.

Later that summer, the group reviewed what we'd learned in light of institutional and departmental policy, practice, and intention. Reviewing CADE materials, we reflected: *Which materials, information, and ideas stood out to us and influenced our thinking about acceleration in developmental education? What else informs our thoughts and beliefs about developmental English and related issues?* As for the latter, one major consideration in adopting a model such as the accelerated learning program (ALP) model, in which prerequisite supports in reading and writing are compressed and packaged as a single corequisite support course, was our approach to reading support. Our philosophical orientation to reading instruction as something done in the service of students' entire college learning experience prevented us from seeing promise in a single course providing reading and writing instruction in support of ENG 1510 only. While ENG 1510 *could* function as a reading-intensive course supported by reading instruction, we recognized the increased efficacy of contextualization via content-area coursework, ideally in the student's chosen area of study, to increase learner motivation and persistence. This stance influenced the ultimate shape and focus of reforms.

We drew these conclusions:

- Developmental instruction should be contextualized.
- Single, high-stakes tests are less useful for placement than cumulative HSGPA.
- Multiple measures for placement should be used to increase access to coursework (not restrict it).
- Support coursework needs to increase student confidence, willingness to collaborate, and likelihood of success.
- What we know as the "contextualized version" of ENG 0410 will be expanded to scale, with all ENG 0410 students taking content-area course(s).

We then established a process for refining and achieving our goals by responding to the following questions:

- Which documents should we focus on to guide our decision-making?
- What data do we need to obtain?
- Which data will best help us explain our plans to other stakeholders? Who are they?
- What processes/entities need to be changed or created?
- What's our timetable?

Of these, the most impactful for decision-making and communicating was the data obtained. Hern's plenary had highlighted the concept of "throughput" in a way that shook us from our satisfaction with ENG 0430 learner performance in ENG 1510. Revisiting our historical retention data through the lens of throughput (Bahr et al., 2019; see Nastal, 2019, for "survival analysis") in particular suggested the reality of developmental outcomes. Whereas we had focused on the strong *pass rates* of learners who had passed ENG 0430 and then gone on to pass ENG 1510 in the subsequent semester during the 2014–2017 academic years, the same data showed only 20 to 37 percent of learners during that same timeframe who had *initially enrolled* in prerequisite developmental writing ever passed first-semester composition (JCC, 2018). By stepping back, we were able to see that while students who *completed* the prerequisite course were likely to also complete college-level composition, a meaningful percentage of learners who *initially enrolled* in the prerequisite course were not. Analyzing completion data from the perspective of throughput confirmed we would benefit from implementing retention strategies relative to writing placement and corequisite support design proposed by CAP, the SUNY Developmental English Learning Community, and others.

Final Push Toward Multiple Measures Placement

Initial reforms had involved shifts in both English placement and curricula. The next iteration required even more parts of the college to shift as well. Having already shepherded initial revisions, and having been integral to ongoing planning, the placement committee ensured preparations for continued placement revisions were tentatively underway prior to initiating system changes. Committee members shared draft plans with IT and information systems staff, and they worked with admissions staff to ensure the college would have mechanisms for collecting various kinds of information from high school transcripts. Like the DS committee, the placement committee included placement and advising staff and faculty from student development, English, math, and the social sciences. This broad committee makeup helped ensure key faculty and staff stakeholder approval of reform proposals. For instance, as the group worked to identify viable success indicators from incoming students' transcripts, history faculty on the committee helped us arrive at the decision to use scores from standardized state exams in American history instead of the English state exam, which was perceived as less rigorous. This choice allayed content-area faculty concerns that placement revisions would increase the number of underprepared learners in their classes. The group was therefore able to effectively ensure multiple measures efforts would be viewed as legitimate by various facets of the college.

In addition to updating placement procedures so that HSGPA was the initial factor considered along with additional success indicators, the English faculty sought at the same time to shift from a prerequisite to a corequisite developmental English curriculum. In previous years, the message heard by JCC's faculty from their colleagues in English had been: If a course requires *any* high-stakes or formal writing, students should take composition first so they could "learn to write." Likewise for reading. Our job, then, was to convince colleagues of the exact opposite and encourage them to open their courses to more first-semester students, especially those in developmental coursework. English faculty therefore undertook an informal educational campaign, sharing information at faculty development workshops and other disciplines' department meetings about language acquisition, constantly highlighting the value of contextualized literacy instruction. This informational campaign regarding literacy, along with more explicit efforts at repositioning ENG 0410 as a reading across the disciplines course, helped garner faculty enthusiasm for reforms generally. One change that ensured this enthusiasm was revision of ENG 0410, which had in the past focused on increasing learner enjoyment of fiction in preparation for later coursework in literature, but had been revised to focus on nonfiction texts, better ensuring support for all introductory courses.

At the same time, JCC was revising its general education curriculum, and decisions about which English composition courses all students should complete were a major component of the redesign. To increase consistency with four-year transfer institutions, the general education committee—which also included full-time English faculty—recommended that all students take ENG 1510 and ENG 1530, the courses revised in recent years to become a true two-semester composition sequence. That the English faculty, DS committee, and placement committee were already proposing to position all learners to take ENG 1510 during their first semester was therefore quite attractive given desired general education revisions: For the first time, all students would be able to make immediate progress toward meeting not only general education requirements, but program requirements. With general education support and advocacy, the English faculty, DS committee, and placement committee felt less burden to make their case in isolation.

These entities spent Fall 2018 presenting at full faculty, curriculum committee, division, and discipline meetings to ensure our vision was communicated consistently yet from various institutional perspectives. To help make a case for multiple measures placement, English faculty relied on Craig Hayward (2017).[6] And regarding elimination of prerequisite developmental English, we relied on California's Multiple Measures Assessment Project Team (2018).[7] Additionally, the humanities program had just completed its five-year program review, including recommendations from an external team including faculty from one peer institution and three transfer institutions. Their suggestions for focusing both the overall program and composition efforts were reflected in our decisions, and we were sure to share their insights.

---

6. Craig Hayward (2017) observed, "The placement of incoming college students into an initial English or math course (developmental vs. college level) has important implications for students' likelihood of enrollment, persistence, and completion (Bailey, Jeong & Cho, 2010; Fong, 2016; Fong & Melguizo, 2016; Hayward & Willett, 2014; Melguizo, Kosiewicz, Prather & Bos, 2014). There is a growing consensus that including additional sources of information beyond placement test scores reduces error in placement decisions. For example, accuracy of placement can be improved by incorporating high school performance information, such as GPA and course grades earned in high school (Belfield & Crosta, 2012; Geiser & Santlices, 2007; Fuenmayor, Hetts & Rothstein, 2012; Ngo & Kwon, 2015; Scott-Clayton, 2012; Scott-Clayton, Crosta & Belfield, 2014; Willett, Hayward & Dahlstrom, 2008; Willett, 2013)" (p.3).

7. The Multiple Measures Assessment Project Team (2018) reported, "A series of regressions using high school grade point average (HSGPA) and ACCUPLACER scores were used to adjust direct transfer-level placement success rates for . . . transfer-level English. These estimated success rates were then compared to estimated 'throughput' rates (the percentage of students completing transfer-level English . . . in a given time frame) of students placed one level below to determine if such remediation would result in higher transfer-level completion or throughput than direct placement into transfer-level coursework. The regression-adjusted success rates were indeed lower than the original success rates of students who had been placed directly into a transfer-level course in the MMAP decision rules data. However, for all HSGPA performance levels in all three gatekeeper courses, the adjusted success rates for students placed directly into transfer-level courses exceeded adjusted throughput rates for students placed one level below transfer. This result suggests that even without any additional supports or course redesigns, the lowest performing high school students would have been more likely to complete transfer-level English . . . if placed directly into these courses as compared to taking below transfer-level remediation" (p. 2).

In August 2018, the placement committee approved multiple measure placement revisions for English, also reviewing concordance data and approving new cut scores for the updated ACCUPLACER, due for implementation in January 2019. In September 2018, English faculty presented the full faculty with information about pending English placement and corequisite plans in anticipation of divisional and curriculum meetings. In October 2018, the full faculty approved a motion to implement English placement revisions (Table 6.4) and to remove ENG 0190, Essential Reading Skills, and ENG 0430, Essential Writing Skills, from the curriculum.

Table 6.4. HSGPA-Based Placement with Multiple Measures Supplement

Multiple Measures Data Points	First-Semester Placement
2.6+ HSGPA through 11th grade	ENG 1510 (first-semester composition) without support
2.0<2.6 HSGPA with one of the following success indicators: • 85+ American History & Government or Global Studies NYS Regents Exam • 500+ SAT Writing • 21+ ACT • 3+ on any AP exam • 85+ in 11th grade ENG course	ENG 1510 (first-semester composition) without support
2.0<2.6 with none of the above success indicators	ENG 1510, ENG 0500, and ENG 0410 (first-semester composition with reading and writing support courses)
<2.0 HSGPA	ENG 1510, ENG 0500, ENG 0410, and Human Development 1300 (first-semester composition with reading, writing, and student skills support courses)

Note. *Placement into ENG 0410 may be overturned via ACCUPLACER reading test. Placement into ENG 0500 may be overturned via guided placement (in-house, untimed placement essay, arranged through ENG department).*

The final, most painful and protracted step in the process of reforming placement involved course requisites. Disciplines across the curriculum had historically used reading and writing placement scores when articulating who may enroll in their courses. Most famously, kickboxing indicated a Composition II prerequisite. Most commonly, introductory courses required "college-level reading" scores to restrict enrollment. Course requisites were strictly enforced by faculty, advisors, and the college's registration system, with requisite codes kept meticulously updated and effective at prompting registration errors. Prior to reform, the number of courses available to students in developmental English was 146, roughly one quarter of the courses in the course catalogue. Changes to placement and developmental English curriculum meant disciplines would need to review their course requisites, reckoning with how these functioned for both matriculated and non-matriculated learners. From January through May of 2019, the implications of revisions to English placement on course requisites across the college's curriculum were recognized, and updates were made. Approximately 300 course requisites were revised and refined, ultimately allowing access to 239 introductory content-area courses, many of which now included those required for various programs.

At the same time, developmental placements reduced drastically. Whereas 25.1 percent of all first-time full-time JCC students had placed into developmental coursework in Fall 2018, reforms resulted in a reduction of learners placed in developmental coursework the following year, to 12 percent of all first-time full-time students. In addition to halving developmental placements, gains were seen in student completion of college-level writing, even when looking at throughput data. Between Fall 2016 and 2018, the percentage of students who had attempted developmental writing and then went on to pass first-semester composition ranged from 32 to 40 percent. In the most recent semesters tracked, that throughput rate has, for the first time, reached 45 percent. Given the number and nature of 2018–2019 adjustments to the factors that play into learner placement and success, it is nearly impossible to control for any one of the interventions described above. However, the college will need to work toward disaggregating data, for in spite of generally positive results, racial disparities appear to be increasing: While students of color have historically made up 25–40 percent of the developmental learner population, that percentage has increased to 49.5 percent in Fall 2018 and to 57.6 percent in Fall 2019 (JCC, 2019a).

The Problem of 11th Grade GPA and Other Next Steps

One group we did not engage as strategically as we might have was the college's concurrent enrollment program. Though proposed success indicators listed in Table 6.4 reference several data points from students' high school years, those selected by the placement committee and English faculty were not useful for high schools' placement purposes. More broadly an issue for *any* student without an HSGPA through the junior year (e.g., students who left prior to junior year completion, current high school sophomores and juniors, some international students), it proved difficult to obtain information for current high school sophomores in particular. English faculty, academic administrators, and counseling center staff met prior to implementation of placement reforms to discuss alternative placement metrics for concurrent enrollment students seeking to place prior to the end of their junior year. Given California research, we considered the possibility of ACT, SAT, AP, and New York State Regents scores, but it was determined none of these scores would be known in time for schedule planning in the high schools, and the process of tracking down scores over the summer would be unwieldy. The decision was therefore made to administer the placement test to all interested high school students, as done in the past. Especially for concurrent enrollment sophomores, research-supported data points would not be available until after schools needed to make decisions about schedules for the following year.

Placement for concurrent enrollment and others without an HSGPA through 11th grade will be a point of ongoing inquiry, especially given concerns that ACCUPLACER reinforces racist educational structures and therefore produces disparate access. In June 2019, English, math, and learning support faculty attended a SUNY-wide discussion on multiple measures in Albany, NY that included progress reports and initial conclusions from seven system institutions taking part in a CAPR study, since updated (Barnett et al., 2020). Subsequent support and advice from state and national research on placement is ongoing, and SUNY itself recently issued its own guidance on placement. While these reports and documents do not address issues relative to concurrent enrollment placement, such a focus is almost certainly forthcoming, as a recent Aspen Institute and CCRC report (Mehl et al., 2020) called for alternatives to placement testing for concurrently enrolled learners.

The Shape of Things

Through placement reform, faculty sought to ensure students would receive instructional support to increase their chances of successful engagement with and completion of college-level coursework during their first semester. The relative ease with which these transitions happened may be due in part to two existing institutional structures. A relatively large full-time English department focused on composition instruction, historically comprising faculty specializing in reading, writing, and literature—and developmental instruction of these—ensured concerted disciplinary effort. Additionally, a college-wide, cross-divisional placement committee was pivotal, inviting ongoing sharing and shaping of ideas and information.

Such existing formations within the institutional network afforded coordinated movement. Specifically, it was the ability of the English department to function both as a unified and distributed force that ensured shared experiences and new insights. While it is not uncommon for community college instructors of reading to work within departments dedicated to transitional studies or developmental studies, with instructors of writing housed separately within English departments, JCC's reading and writing faculty are located in its English department. The largely identical institutional location of such faculty, and the group's ongoing willingness to work and learn together, made for an effective cohort. Further, the placement committee's ability to bring together faculty and staff who are typically dispersed and rarely interact allowed it to function as a hub, both gathering and distributing vital information and data.

Also impactful on placement and curriculum reform is the role of a wide-reaching concurrent enrollment program. That so many learners within JCC's service area complete college composition before arriving as matriculated students leads full-time faculty to maintain certain beliefs about the "typical" Composition I learner. For in a given Composition I classroom, we rarely see students identified by high school teachers or counselors as "good writers." To the contrary, with a concurrent enrollment program reaching most high schools in our service region, we can be assured that learners in our first-semester courses 1) did not excel in high school and therefore were not invited to enroll in college-credit composition courses and/or 2) come to us as adult learners with many years since their last formal education experience. Recognizing this element of the context within which we assign and assess writing, especially given that we as English faculty develop the placement and curricula that reach those "good writers" in their high school years, should force us to constantly reframe our approaches to first-year writing assessment.

Shifts in placement and developmental education began incrementally, yet were swiftly scaled. Due to a tightly networked constellation of policies, it would have been difficult to reform placement in isolation. An institutional shift made space for revision to other systems concurrently, requiring intensive cross-divisional cooperation. After scaling of reforms, prerequisite developmental reading and writing courses have been replaced with contextualized support courses; all learners are placed directly into transferrable, credit-bearing composition coursework, with some placed into support courses largely by virtue of their HSGPA; the number of courses available to DS students has increased substantially; and in Fall 2019, 12 percent all first-time full-time students placed into developmental coursework (JCC, 2019a), essentially cutting developmental placements in half.

Unique to this study was consideration of how academic programs serving non-matriculated students impact placement reforms. It also illustrated how placement reform can coincide with developmental English curriculum reform, even when the latter diverges from more typical IRW and ALP approaches. And it highlighted the affordances of an English department with both developmental writing and reading faculty, as well as the importance of cross-divisional placement committees. As a case study, it necessarily represented largely limited perspectives and would be enriched by additional insights from staff, faculty from other disciplines, and, of course, students.

Acknowledgments

I am grateful for the assistance of SUNY-Jamestown's Office of Institutional Research staff, especially Barb Russell.

References

Adams, P. (2020). Giving hope to the American dream: Implementing a corequisite model of developmental writing. *Composition Studies, 48*(2), 19–34.

Bahr, P. R., Fagioli, L. P., Hetts, J., Hayward, C., Willett, T., Lamoree, D., Newell, M. A., Sorey, K. & Baker, R. B. (2019). Improving placement accuracy in California's community colleges using multiple measures of high school achievement. *Community College Review, 47*(2), 178–211.

Baker-Bell, A. (2020). *Linguistic justice: Black language, literacy, identity, and pedagogy.* Routledge.

Barnett, E. A., Bergman, P., Kopko, E. M., Reddy, V., Belfield, C. & Roy, S. (2018). *Multiple measures placement using data analytics: An implementation and early impacts report.* Community College Research Center. https://ccrc.tc.columbia.edu/publications/multiple-measures-placement-using-data-analytics.html.

Barnett, E. A., Kopko, E., Cullinan, D. & Belfield, C. R. (2020). *Who should take college-level courses? Impact findings from an evaluation of a multiple measures assessment strategy.* Center for the Analysis of Postsecondary Readiness. https://ccrc.tc.columbia.edu/media/k2/attachments/multiple-measures-assessment-impact-findings.pdf.

Carter, S. (2008). *The way literacy lives.* SUNY Press.

Elbow, P. & Belanoff, P. (1986). Portfolios as a substitute for proficiency examinations. *College Composition and Communication, 37*(3), 336–339.

Fain, P. (2013, June 5). Remediation if you want it. *Inside Higher Ed.* https://www.insidehighered.com/news/2013/06/05/florida-law-gives-students-and-colleges-flexibility-remediation.

Hayward, C. (2017). *Validating placement systems comprising test and multiple measure information.* RP Group. https://rpgroup.org/Portals/0/Documents/Projects/MultipleMeasures/Publications/ResearchBrief-ValidatingPlacementSystemswhichUtilizeTestandMultipleMeasureInformationFINAL.pdf.

Huot, B. & Williamson, M. M. (2009). Rethinking portfolios for evaluating writing: Issues of assessment and power. In B. Huot & P. O'Neill (Eds.), *Assessing writing: A critical sourcebook* (pp. 330–342). NCTE.

Inoue, A. B. (2015). *Antiracist writing assessment ecologies: Teaching and assessing writing for a socially just future.* The WAC Clearinghouse; Parlor Press. https://doi.org/10.37514/PER-B.2015.0698.

Jamestown Community College. (2014). *Developmental studies (DS) and developmental course trends.* [Unpublished data]

Jamestown Community College. (2017). *Developmental reading: Success in reading, writing, and retention by enrollment in a writing course.* [Unpublished data]

Jamestown Community College. (2018). *Developmental studies (DS) and developmental course trends.* [Unpublished data]

Jamestown Community College. (2019a). *Developmental studies (DS) and developmental course trends.* [Unpublished data]

Jamestown Community College. (2019b). *Facts and figures.* [Unpublished data]

Jamestown Community College. (2021). *Facts & Figures.* https://www.sunyjcc.edu/about/facts-figures.

Janangelo, J. & Klausman, J. (2012). Rendering the idea of a writing program: A look at six two-year colleges. *Teaching English in the Two-Year College, 40*(2), 131–144.

Klausman, J. (2018). The two-year college writing program and academic freedom:

Labor, scholarship, and compassion. *Teaching English in the Two-Year College, 45*(4), 385–405.

Klausman, J., Toth, C., Swyt, W., Griffiths, B., Sullivan, P., Warnke, A., Williams, A. L., Giordano, J. & Roberts, L. (2016). TYCA white paper on placement reform. *Teaching English in the Two-Year College, 44*(2), 135–157.

Lyiscott, J. (2017). Racial identity and liberation literacies in the classroom. *English Journal, 106*(4), 47–53.

Mehl, G., Wyner, J., Barnett, E. A., Fink, J. & Jenkins, D. (2020). *The dual enrollment playbook: A guide to equitable acceleration for students*. The Aspen Institute; Community College Research Center. https://ccrc.tc.columbia.edu/publications/dual-enrollment-playbook-equitable-acceleration.html.

Miller, K. L., Wender, E. & Finer, B. S. (2017). Legislating first-year writing placement: Implications for Pennsylvania and across the country. *The Journal of Writing Assessment, 10*(1). http://journalofwritingassessment.org/article.php?article=119.

Minnesota Rev. Code Ann. § 120B.13. (2021). https://www.revisor.mn.gov/statutes/cite/120B.13.

Multiple Measures Assessment Project Team. (2018). *AB705 success rate estimates* (Technical paper). RP Group. https://rpgroup.org/Portals/0/Documents/Projects/Multiple Measures/Publications/MMAP_AB705_TechnicalPaper_FINAL_091518.pdf.

National Center for Education Statistics. (2020). *Jamestown Community College*. College Navigator. https://nces.ed.gov/collegenavigator/?q=jamestown+community+college&s=all&id=191986.

Phillips, C. & Giordano, J. B. (2016). Developing a cohesive academic literacy program for underprepared students. *Teaching English in the Two-Year Classroom, 44*(1), 79–89.

Reynolds, N. & Rice, R. (2006). *Portfolio teaching: A guide for instructors* (2nd ed.). Bedford/St. Martin's.

Taylor, T. (2009). Writing program administration at the two-year college: Ghosts in the machine. *Writing Program Administration, 32*(3), 120–139.

Toth, C., Nastal, J., Hassel, H. & Giordano, J. B. (2019). Introduction: Writing assessment, placement, and the two-year college. *The Journal of Writing Assessment, 12*(1). http://journalofwritingassessment.org/article.php?article=133.

Walvoord, B. E. (2014). *Assessing and improving student writing in college*. Jossey-Bass.

Chapter 7. Tracking the Racial Consequences of Placement by Probability: A Case Study at Kingsborough Community College

Annie Del Principe, Lesley Broder, and Lauren Levesque
KINGSBOROUGH COMMUNITY COLLEGE

Abstract: Any placement decision is a gamble on the validity of the mechanism used. The better the placement mechanism matches the actual proficiencies required for success in a future, real-life context, the more accurately it will place students into the best classes for them and the more valid it will prove to be. But what happens if the most obvious, commonsensical approaches to placement that would appear to have the strongest validity—writing tests for placement into writing classes—prove unreliable? Rather than accurately placing students into the "right" class for them, we now know that writing placement tests frequently result in the underplacement of students into developmental courses that are not truly necessary for their success as college writers. Further, writing assessments used for the purposes of incoming college writing placement are part of this pattern and have produced racially inequitable placement patterns for uncountable numbers of students in higher education, including two-year colleges (TYCs). This chapter presents an analysis of racially disaggregated placement data for Kingsborough Community College, part of the City University of New York (CUNY) system, which recently revised its protocol for English placement in an attempt to increase accuracy and racial equity in placement into credit-bearing first-year composition (FYC). The CUNY system shifted from a practice of writing placement via a locally designed and scored timed writing test to an algorithmic placement mechanism—the "Proficiency Index"—that relies heavily on high school GPA. Given the complexities of multiple measures placement for BIPOC (Black, Indigenous, and People of Color) students, we're encouraged to see that the new CUNY policy has resulted in a greater percentage of BIPOC students placing directly into our FYC courses.

Any placement decision is a gamble on the validity of the mechanism used. The better the placement mechanism matches the actual proficiencies required for success in a future, real-life context, the more accurately it will place students into the best classes for them and the more valid it will prove to be. But what happens if the most obvious, commonsensical approaches to placement that would appear to have the strongest validity—writing tests for placement into writing classes—prove unreliable? Rather than accurately placing students into the "right" class for them, we now know that writing placement tests frequently result in the underplacement of students into developmental courses that are not truly necessary for their success as college writers. In addition, as readers of this collection well know, writing assessments used for the purposes of incoming college writing placement are part of this pattern and have produced racially inequitable placement patterns for uncountable numbers of students in higher education, including two-year colleges (TYCs).

Our own TYC, Kingsborough Community College, is part of the City University of New York (CUNY) system, which recently revised its protocol for English placement across all campuses in an attempt to increase accuracy and racial equity in placement into credit-bearing first-year composition (FYC). CUNY shifted from a system of writing placement via a locally designed and scored timed writing test to an algorithmic placement mechanism—the "Proficiency Index"—that relies heavily on high school GPA, an approach that, in other institutions, has been linked to higher placement rates into FYC for Black, Hispanic, and Pell-eligible students (CAPR, 2020). This chapter takes a close look at racially disaggregated data on placement into FYC at our TYC from the first year (two semesters) using the new CUNY algorithm in order to better understand how the new placement is recalibrating the racial makeup of students in FYC. Given the complexities of multiple measures placement for BIPOC (Black, Indigenous, and People of Color) students, we're encouraged to see that, from the limited data we have so far, the new CUNY policy has resulted in a greater percentage of BIPOC students placing directly into our FYC courses. While using a mechanism that relies heavily on high school GPA for writing placement in a TYC isn't without its complexities (Koretz & Langi, 2018), it seems that, in our case, it has resulted in greater racial equity in writing placement for our students.

Context

Kingsborough Community College (KCC) is part of the CUNY system, a 25-campus system spread across all five boroughs of New York City serving 275,000 students per year. CUNY was founded in 1847 as the nation's very first free public institution of higher education and now comprises 11 senior colleges, seven community colleges, and seven graduate, honors, and professional schools. CUNY is headed by a chancellor who acts as the chief executive officer of the system. The chancellor's authority is checked by the Board of Trustees, a governance body that establishes academic policies for the entire system. While CUNY is highly centralized on some policies, on others campuses are allowed some, or a lot of, flexibility, and the Board of Trustees makes those judgements.

Kingsborough is the only community college in the borough of Brooklyn, which, itself, has a population of 2.6 million. KCC is a large community college, with an enrollment hovering around 15,500, serving a diverse student body. According to 2019 institutional research data, KCC students identified as 55 percent female and 45 percent male; 60.1 percent were under 22 years old, 23.8 percent are between 23 and 29, with the remaining 16.1 percent over 30; in 2019, student ethnicity broke down as follows: 29.1 percent Black, non-Hispanic, 36.4 percent White, non-Hispanic, 17.6 percent Hispanic, and 16.6 percent Asian/Pacific Islander. More than a third, 35.6 percent, of Kingsborough students were foreign born, and at least 30 percent spoke a language other than English at home, although this number very likely underrepresents the reality of our students' language diversity. Although tuition costs are quite low—$5,252 for a full-time state resident—75 percent of first-year students received financial aid.

While roughly half of Kingsborough students are enrolled in the associate's program in liberal arts, pursuing one of a number of different concentrations in that degree, the remaining students are enrolled in a range of different degree programs, the five most popular being business, criminal justice, biology, mental health, and accounting. KCC has two large and successful dual enrollment programs that, together, in Fall 2019 comprised fully 31 percent of enrolled students. The "College Now" program trains New York City high school teachers to teach college-level, credit-bearing courses to qualifying NYC high school students as part of their regular course load. The "Early College Initiative" is similar but brings qualifying NYC high school students to the KCC campus for courses taught by college faculty; students in this program attend classes alongside other KCC students. Eighty-five percent of degree-seeking students at KCC are enrolled in transfer programs, with the remainder enrolled in career or terminal certificate programs ("credit students by degree type"). KCC tracks degree completion by collecting three-year graduation rates, which, in 2016, was 33.2 percent of students enrolled in degree programs (Kingsborough Office of Institutional Effectiveness, 2019a). Post-graduation transfer rates from 2016–2019 hovered between 56.2 and 72 percent of total graduates.

Exigence: One Barrier Gone; Time to Knock Down the Next One

In the fall of 2017, two and a half years prior to the eventual implementation of the new Proficiency Index (PI) for placement, CUNY changed its method of assessing exit from remediation, a change that, in retrospect, foreshadowed the eventual change in placement. Prior to 2017, students could only exit remediation in writing by passing the same timed writing test that placed them into remediation in the first place—the locally designed and scored CUNY Assessment Test of Writing (CATW)—thus creating a bookend structure of placement and advancement for students. (See also Charissa Che's chapter in this collection.) For several years, the CUNY-wide Writing Discipline Council (WDC)—a body made up of writing program administrators (WPAs) from across all 18

CUNY community and senior colleges—had been lobbying the CUNY Central administration to discontinue the use of the CATW as an exit measure due to the WDC members' growing sense, based on greater access to disaggregated outcomes data, that it perpetuated racist and inequitable patterns in the population of students who were forced to repeat remedial courses. Fall 2017 marked the very first semester that students exited remedial writing courses on the sole basis of their earned grades in the course. This was a watershed moment for our corequisite writing course, as we watched a much more racially balanced population of students pass through the course, gaining real college credits in FYC and gaining vital momentum in progress toward their degree. Overall, an increase in about five percentage points of students in our corequisite course passed based on the new exit measures, but those changes in pass rates were not allocated equally across racial/ethnic groups. Table 7.1 compares pass rates via the CATW for a typical fall semester with those via course grades. This table shows the difference in disaggregated percentages of students exiting the top-level developmental writing course via re-taking the timed CATW vs. via their grades in the course.

Table 7.1. Exit from Remediation Comparison

	Fall 2016	CATW	Fall 2018	Course Grades
Black Students	56%	61.9%
Hispanic Students	31.3%	63%
Asian Students	68.8%	69.8%
White Students	83.9%	73.3%

Once exit from remediation had been reformed in 2017, all eyes turned toward CUNY's placement practices.

CUNY's recent shift to a new placement protocol (described in detail below in "Unclogging the Pipeline" and "The Proficiency Index for Placement") is part of a much larger national trend in two-year college placement reform away from single standardized tests and toward placement via multiple measures. Over the last several years, many researchers, scholars, and teacher-activists have argued that placement testing not only placed more BIPOC students into remedial courses but also resulted in the underplacement into remediation of a significant percentage of students (Belfield & Crosta, 2012; Scott-Clayton et al., 2014). Whether because students don't fully comprehend the function and importance of placement testing and therefore do not perform at their true ability level or because placement tests aren't valid measures of the complex collection of abilities, habits, and resources necessary to succeed in college writing, placement tests are not reliable predictors of which students will and will not succeed in passing FYC.

As the problems with placement testing became more and more apparent, states and municipalities began to call for changes in their own local systems, perhaps the most well-known being California. In response to Governor Jerry Brown signing AB 705 into law, the California community college system shifted to a variety of placement protocols based on an index of multiple factors from students' educational histories, the most heavily weighed of which is high school GPA because it has been found to be the factor most predictive of students' ability to succeed in English (and math) coursework in college (Bahr et al., 2019). California's shift in placement in response to state-level reform initiatives followed similar legislation in Texas, Minnesota, Tennessee, Oregon, Florida, Connecticut, and Washington state. CUNY's own development of a new placement protocol for its 18 community and senior colleges was set in the context of this national sea change in placement policy and practice.

Unclogging the Pipeline

Amending placement practices and policies at CUNY was a momentous task as remediation had been fundamental to a CUNY education for decades. Since 1999, students who did not place into college-level English and math were required to pass developmental courses at one of CUNY's six community colleges before they could continue their education at the four-year institutions (Jaggars & Hodara, 2011, p. 2). Placement into these courses was determined by two exams. As of October 2010, students took the locally developed CATW, a 90-minute written response to a 250 to 300-word reading passage that was meant to measure students' ability "to do college-level writing in English" (CUNY, Office of Assessment/Office of Academic Affairs, 2012, p. 1). A multiple-choice, computer-adaptive reading test was also required: The COMPASS was administered until it was phased out in 2015, replaced by the shorter ACCUPLACER through 2019. As reforms to remedial education were implemented across the nation, CUNY began to restructure these placement processes and developmental educational pathways, particularly when plans to add a seventh community college, now Guttman, were underway (Jaggars & Hodara, 2011, p. 3).[1] These efforts culminated in the implementation of the PI as the standard placement mechanism in Spring 2020 and the concurrent dissolution of remedial courses.

Stand-alone developmental classes functioned as both a gatekeeper to maintain standards and a means to equip underprepared students for the academy, a view put forth since at least the late 1970s with Mina Shaugnessy's (1977) *Errors and Expectations* and its focus on mechanical competence in CUNY students' writing.

---

1. Notably, Guttman holds the largest endowment of all CUNY community colleges, currently estimated at $15 million, thanks to an endowment from the Stella and Charles Guttman Foundation, highlighting the trend of large philanthropies influencing educational reform.

Two decades later, Marilyn Sternglass' (1997) *Time to Know Them* affirmed this perspective with a longitudinal examination of CUNY basic writers that attests to the power of remediation. These well-known texts were countered by calls against basic writing at CUNY that arose in the 1990s in works like James Traub's (1994) *City on a Hill: Testing the American Dream at City College*. Standardized exams appeared to provide an efficient and consistent measure to place developmental students while still allowing for local interpretation to account for the unique needs of individual programs. By 2011, however, prompted by national trends assessing the efficacy of remediation, CUNY worked with the CCRC to examine placement mechanisms and their effect on student progress. Four years later, the interim chancellor set up the CUNY Task Force on Developmental Education to review research and reimagine remedial placement policies (CUNY Task Force, 2016, p. 2).

Though CUNY's guidelines clearly delineated the boundary between placement into developmental, non-credit courses and college-level, credit-bearing ones, each college had great latitude to structure their remedial educational policies. As such, the length of the developmental sequence varied across campuses as did policies regarding placement and exemption from these courses (Jaggars & Hodara, 2011, pp. 11–12). While some schools used the writing exam for placement, others relied on the reading exam (Jaggars & Hodara, 2011, p. 14). KCC used a combination of reading and writing exam scores along with grades in previous developmental classes and sometimes instructor referral to create a complex placement web for its long developmental sequence (Figure 7.1). The student's knowledge of the sequence, guidance from advisors, and course availability could all affect the number of courses students took.

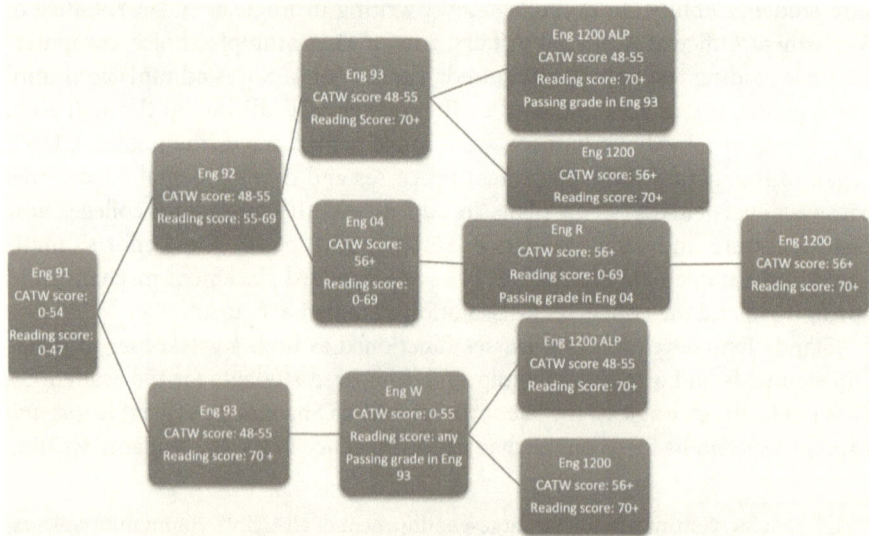

Figure 7.1. Placement pathways and course entrance requirements before implementation of the PI.

Tracking the Racial Consequences of Placement   179

To add to the confusion, entering students were unaware of the great bearing entrance examinations and placement policies could have on their educational plans. For example, on one hand, low placement scores could jeopardize their educational progress as longer pathways to enter credit-bearing courses correlated with greater student attrition (Jaggars & Hodara, 2011, p. 41). On the other hand, students had an equal or even greater chance of passing required, credit-bearing classes if their developmental course sequence was shorter (Jaggars & Hodara, 2011 p. 44). For students entering in Spring 2020, the reading and writing exams were no longer required, and the PI became the standard placement mechanism as more research called attention to the specious validity of placement tests. To help explain the shift to the PI, CUNY Central cited one study that determined that students were far more likely to be misplaced into remediation than into credit-bearing classes. More than a third of students who placed into developmental English classes could have passed the gateway English course with a B or higher while still others could have passed with grades lower than B (Scott-Clayton et al., 2014, pp. 381–382).

At KCC, the English developmental program did not separate reading and writing into separate departments as is the case at other CUNY campuses, though students still had to pass through multiple levels of remediation before they could register for the credit-bearing FYC. Excluding ESL, students with low scores on the placement exams might end up taking seven different remedial English courses, repeating some of these multiple times. As mentioned earlier, CUNY's unusual practice of requiring students to pass the reading and writing entrance exams in order to exit the developmental sequence led to more test-prep and intersession bridge courses, making the barriers out of remediation even higher. The effect of these barriers becomes clearer when examining exactly how placement reform affected students' educational progress. In the semesters before the Proficiency Index was instituted, nearly 40 percent of incoming first-year students placed into an upper-level developmental class; this percentage dropped to about ten percent after changes to placement took effect in Spring 2020. In Fall 2017, for example, approximately 880 students were enrolled in one of the many developmental levels of English while approximately 2,300 students were enrolled in FYC or corequisite FYC.

Figure 7.2. Simplified placement pathway and course entrance requirements after implementation of the PI. Students with a PI of 50-64 could also opt to take a pre-semester workshop through KCC's immersion program that would allow them to place directly into English 1200.

By Fall 2020, when enrollment was down due to the COVID-19 pandemic and the PI was used for placement for the second time, just about 200 students were registered for the one remaining developmental-level class while more than 2,400 students were registered for FYC or corequisite FYC. This difference, discussed in detail in the "Outcomes" section, represents a significant increase in students for whom the PI and corequisite instruction would provide opportunities to earn credit for FYC and eliminate non-credit, remedial coursework that would lengthen the educational path. Figures 7.1 and 7.2 further illustrate how the PI simplified students' educational journeys and laid out a more direct path to earning college credit. Figure 7.1 represents just some of the developmental pathways students could have followed. Note that entering students could begin this sequence at English 91, English 92, or English 93, based on their test scores. They would exit remediation only after passing the reading and writing exams that initially placed them into developmental education.

CUNY's new placement policies relied on robust corequisite course offerings that would replace the developmental sequence. KCC established its own corequisite course, the Accelerated Learning Program (ALP), for FYC in Spring 2013, long before the PI was developed, following a visit from Peter Adams, who popularized the method at the Community College of Baltimore County. The program began as a small pilot, just five sections that did not even appear on the school's scheduling platform. For several years, only students who narrowly missed entrance to the credit-bearing FYC were placed into the course. These students were mainstreamed into designated sections of FYC and also received an additional hour of instruction with their professor each week; within a few years, supplemental instruction was increased to two hours. In these first semesters, corequisite students could only exit by passing the CATW. After CUNY recognized that it was not legally feasible to mandate different exit requirements from students in the same course, they retroactively passed those who had failed due to their score on the CATW. KCC took this change in CUNY policy as an opportunity to amend assessment practices of the corequisite sections of FYC and began to evaluate students by portfolio assessment in Fall 2017, which, based on a few years of student outcomes data, appears to favor White students less than the exam had.

The Proficiency Index for Placement: Medical Discourse in the Name of Equity

Although the data made clear that English placement needed to be reformed, it would take extensive outreach and communication to explain these new policies to the many affected programs throughout CUNY. After the CUNY Task Force on Developmental Education—comprised of chairs of the discipline councils, administrators from two- and four-year CUNY colleges, and members of the Office of Academic Affairs (OAA)—had established placement recommendations, the OAA was charged with implementing these changes by establishing the PI (CUNY, 2019). As local campuses were not involved in crafting the algorithm, information about the PI trickled to campuses by way of memos from CUNY Central and information shared by members of the CUNY Writing Discipline Council. This communication was supplemented with the CUNY English Summit in October 2018, a day-long event where representatives from CUNY Central, including the interim chancellor, The Community College Resource Center (CCRC), corequisite scholars, and CUNY faculty, explained the new policies, their potential benefits to students, and new pedagogical models, all with the celebratory air of embarking on a new era.

CUNY administration gave the new policies a medical frame, explaining at the summit that "our new placement practices aim to assign each student to the minimum effective dose of developmental supports" (CUNY, 2018). These "doses" were to be administered via "the Proficiency Index" (PI) algorithm. Like new multiple measures placement indexes in other states and municipalities, the PI would draw on multiple measures from a student's educational record to generate placement based on predictive probability, calculating students' chances of success by weighing high school GPA, scores on the statewide Regents exam, and, if available, SAT scores. Based on this formula—established by studying years of data on students' performance in developmental, corequisite, and credit-bearing courses—students with approximately a 65 percent chance of scoring C- or higher would be placed in FYC. Students who needed some "light developmental support" based on their range on the PI would be placed in corequisite, credit-bearing courses. Students with the lowest PI would not register for CUNY classes but instead a special, stand-alone program called "CUNY Start"; though the semester-long program is not covered by financial aid, the current cost of $75 is meant to make it accessible to most students. The full-time program includes both reading/writing and math and meets for 25 hours a week, while the part-time version includes either reading/writing or math and meets for 12 hours a week. While campuses were encouraged to experiment with different corequisite models, the PI itself would not be discussed, piloted, or adapted but rather uniformly applied as of Spring 2020 to all incoming students at CUNY's campuses. Along with this change, schools were given explicit instructions to end all stand-alone developmental course offerings, which KCC has slowly phased out through the Fall 2021 semester.

To explain the all-encompassing nature of the reform, CUNY continued the medical metaphor at the 2018 summit: "Students who fail remediation are most likely to drop out of college. Failing English is not about English. It is not the disease. It is the symptom" (CUNY, 2018). Throughout the day, administrators adapted the very medical ideology that Mike Rose had long ago critiqued in discussions of remediation, a term he urged universities to abandon to avoid the peculiar system of providing students "entrance to the academy while, in various symbolic ways, denying them full participation" (Rose, 1985, p. 357). More than three decades later, this jargon was invoked more in a therapeutic sense than a pathologizing one to dismantle developmental education and so launch a more just form of placement. Though administrators at the summit repeatedly emphasized that the changes were not to be top-down or free from discussion, it was clear that the disease they had diagnosed—remediation and long pathways to enter credit-bearing courses—could only be cured with system-wide placement reform and corequisite models of education rather than a constellation of different reforms enacted at different colleges in the system.

Reactions to the Proficiency Index

The separate but related issues of placement reform and the resulting reduction of developmental course offerings caused varying degrees of distress among faculty. Updates about placement reform and the new Proficiency Index were regularly discussed at department meetings, where instructors expressed some concern that standards would be lowered or would become unreliable without standardized tests to determine placement. Moreover, while the implementation of the PI caused some friction, the reduction and eventual elimination of the well-established developmental sequence had more direct bearing on faculty labor.

The phasing out of stand-alone developmental courses ran against the experience of instructors who spent years working closely with students enrolled in developmental English courses. These instructors well understood the findings that informed CUNY's decision to amend placement: Many students who ended up in developmental English did not continue in their studies. However, they argued, students' "weak literacy skills" were justification that the courses were necessary, not that they should be abandoned. If many struggled or failed after a semester, the idea of dropping them into the credit-bearing FYC course seemed reckless and even unethical, instructors argued. The shift in placement policies, thus, countered the oft-expressed local wisdom that those students who made it through the developmental sequence and finally enrolled in FYC were the most prepared. These former developmental education students' strengths in FYC were taken as tangible proof of the success and validity of developmental education. Figure 7.3 shows the percentages of students from each English background who passed through our FYC 1 course in Fall 2018.

Of course, the success in FYC of students who had persisted and made it through KCC's prodigious dev ed sequence was a self-fulfilling prophecy. Few faculty in our department openly voiced the critique that, since our dev ed English courses were often run as prep courses to our FYC and since a significant percentage of students cooled out in that sequence, it was truly unsurprising that those students who actually passed through the dev ed machine might easily pass FYC. Very few asked aloud whether those students might have passed FYC to begin with. Instead, to many instructors, shortening the educational pathway felt like a neoliberal justification to cut costs.

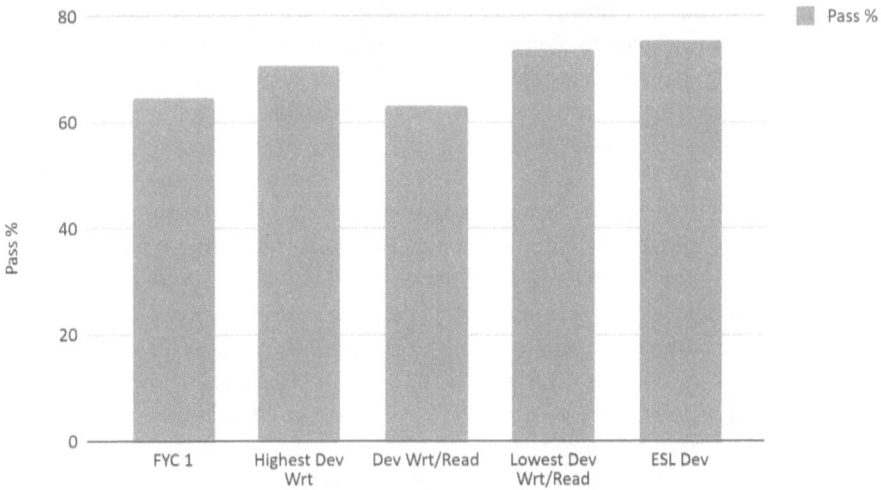

Figure 7.3. FYC pass rates by first English course.

Dire predictions and contradicting rumors ensued. The idea that the PI was the administration's plan to rid CUNY of the most unprepared students ran alongside the fear that faculty would be pressured to pass all students through a form of college-level social promotion, a capitulation to an empty form of the now popular term "student success." Another continuing concern was that FYC would devolve into a remedial-level course since, prior to implementation of the PI, KCC had reserved the corequisite model for high-scoring developmental students. Even if some found it counterintuitive to abandon placement tests and developmental courses, there was little faculty recourse except to request a teaching schedule that did not include FYC or the corequisite form of the course. The CUNY-wide changes would no longer be subject to local adaptations. Individual CUNY campuses would no longer have the authority to devise their own system for interpreting placement based on the PI, nor would campuses be allowed to generate their own versions of the PI. Because CUNY is a centralized system in which students often take classes on different campuses throughout their educational careers, the PI benefits students by standardizing placement determinations that had historically varied widely at the developmental level. Because placement via the PI is consistent across campuses, CUNY has not been part of national experiments in directed self-placement, as the new system does not allow for local interpretations by faculty or by students.

In contrast to the very practical concerns of the faculty in our college who teach developmental and FYC courses, members of the CUNY-wide WDC (Writing Discipline Council) focused on the potential for PI placement to create a more socially just FYC ecosystem for CUNY students. At the monthly meetings of the 18-member body—composed of WPAs and course coordinators from across the system—most attendees expressed relief that the complex and expensive internal

CUNY mechanisms for testing incoming students' writing ability via the CATW test would fade away and be replaced with a new approach to placement. A strong percentage of the WDC was familiar with changes to placement already afoot in other parts of the country and was excited that this change was coming to our system and understood, and believed, what research demonstrated about the racist, oppressive patterns perpetuated by placement via testing. Perhaps the difference in perspective between WDC members and the community of FYC teachers at KCC can be attributed to the fact that, as is true at many TYCs nationally, the majority of faculty who teach writing at KCC do not have professional disciplinary identities in a writing studies field (Del Principe, 2020). While they have spent most of their careers teaching writing, they identify as literary scholars or creative writers in the professional work they produce outside the classroom. While WDC members were generally in favor of the shift to placement via the PI, they recognized that major changes in placement would result in major changes in the administration and structure of FYC programs and anticipated the significant work that would be necessary to grow, redesign, and eliminate various different parts of their campus' writing sequence.

Outcomes

From our current perspective one year into the transition to CUNY's new placement mechanism, we have begun to see some promising changes for students as a whole and for certain groups of students in particular. Figure 7.4 shows the percentage of incoming students placing into either the highest level of developmental writing or into credit-bearing FYC. In Fall 2017–Fall 2019, on average per semester, 618 students placed into developmental courses and 1,333 students placed into FYC. In Spring–Fall 2020, with the new PI, on average per semester, 222 students placed into developmental courses and 1,936 placed into FYC.

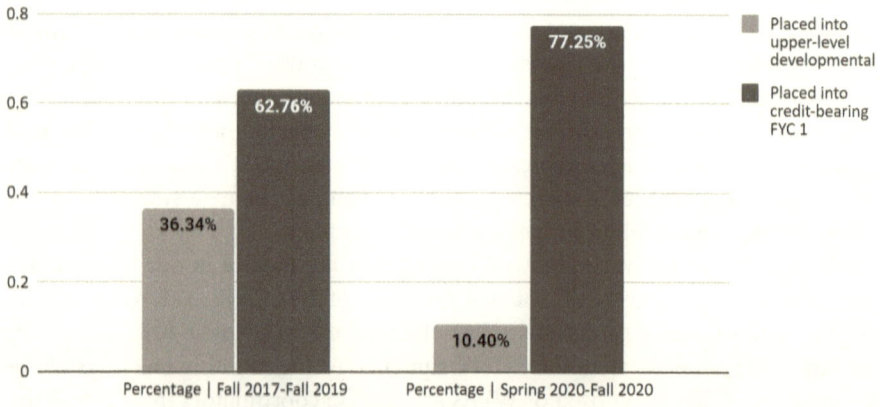

Figure 7.4. Placement pre- and post-Proficiency Index.

Looking more closely, we can see other trends. In comparing both the Spring and Fall 2020 placements (using the new PI) to those from 2018–2019 (using the former CATW & ACCUPLACER placement), we can see that many more incoming first-semester students are placing into a credit-bearing English course—either a corequisite or regular section of FYC—as a result of the new PI. The first semester the PI was used to determine placement in English—Spring 2020 (placement population $n=646$)—there was a slight jump in the percentage of students placing directly into FYC (from 50.2% to 52.5%), and there was a sizable increase in the percentage placing into our coreq/ALP course (from 4.95% to 16.7%). This resulted in an overall change in spring placement into credit-bearing English from 55.15% to 69.2%—a 14.05% increase—for incoming students and led to an explosion in sections of our coreq course offerings as this shift resulted in 80 more students placing into our coreq courses.

While the spring placement shift is certainly significant, the bulk of incoming students enter our college in fall semesters, and Fall 2020 (placement population $n=1,744$) is when we saw the true extent of the new PI's effect on placement into credit-bearing English courses. Even with the national decrease in enrollment in Fall 2020 due to the COVID-19 pandemic, we experienced a significant 17.6 percent overall increase in placement into FYC for incoming students in Fall 2020 as compared to Fall 2018/2019. Further, there was even more growth in the percentage of incoming students placing directly into FYC (from 64.2% in Fall 2018/2019 to 72.9% in Fall 2020) and a parallel jump in coreq placements (from 3.6% in Fall 2018/2019 to 12.4% in Fall 2020), resulting in even more relative growth for our coreq course.

While we know that more incoming students overall are now placing into FYC, are all student groups benefiting equally from this new placement mechanism? When we look closely at the disaggregated placement percentages from Spring and Fall 2020, we can see that several racial/ethnic groups appear to have benefitted from the PI. In particular, White, Black, and Asian students all had noticeably and similarly higher placement rates into FYC than those same groups had in the previous year. In Spring 2020, 21.8 percent more White students, 16.2 percent more Black students, and 12 percent more Asian students placed into FYC (Figure 7.5), and those increases in placement resulted in larger numbers of these students placing into FYC that semester (Figure 7.6). Figure 7.5 shows the rates at which different student groups placed into FYC in Spring 2019 and 2020. Figure 7.6 shows the total numbers of students in different groups placing into FYC in Spring 2019 and 2020.

The parallel statistics for Fall 2020 tell a somewhat similar story, with 22.7 percent more Asian students, 19.4 percent more Black students, and 15.8 percent more White students placing into FYC (Figure 7.7), which created a somewhat different demographic mix of students in credit-bearing English than in previous semesters (Figure 7.8). Hispanic students, too, have benefited from greater placement into FYC via the PI, but their placement percentage hasn't increased as much as other groups. The reality is that a relatively higher percentage of incoming Hispanic students had previously been placing into FYC via the former placement tests (Figures

7.5 and 7.7), and their more modest increases in placement via the PI bring their numbers into line with placement for other groups (Figure 7.8). Figure 7.7 shows the rates at which different student groups placed into FYC in Fall 2019 and 2020. Figure 7.8 shows the total numbers of students in different groups placing into FYC in Spring 2019 and 2020.

Given the complexities of multiple measures placement for BIPOC students, we're encouraged to see that, so far, the CUNY PI has resulted in a greater and more equitable and racially representative cohort of students in FYC. Because placement that relies heavily on high school GPA has been shown to have negative differential impact for Black students and because high school GPA is the factor most heavily weighed in the PI algorithm, we were concerned that we might see greater patterns of inequity in placement for these students (Scott-Clayton & Stacey, 2015). In our case, it seems that CUNY's inclusion of other factors in the PI and KCC's comparatively high rate of traditionally aged college students mitigated the problems caused in other systems by the dominant use of high school GPA as a placement indicator.

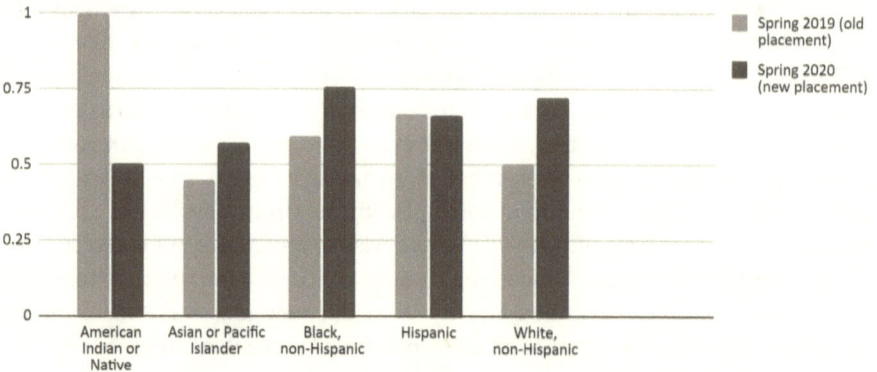

Figure 7.5. Spring placement into FYC, disaggregated percentages.

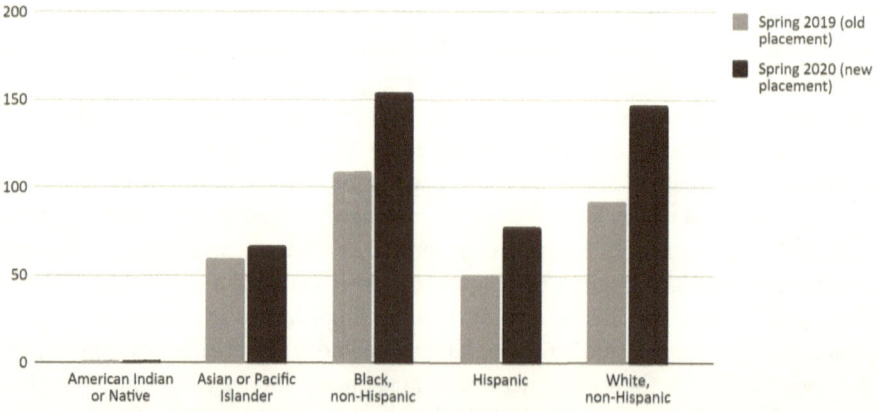

Figure 7.6. Spring placement into FYC, disaggregated population totals.

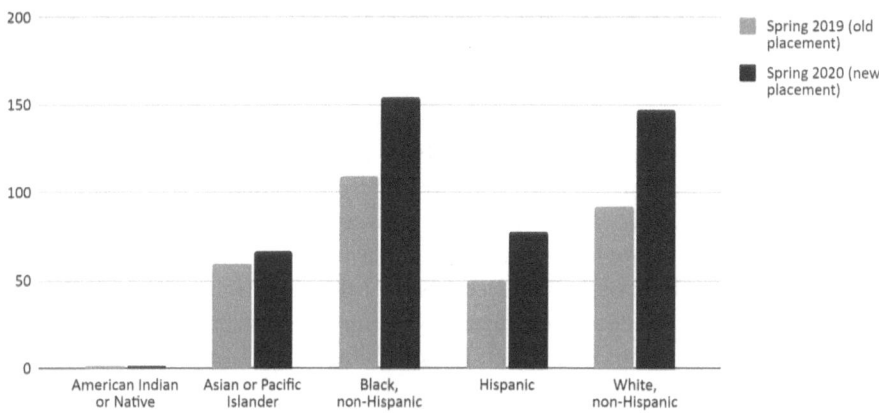

Figure 7.7. Fall placement into FYC, disaggregated percentages.

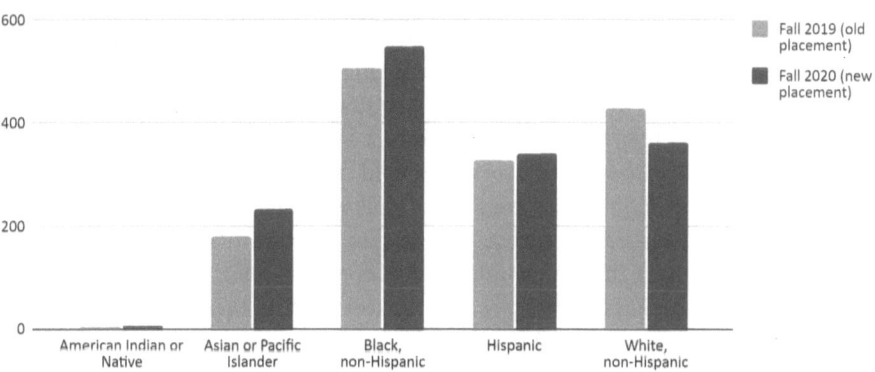

Figure 7.8. Fall placement into FYC, disaggregated enrollment totals.

Consequences

CUNY's overhaul of placement policies radically altered the nature of the KCC English department by eliminating the long pipeline to reach credit-bearing FYC. In Spring 2013, when ALP was first piloted in our department, we offered seven different developmental-level courses, not including ESL offerings and the externally run CUNY Start program, amounting to over 100 sections of classes that enrolled close to 2,000 students. By the Spring 2021 semester, the first full year after the PI was instituted, only seven developmental sections of a single course remain, and CUNY is encouraging KCC to eliminate it completely. Instead of these developmental courses, roughly 30 sections of an ALP-style corequisite FYC course were offered, serving between 250 and 300 students. The new structure means that hundreds of students who would have placed into the lowest level of remediation will be moved to the pre-semester, intensive CUNY Start, providing students the opportunity to place into ALP or regular FYC during their first semester in college.

An unexpected outcome of the implementation of the PI and the vacuum of developmental courses has been a shift in administrative job responsibilities. Due to the awkward configuration of the corequisite ALP course on the school's scheduling system, the ALP coordinator's position had been filled with clerical tasks, drafting schedule spreadsheets, verifying course information was presented correctly, updating and collecting contracts from students, and distributing information to advisors. As the program grew and the course was administratively reconfigured, providing resources and workshops for new ALP faculty now comprise the bulk of the required labor. At the same time, as the number of developmental classes decreased, faculty who managed the hundreds of sections of developmental courses found their responsibilities distributed to other administrative duties in the department or reallocated to teaching a full load of courses.

Lessons

Like so many TYCs across the country, Kingsborough has learned that its previous approach to determining which students may enroll in FYC—giving them a writing test—resulted in much less racially equitable and less racially valid access to credit-bearing English. The previous direct testing approach, which seemed commonsensical to most faculty, served to hold decades of students, and a higher percentage of BIPOC students, back from making meaningful progress toward their degrees and served to segregate them into an educational holding pattern or limbo from which too few would ever successfully exit. Instead of evaluating qualities of students' writing as a means of placing them, relying on their past behavior patterns as high school students, as evidenced in their high school GPAs, among other factors, has created cohorts of students in our FYC classrooms that more closely resemble the demographic makeup of students who enroll in our school. While Holly Hassel and Joanne Baird Giordano (Gilman et al., 2019) were wise to warn of the dangers of relying on high school GPA for placement of returning adult students, the fact that KCC's entering first-year students tend to skew young, with 60.1 percent under 22 years old, means that the vast majority of our students attended high school in New York City and have local, relatively recent, educational records, making this placement approach a good match for our population.

CUNY's new approach to placement relies on the probability that the constellation of habits and behaviors that students used to succeed in high school will allow them to succeed as college writers, too, and this is one important result that we cannot yet evaluate. Because our institution's shift in placement policy overlapped with the nation's urgent shift into remote schooling due to the COVID pandemic, student grade outcomes data from Spring and Fall 2020 are hopelessly confounded. It is impossible to tease the "COVID effect" out of the pass and grade rates, for example, from those semesters to try to gauge how students placed by the PI fared in FYC because their performance was so utterly influenced by the full shift to schooling and living from home while still working, caregiving, grieving, and attempting to stay healthy. As time moves forward and the COVID emergency recedes over the next few semesters, we will watch pass and performance rates in our FYC courses quite closely to see how students—on the whole, and BIPOC students in particular—are faring in the course.

Perhaps most interestingly, this shift in placement forces our English department and writing program to confront several key questions: What is good writing? What does success in a writing course look like? What should it look like, in order to be fair and valid? And are those the same things? Before the shift to the PI, our writing program had already begun to work with a large committee of faculty to rethink and redesign our courses in light of the sea change toward antiracist scholarship, pedagogy, and assessment in writing studies. This work had already started to inspire faculty to question many of their deeply held beliefs about what "good writing" in college might look like and what the structural function of a course like FYC might be in the larger educational and social justice ecosystem of a diverse TYC in a large urban center. By placing a larger percentage of BIPOC students directly into their FYC classes rather than filtering them through a complex mechanism of developmental courses, the PI has forced these faculty to recalibrate their own understandings of what they are trying to teach and assess in their classes and how that may, or may not, serve their students well. As our department and college absorb the shift from restrictive gatekeeping to gate-opening, the college itself must examine and revise the ways it assesses and supports student success for a more fair and just society.

Acknowledgments

We'd like to acknowledge the support of Kingsborough's Office of Institutional Effectiveness (OIE) in providing us with data to help illuminate patterns in disaggregated placement information for our students. That data wasn't easy to locate, and our OIE thought outside the box to generate it for us.

References

AB 705: The Law & Your Rights. (n.d.). https://ab705.org/what-is-the-law.
CUNY. (2018, October 26). CUNY English Summit. Borough of Manhattan Community College–CUNY. New York, NY, United States.
CUNY. (2019, November 14). Frequently asked questions OAA-19-01: CUNY developmental education policy changes. https://www.cuny.edu/academics/academic-policy/dev-ed-faq/.
CUNY, Office of Assessment/Office of Academic Affairs. (2012). CUNY assessment test in writing (CATW). http://www.cuny.edu/wp-content/uploads/sites/4/page-assets/academics/testing/cuny-assessment-tests/test-preparation-resources/CATWInformationforStudentsandpracticeweb.pdf.

CUNY Taskforce on Developmental Education. (2016, June 1). Report of the CUNY task force on developmental education. https://www.cuny.edu/wp-content/uploads/sites/4/page.

Del Principe, A. (2020). Cultivating a sustainable TYC writing program: Collaboration, disciplinarity, and faculty governance. *WPA: Writing Program Administration*, 43(3), 54–72.

Gilman, H., Giordano, J. B., Hancock, N., Hassel, H., Henson, L., Hern, K., Nastal, J. & Toth, C. (2019). Forum: Two-year college writing placement as fairness. *Journal of Writing Assessment*, 12(1). http://journalofwritingassessment.org/article.php?article=139.

Jaggars, S. S. & Hodara, M. (2011). *The opposing forces that shape developmental education: Assessment, placement, and progression at CUNY community colleges* (CCRC Working Paper No. 36). Community College Research Center, Teachers College, Columbia University. https://ccrc.tc.columbia.edu/media/k2/attachments/opposing-forces-shape-developmental.pdf.

Kingsborough Office of Institutional Effectiveness. (2019a). *KCC Fall 2019 at a glance*. https://www.kbcc.cuny.edu/irap/documents/IP2019/2019KBCCataGlance.pdf.

Kingsborough Office of Institutional Effectiveness. (2019b). *National origin countries of birth second language background*. https://www.kbcc.cuny.edu/irap/documents/IP2019/NationalOrigin.pdf .

Koretz, D. & Langi, M. (2018). Predicting freshman grade-point average from test scores: Effects of variation within and between high schools. *Educational Measurement: Issues & Practice*, 37(2), 9–19. https://doi.org/10.1177/2332858416670601.

Rose, M. (1985). The language of exclusion: Writing instruction at the university. *College English*, 47(4), 341–359.

Scott-Clayton, J., Crosta, P. M. & Belfield, C. R. (2014). Improving the targeting of treatment: Evidence from college remediation *Educational Evaluation and Policy Analysis*, 36(3), 371–393. https://doi.org/10.3102/0162373713517935.

Scott-Clayton, J. & Stacey, W. G. (2015). *Improving the accuracy of remedial placement*. Community College Research Center, Teachers College, Columbia University. http://ccrc.tc.columbia.edu/media/k2/attachments/improving-accuracy-remedial-placement.pdf.

Shaughnessy, M. P. (1977). *Errors and expectations: A guide for the teacher of basic writing*. Oxford University Press.

Sternglass, M. S. (1997). *Time to know them: A longitudinal study of writing and learning at the college level*. Lawrence Erlbaum Associates.

Traub, J. (1994). *City on a hill: Testing the American dream at City College*. Da Capo Press.

Chapter 8. Mind the (Linguistic) Gap: On "Flagging" ESL Students at Queensborough Community College

Charissa Che
QUEENSBOROUGH COMMUNITY COLLEGE

Abstract: Across City University of New York (CUNY) campuses, less than half of students assigned to developmental courses have finished them by the end of their first year. In response, CUNY began implementing placement reforms in Spring 2020: Instead of a placement test, students are now evaluated based on their Proficiency Index (PI) score, which considers their high school GPA, and SAT and Regents scores. Further, first-year students who have spent at least six months in an institution where English is not the primary language would be "flagged" as potential ESL students. This definition of an "ESL student" excludes those who have only attended school in the U.S., yet may still need supplemental English instruction. Placement reforms strive to close racial gaps; however, the multiple measures used to determine students' placement are still rooted in Standard English ideologies. The stakes for this shortcoming are high at Queensborough Community College (QCC), one of the most diverse two-year campuses in the nation. This chapter argues that amid reforms, we should problematize how we regard "ESL students." QCC students' PI scores and final grades demonstrate the broader efficacy of the reforms, and interviews with the ESL Discipline Council reveal ongoing efforts to reform ESL student placement. Students and English faculty provide first-hand insight on their experiences with the placement process, and in their English classes. With additional guidance from second-language writing literature, this piece demonstrates the need to reconsider the complexities of "ESL student" identities for more equitable writing placement.

To create more equitable educational opportunities, two-year colleges have been increasingly moving away from standardized placement tests as a way to determine an incoming student's "college readiness." Across City University of New York (CUNY)[1] campuses, less than half of students assigned to developmental courses have finished them by the end of their first year (CUNY Task Force on Developmental Education, 2016), and African American and Hispanic students are almost twice as likely as their White and Asian peers to be assigned to developmental education (Office of Academic Affairs [OAA], 2020b).

---

1. Unless a specific CUNY campus is specified, "CUNY" will refer to the university system as a whole, and will be used interchangeably with "CUNY Central" and "the university."

CUNY began implementing placement reforms in Spring 2020. Instead of a placement test, students who do not meet benchmark scores on the SATs, ACTs, or New York State Regents exam are now evaluated based on their *Proficiency Index* score, which takes into consideration any relevant and available high school exit scores, such as overall high school GPA and subject-specific SAT and Regents scores. (The Regents are administered to seniors in New York State high schools. They are given in four subjects, including English language arts. Results are used for student high school graduation requirements, school quality reports, and teacher development and evaluation.) Those who do not meet the target score would be enrolled in either corequisite credit-bearing classes or developmental "interventions" (NYC Department of Education, 2021; OAA, 2019).

The stakes for these reforms are high at Queensborough Community College (QCC), one of the most diverse colleges in CUNY, and the nation. The CUNY Office of Institutional Research (OIR) breaks down the ethnic and racial backgrounds of all QCC students:

> Twenty-nine percent of all degree and certificate seeking students—national and international—were Hispanic, 28 percent were Asian or Pacific Islander, 28 percent were Black, and 14 percent were White.... Asian or Pacific Islander students make up a larger percentage of the non-degree population, standing at 38 percent for Fall 2019. (OIR, 2020)

QCC students come from 123 countries and speak 79 different languages. Twenty-two percent were born outside the United States and have come from every continent of the world, except Antarctica. Students of color are more likely to experience the negative effects of assessment given rigid institutional requirements (Poe et al., 2014), and what's more, this disparity is even more apparent in community colleges. QCC students demonstrate the need to examine the complexities of student identities in relation to writing placement practices—given that country of birth, being multilingual, or speaking English as a second language in and of themselves do not necessarily signal a particular linguistic proficiency.

The Office of Academic Affairs (OAA) determined that first-year applicants who have spent at least six months in an institution where English is not the primary language would be "flagged" and receive an "ESL indicator." While the Developmental Education Task Force has moved away from standardized testing for all incoming students, the ESL Discipline Council voted to continue using the standardized CUNY Assessment Test in Writing (CAT-W) for "flagged" students, "while it works with OAA (the Office of Academic Affairs) to develop better ESL placement tools" (OAA, 2019).[2]

---

2. The term "ESL" can be problematic in referring to students in that it may suggest an inherent deficiency in English, or an inferiority to their English as a first language (EFL) peers. However, for the purposes of this chapter, the term "ESL" will be used in line with

Unfortunately, before these new placement plans could be implemented and their effectiveness measured, the COVID-19 pandemic arrived, and New York City schools moved to remote learning. Incoming Spring 2020 first-year students have not been able to take their in-person Regents exam in high school, so their Proficiency Index would rely solely on their SAT scores and/or high school GPAs. "Flagged" ESL students would have even fewer materials to determine their placement, especially if they also lack a domestic high school GPA. Whereas "flagged" students who don't meet the benchmark scores of these entrance exams would have taken the in-person CAT-W, or the CUNY Assessment Test in Writing, for ESL course placement, the exam was replaced with the last-minute creation of the online ESL Diagnostic assessment, or the ESL-D. Importantly, Linda Evangelou, assistant dean for New Student Enrollment Services at QCC, notes that remotely administering the ESL-D in lieu of the CAT-W posed particular difficulties for students facing a linguistic gap. "Testing the ESL students was the population most impacted by COVID-19," she says (L. Evangelou, personal communication, July 9, 2020).

Despite the sizable percentage of students who speak English as a second language, the multiple measures used to determine their Proficiency Index scores are still rooted in standardized English ideologies. Further, statistics can only tell us so much and omit the very tangible experiences of college personnel and students "on the ground"—besides, as of yet, a "breakdown" of CUNY's student population by the university does not correlate those who speak English as a second language with their race/ethnicities or countries of origin. Instead of being considered in conjunction with each other, these factors are measured separately by CUNY, discounting how these backgrounds can work together to shape a student's level of preparedness for first-year writing.

This chapter will examine CUNY's continual efforts to account for incoming students' backgrounds in ESL placement reform by foregrounding the perspectives of administrators and English faculty. Altogether, these perspectives aim to complicate longstanding conceptualizations of "ESL students"—and shed light on the difficulties of establishing placement methods that holistically account for the language competencies of ESL students. (Given my problematization of the "flagging" process, and the problematic negative connotations that can come from "flagging" something or someone, the term will be used in scare quotes throughout this chapter. Similarly, to delineate the use of "ESL" to refer to students themselves from "ESL" as a concept, the term will be in scare quotes when used as a concept.) The hope is that we as instructors, curriculum developers, and administrators may have richer, more nuanced considerations in mind as we move toward devising more equitable writing classroom placement practices that foster academic advancement.

First, this chapter will explain the multiple *exigencies* motivating CUNY's recent placement updates, and their specific implications at QCC, where multilingualism is the norm. Second, I will discuss *the mechanics* of the key placement

---

the language used by CUNY to refer to students who have been "flagged" as "ESL."

routes currently in place by outlining the roadmaps for "non-ESL" students and those "flagged" as "ESL," and providing sample placement exams and sample exit exams from CUNY's developmental programs (see Appendix C). Third, the *efficacy* of these key changes in ESL placement will be examined by analyzing student outcomes data from QCC's Director of Institutional Research and perspectives from administrators and English department faculty. The final section of this chapter will propose *implications of current placement measures* and *potential avenues for improvement* in ESL placement reform going forward.

Exigencies for Placement Reform

For nearly half a century, CUNY has implemented standardized placement exams for all incoming first-year students. These exams would be taken if students did not meet benchmark SAT, Regents, or ACT scores. "This [process] dates back to 1978; we were administering some type of placement/proficiency exam," said CUNY Director of Testing Melissa Uber, referring to the ACCUPLACER reading exam, the CAT-W, and the math proficiency exam. However, she explained that those at the OIR have noted over time that these measures were not necessarily the best predictors of students' "gateway" writing class outcomes. Indeed, misplacement into remediation is much more common than misplacement into college-level courses. The university's Policy Research unit found that a student's high school GPA was often the best indicator of their college success. (M. Uber, personal communication, January 9, 2021; July 9, 2020; OIR, 2019; Scott-Clayton et al., 2014).

After realizing the lack of correlation between placement exams and student outcomes in their first-year composition courses, the university began to research other ways to gauge its incoming students' reading and writing aptitudes. The idea for a *Proficiency Index* (PI) *score* was born: a multiple measures assessment which aims to be a more holistic way of assessing students' readiness for first-year writing classes. The PI score took into consideration high school GPA, English Regents scores, and other relevant student background data for their writing placement. Whereas reading and writing proficiency were separately assessed with the ACCUPLACER and CAT-W exams, respectively, the PI score makes no distinction between the two skills in an incoming student's placement.

In the case of *ESL students*, anticipating outcomes was further complicated given that the CAT-W included culturally specific (American) content that was difficult to grasp for international students, or students who grew up within a different heritage cultural context. To be more considerate of its now-exclusively ESL student test-takers, the CAT-W was slightly revised: The ESL Discipline Council had to approve the readings to assure the content was "ESL sensitive" (not too culturally specific) (D. Rothman, personal communication, January 6, 2021; a sample of the CAT-W and scoring rubric can be found in Appendix C). Pragmatically, ESL placement was difficult because international students and domestic students who have spent time learning abroad often lacked transferrable high school diplomas and did not take the SAT, Regents, or ACT.

Executive vice chancellor and university provost José Luis Cruz explained that these recent placement changes aimed to improve educational equity for CUNY's student body, which largely comprises first-generation students, immigrants, and under-represented communities. "It is especially important that we embrace evidence-based practices that will allow us to better help them meet their full potential," he writes (OAA, 2019). But how equitable is equitable *enough*? Is there a placement measure, or measures, that could adequately account for the myriad variables that could influence an ESL student's success in a writing course? Is it inevitable that some students will slip through the cracks no matter how inclusive the placement method is—and what are the possible implications for ESL students who do not receive the writing instruction they need?

The factors behind a student's English language proficiency are manifold. For one, there is the consideration of *race and ethnicity*. Historically, the QCC student body has been "majority minority"; in other words, it is predominantly non-White. According to the 2019–2020 QCC Factbook, 3,203 first-time freshmen enrolled in Fall 2019. Of these students, 30 percent were Black and non-Hispanic, 30 percent were Hispanic, 22 percent were Asian or Pacific Islander, 11 percent were White or non-Hispanic, six percent were "Nonresident Alien," and one percent were American Indian or Native American (OIR, 2020). While there is no inherent connection between a student's racial or ethnic background and their English proficiency, language education is rooted in histories of white supremacy and colonial expansion—and, as Von Esch et al. (2020) wrote, "Who gets to define what counts as language ultimately shapes the potential of those learning it" (p. 395). They listed several ways in which the two influence and inform each other: 1) standard language ideology and racial hegemony, 2) the idealized native speaker with racial labeling, 3) racial hierarchies of languages and language speakers, 4) racialization and teacher identity, and 5) race-centered approaches to pedagogies and educational practices (Von Esch et al., 2020, p. 397). Language teaching and race are inextricable, and while our first-year writing pedagogies are moving away from racist epistemologies, it remains that many of our assessment practices still evaluate students' English proficiency in light of its "standardness" (see: proximity to Whiteness).

What's more, a student's *linguistic background* complicates place-based assumptions of English linguistic proficiency. While QCC freshmen came from 62 and 75 different countries in Fall 2018 and Fall 2019, respectively, the vast majority of QCC students were born in the US, are New York City residents, and live in Queens (OIR, 2020; a more thorough breakdown of student demographics starting from Fall 2016 can be found in Appendix A). Indeed, most QCC freshmen are first-generation Americans and children of immigrants from non-White countries, which often means they speak a language other than English at home, and/or speak a language other than English as a first language. The most recent data shows that over 35 percent of Fall 2018 freshmen speak a language other than English at home; Spanish, Chinese, Bengali, Creole, and Urdu were the most prevalent non-English languages among freshmen.

Whether a student has spent at least six months at a non-English-speaking institution—the "flagging" criterion for a potential ESL student—arguably does not account for the above considerations. This criterion conflates various culturally informed approaches to English instruction abroad and overlooks their potential efficacy. Further, it excludes domestic students who have only attended school in the US yet may still need supplemental English instruction, as well as students who have experienced domestic diaspora across locations in which English is not the primary language.

Roadmaps for Placement

The roadmaps in Figure 8.1 and Figure 8.2 have been constructed based on information in the September 4, 2019, OAA Academic Policy Brief, "Policy for the Use of CUNY's Proficiency Index in Developmental Education Assignments." The first roadmap outlines the placement process for ALL incoming students (ESL or otherwise), and the second displays the trajectory for those "flagged" as potential ESL students. (For explanations of relevant key terms as they pertain to the conversation surrounding student placement in QCC, and CUNY broadly, see Appendix B.)

Note how the writing placement trajectory varies significantly between those who are "flagged" as potential ESL students (Figure 8.2) and those who are not (Figure 8.1). Given that the ESL Discipline Council is still in the process of honing their procedures, Figure 8.2 is more nuanced, allowing students to be placed in credit-bearing courses by multiple measures.

As shown in Figure 8.2, "flagged" ESL students can still be placed into a matriculated first-year writing class: If their English SAT and Regents exams scores meet the appropriate benchmarks, they would be assigned a PI score and conform to the placement process of their non-ESL-"flagged" peers. However, if they do *not* meet the benchmarks, they would be required to take the ESL-D, or the ESL-Diagnostic Assessment, and be placed into an ESL program recommended by the college. (For a list of developmental and interventional coursework open to these students, see Appendix B.) Created to replace the CAT-W in the wake of the COVID-19 pandemic and a lack of access to in-person testing facilities, the ESL-D was given to incoming students as of Fall 2020 if they were "flagged" as potential ESL students (see Appendix D for a sample ESL-D; Office of the Executive Vice Chancellor and University Provost, 2020).

The timed, online assessment comprises two sections: The first asks students to read a passage and write an essay that explains the passage's "main point," give an explanation for why they believe this is the "main point," and draw connections between the passage and their personal experiences and/or prior knowledge. The second section is a take on directed self-placement: A survey asks students to consider the ease with which they were able to complete the first section; describe the type of English language instruction they have previously received; assess their level of comfort with reading, writing, listening, and speaking in English; and gauge which skills they believe they need instruction on. Professor David Rothman explains that a few amendments have been made to the ESL-D:

> For Spring 2021 ESL Diagnostic testing, students no longer have a 2–3-day window to complete their writing sample. Once they start the test, they have two hours to complete the task. Also, the student survey, which is included with the writing sample, has been broadened to give the placement team more info about the students' experience with academic English. (personal communication, January 6, 2021).

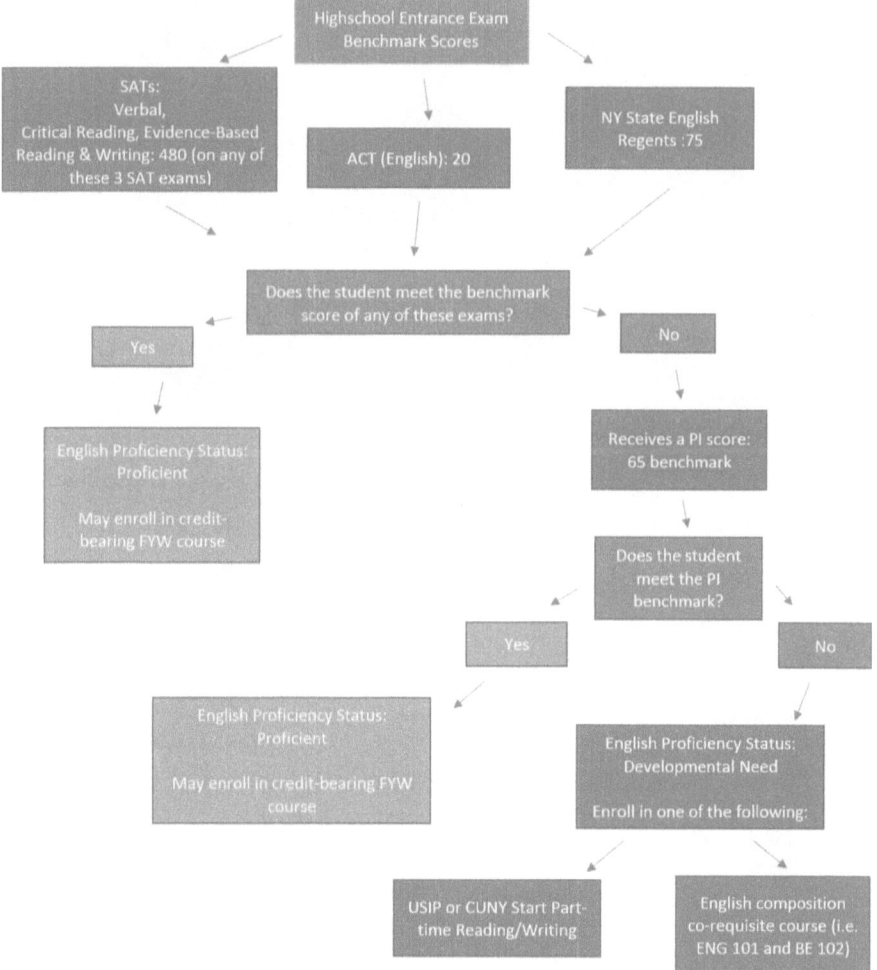

Figure 8.1. Flowchart outlining the placement process for ALL incoming students.

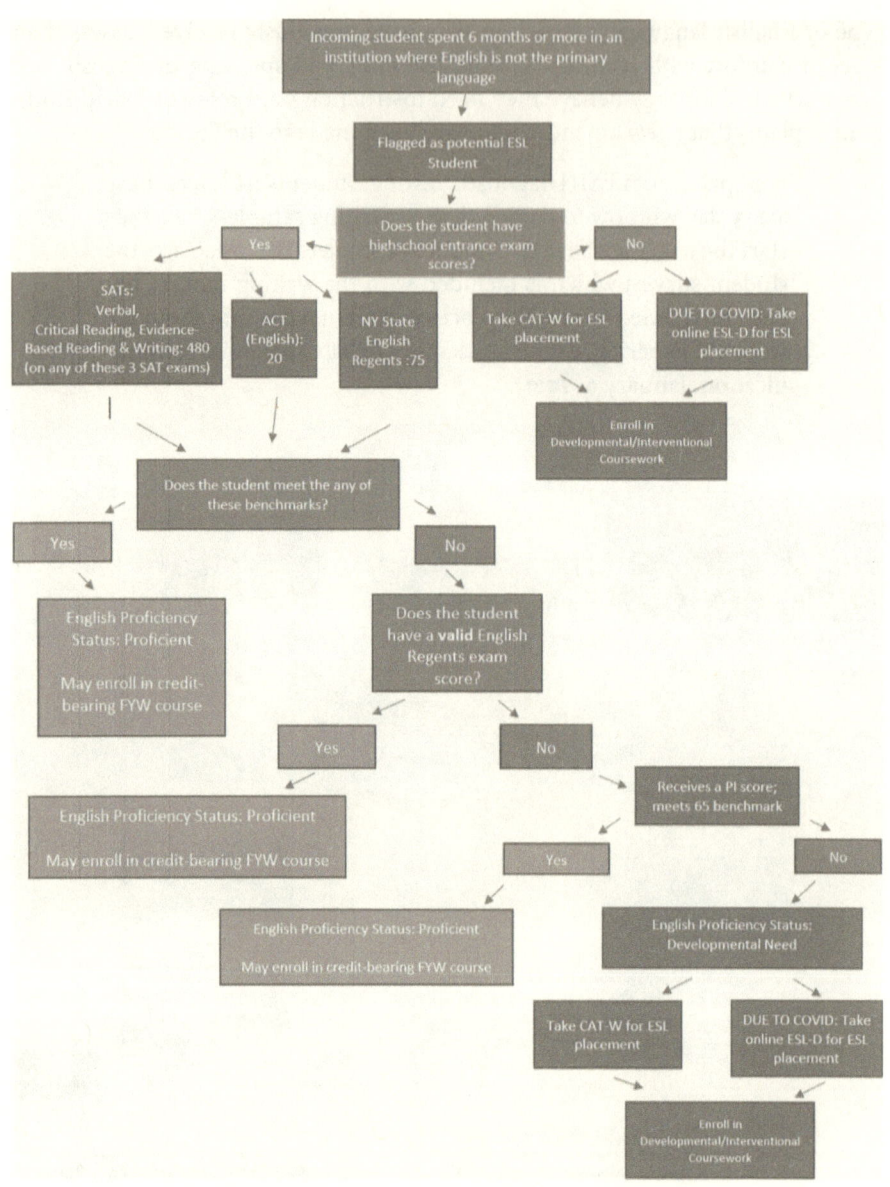

Figure 8.2. Flowchart for the students who have been "flagged" as potential ESL students.

Efficacy of New ESL Placement Protocols

Student Outcomes Data: Comparing Pass Rates Between NES and NNES Students

In Table 8.1, Elisabeth Lackner, the Director of Institutional Research and Assessment at QCC's OIR, has provided aggregated data for the ENGL 101 pass/completion rates of "Native English Speakers" (NES) and "Non-Native English Speakers" (NNES) respectively, for the semesters of Spring 2019 through Fall 2020. The outcomes of Spring 2019 and Fall 2019 (pre-PI) are compared with those of Spring 2020 and Fall 2020 (post-PI) to note any differences in outcomes before and after CUNY's new placement changes. Students receiving a grade of A to D- have passed;[3] students may also opt in for No Credit (NC): This option was developed in the wake of the pandemic and is available to passing students whose grade can nonetheless severely damage their overall GPA. The percentages of enrolled NES and NNES students who passed ENGL 101 are provided for each term.

Table 8.1. ENGL 101 Pass/Completion Rates of NES and NNES From Spring 2019–Fall 2020 (Counting all grades of A to D-, including CR* as passing)

	NES Students		NNES Students	
	% Enrolled	Pass Rates	% Enrolled	Pass Rates
Spring 2019	52.0%	64.0%	19.5%	72.4%
Fall 2019	66.8%	67.1%	23.1%	74.2%
Spring 2020	53.7%	55.0%	33.0%	69.9%
Fall 2020	63.1%	52.8%	27.6%	59.5%

* Students receiving a passing grade can elect to receive a CR (Credit). CR allows students to enroll in subsequent classes and is neutral in the student's GPA.

Perhaps due to similar challenges faced from COVID and the new PI, there is a significant drop in pass rates for both student groups since the placement updates were implemented in Spring 2020—for NES, the difference is up to 14.3 percent, and for NNES, it is 14.7 percent. For both groups, pass rates are the lowest they have been in Fall 2020. Not shown, but as expected given QCC's student demographics, most of enrolled NES students were non-White; the percentage of White NES enrolled in Spring 2019 and Fall 2019 was 6.7 percent and 9.4 percent, respectively, and in Spring 2020 and Fall 2020, six percent and 9.2 percent, respectively.

---

3. However, those receiving a C- or below would not be able to transfer their credits to another CUNY college.

However, the data also shows that regardless of semester, NNES students on the whole performed better than their NES peers. While the factors for these differences cannot be drawn from this data alone, the diverse linguistic backgrounds, countries of origin, race, and ethnicities of incoming QCC students beg the question of which students have *not* been "flagged" as ESL via CUNY's six-month criteria yet could have benefitted from supplemental NNES support, given that the pass rates for the latter group are consistently higher.

This disparity demonstrates the need to develop placement methods that go beyond the dichotomy of "native" versus "non-native" English speakers and to think about finer student distinctions; otherwise, we risk perpetuating the inequities our reforms seek to resolve in the first place.

Administrative Standpoints: Comparing the CAT-W with the ESL-D

Although quantitative data can give us a cursory view of the overall success rates of ESL and non-ESL students, first-hand perspectives from QCC administrators and faculty can contextualize this data and help us understand the factors that have possibly influenced student outcomes. For instance, given a rift between CUNY Central and individual CUNY campuses on how to best adjust to the move to online placement, Evangelou recalls facing conflicts of interest. In March 2020, her office crafted a "local business practice" based on directed self-placement for ESL students to address the lack of on-site testing. However, the practice was scrapped when the university decided that all CUNY colleges should wait until a CUNY-wide practice was developed. "It was frustrating because we had over 200 students who had matriculated and were waiting for direction," says Evangelou (L. Evangelou, personal communication, July 9, 2020).

When the university notified ESL students that they had to take the ESL-D in mid-June 2020, there was still not a system in place for how it would be assessed. A lack of communication between CUNY Central and its campuses in turn led to a communicative disconnect between the campuses and their students. "Locally we did not have much information on the process and the launch seemed very hurried. We were inundated with calls from students saying they took the test, 'Now what?' We had no answer," recalls Evangelou, adding that because the onus was on QCC to answer students' questions, students often saw these shortcomings as stemming from the college itself, rather than the university as a whole (L. Evangelou, personal communication, July 9, 2020). An assessment system was ultimately established: Students' ESL-D essays would not be scored; instead, they would be evaluated, and alongside their metacognitive survey responses in the Diagnostic's second section, administrators would assign "placement milestones" on a student's record and provide recommendations for course placement. As the administrator for running this process at QCC, Rothman and a team of four other CAT-W-certified readers work in Microsoft Teams to evaluate the writing samples of incoming ESL QCC students.

Testing setting aside, a fundamental difference between the CAT-W and ESL-D lies in their structure. As an ESL Discipline Council member, the head of the English department's English language learner committee, and a member of the Proficiency Index implementation team, Rothman explains the methodical process by which the former was administered and scored. He described the CAT-W as a "tightly honed practice" comprising sample essays to norm readers on the evaluation process. Grading would be carried out in a conveyor belt fashion, overseen by a chief reader: When a CAT-W essay would receive similar scores from first and second readers, a third reader would review and re-score the given essay. Further, if one reader passed an essay and the other didn't, a third reader would break the tie. In contrast to this systematic process, only one reader evaluates each ESL-D student essay, which presents a greater chance of reader bias and limits the areas of expertise that multiple readers would otherwise lend to the process (D. Rothman, personal communication, January 6, 2021).

Furthermore, the CAT-W provided fewer opportunities for students to plagiarize or receive outside help, as students were required to take it at a CUNY testing center with proctors enforcing protocol. Because it is taken at home, the ESL-D cannot be as strictly enforced. Students are free to consult friends, family members, and the internet for help. Google Translate, for one, can be used as a workaround to write an essay in an unfamiliar language. "When this happens, you're not getting a valid placement," says Rothman. For him, a student's level of English competency is more accurately measured when writing is done in a controlled setting, away from any opportunities to consult outside help. Still, circumstances considered, the protocol does the job for now: "I'm glad that we're doing something rather than nothing," he says, adding that on the plus side, the looser protocol of the ESL-D makes for much more efficient evaluations; a scorer may read up to 15–18 essays in an hour (D. Rothman, personal communication, January 6, 2021).

Since its establishment, changes have been made to the ESL-D to curb the possibility of plagiarism and the use of outside help. As of Spring 2021, students no longer have a two to three-day window to complete their ESL-D writing sample. Instead, they have two hours to complete the task, in one sitting. Additionally, the student survey portion of the diagnostic has been broadened to give the placement team more information about the students' experience with academic English. Yet, some challenges linger. The time it took to launch the ESL-D meant matriculated students waited months before being able to be advised and registered. To date, ESL students who deferred their enrollment have not been contacted to take the test. As placement milestones could not be given to already-admitted students, a separate system needed to be created to place them.

Faculty, on the Merits of "Flagging" Criteria

It is important to note that discussing the efficacy of CUNY's Spring 2020 placement reforms inextricably considers *the new placement procedures themselves* and their *timing*—the move to online learning (namely, the learning management system Blackboard) during a pandemic. This intersection of circumstances means the "root" cause of any changes in student outcomes cannot easily be attributed to one specific factor. With this in mind, QCC English faculty reflected on key factors that may have impacted their ESL students' performance before and after Spring 2020. These ranged from a lack of peer and faculty interaction, the lack of non-verbal cues, the lack of urgency yet greater flexibility that came with asynchronous classwork, limited access to necessary technology, and general life circumstances (Che, 2023). In evaluating the efficacy of the ESL "flagging" process, some key themes were found in faculty responses: the need for us to move beyond place-based assumptions of a student's ESL status, to consider students' multiple language proficiencies, and to not think of a "passing" exit score as synonymous with English proficiency.

For some faculty, the shortcoming of the six-month criteria came in its assumptions of a student's English proficiency based on place of instruction. Madi S.[4] thinks that the flagging rule is fine "in theory"; however, "many times students can be ELL even if they have attended an English speaking school." Factors such as diaspora and generationality challenge educational locality as a sole determinant of English proficiency. Though CLIP Instructor Anthony Prato agrees that any student who has spent at least six months in a non-English learning environment should be flagged as an ESL student, he believes the criteria should be expanded (personal communication, April 22, 2021). "This ... guideline likely missed many Generation 1.5 students," he says. "If a student moves from China to NYC at age 13, and then completes 4 years of high school, I imagine this student would not be labeled as an 'ESL student.' In fact, he/she could have easily graduated [from] a typical NYC high school without the English skills necessary for even basic community college courses." The flagging criteria overlooks students who have largely or only been educated domestically in English-speaking contexts, yet may still need supplemental English instruction. A student who has only studied in an English-speaking context can be just as prepared—or unprepared—for first-year writing as a student who has studied in a non-English speaking context.

Other faculty believe students' rich linguistic backgrounds are not adequately accounted for in the placement process. Corona points out that "fully bilingual students ... may present as ESL," and that they may in fact be proficient in English. Considering a student's linguistic background also means taking into account the possibility that they have more than one first language and may therefore possess what Suresh Canagarajah (2006) deemed a "poliliterate orientation to writing"; these students would be "simultaneously bilingual" or multilingual (pp. 583, 587).

Just as a student can be proficient in multiple languages at once, merely identifying a student as ESL does not account for the level, or type, of additional English instruction they need. "[The flagging criteria] does not address the depth

---

4. Pseudonym

of the student's unfamiliarity with English," says Emanuele. A student's "depth" of English language knowledge can also be undetectable when looking at high school exit exam scores: Passing does not necessarily mean proficient. Rothman asks, "What about ELL students who struggle through an American high school experience, but manage to pass with decent enough grades to avoid an ESL placement?" Gina makes a distinction between the accuracy of high school exit exams and a college's own placement methods in determining an ESL student's rightful English proficiency. "Some leave high school with passing Regents scores, but cannot read and write well, especially not at the college level," she says, adding that these students have a greater chance of failing English 101. A rift between high school exit procedures and college entrance exams can often lead to the misplacement of students in ESL courses, given that collaborations between secondary and post-secondary institutions are often absent during students' transition to college. Even though the Accelerated Learning Program (ALP) was conceived to mitigate the learning gaps this rift presents, it has often served to merely shift the locus of failure to these classes. (Since the implementation of the ESL-D, many of Rothman's ESL students have continued to excel; however, he is noticing an increase in lower-performing ESL students in his remedial ALP classes.)

Jacobowitz took issue with the flagging criteria given the psychic effects being "flagged" can have on a student. "I don't know if this 'flagging' makes students feel singled out in a bad way or in a helpful way," she says. Diaz, meanwhile, wondered if placing students based on their English proficiency is prudent to begin with. "I worry that ESL students will be placed together and won't have contact with native speakers," she says. While these faculty's concerns do not fit under the main themes found across faculty responses, they signal the need to consider the unseen matters of "flagging"—how students may internalize having been "flagged," similar to the stigma that already surrounds being "ESL," alongside what students may miss if they are placed in an ESL sequence.

Overall, English faculty are well aware that what constitutes an "ESL student"—that is, a student requiring additional English language assistance—is much more complicated than its flagging criteria posits. So we don't unnecessarily place first-year-writing-ready freshmen into interventional courses, we need to cast aside the Eurocentric notion that receiving an English education in a non-English speaking context signals a deficit. Conversely, so that students who do need additional support don't fall through the cracks, we need to adapt more flexible ESL "identifiers" that are not bound by place or exit exam scores, but instead look at a student's multiple language proficiencies, the depth of their English knowledge, and their specific English language competencies and needs.

Conclusion: Implications and Avenues for Improvement

Based on their experiences with placement design and scoring entrance exams, QCC administrators offer suggestions on how current roadblocks to effective ESL student placement could be remedied—as well as efforts currently being made to do so. Alongside moves to streamline exit exams and re-introduce the CAT-W upon the resumption of in-person learning, some key faculty suggestions include: adding a *speaking component* to placement, *giving students more say* in where they should be placed, *being clearer* with incoming students on the intricacies of the placement process, establishing *more accommodating testing conditions,* and *placing less capital* on high school exit scores.

Building on Existing Measures Within the PI, CAT-W, and ESL-D

Flaherty said during a Spring 2021 composition committee meeting that the CUNY Language Immersion Program (CLIP) is working to develop a more streamlined pathway for students who pass the program and move toward matriculation, by standardizing the CLIP exit exam to coincide with classwork, the class final exam, and the ESL-D. Additionally, per an ELL Discipline Council meeting handout from January 2020, the council has expanded its ESL "flagging" process to *potentially* include students who have graduated from a secondary school where the language of instruction is English and who have completed at least one semester in a non-English secondary school environment and those who completed their High School Equivalency Examination (GED, TASC, HiSet) in a language other than English.

ESL placement may revert to familiar protocol soon should in-person classes resume; "[M]y understanding is that the CAT-W will return briefly and will be replaced by another assessment for Fall 22 cohort," Flaherty states. Some instructors point out that the CAT-W had its merits, *but could use a few tweaks*. Rothman believes it is "more accurate" in identifying ESL students than the ESL-D, and Anderst believes its uses could be more flexible—"since it was both a placement exam and an exit exam." Professor J also saw some flaws in the CAT-W, yet also acknowledges its strengths. "The old CAT-W had some false positives for remediation and false negatives for not needing it, but it seemed pretty good," he says. "With that said, it is very hard to disentangle having spent so much time using that line as a marker to objectively say whether it was accurate." If the CAT-W were to be reinstated in what Rothman describes as its "more culturally-sensitive" form, we may be able to observe its efficacy in ESL student placement. However, we would still be conducting this observation through an all-too familiar lens of the CAT-W. The assessment has been in place for so long that instructors don't have another measure by which to assert placement effectiveness. Perhaps it's not enough that we tweak it, as much as we need to overhaul it.

At the composition committee meeting, some English faculty expressed what seemed to be an essential missing piece of the ESL-D: *a speaking component.* "That would be so easy to tell the students apart, non-native student English speaker and a native English speaker," one colleague commented. Leah echoes, "Having a current writing sample alongside an in-person conversation with students about placement would be so great." However, Rothman disagrees, believing a student's oral English proficiency is irrelevant to their readiness for a first-year writing course. "All the benchmarks are based on literacy, reading and writing. So I don't see where the need comes for any oral [component]; it doesn't fit the course," he says. This debate around which English language proficiencies—speaking, reading, writing, and listening—should be factored into the "flagging" equation, and which should be overlooked, is a salient one. If we were not to assess a student's oral proficiency, what information about a student's English competencies that would be useful in the writing class (say, for the purposes of accommodating group work or presentations) might we miss? Conversely, if we test for oral proficiency even if ENGL 101 doesn't teach it, what would be the rationale—to identify ESL *learners* or just overall ESL *individuals*?

Logistically, more considerate testing conditions could better students' performance and not bind them to the stressors of test-taking. If CUNY and QCC were to reinstate standardized exams, Gina says, "they must be fair, and more accommodating. Asking an ESL student to read and respond to a passage in 90 minutes is not always fair."

Furthermore, the PI for some is still lacking, despite its aim to be a more holistic multiple measures replacement for standardized exams. "I think we need more than the CUNY Proficiency Index because grades on the Regents exams are grossly inflated," Gina says. Until the CAT-W is reinstated, Rothman reminds us that a student's test-taking abilities, whether in a high school exit exam or a writing placement measure, do not necessarily reflect their English proficiency. "We should . . . re-evaluate the current system in which some under-prepared ESL students may well place out of taking a writing placement due to their high school grades," he says. "As we all know, sometimes grades reflect effort more so than competence in a skill area." Echoing his previous allusion to the rift between high school exit testing and college placement methods, Rothman touches on a key distinction between the skill of test-taking and the act of reading and writing itself: The latter is something that ESL and non-ESL students alike may struggle with due to time constraints, anxiety, learning disabilities, and other factors, and may not be an accurate indicator of their competency in a subject area.

Fostering Agency and Greater Transparency with Students

Other faculty call for *more transparency* offered to students on their placement options. "At non-CUNY institutions where I've taught, there has also been a category for students who were born in the US, but grew up in a family that spoke a different language at home," says Lago, adding that knowing what languages her students spoke at home would be especially useful in a distance learning environment. In this statement, Lago challenges strict place-based criteria for ESL "flagging" so as to not overlook students born in the United States. For any student who may lack English reading comprehension (and arguably, any incoming student despite English proficiency), Lago says students need to be better informed of what each interventional program entails before entering one. "I think they have to know ahead of time what that placement means," she says. "Unfortunately, students who have weak English language mastery may not understand the structure and requirements of the ALP sequence." As CUNY continues to revise its placement roadmaps, perhaps something in the form of one-on-one consultations with placement administrators, or small orientation courses, could help in clarifying any questions incoming students may have about where they would fall in the placement path—and what course options would be available to them as a result.

Alongside educating students on the placement process, faculty advocate for *more nuanced, agentive placement methods*. Anderst and Diaz believe more credit should be given to students to already be cognizant of where they are on their "college writing readiness." "Most students are aware of their level of proficiency and want to progress at the right pace," Diaz says. "A student's own input is very important," Anderst agrees, adding that a directed self-placement model could enable assessors to gauge students' reading and writing experiences in ways that aren't captured by the fact of having spent time abroad. However, she acknowledges that this "holistic approach" would be costlier to implement.

Their colleagues echo the potential for a more self-determined placement approach, but with a subtler approach, given the uncomfortable and perhaps stigmatizing spotlight that might come from directly inquiring about a student's language competency. Rothman considers "a gentle sort of survey for a 101 course . . . to find out about their languages that they speak." Kathryn[5] concurs, adding that the survey could also ask about students' interests, majors, and what particular topics interest them. "If you find something that students latch onto, they're more likely to engage than if it's something that . . . is just so foreign to them for whatever reason," she explains. "Maybe you can census and say you're thinking of assigning a text and you want to assign something that, you know, will engage them." Asking questions not just about a student's language background, but also their overall interests academically or otherwise, can give instructors a more personalized sense of what class materials and praxis can best engage their students each semester, thus potentially yielding more motivated and effective writing.

Mobilizing ESL Students' Assets in Placement Materials

In interviewing English faculty on what they believe to be some of their ESL students' assets, there was a recurring theme: English instruction in a classroom whose lingua franca is not English can indeed be more rigorous in areas such as academic writing and mechanics than in some English-speaking classrooms. Prato claims that students' prior English training can have beneficial or

---

5. Pseudonym

detrimental implications for their academic success: "Some students have experienced somewhat rigorous academic backgrounds in the past (in their native countries) and these backgrounds better-prepare them for CLIP and college writing in general" (personal communication, April 22, 2021). Rothman notes his ESL students' prior instruction has taught them to prioritize certain skills and topics when they enter the writing classroom:

> Many of my students have strong study habits. They are willing to work hard through the drafting process to produce a stronger final draft. Many of my students place a high value on 'language related' instruction. They do not doubt that they need to improve these skills in order to be successful in college.

These students' personal experiences and ways of thinking can also work to their advantage. Anderst says, "Some of my ESL students have a lot of education from another country and bring to the class experiences and ideas and thinking skills that enrich the papers they write."

Others acknowledge that precisely because their ESL students learned English as a second language, the learning skills they've picked up are more methodical than English instruction in an English-speaking classroom. "Many ESL students have studied English from a structural perspective in the act of acquiring a second language and often have a greater vocabulary around issues of grammar and sentence conventions that make conversations grammatical and structural issues easier to navigate," says ENGL 101 instructor Aliza Atik. ESL students can also be more creative in their prose. "They come up with interesting ways of conveying their ideas, sometimes even poetic," says Jordan Schnieder. Susan Jacobowitz echoes, "I think the strength is in the stories. . . . Sometimes there is an unusual way of stating something that is very poetic." Elise Denbo believes that multilingual students have a rich repertoire of language resources to draw upon, and tapping into it can in fact boost their confidence as writers. "Often . . . ESL students bring the 'flavor' of their language to their writing, using metaphors, terms, figurative language in special ways, bringing the rhythms of their language to the writing of English," she says.

In observing these assets at work in the writing classroom, perhaps we can consider ways to mobilize them in our placement practices. If ESL students have commonly been observed to have regimented studying skills, motivation to rewrite a piece, a definitionally-based understanding of grammar, and "poetic" ways of expressing their thoughts, why not think of ways we can offer them opportunities to demonstrate these skills on the CAT-W, the ESL-D, or their interventional coursework exit exams? "Many appreciate hearing how their voices add to their writing and to the language," Denbo says. Acknowledging the different meaning-making practices of students who have studied in other cultural and linguistic contexts can not only be a more equitable way to place them in writing classes; it can also be empowering and instill in them the belief that the knowledges they have brought with them to U.S. higher education are valuable, and useful.

Instructors, Adapting in the Meantime

It is unclear whether or when placement procedures for incoming QCC (and CUNY, broadly) students will be finalized, and what these procedures would look like. English faculty in the meantime continue to brainstorm ways they can best accommodate the ESL students that have been placed in their classes through their own pedagogies and assessment practices. Corona wishes she could see her students' writing before classes begin, but as things are, she finds a colleague's precursory research on her students potentially helpful: "She goes into CUNY First[6] and looks up information on every student in her classes to get a sense of their placement," she says. "Just getting that information would be helpful in the formation and development of an introductory English course."

As placement reforms continue to be in flux, Prato (personal communication, April 22, 2021) believes faculty should also rethink the *type of writing instruction itself* that we provide ESL students so they can successfully navigate non-academic spaces. "Most ESL students in CLIP speak/write little or no English outside of the classroom environment," he says. "They need to learn the basics of English dialogue in real-life situations.... A non-native speaker ... can 'get by' in an academic environment due to technology," he adds, referring to translation technologies. "But when that person graduates, he/she will unlikely be able to communicate effectively in the real world. What good is it to be able to summarize an article when you cannot even ask someone where the nearest bus stop is located?" Indeed, Prato's call for a more expansive writing curriculum echoes Kip Strasma and Paul Resnick's (1999) emphasis of "literacy" at the two-year college as needing to not only include reading and writing, but also workplace literacies and civic literacies.

CUNY's new placement measures have taught faculty and administrators the difficulties of adapting to an online environment, and the particular challenges they pose to ESL students. Strong stances have been taken on the CAT-W, PI, ESL-D, and the criteria by which potential ESL students are identified. At the same time, the timing of these measures working in concert together leaves many questions unanswered. Former English department chair David Humphries believes it is "too soon to tell" these reforms' effectiveness. And Lago perhaps sums it up best: "Since the placement changes occurred in the midst of the pandemic, it's hard to parse out all the factors that impact a student's success." As the pandemic ebbs and NYC schools begin to move back to in-person learning, we should begin to see which post-Spring 2020 factors—the move to online learning and the new placement measures—coincide with specific ESL student outcomes.

---

6. Online platform used by students to enroll in classes, and by faculty to view course information

Until then, it is our hope that our pre-existing and newly gained knowledge of ESL students' assets, nuanced backgrounds, and challenges can leave us with better guidance on how to fairly determine ESL "flagging" criteria and placement roadmaps. Holly Hassel (2013) stressed the importance of considering two-year college students' intersectional identities as we work toward more equitable teaching and assessment praxes: "Future areas of research must explore how class, race, and other forms of difference disproportionately impact students at two-year campuses and how we can and should address them" (p. 349). By challenging monolithic assumptions of what makes an "ESL student," we may begin to develop more agentive, personal, equitable, and accurate placement protocols for our diverse community college students.

Acknowledgments

To my generous and kind colleagues at the QCC English department and my students.

References

Accelerated Study in Associate Programs (ASAP). (2020). *Counselor's corner.* Queensborough Community College. https://www.qcc.cuny.edu/asap/counselor-Corner.html.

Canagarajah, A. S. (2006). The place of world Englishes in composition: Pluralization continued. *College Composition and Communication, 57*(4), 586–619.

Che, C. (2022). *The challenges posed by COVID to ESL community college students* [Unpublished manuscript]. Department of English, Queensborough Community College.

CUNY Language Immersion Program (CLIP). (n.d.). *Sample CLIP exit exam.* [Unpublished data]. CUNY.

CUNY Language Immersion Program (CLIP). (2018, February 8). *Scoring guidelines for the CLIP essay rubric.* [Unpublished data]. CUNY.

CUNY Task Force on Developmental Education. (2016, June 1). *Report of the CUNY Task Force on Developmental Education.* CUNY. https://www.cuny.edu/wp-content/uploads/sites/4/page-assets/about/administration/offices/undergraduate-studies/developmental-education/Proposed-Recommendations-of-RTF-06.17.16.final.pdf.

Hassel, H. (2013). Research gaps in teaching English in the two-year college. *Teaching English in the Two-Year College, 40*(4), 348–349.

NYC Department of Education. (2021). *NY State high school Regents exams.* https://www.schools.nyc.gov/learning/testing/ny-state-high-school-regents-exams.

Office of Academic Affairs (OAA). (2019, September 4). *Academic policy brief OAA-19-01: Policy for the use of CUNY's Proficiency Index in developmental education assignments.* CUNY. https://www.cuny.edu/wp-content/uploads/sites/4/page-assets/about/administration/offices/registrar/resources/OAA-19-01-Policy-Brief-Technical-Guidance-FAQs.pdf.

Office of Academic Affairs (OAA). (2020a). *Sample ESL-D Assessment.* [Unpublished data]. CUNY.

Office of Academic Affairs (OAA). (2020b). *Testing FAQs.* CUNY. https://www.cuny.edu/academics/testing/testing-faqs/.

Office of the Executive Vice Chancellor and University Provost. (2020, July 14). *Update #16 CUNY COVID-19 guidance on academic continuity.* CUNY. https://www.cuny.edu/coronavirus/academic-continuity/guidance-on-academic-continuity-to-campuses/#updated.

Office of Institutional Research and Assessment (OIR). (2012). *CUNY Assessment Test in Writing (CATW) student handbook.* CUNY. https://www.cuny.edu/wp-content/uploads/sites/4/page-assets/academics/testing/CATWInformationforStudentsandpracticeweb.pdf.

Office of Institutional Research and Assessment (OIR). (2019). *Total enrollment by undergraduate and graduate level, full-time/part-time attendance, and college, Fall 2019.* CUNY. https://www.cuny.edu/irdatabook/rpts2_AY_current/ENRL_0001_UGGR_FTPT.rpt.pdf.

Office of Institutional Research and Assessment (OIR). (2020). *2019–2020 factbook.* QCC https://www.qcc.cuny.edu/oira/docs/Factbook-2019.pdf.

Office of Policy Research. (2019, March). *The CUNY approach to developmental education reform: New placement plans.* [Unpublished data]. CUNY.

Office of Undergraduate Studies, Academic Programs & Policy. (2021). *Developmental education.* CUNY. https://www.cuny.edu/about/administration/offices/undergraduate-studies/developmental-education/#1495476147062-1732421c-e5d7.

Poe, M., Elliot, N., Cogan, J. A., Jr. & Nurudeen, T. G., Jr. (2014). The legal and the local: Using disparate impact analysis to understand the consequences of writing assessment. *College Composition and Communication, 65*(4), 588–611.

QCC English Department. (2020a). *English Department new student placement for Winter and Spring 2020.* [Unpublished data]. QCC.

QCC English Department. (2020b). *Grading guidance—Fall 2020.* [Unpublished data]. QCC.

Scott-Clayton, J., Crosta, P. M. & Belfield, C. R. (2014). Improving the targeting of treatment: Evidence from college remediation. *Educational Evaluation and Policy Analysis, 36*(3), 371–393.

Strasma, K. & Resnick, P. (1999). Future research in two-year college English. *Teaching English in the Two-Year College, 27*(1), 106–114.

Von Esch, K. S., Motha, S. & Kubota, R. (2020). Race and language teaching. *Language Teaching, 53*(4), 391–421.

Appendix A: Student Demographics, QCC 2019–2020 Factbook

QCC First-Time Freshmen by Country of Birth: Top Ten Non-USA

	Fall 2016		Fall 2017		Fall 2018		Fall 2019	
	Country	Heads	Country	Heads	Country	Heads	Country	Heads
1	China	125	China	86	China	101	China	102
2	Jamaica	51	Guyana	45	Jamaica	58	Guyana	68
3	Bangladesh	41	Jamaica	44	Guyana	46	Jamaica	62
4	Guyana	40	Bangladesh	31	Bangladesh	42	Dominican Rep.	45
5	Haiti	39	Haiti	30	Dominican Rep.	30	Haiti	42
6	Dominican Rep.	36	Dominican Rep.	29	Haiti	26	Bangladesh	40
7	Ecuador	34	Pakistan	22	Ecuador	23	Ecuador	35
8	South Korea	28	India	20	Columbia	19	India	28
9	India	27	Columbia	19	South Korea	19	Pakistan	27
10	Pakistan	24	Ecuador	18	India	18	Mexico	24

QCC First-Time Freshmen Native Languages: Top Five Languages Other Than English

	Fall 2015		Fall 2016		Fall 2017		Fall 2018	
	Language	Heads	Language	Heads	Language	Heads	Language	Heads
1	Spanish	244	Spanish	234	Spanish	243	Spanish	169
2	Chinese	161	Chinese	115	Chinese	93	Chinese	96
3	Bengali	38	Bengali	44	Bengali	34	Bengali	37
4	Creole	30	Creole	30	Urdu	32	Creole	19
5	Urdu	29	Urdu	24	Creole	23	Urdu	15

Note: Due to a change in the admissions application, data for Fall 2019 is not available

Percent of First-Time Freshmen Who Speak a Language Other Than English at Home

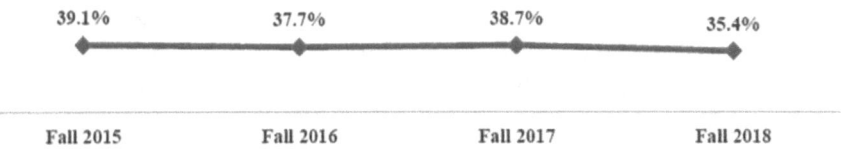

Source: CUNYfirst and CUNY IRDB

Appendix B: Definitions for Understanding Incoming QCC Student Placement

a. *Administrative Offices:*

- **The Office of Academic Affairs (OAA):** Oversees CLIP and CUNY Start[7] (see Developmental Coursework below). Supports faculty, staff, and students by collaborating with other administrative divisions. Aims to facilitate, disseminate, and implement assessment and strategic planning across the college (OAA, 2020b).
- **CUNY Task Force on Developmental Education:** Established by the OAA. Members include faculty chairs or co-chairs of the Mathematics, Reading, and English Discipline Councils, four chief academic officers from colleges offering developmental instruction and two from senior colleges, and members of the central OAA. Members deliberate on issues regarding "placement into developmental coursework, developmental instruction and supports for students, and the criteria for determining readiness to exit from developmental instruction" (CUNY Task Force on Developmental Education, 2016).
- **ESL Discipline Council:** Per council member David Rothman, a cohort of TESOL faculty that discusses and works toward "the resolution of issues relevant to CUNY's ESL population." Rothman defines an "ESL student" as one who lacks adequate English language competence, and works with the OAA "to develop better ESL placement tools" (OAA, 2019).
- **The Office of Institutional Research and Assessment (OIR):** Aims to "provide official, accurate, unbiased, and useful information and analysis to support institutional planning, assessment, decision-making, and reporting obligations." Works across CUNY campuses to gather data "for daily operations, decision-making, and assessment support" (OIR, 2020).

b. *Developmental and Interventional Coursework:*

- **CLIP (ESL students):** *CUNY Language Immersion Program*. A developmental "intervention" available to "flagged" ESL students who do not meet benchmark entrance requirements and are in need of improving their English language skills (QCC Student Affairs, 2020). Recommended for students who have received a PI score of 39 or lower.
- All CLIP instructors are full-time and have TESOL (or related) training: Students learn writing, reading, listening, and speaking skills through "focused academic content," according to Flaherty. The program integrates advisement with "college knowledge." Students may take the

---

7. CUNY Start is not a suggested pathway for ESL students, and is therefore not listed under Developmental Coursework.

program for up to three terms (two semesters and a summer term). A score of at least 75 percent on the exit exam is needed for a student to be deemed "proficient" and advance to ENGL 101. (See sample CLIP exit exam and scoring rubric in Appendix C.)
- CLIP courses are offered at four levels: beginner, intermediate, upper intermediate, and advanced. While students are directed to CLIP by a single measure that prioritizes writing and reading, Flaherty explains that students are placed into their appropriate levels based on multiple measures: They complete "a combination of an essay, a listening diagnostic and in the first three to four days of class they have one on ones [during] their small group conversations with their instructors that will then perhaps shift their placement."
- **ENG 90 (ESL students):** ESL Reading and Writing. Six-hour integrated reading and writing course to support English Language Learners. For ESL students with a PI score of 40–48. Any ESL students with a PI score of 50–64 may also register with an advisor.
- **USIP (ESL and non-ESL students):** *The University Skills Immersion Program.* Intended for students that are required to complete a math, reading, or writing developmental course prior to their matriculation. Includes tuition-free workshops and courses that are usually offered before the fall semester and between or during semesters (Office of Undergraduate Studies, Academic Programs & Policy, 2021).
- **BE 29:** Developmental Reading/Writing Workshop for Continuing Students. Offered by USIP. Six-week combination reading and writing summer workshop open to any returning student who must satisfy a remediation need. This includes those who are repeating BE 102, or exiting ENGL 90. Also eligible are students exiting CUNY Start with a developmental need in English and students exiting CLIP who have been advised by their instructors to take ALP. Students who pass the workshop would be eligible to take ENGL 101.
- **ALP (ESL and non-ESL students):** *Accelerated Learning Program.*
4. Dual enrollment program comprising ENGL 101 (English Composition) and BE 102[8] (Developing Competence in Reading, Writing, and Study Skills). For students determined to need developmental writing support. While BE 102 is non-credit-bearing, ALP students must pass it and ENGL 101 in order to advance to ENGL 102 (English Literature).
5. According to QCC's English department "New Student Placement" outline for Winter and Spring 2020, new students with a PI score of 50–64 or a CAT-W score of 49–55 may take ALP (QCC English Department, 2020a). (As stated previously, the ESL-D replaced the CAT-W to determine their placement upon the COVID-19 shutdown.)

---

8. As of 2022, BE 29 will be referred to as ENGL 99.

Appendix C: Sample Placement and Exit Exam Materials

The CATW uses an analytic scoring guide, called a rubric, to evaluate student writing samples. Each test is scored independently by two faculty raters and both raters assign scores in each of five grading categories.

The Five Scoring Categories

1. "Critical Response to the Writing Task and the Text": This category emphasizes your ability to complete the entire writing task and to demonstrate understanding of the main ideas in the reading text, using critical analysis, and integrating your own ideas and experiences to respond to the main ideas in the text

2. "Development of the Writer's Ideas": In this category you are evaluated on your ability to develop your ideas (for example, by using summary, narrative, or problem/ solution) in a clear and organized way. Your response should include both general statements and specific details and examples. These details and examples can be drawn from your personal experiences, what you have read, or other sources. You must make specific references to ideas in the reading with these details and examples.

3. "Structure of the Response": This category evaluates your ability to organize ideas into an essay that supports a central focus, or thesis. The structure of your essay is evaluated for evidence of clear connections between ideas and the use of appropriate language to convey these connections.

4. "Language Use: Sentences and Word Choice": This category evaluates the degree to which you demonstrate sentence control and variety in sentence construction. This category also evaluates your ability to use appropriate vocabulary to make your ideas clear.

5. "Language Use: Grammar, Usage, and Mechanics": This category evaluates your ability to follow the conventions of standard American English language use in terms of grammar and mechanics (i.e. punctuation, spelling, use of capitals, etc.), so that your meaning is clear.

Copyright © 2012 The City University of New New York

Figure 8.C1. Sample CAT-W and rubric.

Appendix D: Sample ESL-D Placement Exam Web Pages

Webpage Section 1

Time remaining: 00:12 min:sec

Full Name: Sarah Truelsch

EMPLID: 789xyz

Section 1

Directions: Please read the passage below and write an essay in English. You will have 120 minutes to write your essay, and you may use a dictionary, including a bi-lingual dictionary. You are expected to write this essay by yourself, with no help from any other outside sources. Your essay should do the following:

1. Explain the main point the author is making.
2. Share what you think (your opinion) about the author's main point.
3. Support your opinion about the author's main point by connecting it with your personal experience and/or what you have read, seen, learned about in school and/or on TV or social media about the topic.
4. Once you have finished your essay, be sure to review your writing and make any changes or corrections that will help the reader clearly understand the points in your essay.

"Reading Passage"

by Author

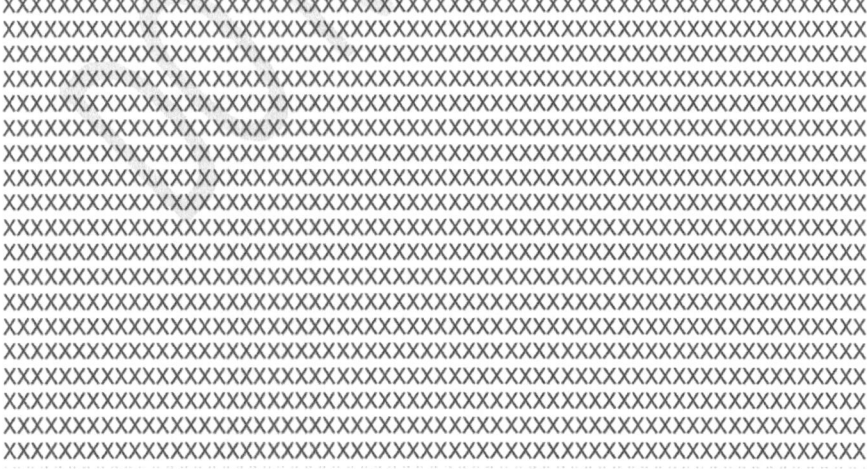

Sample ESL-D Placement Exam Web Pages, Continued

Section 2

Directions: Please fully complete the following questions. You must respond honestly and truthfully to the questions because your responses will be used to help you register for the English class that is best suited for you! If you get placed into the wrong class, you will have to b moved. Please help us understand your English level.

You must complete this section in order to submit your response to the ESL Diagnostic Assessment.

Please click on the response that best matches your understanding of the reading.

How comfortable were you with the reading that you were given to use to write your essay:

- I was very uncomfortable with the reading, and I understood almost none of it.
- I was quite uncomfortable with the reading, and I understood a little of it.
- I was uncomfortable with some parts of the reading, but I was comfortable with other parts.
- I was comfortable with most of the reading, but a few parts of it were unclear.
- I was very comfortable with the reading, and I understood all of it.

Please click on the response that best matches your experience.

I needed to use a translation dictionary to understand the reading and write my essay.

- All the time, as I was reading the text.
- Frequently, as I was reading the text.
- Sometimes, as I was reading the text.
- A few times.
- Never, as I understood every word.

Sample ESL-D Placement Exam Web Pages, Continued

How many years of high school did you complete in the U.S.?

- 1 year.
- 2 years
- 3 years
- 4 years
- I did not attend high school in the U.S.

Please describe in as much detail as possible the type of writing you practiced or you learne and what language instruction, including grammar, you had in your English Language Arts (ELA) class (if you took it in a U.S. high school), or in your English class (if you took a language class in another country).

Please write your answer in one paragraph, using sentences, **NOT** a list, in the blank space below:

Sample ESL-D Placement Exam Web Pages, Continued

How would you describe your ability to speak in English and be understood by other people

- I get nervous about speaking in English; people have trouble understanding me.
- I get nervous about speaking in English; people often ask me to repeat what I said.
- I rarely get nervous speaking in English, but sometimes people do not understand me.
- I am quite comfortable speaking in English, and most people understand me.
- I am fine speaking in English, and everyone understands me easily.

If you could place yourself into an English class in college, based on what YOU think of you English language ability in speaking, reading writing and listening, which class would it be:

- I need a lot of language instruction, in all skills areas: speaking, reading, writing and listening.
- I need instruction in speaking, but I am fine with reading and writing.
- I need instruction in reading and writing.
- I need instruction in writing only.
- I think my language skills are good enough to take a College Composition class.

Appendix E: Sample CLIP Essay Prompt

An Environment

An environment is everything around us. A physical environment is everything that someone can see, hear, smell and touch. It also includes invisible things, such as chemicals in the air. A social environment contains the people someone interacts with, such as family or friends. An online environment includes all the places on the Internet that someone visits, such as YouTube and social media sites like Facebook and Instagram. People are always in an environment. However, they don't often think about how it affects them. Here are some ways it does.

Many studies have shown that the physical environment affects us. The exhaust from cars or factories can increase the risk of having a heart attack. This type of pollution can also make health conditions like asthma worse. The environment can also affect our mental health. A recent study compared people walking in a park with people walking on the street. It found that people walking in a park had significantly lower levels of negative emotions and anxiety.

A social environment can influence someone in many ways. It certainly influences how they behave. David, a 16 year old, explains how his social environment influenced his behavior. He remembers, "I smoked my first cigarette when I was 11. I didn't want to, but all my friends were smoking and I didn't want to be out of the group." David's experience is not unique. Friends in a person's social environment influence that person's behavior.

An online environment can also have a powerful effect on someone. The online environment encourages people to shift their attention. When online, everything is just "one click away." For example, while someone looks at a social media post, they click on a link to a YouTube video. This constant shifting of attention negatively affects their ability to focus. In fact, research has shown that people who repeatedly click from one website to another have more difficulty focusing—even when they are not online.

An environment is not only around us. It also affects us in many ways.

Writing Directions: Read the passage above and write an essay about it. Summarize the main ideas of the passage in your own words. In addition, explain how one or more ideas in the passage relate (connect) to something you have experienced, seen, read, and/or learned in school.

Only a small part of your essay should summarize the passage, but make sure to include all the author's main ideas. Most of the essay should explain how one or more ideas relate to something you have experienced, seen, read, and/or learned in school.

Remember to review your essay and make any changes or corrections that will help your reader clearly understand your essay. You will have 90 minutes to complete your essay.

Appendix F: Scoring Guidelines for the CLIP Essay Rubric (2/8/2018)

Overall Guidelines

Choose the score with the criteria that best describe the essay.

In some cases, the essay will meet all three of the criteria for a score. In other cases, the essay may not meet one of the criteria for a score. The essay should not be disqualified for a score because it does not meet one of the criteria. Instead, choose the score whose criteria most closely describe the essay.

Think of "competent" as equivalent to a C+ level of performance for an in-class essay exam in the highest level CUNY developmental writing class. An in-class essay means an essay like the CLIP essay in which, within 90 minutes, the student summarizes and responds to a prompt that they have not previously read. The highest level developmental class at CUNY is the class that now uses the CATW as a final exam. Refer to anchor papers A and C for components that reach a "competent" level of performance.

When reading the essay, do not translate from ESL interlanguages to English. Read at a normal pace and do not re-read to try to determine meaning. Anything that is not comprehensible to a reader unfamiliar with ESL writing or speech should not receive credit for any components. It's helpful to read the words the student writes one at a time and determine what, if anything, these words communicate. It is especially important to use this strategy with summaries, since the scorer already knows the content.

Lack of clarity due to word choice, sentence structure or grammar can also lower the scores in critical response, development and organization. If parts of the essay are unclear to the extent that a student is unable to articulate a clear response, to competently develop ideas, and/or to construct a well-organized, unified paragraph, this can lower the scores for critical response, development, and/or organization.

When evaluating whether a student "almost never," "sometimes" or "mostly" achieves a level of performance, think of these terms in reference to a four to five paragraph essay. Therefore, an essay with just one or two short paragraphs can never "sometimes" or "mostly" achieve a level of performance in critical response, development, organization, word choice or grammar. *An essay with four or fewer independent sentences should never receive a score above "1" in any category*

Critical Response

Only parts of the student essay that are summarized or paraphrased should be evaluated for the summary. Any text that is copied (or very, very closely copied) should not receive any credit towards summarizing. Read the prompt four or five times before you score so you remember the key phrases. Underline the main points to quickly check for copying.

Make sure to evaluate if the student is accurately summarizing the main points of the essay. Always ask if reading the words on the student's essay gives you an accurate understanding of the main points. Misrepresentations of the main points (even if they include some information from the text that is accurate) should receive no credit towards summarizing. The essay should be evaluated on summarizing the main points of the prompt. Merely stating facts from the prompt does not constitute summarizing.

If the student does not summarize the article, or summarizes it poorly, look at the other two components of the critical response score—relating and integrating and focusing on the task—to determine the score. The student should receive the score that best describes the essay. Generally, this means that two of the three criteria for the score describe the essay. Since an essay without a summary is not "almost always" focused on the task, an essay without a summary in the student's own words should never be given a score of 6. However, the essay could possibly receive a score of 4 or 5, depending on how well the student relates and integrates idea(s) from the article and stays focused on the task.

When evaluating "focus on task," evaluate how well the student has actually summarized and responded to the prompt. For example, if the summary copies almost all the text from the prompt, or if the summary is inaccurate, the student has not focused on the task of summarizing. If the student discusses something unrelated to an idea in the article, the student has not focused on the task of responding.

When evaluating whether a student responds to an idea related to the passage, students should not be penalized for responding to an idea from the passage that is not a main idea. For example, the prompt "Feeling Lonely? Too Much Time on Social Media May be Why" concedes that "Social media sites are a good way to keep in contact with people." Since the article is focused on how social media leads to loneliness, this is not a main point. However, a student should not be penalized for responding to the concession ("Social media sites are a good way to keep in contact with people").

<u>Development</u>

When evaluating how well the student develops ideas, focus on the development of ideas, not the development of a paragraph. For example, an essay could include paragraphs with two unrelated, but competently developed ideas. If the ideas are competently developed, the student should receive a higher score for development. The issue with unrelated ideas in paragraphs should be reflected in the score for organization, not development.

Statements that are completely inaccurate should not receive credit for development. For example, if a student states that people who don't know a second language cannot get a job, that statement should receive no credit towards development.

Organization

The student should not be penalized for responding to more than one idea. The writer's central focus, and the organizational structure that supports that focus, can be a summary, followed by three paragraphs, each with an explanation of how a different idea from the passage is related to what the student has experienced, seen or read, and/or learned in school. The student may choose to include a statement at the end of the first paragraph previewing that this is what the essay will do. However, the student may also signal that s/he will be responding to three different ideas with signal phrases such as "one idea that relates to my life is," "another idea that relates to my life is."

Word Choice

Since there is some gray area between intermediate and advanced vocabulary, **focus on the total number of intermediate or advanced words in the essay when scoring for Word Choice.**

Sentence Structure, Grammar and Mechanics

The words "comprehensible," "impedes comprehension," or is "incomprehensible" mean comprehensible, impedes comprehension or incomprehensible for a reader unfamiliar with ESL writing and speech. To help approach how a reader unfamiliar with ESL interlanguage would comprehend or not comprehend parts of an essay, scorers should not re-read sentences or phrases that they find confusing.

Text that is a copy of phrases from the text (or a near copy) should receive no credit for demonstrating proficiency in sentence structure, grammar, or mechanics.

Part Three. Pandemic-Precipitated Placement Reform

Chapter 9. Pandemic Placement at Cuyahoga Community College: A Case Study

Ashlee Brand and Bridget Kriner
Cuyahoga Community College

Abstract: The onset of the COVID-19 pandemic in March 2020 created an exigency for placement reform at Cuyahoga Community College (Tri-C), a multi-campus, urban community college located in Cleveland, Ohio, and its suburbs. These reforms were designed to accommodate remote administration of placement tests into the range of developmental and first-year composition classes offered at the institution, as it was not possible to continue with the current system of ACCUPLACER Reading and WritePlacer instruments without the availability of a proctored testing environment. The resulting system utilizes multiple measures—i.e., high school GPA and ACT/SAT scores along with informed self-placement and expert-reader assessment by English faculty—to place students in the most appropriate English course. This case study of the reformed "pandemic placement" system includes a description of the design process, draws on quantitative data on placement and success rates for students placed using the new system, and discusses responses from a qualitative survey of English faculty involved in the design and implementation of the system.

Cuyahoga Community College, regionally known as Tri-C, is Ohio's largest and oldest community college and consists of four campuses and sites serving over 55,000 credit and non-credit students annually. Tri-C has the lowest tuition in Ohio, offers over 200 degree and certificate options, and runs more than 1,000 credit courses each semester. At the start of the Fall 2020 semester, approximately 19,000 students were enrolled for credit-bearing courses. The students who attend the institution represent a diverse demographic: Six out of ten students are female, and 40 percent are from historically underrepresented communities. As reported in the 2020 Diversity Report, students identify as the following ethnicities: 53 percent White/Caucasian, 23 percent African American/Black, five percent Asian, four percent Hispanic/Latino, six percent multiracial, and nine percent unknown. The average student age is 26.8 but ranges from younger than 15 to older than 75, and students are represented from more than 40 countries. In addition, 60 percent of students can be considered low-income as indicated by their receipt of Federal Pell Grant Aid. One of the college's fastest growing student populations is students who dually attend high school and college; more than 3,500 students are part of the state's College Credit Plus program at Tri-C (Cuyahoga Community College, 2019).

Tri-C has placed an extensive focus on improving graduation rates, and in 2019, the college increased its Integrated Postsecondary Education Data System (IPEDS) graduation rate from four percent for the 2011 graduating class to 19 percent for the 2018 class (Cuyahoga Community College, 2020). Equity remains a concern, as graduation rates for Black students have increased but are still less than half of those for White students (Jenkins & Griffin, 2019). The college has focused on prioritizing IPEDS graduation rates through a wide variety of initiatives centered on retention and student success, including mentoring programs, guided pathways, first-year experience (FYE) courses and programs, and direct student outreach. These efforts are continuing to positively impact graduation rates for students, and the college ranks first in Ohio and 25th in the nation in the number of associate degrees conferred in all disciplines (Jenkins & Griffin, 2019). A multi-campus, urban community college located in Cleveland, Ohio and surrounding suburbs, Tri-C offers more than 500 sections of first-year composition and developmental English each academic year in seated, asynchronous online, and hybrid modalities that run for 16-, 14- or 8-week terms. In addition, the college began offering classes in a synchronous online modality, new to Fall 2020, due to needs arising from the COVID-19 pandemic. There are more than 400 full-time faculty at Tri-C, consisting of tenured and tenure-track faculty who are members of the American Association of University Professors (AAUP). The English department consists of just over 40 full-time tenure-track and tenured faculty across the four campuses and in Spring 2021 had 85 English faculty who are part-time, contingent faculty assigned to teach courses. There are additionally 20–25 contingent faculty who were not assigned that term due to lack of additional sections. At the start of the 2020–2021 academic year, both full-time and contingent faculty combined were 84.7 percent White and 15.3 percent from historically underrepresented racial and ethnic groups, 77.5 percent 40 years or older, and 67.6 percent female-identified. These faculty demographics have been constant since 2016. There are a handful of English lecturers (one-year full-time, non-bargaining unit positions) for the 2020–2021 year, but no new tenure-track hires were made at the conclusion of Spring 2020 due to the pandemic and its impact on the institutional budget. Further, there will not be any additional tenure-track hires for the 2021–2022 year.

Faculty roles are such at Tri-C that there is not a writing program administrator (WPA) at the college or someone who functions in such an administrative role as might be seen as a lead for the composition program or writing placement. Instead, faculty members take on additional service to the college in the form of committee involvement in addition to teaching a 30-credit annual workload, typically split into two 15-credit semesters. For many English faculty, this equates to teaching 4–5 courses each semester, as first-year composition courses count as 3.6 units, developmental English courses (integrated reading and writing) count as 6 units, and literature courses count for 3 credits towards faculty workload. Certain service responsibilities provide a course reduction in varying amounts towards total faculty workload, including both shared college governance roles and the work typically associated with a WPA position at a four-year institution.

The collective group of full-time English faculty is known as the English Counterparts group, and this group's English Placement Taskforce assumed a leadership role focused on the college's placement research, recommendations, and processes in earlier placement reform in 2012 as a response to the creation of the Ohio Remediation Free Standards,[1] which were implemented in 2012 and codified statewide standards for college readiness that relied heavily on standardized tests, including ACT, SAT, and WritePlacer. High school grade point average is not currently included with a statewide minimum GPA for college readiness. According to the Ohio Department of Higher Education, the standards seek to "establish uniform statewide standards in mathematics, science, reading, and writing that each student enrolled in a state institution of higher education must meet to be considered remediation-free." Tri-C's English Placement Taskforce responded to these standards through an initial placement reform that adopted WritePlacer and ACCUPLACER Reading in 2012 (see "ACCUPLACER/ WritePlacer" section in Table 9.1) because faculty desired to have students produce an essay as part of the placement process.

During Spring 2012, in order to implement these reforms, faculty serving on the Placement Taskforce led efforts among English faculty to identify placements for English that aligned with our curriculum and the Remediation Free Standards. We engaged in national research, pilot testing, and rigorous norming sessions to align WritePlacer scores with courses and curriculum. Our norming sessions sought to enact a process that we later learned was similar to an expert reader model to see which course faculty would place a student WritePlacer sample into to help identify our cut scores. This norming process aligns with Peggy O'Neill's (2003) description of William L. Smith's work distinguishing between holistic scoring and placement: "a key to understanding the validity research Smith conducted is to understand the difference between holistic scoring—a procedure for evaluating texts—and placement—the decision that is made about the writer based on the results of an evaluation" (p. 52). This shift to WritePlacer occurred at Tri-C before COMPASS stopped being available in December 2016 (Table 1). The transition from COMPASS to WritePlacer and ACCUPLACER Reading also marked a renewed focus on substantive placement reform at the college, including expansion of the Accelerated Learning Program (ALP) corequisite model and a two-week bridge course, which had previously begun in 2011, and sought to provide more in-depth review of students' writing abilities and more authentic placement prior to the start of a 14-week term. The changes in placement resulted in a decrease of placement into standalone developmental English courses, as well as an improved success rate in the first-year composition course (ENG 1010). For English faculty, the work on reforming placement methods at this time instilled faculty expertise and involvement into the

---

1. https://www.ohiohighered.org/college-readiness

placement process, decisions, and evaluation at the college. The original Placement Taskforce still remains in the form of an English placement committee and consists of between six to ten full-time English faculty who monitor placement data and make recommendations to the full English counterparts regarding placement cut scores and process changes as necessary.

At the start of academic year (AY) 2019–2020, the college had been seeking additional placement reforms as a participant in the Ohio's Strong Start to Finish Initiative,[2] the goal of which is to increase the number of students completing gateway courses within their first academic year. English faculty proposed a series of adjustments to placement processes, as well as curricular revisions to its standalone developmental English offerings—ENG 0980 and ENG 0990 (six-credit integrated reading and writing courses). At the onset of the COVID-19 pandemic and the resulting campus closures, the implementation of these reforms was under consideration by faculty and administration (Table 9.1).

Table 9.1. Institutional Placement Instrument Timeline

Time Period	Instrument
Before December 2016	COMPASS
January 2017–March 2020	WritePlacer & ACCUPLACER Reading
April 2020–present	Faculty-designed placement system

Pandemic Placement System

In AY 2019–2020, prior to campus closures, 3,194 students were placed using WritePlacer and ACCUPLACER Reading exams, which were administered on campuses in proctored environments, as well as at area high schools to determine students' qualifications for College Credit Plus (CCP),[3] Ohio's statewide dual enrollment program. All administration of standardized assessments ceased in mid-March 2020 due to campus closures related to COVID-19.

The unexpected closure of all of the college's campuses and the transition to online course delivery and remote work in March 2020 presented a serious placement-related dilemma. Because the college could no longer proctor WritePlacer exams in person in its physical testing centers and because no remote proctoring options were readily accessible, a system needed to be developed and implemented quickly in order to prevent a prolonged interruption to student enrollment in Summer and Fall 2020. Since ENG 1010 or ENG 1010-readiness is a prerequisite for courses across myriad disciplines, not administering the institution's traditional placement tests was anticipated to have devastating effects. As was also the case throughout

---

2. https://www.ohiohighered.org/SSTF
3. https://www.ohiohighered.org/collegecreditplus

the country, students did not have ACT or SAT scores due to cancellations of standardized tests, presenting a kairotic moment to revisit discussions about placement, authentic writing assessment, and the expertise of faculty in determining where students could be most successful in their first English course at the college. While the discussion of using high school GPA for placement had been present for years, the immediacy of the reforms that took place in April 2020 was the result of WritePlacer and ACCUPLACER's Reading test not being able to be administered during a period of campus closure and statewide shutdown due to the pandemic as all services were forced into a remote environment.

A committee of English faculty composed of members of the English placement committee and counterparts chairs convened in late March 2020 to develop a proposal for what—at the time—was to be a one-year temporary placement system in the absence of proctored WritePlacer assessments on campus. The pandemic's institutional shutdown of standardized, proctored testing had afforded us the opportunity to enact our own assessment tool, which Richard Haswell and Susan Wyche-Smith (1994) had been calling for more than two decades prior when they recognized that teachers should be leery of tools others made and instead that they "should, and can, make their own" (p. 221). Over the course of the ensuing four to five weeks, these faculty collaborated with college leadership and testing center staff to design and implement a fully remote system that would eliminate the need for either in-person or remote exam proctoring. While the timing of this in the middle of a semester definitely posed institutional challenges, it afforded the opportunity for rethinking placement at the college to better align with best practices in the field, which eschew reliance on high-stakes standardized assessments and move towards multiple measures and directed self-placement methods (Klausman et al., 2016).

Placement Ideology

Writing placement, as noted by other scholars, plays a critical role at two-year colleges of opening or closing doors to economic opportunity, personal or professional advancement, or education in any form; thus, the implications of placement decisions on these students specifically are finally beginning to receive attention deserved in the field (Toth et al., 2019). As such, a growing body of research indicates that high school GPA is strongly predictive of success in college courses (Allensworth & Clark, 2020; Vinaja, 2016).

Further, discussion of writing placement at two-year colleges centers on fairness, equity, and the local setting surrounding placement decisions. While supportive of multiple measures, Holly Hassel and Joanne Baird Giordano encourage community colleges to proceed with some caution when using high school GPA for direct placement in English due to the diverse nature of student populations with regard to limited college preparatory coursework and also call for placement to be aligned with local curriculum and pedagogy in the teaching of writing (Gilman et al., 2019). For these reasons, Tri-C opted to develop a system for placement assessment using high school GPA and high-stakes assessments in combination with both directed self-placement (DSP) and expert reader assessment models. The latter methods allow for refinement of the placement assessment process, specifically for students who might benefit from either a corequisite course in addition to the gateway course or an honors version of the gateway course.

Pandemic System Design

After numerous collaborative sessions, the team of placement committee members and faculty leaders devised a system that combines multiple measures assessment (MMA) and directed self-placement (DSP). Multiple measures assessment includes standardized college entrance exam scores, i.e., ACT and SAT, and high school grade point average to place students into English courses and self-directed placement along specific pathways (corequisite models and honors). These measures would be confirmed through transcript and test score submission to the college's Registrar's office as part of the admission process. Students are requested to submit these materials at the point of admission and enrollment in a program of study.

In addition, some incoming students could have placement waived if they met minimum criteria in other ways. For example, students may not be required to take the English placement test if they present at the point of admissions with an earned degree (associate's, bachelor's, or higher), a grade of C or better in college-level English from an accredited institution of higher learning, successful (C or better) completion of developmental English within the last two years at another Ohio community college or university, satisfactory standardized test scores, satisfactory high school grade point average (GPA), or English placement test scores from Tri-C (Table 9.2). Prior placements using pre-pandemic approaches were identified as remaining valid for two years from the original date of testing or high school graduation.

Table 9.2. Measures Correlated to English Course Placement

English Measure	GPA or Score Range	Placement
Cumulative High School GPA	3.8 and higher	ENG 1010 Honors
	3.0–3.799	ENG 1010
	2.6–2.99	ENG 0900 <u>and</u> 1010 or ENG 1001 <u>and</u> 1010
	2.599 and lower	Take English placement test

English Measure	GPA or Score Range	Placement
SAT Reading & Writing Score	570–800	ENG 1010 Honors
	480–569	ENG 1010
ACT English Sub Score	25–36	ENG 1010 Honors
	18–24	ENG 1010
ACCUPLACER WritePlacer Score	7 or 8	ENG 1010 Honors
	6 <u>and</u> ACCUPLACER Score Next Gen. Rdg 261–300 or Classic Score 90+	
	5 or 6 <u>and</u> ACCUPLACER Score Next Gen Rdg. 200–260	ENG 1010
	4	ENG 0900 <u>and</u> 1010 or ENG 1001 <u>and</u> 1010
	3	ENG 0990
	2	ENG 0980
	0–1 <u>and</u> ACCUPLACER Score Next Gen Rdg 220–300 or Classic Score of 28+	ENG 0980
	0–1 <u>and</u> ACCUPLACER Score Next Gen Rdg 200–219 or Classic Score of 9–27	Aspire Program (non-credit)

Students who qualify for college-level English with the help of a supportive course have the option to choose between pairs of courses, either ENG 900 with ENG 1010 (a two-week long Bridge[4] + 14-week Gateway) or ENG 1001 with ENG 1010 (Community College of Baltimore County (CCBC) model ALP corequisite +Gateway). Using the directed self-placement model (Toth, 2019), students are

---

4. The two-week ENG 0900—Transition to College English—course has been offered at the college since 2011 and takes place in the first two weeks of the 16-week semester, is a pass/fail course, and serves to allow more intensive assessment of what students can do as writers. The curriculum focuses on extensive writing and revision and mirrors the academic expectations of an ENG 1010 course with regard to compositions. Upon successful completion, these students immediately enroll in a 14-week, stand-alone gateway ENG 1010 college composition course or another course as determined by faculty assessment of an end portion. Since inception, the institution has seen a pass rate of greater than 90 percent in this two-week offering.

encouraged to enroll in whichever of these options they feel is most appropriate. Similarly, students who present at the point of placement with a history of high achievement as demonstrated by standardized test scores or high school GPA are given the option to enroll in either ENG 1010 or ENG 101H (honors version of ENG 1010). Students in both these categories receive course descriptions along with guiding questions in order to help them to decide to enroll in the best option for them (Table 9.3).

Table 9.3. Directed Self-Placement for Selected Courses

Course Options	Qualifying Measure(s)	Directed Self-Placement Language
ENG 1010 or ENG 1010 Honors	3.8 GPA or higher high school English Taken an Honors English course at the junior or senior high school level Taken AP English in high school but do not have test scores	What is the difference between Honors English Composition I (ENG 101H) and College Composition I (ENG 1010)? Honors classes do not involve doing more work than non-Honors classes. Rather, Honors classes have these characteristics: Smaller class sizes with fellow Honors students; May emphasize seminar-style discussion; Typically involve a "deep dive" into course material; May be theme-based; May involve individual or group projects; May involve extracurricular learning opportunities.
ENG 0900 and ENG 1010	Placement test score of 4 Cumulative high school GPA 2.6–2.99 WritePlacer Score of 4	If you answer yes to most of these questions, this option might be the placement for you: Have you ever written a paper of 4 pages or more using outside research? Did you receive mostly B's or higher in your high school English courses? Do you think that you would benefit from a quick "brush-up" before your ENG 1010? Do you enjoy reading and writing outside of school?
ENG 1001 and ENG 1010	Placement Test score of 4 Cumulative high school GPA 2.6–2.99 WritePlacer Score of 4	If you answer yes to most of these questions, this option might be the placement for you: Would you like to have more help from your professor to help you in the course? Did you receive mostly C's or lower in your high school English courses? Do you lack confidence in your writing or feel anxious about writing?

Students without either a high school GPA of at least 2.6 or a recent enough standardized test score are placed into a course based on a writing sample completed in response to a prompt, which is assessed by full-time English faculty members. The English placement committee designed the prompts and developed training materials for faculty assessors to place students based on their expertise and knowledge of the college's curriculum. Students who need to submit a writing sample through this process make an appointment through an online system administered by testing center staff. The appointment must be made at least 24 hours in advance. Upon completion of the appointment intake process, students receive an email with testing information, guidelines for writing the essay response, and a sample prompt. At the time of the actual testing appointment, a testing center staff member emails an essay prompt to the student, who then has two hours to return a completed essay to the staff member. It should be noted that this system was designed to minimize in-person contact at campus facilities. Each prompt includes a very short passage or quote (e.g., "When there's a setback, someone with a fixed mindset will start thinking, 'Maybe I don't have what it takes?' They may get defensive and give up. A hallmark of a successful person is that they persist in the face of obstacles, and often, these obstacles are blessings in disguise."—Carol S. Dweck) and calls for students to respond to a question derived from the passage (e.g., Please write an essay in response to this question: Can obstacles sometimes be "blessings in disguise"? Explain why or why not). In cases where the passage provided contains a term that could require definition, it is provided in simple terms (e.g., A definition of *hallmark* is a quality or characteristic of something.). All prompts were designed in this format; the goal in the design is to be able to assess how students respond to the complex ideas set forth in the passage, while still offering a clear question for students to consider. This type of writing task is consistent with the curriculum of the first-year composition courses. These original prompts, developed by the placement design team, are rotated by the testing center staff based on the reader assigned.

Upon receipt of the completed essay, the testing center staff member forwards the essay to a faculty reader from a team of readers composed of full-time English faculty, who has 48 hours to assess the student essay and return a score to the testing center staff member, who provides the student with a score and applicable course placement information and enters the score into the student's record. The faculty member who completes the assessment enters the scoring data into a separate tracking system maintained by members of the placement team. Faculty are compensated by the college for scoring these essays; scoring is not part of the faculty member's primary responsibilities and is not release time eligible. To make the system accessible, email was used for staff to transmit prompts to students and for students to return writing samples, as the technology requirements for third-party proctoring (e.g., camera, high speed internet access) could make the process much more difficult for students. However, there is recognition by the faculty committee that even the utilization of email for this process may still constitute a barrier for some students. To mitigate this issue, testing centers on all campuses provided limited on-demand testing on specific days on site where students could complete the writing sample using college computers.

Pandemic System Assessment Process

To prepare for the assessment of student placement essays, readers participate in a brief training developed and hosted by the placement design team to inform them about both logistics of the scoring process and assessment criteria, which are provided to the team of readers in the form of a rubric[5] (Table 9.4). Sample essays developed by the placement design team for each of the possible scores are also given to the faculty readers to serve as a reference point for norming assessment processes. During the assessment process, there are cases where the faculty member is presented with an essay that they have difficulty scoring for a variety of reasons. That reader may contact another member of that month's reading team for a second opinion. In these cases, the two readers confer on the essay to determine an appropriate score, which at first consideration would align with criterion-referenced assessments, except that the placement course levels were originally normed by teams of faculty readers who regularly teach the courses, thus beginning the focus on consistency in scoring from an approach more closely aligned with expert reader models.

Readers also pay close attention to multilingual linguistic traits in student-submitted writing to address the possibility that students who were non-native English speakers may have taken the English placement test by mistake; to make these determinations, faculty readers rely on their experience teaching writing courses to both native and non-native speakers of English. Because the intake process for the college requires students to self-identify whether or not English was the "first language they learned to speak or write" to determine whether ESL or English placement is needed, there was some concern about whether students who may be ESL would select the English placement in error. In the event that strong ESL markers are detected in the student essay by the initial reader, the essay is referred to an ESL faculty member for further evaluation and collaboration between departments. This referral could result in the student needing to take a separate ESL placement test that consists of a grammar, listening, and writing component. ESL placement and English placement are two separate processes

---

5. In an effort to maintain consistency with the previous placement scoring system and avoid confusion among staff who were also working remotely, as well as personnel and staffing changes due to voluntary separations, retirements, and budget cuts, the same numerical codes were kept in place in Banner [information management system for student record keeping] but applied to the original rubric developed by the placement design team. Additionally, this allows for longitudinal data studies later comparing the old system (WritePlacer) with the new system (high school GPA or the departmental test) in more direct ways as both were normed to our curriculum and courses.

at Tri-C, and the two departments have separate courses and curricula. In cases where there is insufficient writing to complete an assessment (typically less than 100 words) or when a student exceeds the time required without an ADA (Americans with Disabilities Act) accommodation, the faculty reader has the option of not returning a score and asking for the student to repeat the test with a different prompt. If a reader detects evidence of academic dishonesty in the student essay, the student is automatically asked to retest using a prompt specifically designated for this purpose. Up to this point, cases of this nature have been quite rare; there is not sufficient evidence to provide any analysis of what, if any, effect this practice might have on enrollment.

Table 9.4. Criteria for Tri-C English Placement Test Assessment

Score	Course	Essay Characteristics
0–1	ASPIRE	Essay lacks organization, development of ideas, and paragraphs. There is no evidence of a thesis statement (main idea). There are many errors in sentence structure, punctuation, mechanics, and spelling.
2	ENG 0980	Essay exhibits numerous grammar and mechanical errors (capitalization and punctuation) at the sentence level including sentence boundary errors (run-on sentences, sentence fragments). There is a lack of organization and development of ideas. Details may stray from thesis (main idea).
3	ENG 0990	Essay contains many errors in grammar, mechanics (punctuation), and sentence structure (run-ons and fragments). There is a thesis (main idea), but the essay lacks some development (details) and organization and may contain mistakes in paragraph structure.
4^6	PAIRED COURSES	Essay contains some errors in grammar, mechanics, and sentence structure (run-ons and fragments). There is a thesis (main idea) and some details that help develop that thesis, but there are also a few errors in organizing those details.
5	ENG 1010	Essay demonstrates ENG 1010–readiness including a strong thesis that clearly answers the prompt, details that help develop the main idea, organized ideas and paragraphs that support the thesis. There are a few minor grammar and sentence structure errors, but nothing that prevents understanding of the central idea.
7^7	ENG 101H	Essay meets all qualities of a score of 5. In addition, it exhibits advanced readiness in vocabulary, critical thinking, sentence variety, and richness of language.

---

6. Students with a score of 4 are placed in one of two course combinations (both ENG 1010 and a supportive course).

7. There is no 6. The score of 7 was intentionally chosen to be consistent with WritePlacer numbering so as to avoid confusion within student records and among staff.

Reactions

During the training sessions for new readers in Summer 2020 and early Fall 2020, many experienced and returning faculty readers shared their experiences with new readers. These responses often expressed the pedagogical value in the conversations among peers and further demonstrated a positive impact of the quick change in the system. Of the 44 full-time members of English Counterparts, a total of 18 faculty members served as readers throughout the process for at least a month. Of these 18, all scored essays for more than one consecutive month, with many readers—a core group of approximately 12—scoring consistently from May 2020–December 2020 without any months "off" from doing so. At this time, the process seems to be sustainable, as many faculty readers have found the work meaningful and rewarding. A preliminary call for readers for Spring 2021 has also demonstrated strong interest in engaging in this process, as a wide variety of faculty showed interest in participating—tenured and tenure track, as well as some that are not heavily involved in other service to the college. More than 20 out of 40 full-time faculty members have responded with interest to score for at least one month in Spring 2021. This level of engagement and dialogue among English tenure-track and tenured faculty in the placement process is unprecedented. Beyond engaging in consults and training sessions, readers communicate regularly by email to troubleshoot, engage in discussion about curriculum and teaching (often triggered by a placement essay or score), and through regular meetings of the placement team. The readers also are actively engaged in revision to prompts and other components of the process, even if they do not actively serve on the smaller placement core team.

Faculty readers and members of the design team who responded to a survey about their experiences overwhelmingly reported positive reactions to the experience of the reformed system. They noted enjoyment of both the experience of working closely with colleagues on the project and of the actual reading of student essays. Further, most respondents noted that the system was simple and easy to use from the reader perspective. As one respondent commented,

> The implementation of the system was smooth and easy, especially because those instructors involved had long been desiring and discussing such a system. Personally, I found the system to be well-constructed and helpful to the user; it took little time to get used to and use correctly.

Designing and implementing these reforms during the pandemic was a collaborative experience among the full-time English faculty, testing center staff, and college administration. As one faculty member said,

> The collaboration that happened between faculty, staff, and administrators was unprecedented. I'm still surprised we were

able to pull something together in such a short amount of time. It wasn't easy, and it took a lot of work, but I feel grateful to have been a part of something like this.

Another noted, "The camaraderie and collaborative spirit shared among the group of faculty readers were particularly encouraging, helpful, and pleasant." At a time when many experienced isolation and disconnection from the institution, this sense of connection identified by faculty readers is an important reaction.

There was not noticeable resistance as there was a shared understanding that a form of placement had to be implemented by both faculty members and members of the administration due to the direct relationship between placement and enrollment. However, there were some concerns expressed by other faculty counterparts groups (ESL and psychology, for example) after the changes were implemented just prior to the start of the Fall 2020 term. These concerns were primarily focused on questions about potential cheating in an unproctored setting, as well as some other discipline faculty members' perceptions of high school GPA as a faulty mechanism for placement. It is worth noting that even some English faculty had initially shared these concerns about using GPA as a placement tool. As one English faculty member stated,

> I was extremely hesitant to use high school GPA for placement. After looking at the national data and seeing how other schools across the country have had great success, I felt more comfortable. Now that we're starting to see that our own data mirrors the rest of the country's, I feel much more at ease keeping this multiple measures system.

As this faculty member points out, the English placement committee responded to these concerns with national evidence supporting the use of high school GPA for placement and indicated the intention for continued monitoring of student success data as the semesters and year went on.

The college's ESL department also faced declining enrollment in AY 2020–2021 due to the pandemic and other factors stemming from immigration policies and national changes impacting international students, as well as travel barriers due to the COVID-19 pandemic. ESL faculty expressed concerns that pandemic processes were not adequately identifying students who may be better served by ESL placement due to the new unproctored English assessment tests, as well as concerns about potential academic integrity issues surrounding placement with ESL students. This led to dialogue and collaboration with ESL faculty seeking to further provide students with appropriate student-direct questions to identify whether ESL or English placement would be needed and the creation of a tool by ESL colleagues to aid ENG readers, if needed. In addition, the collaboration between the two departments also led to the development of a formal referral process between the two disciplines at the point of placement that would allow the best placement decisions to be made based on collaborative assessment of ESL placement measures and ENG placement measures.

Conclusions

The college has been using high school GPA in addition to standardized assessment scores (ACT and SAT) and a departmental essay test for English placement for just over a year now. We have remained fully virtual for all testing provided and have not resumed on-campus placement testing on a regular basis throughout the pandemic, with the exception of a few on-campus enrollment days where students were permitted to walk on campus and take a placement test. However, for the entire year, under 30 students in total took advantage of this opportunity.

From May 2020–April 2021, the college completed 9,586 total English placements, across all measures and methods. Of this number, 53 percent (5,081) of placed students enrolled in courses (Table 9.5). We also saw 5,545 students placed into English courses based on high school GPA, with 2,523 of these students enrolling in courses.

We were initially concerned when we learned that 47 percent of all placed students did not enroll for courses; however, we learned that this aligns historically with college placements and admissions processing outside of the pandemic. For many students who apply to the college, we are not a "first-choice" institution; for other students, outside factors result in their decision to not enroll in courses after beginning the application process (employment, financial aid, family or caregiver obligations, etc.). We were concerned about this early on and thought the fully online placement process or pandemic might be negatively impacting student completion of the placement process or deterring them from starting. However, we learned that the loss of potential students from placement to registration is not atypical, and it is not unique to the pandemic or a change from previous use of on-campus testing with WritePlacer.

Table 9.5. Total Students Placed May 2020–April 2021

	# Admitted Students	# Enrolled Students	Measure
	4,025	2,546	English Essay test
	5,545	2,523	HS GPA
	13	12	WritePlacer
Total	9,583	5,081	

In addition, there were 74 instances in which a faculty reader identified a student placement essay as unable to be scored and requested that the student be given a retest. Most often, readers indicate that this occurs when the submission is too short to determine a placement. Students who choose to attempt the essay test again are not part of the data termed "retest" as these students will have multiple attempts. In such cases, students are placed with the highest earned placement of all attempts. At this time, we have not reviewed the year's historical data to see what patterns may emerge from retests that students take. A total of 17 students were referred by English placement readers to ESL placement for assessment, which we find to be a lower number than we may have originally anticipated.

During the first few months of the process, we found some instances in which a student was given a placement test but had already received a placement based on GPA or ACT or SAT scores. Therefore, during the month of August, which was our busiest month for essay placements scored (total of 834), we sought to engage in research to see how widespread the "leakage" of our admissions and institutional process was as a way to address it so that students did not take an assessment they did not need to take. We identified approximately eight to ten percent of the students in that month who already had a placement based on high school GPA, ACT, or SAT. Many of these students were those who had placed into our accelerated offerings—either the 14-week corequisite ALP (ENG 1001 and ENG 1010) or the 2-week bridge course—so we hypothesize that they attempted to retest as a way to place into a standalone ENG 1010 course. We worked with our registrar's office directly to help develop direct messaging to students that either communicates a placement after the review of their high school transcript or refers them to placement testing. We have not seen a recurrence of this situation in later months.

Approximately 22 percent of all students placed into developmental English in Fall 2019, but as of Spring 2021, we are currently placing between four and five percent of students into developmental courses. Despite our transition from WritePlacer to GPA or a departmental essay, the success rates in ENG 1010 have remained within the ranges seen over the last five years (66–69%). The success rate for our gateway English course has remained constant this year—and while we do not know if this will remain in subsequent terms or post-pandemic, it is promising and worth continued monitoring. We also hypothesize that the use of faculty readers who teach the courses in the curriculum sequence could be having a positive impact on placement of students into honors-level first-year composition, which saw placements increase by 7.2 percent through the end of Fall 2020.

Emerging Considerations and Impact

We have found that there is strong value in faculty engagement and ownership of the placement decisions, especially in the use of authentic assessment as one of multiple measures. One faculty member said, "The key component of the system, faculty reading student essays, is the essence of authentic assessment; faculty who teach the courses are uniquely qualified to correctly place students." As faculty have long felt frustration with finding students who were significantly underqualified or overqualified to be in a particular course, implementing a system where their experience and firsthand knowledge is leveraged to find the best fit for a given student is quite powerful. Another faculty member described the relationship between reading placement essays and teaching in the classroom: "With so much experience in the classroom reading and grading essays, it was very easy to move into reading and placing new students into the correct courses for their skill levels." As one faculty reader said,

> We recognize critical thinking that may be hidden by typographical errors, often the result of composing an essay on a phone. Experienced readers know the difference between a basic writer[8] and a student who may not have understood the stakes of the assessment. When we aren't sure, we have one another. Standardized tests cannot do this, and the consequences of either over-placing or under-placing a student may be profound.

Another colleague reiterated this sentiment: "In many ways, the placement process not only allowed us to place students based on actually looking at their writing (instead of a computerized test) but also norm our assessment methods with our peers." These faculty member experiences reiterate the value of a human reader who can recognize the affective components and potential of students that a computerized assessment recognizing algorithms and semantic patterns may not readily identify. During consultations, it was not uncommon for faculty readers to engage in discussions about the potential for success in a course that a submitted essay demonstrated.

Another identified ways in which participation has informed pedagogy:

> I have gained insight not only into what students can do currently but what they need. Having this early access to student writing has informed my approach to the early weeks of the semester. If students are placed into the course that best suits their needs, and I am better prepared to greet them, then positive outcomes will follow. For this experience, I am a better writing instructor.

The first ten months of the pandemic placement process afforded opportunities for collaborative dialogue and direct faculty engagement in placement of students at the college that appear promising. As a result, despite the original pandemic placement agreement between the administration and union expiring in May 2021, an agreement has been reached to approve a one-year extension into the 2021–2022 year, allowing the identification and analysis of placement data,

---

8. The authors acknowledge that this is a contested term. To clarify, "a student who might benefit from additional support in the form of a developmental or corequisite course" would more effectively capture the intent.

processes, and faculty experiences in a more robust way before revisiting again in 2021. In addition, the revised developmental English sequence curriculum was revisited, and alternatives were proposed for consideration based on changes in placements and course delivery options. The past year has prompted an escalation of conversations among faculty and administration surrounding placement, largely as a result of a forced remote environment due to the pandemic. We now eagerly await more robust data from which to continue to revisit our placement measures, consider revisions to these measures based on student success and faculty member feedback regarding student success, and to investigate additional tools and platforms from which to continue process improvements.

Just over a year into this significant change in placement practices at the college, we await data from which to further conduct more robust comparative analysis regarding student success and progression into courses beyond those in which they place. The work has been informative with regard to placement practices at Tri-C and increased the involvement and engagement of full-time English faculty in the placement decisions of incoming students. We recognize that it is still early in the implementation of new placement measures and processes and that we have only a partial picture of the overall impact, as well as that, due to the pandemic, much of the data has to be analyzed in a limited context. Thus far, the impact on students appears to have promising implications that we are eager to continue to study, and faculty perceptions about the impact of the change on their courses appear promising. The unintended consequence of more robust faculty-to-faculty conversation about placement practices, expectations for students in the courses and teaching practices to further support students, and assessment of writing in general also presents significant further opportunities for research and directly impacting student success.

Acknowledgments

We would like to thank our tenured and tenure-track members of English Counterparts college-wide who worked diligently to respond to the need to continue placement during the pandemic, especially the members of the ENG placement team: Amy Cruickshank, Lorrie DiGiampietro, Lindsay Milam, Luke Schlueter, David Sierk, and Patrick Stansberry. We would also like to thank Dr. Terri Pope, Dr. Claire McMahon, Chandra Arthur, and Rob Stuart for helping us gather data to work on this chapter.

References

Allensworth, E. M. & Clark, K. (2020). High school GPAs and ACT scores as predictors of college completion: Examining assumptions about consistency across high schools. *Educational Researcher*, 49(3), 198–211. https://doi.org/10.3102/0013189x20902110.

Cuyahoga Community College. (n.d.). *AQIP systems portfolio 2017.* Retrieved May 1, 2021, from http://www.tri-c.edu:443/about/accreditation/documents/2017-aqip-systems-portfolio.pdf.

Cuyahoga Community College. (2019). *Tri-C at a glance.* https://issuu.com/lj719/docs/17-1596-at-a-glance_6-17_web?e=2373789/54362852.

Cuyahoga Community College. (n.d.). *Redefining access at Tri-C.* https://www.tri-c.edu/news-and-events/news/redefining-access-at-tri-c.html.

Diversity and Inclusion. (2020, September 10). Issuu, Retrieved May 1, 2021, from https://issuu.com/lj719/docs/20-0578_diversity_and_inclusion_-_diversity_report.

Gilman, H.; Giordano, J. B; Hancock, N.; Hassel, H.; Henson, L.; Hern, K., Nastal, J. & Toth, C. (2019). Forum: Two-Year College Writing Placement as Fairness. *Journal of Writing Assessment,* 12(1). Retrieved from https://escholarship.org/uc/item/4zv0r9b2.

Haswell, R. & Wyche-Smith, S. (1994). Adventuring into writing assessment. *College Composition and Communication,* 45(2), 220–236.

Jenkins, D. & Griffin, S. (2019). *From pockets of excellence to engaged innovation at scale: Guided pathways reforms at Cuyahoga Community College.* Columbia University, Teachers College, Community College Research Center. https://ccrc.tc.columbia.edu/media/k2/attachments/guided-pathways-case-study-1-tri-c.pdf.

Klausman, J., Toth, C., Swyt, W., Griffiths, B., Sullivan, P., Warnke, A. & Roberts, L. (2016). TYCA white paper on placement reform. *Teaching English in the Two-Year College,* 44(2), 135–157. https://cdn.ncte.org/nctefiles/groups/tyca/placementreform_revised.pdf.

Ohio Department of Higher Education. (n.d.). *College readiness and P-16 connections.* Ohio Higher Ed. https://www.ohiohighered.org/college-readiness.

O'Neill, P. (2003). Moving beyond holistic scoring through validity inquiry. *Journal of Writing Assessment,* 1(1). https://escholarship.org/uc/item/4qp611b4.

Toth, C. (2019). Directed self-placement at two-year colleges: A kairotic moment. *Journal of Writing Assessment,* 12(1). https://escholarship.org/uc/item/6g81k736.

Toth, C., Nastal, J., Hassel, H. & Giordano, J. B. (2019). Introduction: Writing assessment, placement, and the two-year college. *Journal of Writing Assessment,* 12(1). https://escholarship.org/uc/item/8393560s.

Vinaja, E. A. (2016). High school GPA and english graduation examinations: Predicting college english placement and english 101 final course grades (Order No. 10149277). ProQuest Dissertations & Theses Global. (1831587980). https://digitalcommons.liberty.edu/cgi/viewcontent.cgi?article=2305&context=doctoral.

Chapter 10. A Complement to Educational Reform: Directed Self-Placement (DSP) at Cochise College

Ella Melito
COCHISE COLLEGE

Erin Whittig
UNIVERSITY OF ARIZONA

Cathy Sander Matthesen
COCHISE COLLEGE

Denisse Cañez
COCHISE COLLEGE

Abstract: While many two- and four-year institutions have pivoted to directed self-placement (DSP) as a response to ethical and social justice concerns (Toth, 2019), at Cochise College, DSP was initially implemented as an emergency alternative to ACCUPLACER in the face of a worsening COVID-19 crisis and impending restrictions to in-person test proctoring. With support and buy-in from upper administration, the English department launched a full-scale pilot of DSP as a placement approach for all incoming Fall 2020 students. This case study describes the institutional context and Cochise's history of developmental reform from which the DSP emerged, the development of an "emergency" DSP and its evolution to a full-blown pilot alternative placement process, and our preliminary conclusions about DSP effectiveness and sustainability. Through the process of designing and implementing DSP, we have come to a fuller understanding of how placement testing works in concert with other developmental education reform initiatives and how it correlates with student success. In reflecting on this process, we've begun to see that while institution-wide buy-in and collaboration are necessary for placement reform, our collaborations have also exposed other practices and policies that must be addressed in order for DSP to be successful. We have come to understand that the COVID-19 pandemic provided us a rare opportunity for both immediate and continuing educational reform. Our preliminary data supports our decision to abandon our status quo placement tools in favor of the holistic and more personalized placement approach of the DSP.

Early in the COVID-19 pandemic, the Community College Research Center (CCRC) at Columbia Teachers College created a dedicated webspace for resources and research on the impact of COVID-19 on the nation's community colleges. Unsurprisingly, many of the early reports, blog entries, and news items posted center on concerns about remote learning, inequity in attainment, enrollment, transferability of pass/fail grades (a measure implemented by many higher education institutions), and the effect of all the above on fiscal stability (Glatter, 2020). Less apparent in these early conversations is how the pandemic would wreak havoc on two-year (and four-year) institutions' placement testing capabilities. A blog entry from September 2020 briefly notes adjustments a few colleges made in response to limited or no in-person testing (Lopez et al.), but by and large, we lacked a full picture of what such adjustments looked like.

A year into the pandemic, the on-the-ground stories of placement and testing professionals who had to pivot quickly in Spring 2020 began to emerge (Bickerstaff et al., 2021; Ockey, 2021). Cochise College, a two-year Hispanic-Serving Institution (HSI) in rural southeastern Arizona, faced a challenge similar to what we see in these emerging stories: How do we develop or adopt alternative placement exams in the event that social distancing protocols or remote proctoring limitations would prevent us from proctoring students taking the ACCUPLACER/WritePlacer exams?

While Cochise had already been using multiple measures placement for a few years, students who didn't meet the requirements of that process typically had to sit for the ACCUPLACER exam in the college's testing center to receive a placement in a writing course. Faced with a severely limited timeline—Fall 2020 students would begin taking placement tests in less than two months—the English department made a decisive move to implement a directed self-placement (hereafter, DSP) process as an alternative for students who could not be placed by multiple measures.

In this chapter, we will describe the institutional context and Cochise's history of developmental reform from which the DSP emerged, the development of an "emergency" DSP and its evolution to a full-blown pilot alternative placement process, and our conclusions about DSP effectiveness and sustainability. In sharing our story, we focus on how this process informed many of our unquestioned assumptions about what determines student readiness and success. While DSP was originally a response to an institutional challenge to provide alternative, remote placement options, the process of designing and implementing our DSP process allowed us to understand more fully how placement testing works in concert with other developmental education reform initiatives and how it correlates with student success. In reflecting on this process, we've begun to see that while institutional buy-in and collaboration are necessary for placement reform, our collaborations have also exposed other practices and policies that must be addressed in order for DSP to be successful.

Background

Institutional Context

Cochise College is a Hispanic-Serving Institution (HSI) comprising two main campuses in southern Arizona—Sierra Vista and Douglas—and maintaining centers in downtown Sierra Vista, Benson, Willcox, and Fort Huachuca. Cochise College continues to develop as a learning community by focusing on teaching and learning, access and diversity, and the use of technology and innovative instruction. Cochise College's 255 faculty members and 321 staff members provide education and training, in both online and face-to-face formats, including degree and certificate-level programs, community education, skills upgrading, developmental education, and educational programming for special populations to address barriers to participation in education and employment.

Our mission is largely shaped by the needs of the surrounding communities: rural southern Arizona communities, as well as border commuters from Mexico. Since we are situated so close to the U.S./Mexico border, the majority of our students are Hispanic/Latinx (44.5 percent in Fall 2020); many of these students are served by our Douglas campus, but we also serve a large contingent of military students on the Sierra Vista campus (from the Fort Huachuca military base). In Fall 2020, our total enrollment was 3,327 (excludes some active-duty military students in specified training programs, department of corrections students, and high school students). Of these students, 42.3 percent identify as male and 57.7 percent identify as female.

The English department at Cochise College is part of the Liberal Arts division. Often, the English and reading departments work closely on curriculum reform; student success initiatives; and placement testing research, implementation, and monitoring. Further, collaboration occurs between the English department and the Cochise College writing lab, which falls under the purview of the student success division.

As of Fall 2020, the English department employed nine full-time faculty members, six of whom identify as female and three as male. The faculty's educational backgrounds include eight masters degrees in a related field (e.g., literature, creative writing, English) and one Ph.D. in rhetoric, composition, and the teaching of English.

History of Curriculum and Placement Reform at Cochise

Before our introduction to DSP, Cochise College English faculty were already engaged in curricular and placement reforms to more effectively serve our population. We have been actively using research to guide our developmental education reform. Cochise College's reform movement contextualizes our transition to DSP and positions us to recognize DSP as a complement to our other reform initiatives. Prior to 2017, the English composition sequence at Cochise College consisted of three developmental education writing courses (Figure 10.1) into which students were placed via ACCUPLACER, followed by the for-credit, required writing courses.

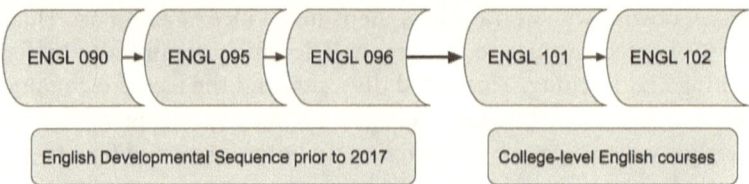

Figure 10.1. English developmental sequence prior to 2017. Note. ENG 096 was originally ENG 100, but articulation agreements with other AZ institutions forced a course number change to ENG 096 in 2018. The course outcomes are exactly the same.

Developmental English students, however, were languishing in lower-level courses in this period prior to any developmental education reform. A review of data from 2014–2016 reveals the adverse impact of a multicourse developmental program: We tracked transfer rates of students enrolled in developmental courses (reading or English) as well as students not enrolled in these courses. After tracking students over a six-year period (beginning in 2014), we found that students who had not enrolled in a developmental reading or English course achieved a transfer rate of 22.2 percent, while students enrolled in these courses achieved a 15.4 percent transfer rate (see Tables 10.A1 and 10.A2 in Appendix A). We saw this same trend continue with each tracked developmental and non-developmental cohort in subsequent years.

Further, from 2014–2016, students who began at the very lowest-level developmental course (i.e., ENG 090) had a lower rate of successful completion of ENG 101 than students who began the developmental sequence in higher-level developmental courses (i.e., ENG 095 or ENG 096)—31 percent versus 47 percent or 70 percent (Table 10.1).

Recognizing that these programs were not adequately serving or meeting the needs of its students, Cochise College began to engage in researching and implementing different support models to make its writing and reading programs more effective for its population. A 2014–2015 annual report to the governor stated that Cochise College had "begun exploring ways to reinvent developmental education because a high percentage of incoming students require pre-college-level instruction" (Rottweiler, 2015). At the time, Cochise College was specifically interested in redesigning its developmental and general education reading and English course offerings. Cochise asked Hanover Research—a private research and analytics firm—to study best practices in community college English and literacy instruction, particularly as they relate to developmental college preparation courses and their impacts on student outcomes. Hanover Research provided Cochise College with an overview of trends and issues in developmental education, as well as an overview of best practices in developmental English placement and course and curriculum design (Hanover Research, 2016).

Table 10.1. Average Percent and Time to Pass ENG 101 for Students Enrolled in Developmental ENG

	Initial Course Placement		
	ENG 090	ENG 095	ENG 096
Average % of students completing ENG 101 with a passing grade (A, B, C)	31%	47%	70%
Average # of terms to complete ENG 101 with a passing grade (A, B, C)	5.6	4.6	3

Additionally, we looked at various developmental education models at other community colleges in the state of Arizona, reviewed the Accelerated Learning Program (ALP) scholarship, and attended several conferences held by the Arizona Association for Developmental Education. In 2018, Cochise College signed a contract with Complete College America (CCA), a national organization that helps colleges and universities reshape their policies, perspectives, and practices as a way to increase economic opportunity, social mobility, and racial justice. CCA initiatives focus on improving retention, completion, and transfer rates of students. A push to align with the CCA framework initiated conversations about strategies to reduce the number of courses in our developmental sequence. During two waves of developmental education reform (Figures 10.2 and 10.3), the developmental English courses were ultimately reduced from a sequence of three to two: We now only offer ENG 095, a basic writing course focusing on grammar and paragraph development, and ENG 096, an intermediate writing course that focuses on grammar, essay development, and research skills.

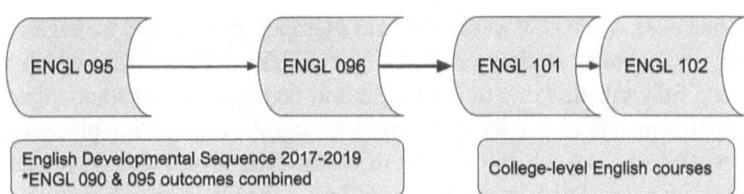

Figure 10.2. First-wave reform English course sequences (2017–2019).

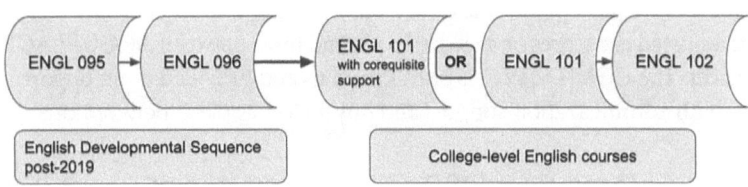

Figure 10.3. Second-wave reform English course sequences (2019–2021).

In Fall 2020, we opened corequisite English 101 courses on both the Sierra Vista and Douglas campuses. The corequisite ENG 101 course incorporates a separate support lab that is capped at nine students. The English department implemented corequisite support models as a way to improve retention, completion, and transfer rates of students in developmental education programs.

During the first-wave reform (Figure 10.2), multiple measures were implemented for placement into the English composition courses. Students must have received one of the following within the last three years to be placed into first-year writing courses:

- a score of 480 or above in the SAT Evidence-Based Reading and Writing (EBRW) section
- a score of 20 or above on the ACT
- a grade of B or better in a 12th grade English Honors course

If a student could not be placed using the multiple measures criteria, then the student took the ACCUPLACER exam to determine first-year writing course placement. The majority of our students were placed by ACCUPLACER.

It was during this second-wave reform (Figure 10.3)—in which multiple measures/ACCUPLACER placement was in place—that the COVID-19 crisis forced us to reconsider and redesign our placement protocols. After adjusting multiple measures cut offs for COVID (i.e., changed SAT/ACT currency from three years to five years), we still had a significant number of students who needed to be placed by ACCUPLACER. However, amidst quarantines and shutdowns, ACCUPLACER's proctoring requirements posed potential problems for students accessing the exam. Our exploration and subsequent adoption of DSP was initiated by the need to create remotely accessible placement exams that would not require active proctoring.

Furthermore, while DSP was initiated as a temporary measure, we began to see it as a viable replacement option for ACCUPLACER/WritePlacer, with which we had never been fully satisfied due to the length and taxing nature of standardized testing. Our students often take the mathematics, English, and reading placement tests in consecutive sessions which can lead to testing fatigue and disengagement from the placement exam. Students reported randomly answering questions and quickly moving through the placement exams when they begin experiencing testing fatigue. We wondered whether this unfocused response to the placement exam may contribute to inaccurate placement, but rather than seeking out an alternative placement tool, we adjusted cut scores or switched back and forth between ACCUPLACER and WritePlacer. The COVID-19 crisis both forced us and provided us an opportunity to explore, with administration support and buy-in, other placement options.

Designing DSP: Collaboration is Key

While many scholars have begun to view DSP as a way to address ethical and social justice concerns (Inoue, 2009; Kenner, 2016; Poe & Inoue, 2016; Toth, 2019), at

Cochise College, DSP was initially a temporary response to a crisis. In the thick of this crisis, we understood only that we had to act swiftly and decisively. We implemented DSP as a standalone project with the mindset of returning to the status quo placement procedure once the pandemic subsided. DSP was poised to launch after a three-week development phase. The English DSP Pilot Phase I began on May 13, 2020, and ended on June 8, 2020, with over 100 students participating. The dean of liberal arts then supported the English DSP's launch as a full pilot (DSP Pilot Phase II), requiring all incoming placement-seeking students to participate in the DSP.

In this section, we will describe how we developed the Cochise College English DSP, where it "lives," and how students enroll in the English course once they have chosen a course. Given that we had just two months to design and implement our "emergency" procedure, we have chosen to focus on the cross-institutional collaboration and institution-wide partnerships that were integral in ensuring its swift creation, rollout, and accessibility. Without this collaboration, the DSP could never have been functional in such a short time.

Cross-Institutional Collaboration

Serendipitously, Cochise College English faculty members had recently been introduced to DSP through two key sources: a presentation on DSP by Christie Toth at an annual statewide gathering of university and community college English instructors and the *TYCA White Paper on Placement Reform* (Klaussman et al., 2016). Recalling what we'd recently learned, in early April 2020, the English department chair contacted the University of Arizona (UA) writing program, which had been employing a directed self-placement approach since Spring 2018, to explore their tool as a model for those students the testing center could not accommodate.

While the University of Arizona's own DSP was developed over a nearly three-year period, it grew out of a similar "kairotic moment" (Toth, 2019): when the College Board announced a new scoring system for the SAT to be implemented in March 2016, UA's writing program was using a combination of SAT/ACT scores and high school GPA to determine writing placement. However, writing program administrators had been considering DSP since 2015 for a variety of reasons: to address a lack of curricular awareness and agentive educational decision-making in our incoming cohorts, to gather more information about students reporting dual enrollment, and to re-examine and re-articulate the intended audiences and purposes of the first-year writing course sequence.

Initially, the most salient feature of UA's placement process for Cochise was the fact that the entire process is completed online (using Qualtrics, a robust survey-building platform). Being able to provide the process online to any student would address Cochise's immediate need for accessible, remote placement. Further, the specific components of UA's DSP also appealed to Cochise DSP developers and appeared adaptable to our local context, specifically, course information, the self-assessment survey, a course recommendation (based on self-assessment responses), and a writing task where students are asked to reflect on the information they've been provided and state which course they wish to take.

In partnership with the University of Arizona writing program's assistant director for placement, the Cochise English department began developing the DSP "course" in Moodle, our learning management system (Figure 10.4). The English DSP course guides students through a series of videos that acquaint them with each of the first-year writing courses Cochise College offers. Students taking the English DSP course then participate in self-reflective activities that ask them to think about previous writing experiences and their learning preferences (see Appendix B), culminating in a reflective writing activity (Figure 10.5).

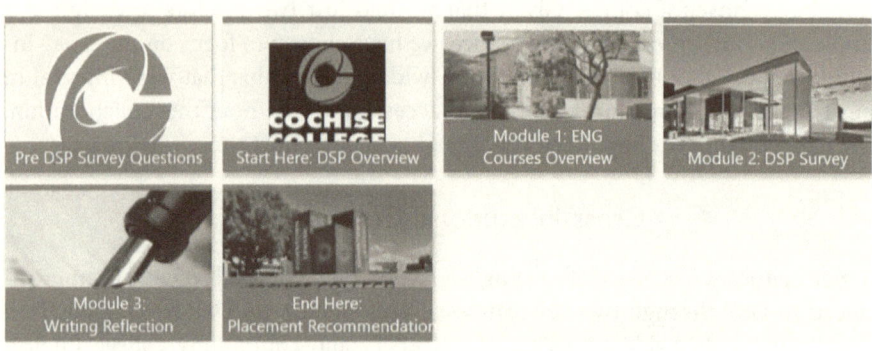

Figure 10.4. Cochise College tile design for DSP course.

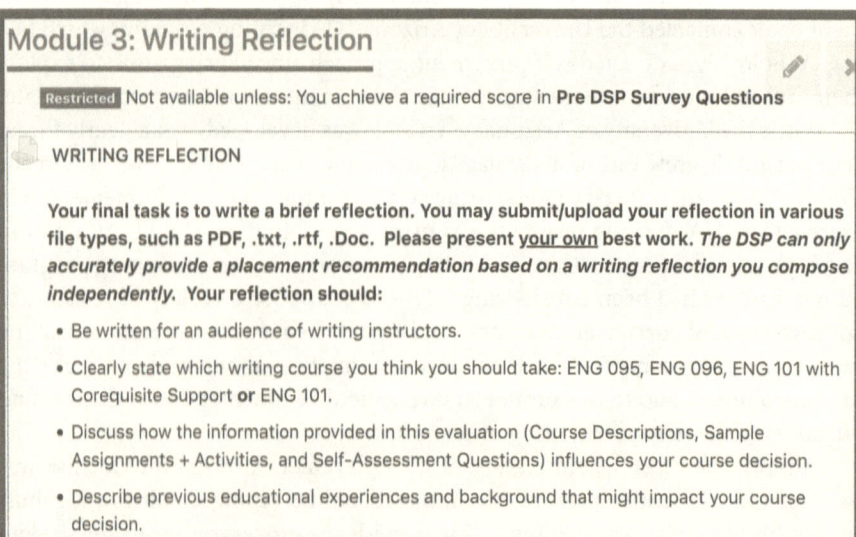

Figure 10.5. Post-DSP survey writing reflection.

When the student completes the DSP course, a specific course recommendation is generated. Once a student receives a placement recommendation, an alert is sent to the testing center director, who removes enrollment blocks to enable the student to register. The testing center director and all advisors also have access to student placement recommendation equated scores (see Appendix C) in our student management system. Note: We are working to ensure the students do not see the raw placement scores; we want them to see only their *recommended* placement. The advisors have access to each student's responses to the DSP survey questions, raw scores, and writing samples housed in Moodle.

Institution-Wide Collaborations

As we moved from "emergency" design and implementation into full-scale pilot phases, we experienced a number of epiphanies about the far-reaching effects of DSP on the institution and its stakeholders. We fielded daily inquires from our centers and departments on both campuses about how the DSP would affect their processes, policies, and programs, but were nevertheless inspired by the way the DSP pilot provided the opportunity for collaboration among many departments, staff, and administrators. Having initial buy-in from our dean of liberal arts and the student success dean very likely helped pave the way for DSP development and implementation; had we encountered resistance from upper administration, other critical partnerships might have been more difficult to establish. Despite what we've perceived as the critical role of buy-in in our own DSP implementation, this concept is relatively unexplored in DSP scholarship (see Moos & Van Zanen, 2019), especially as it relates to the myriad departments, staff, and other stakeholders who can make or break a placement reform like DSP. Ultimately, we learned that placement reform requires college-wide collaboration and buy-in. Furthermore, it is through such extensive collaboration and communication that we have begun to see how placement reform can expose the seemingly benign institutional processes and policies that can have adverse effects for our students. In some cases, our collaborations led to improvements, streamlining, and better communication; in other cases, we are still grappling with the issues surfaced by our placement reform efforts.

An early issue we faced was with access: Since Moodle is intended as a learning management system for already-enrolled students, we had to collaborate with our learning management administrator (LMA) to ensure the DSP "course" was accessible to incoming students, functioned properly, and adequately stored all the data we needed on each test taker. The LMA was able to find creative and viable solutions to allow incoming students access. Additionally, our web administrator (WA) created a standalone DSP website that introduces new students to the English DSP and provides buttons that direct students to the English DSP. The WA also added direct links to the English DSP on the testing center and counseling and advising websites. The testing center director monitors the DSP, directs students to the DSP page, and ensures students are able to access DSP. Once a student has completed the DSP, the testing center director receives an alert via an email message prompting them to remove any enrollment block and add notes to the student's placement recommendation in Banner (Cochise's student management system).

We also recognized early on the critical role that advisors play in supporting students' placement decisions (see Saenkhum, 2016). Our advisors were given access to check the students' raw scores and placement recommendations from the DSP surveys and to read students' reflective essays, allowing them to gain a more holistic understanding of the student and their placement needs in order to support students' decision-making. To ensure that advisors and students resist applying a skills-based testing mentality to DSP (e.g., some students have requested to retake the DSP for a better score/placement recommendation), we developed training information for advisors. The training reiterates that the DSP is a tool designed to guide a student through self-reflection, so completing the process again to manipulate the result and recommendation is not ideal. We also emphasized both to advisors and students that if a student does not feel comfortable with their placement recommendation, they are permitted to select a different course option. If a student would like more help selecting a course, then they can discuss the placement with an advisor. In addition to this training, we provided advisors with a training video to help them navigate the English DSP housed on Moodle and access all student information related to DSP placement recommendation.

As we continue to use the DSP, we desire to create a culture among faculty and staff that fosters trust in students to select the first-year composition course that aligns with their overall educational goals. To do this, we understand the importance of keeping lines of communication open between the English department and the advisors. We are quick to respond when issues arise, such as old placement policies conflicting with the spirit/philosophy of the DSP. We invite our advisor who acts as the English department liaison to department meetings and DSP training events, and we host touch-base meetings to candidly discuss how placement affects advisors and their interactions with students.

An unforeseen, yet welcome, outcome of our collaboration with advisors was that it allowed us to promote the English corequisite pilots on the Sierra Vista and Douglas campuses. Using the DSP recommendation, writing samples, and collaboration with the student, advisors encouraged students to participate in the English corequisite pilot. If the DSP recommends placement into ENG 096, a developmental course, but the student does not feel ready for English 101 and wishes to bypass a developmental course, the corequisite course has emerged as a wonderful placement option; it is a nice compromise. The corequisite provides students more support and guidance throughout the semester in a transferable, credit-bearing course. When the student completes the English corequisite course, they receive credit for English 101.

Despite the training and conversations, we have still encountered entrenched mentalities regarding placement along with outdated placement policies that conflict with students' ability to self-place. We are just beginning to establish connections and open conversations with ArmyIgnitED advisors, for example, who treat the DSP placement recommendation as a hard-and-fast placement, and only allow enrollment into a higher course if the student goes through an approval process. We encountered a similar issue with one student in a particular program trying to enroll in ENG 101 when they'd received a recommendation for ENG 096. The program would only admit students who had received a placement of ENG 101. The student's advisor felt uncomfortable allowing the student to choose an English 101 placement and self-enroll in the program. The student was eventually permitted to enroll in the program by obtaining approval from the dean overseeing the program. While it is encouraging to know that students can get around such obstacles, these inconvenient approval processes undermine students' ability to make their own course decisions. While we want to protect students' choices, we also want to be sensitive to our current position; we are very much in a transition phase in that we are adopting a placement tool that is philosophically different from skill-based, standardized placement tools we have historically used on our campuses. Our goal is to build relationships through collaboration, education, and conversations so that when placement issues present themselves, we can work together to resolve them.

There have also been some concerns that there might be financial aid disbursement and allocation challenges associated with DSP recommendations, especially for those students who choose to deviate from the DSP placement recommendations when enrolling in courses. However, the financial aid advisor collaborated with the DSP development team to add information to the Cochise College catalog to address DSP recommendation and financial aid disbursements. Since the financial aid advisor supports allowing students to make placement choices, students may choose to enroll in English courses both lower or higher than the placement recommendation without fear of losing financial aid. If a student makes a course selection "higher" than the placement recommendation and fails the course, they are still eligible for financial aid; however, the financial aid advisor may request the student enroll in the original course the DSP recommended.

Perhaps one of the most complex and ongoing issues surfaced by the shift to DSP has to do with our English language learners (ELLs). The dean of student success and the English as a Second Language (ESL) faculty have worked closely with the DSP development team to ensure that we still identify students who may be ELLs at placement, since Cochise College does not have published English proficiency requirements (e.g., TOEFL, IELTS) for admissions. The ACCUPLACER exam at Cochise College was designed to capture demographic and ELL indicators (e.g., primary language, home language, primary language of instruction) at the beginning of the placement exam. If a student was identified as ELL, they were directed away from the ACCUPLACER exam and provided a separate ESL placement exam. Like many other institutions, Cochise College offers an English for Academic Purposes Program that helps students improve their skills in oral communication, reading, grammar, and writing as preparation for continued higher education at Cochise College and beyond. This is a for-credit program, and eligible students may receive financial aid. Our ESL courses in the English for Academic Purposes Program particularly serve and benefit students on the Douglas Campus, where we serve a significant population of students from Agua Prieta, Sonora, Mexico and Naco, Sonora, Mexico along with other international students. When we developed the DSPs in Moodle, we initially did not integrate a mechanism to identify ELLs for this program. While transitioning into a DSP Pilot Phase II (discussed in more detail below), we coordinated with the dean of student success to ensure ELL students were identified via an ESL pre-survey, which is housed on the DSP website. Once the pre-survey is completed, links to the DSPs are then visible and active. Because it is possible for students to bypass the ESL pre-survey and access the DSPs, the ESL pre-surveys are also embedded into both the English and Reading DSPs. While these testing redundancies are currently necessary, we hope to find a way to identify ELL students without also embedding the ESL pre-survey directly on the testing page website and into each DSP.

From Planning to Piloting

The Cochise College English DSP Pilot Phase I began on May 13, 2020, and ended on June 8, 2020, with 134 students participating. Although the sample size is too small to draw final conclusions about the effectiveness of the DSP, our initial data and informal student and administrative feedback suggest that allowing students to make placement choices did not seem to significantly change placement of students across our courses. Table 10.2 provides a snapshot of a comparison between ACCUPLACER and DSP placement.

Table 10.2. Comparison of ACCUPLACER Placements and DSP Placements

	Initial Course Placement		
	ENG 095	ENG 096	ENG 101
ACCUPLACER June 2017–June 2020 ($n=3,805$)	14%	47%	38%
Directed Self-Placement May 2020–June 2020 ($n=134$)	8%	41%	40%

We are beginning to see that DSP has the potential to challenge our notions of what determines college-level writing readiness and what predicts student success. A student's agency in course selection could increase their engagement and commitment in their courses (see Moos & Van Zanen, 2019). In one conversation with a student about placement and the effectiveness of their ENG 101 corequisite course, the student shared that the DSP ultimately helped them to commit to enrolling in courses. There was a significant gap between their high school experience and their interest in a college experience. They feared the academic gap would make their skills a little rusty and cause them to place into a developmental course. Their academic goals were clearly set—they wanted to get into college, get through coursework as quickly as they could, and enter the workforce in order to support their young family. They decided that if they tested into developmental courses, they would not attend college because degree completion would take too long and cause a financial strain. While the DSP tool did recommend a developmental placement, the student conversed with an advisor and determined that ENG 101 with corequisite would effectively meet their needs. Knowing they would receive academic support and ENG 101 credit, the student decided to enroll in the corequisite class and begin pursuing their degree. They went on to receive an "A" in ENG 101. By learning about this student's DSP experience—and others' experiences—we are given a glimpse into factors about a student that impact their success that cannot be measured by ACCUPLACER scores, such as engagement, motivation, and learning preferences.

In addition to many discoveries as we implemented the DSP, our examination yielded important realizations about placement: 1) students typically follow the DSP's placement recommendation, 2) the DSP is responsive and dynamic, 3) the DSP fosters communication among students, advisors, and faculty, and 4) the DSP placement tool has potential to improve rates of completion, transfer, and disproportionate placement in relation to race, class, gender, and linguistic background.

First, we were initially concerned some students would self-place into a course they were unprepared for; however, we came to understand that many students would select the course that would best meet their skill level and academic needs. Early results from DSP Pilot Phase I are beginning to dispel some of our initial placement concerns. We discovered that 50 percent of students who participated in the DSP enrolled in the course the DSP recommended and only two percent of the students chose a higher-level course (the remaining percentage of students had not yet enrolled in an English course at the time data was collected). Knowing how students respond to DSP recommendations is important as we move forward in ensuring that students are getting the best possible placement experience.

Also, because our DSP tool was locally designed, managed, and administered, it is nimble. Asao B. Inoue and colleagues (2011) asserted that "DSP makes clear how course placement processes should be 'site-based' and 'context-sensitive'" (p. 1). We can make adjustments to the tool by adding or changing survey questions and altering cut scores for placement recommendations. We can do this based on trends, classroom experiences, and data. Recognizing that "successful course placement may be measured differently than conventional validity inquiries" (Inoue et al., 2011, p. 2), we do hope moving forward to capture student satisfaction rates through student surveys. Student responses also have the power to drive DSP adjustments and changes (Gevers & Whittig, 2019).

We also found that the DSP fosters more holistic communication with students, especially student-advisor communication. As students move through DSP modules, they are not only exposed to the writing curriculum at the college, they are invited to reflect on their prior learning experiences. When students complete the DSP, they often meet with advisors to discuss placement options; advisors' insight into the students' abilities now goes beyond a cut score or standardized test score. Our hope is that students' agency in course selection increases engagement and commitment in their courses.

Finally, while designing and implementing the DSP, we have been increasingly exposed to scholarship on DSP and placement reform (see Kelly-Riley & Whithaus, 2019; Klausman, et al., 2016), so we are now beginning to recognize how placement is potentially pivotal in improving transfer and completion rates and disproportionate placement of students of color and students from low-income and working-class backgrounds into developmental courses. Currently, we can provide only a broad picture of results, but we've learned a valuable lesson about data collection, and we now understand the importance of disaggregating data to determine disproportionate placement of students related to race, class, gender, and linguistic background. Moving forward, we have greater insight about the type of comparative data we need to collect to make informed decisions.

Conclusion

After receiving broader training (a Fall 2020 workshop on DSP for all English faculty), reviewing the early data, and considering faculty input, in October 2020 we decided to launch a DSP Phase II pilot that would span a three-term period and allow us to grow our sample sizes. We intend to systematically move through three phases: data collection, interventions, and methods of results interpretations. We plan to collect student survey responses regarding their self-placement course choices versus DSP recommendations, developmental placement demographics, ACCUPLACER/DSP placement data and course completion and pass/fail rates, and faculty perspectives on DSP adoption. We will also implement additional faculty and staff training, and educate students on the importance of the first-year writing course selections. We intend to learn more about interpreting disaggregated data so that we can readily see whether the DSP mitigates disproportionate placement related to race, class, gender, or linguistic background.

It is only in hindsight that we have come to understand that the COVID-19 pandemic provided us a rare opportunity for both immediate and continuing educational reform. Even though we were in a moment of crisis, the pandemic opened a space for us to have a more concentrated focus on understanding our population and meeting their needs. The DSP inspired us not only to increase our awareness of our students' needs, but also to revisit our curriculum sequence, reconsider and reevaluate the effectiveness of all our reform initiatives, question whether we are truly serving and meeting the needs of our student population, and form crucial institution and cross-institution partnerships. As we review our preliminary data and begin hearing stories from students about how the DSP personally impacted their decisions to both enter college and select courses, we are confident that we will not be readily returning to our status quo placement tools, instead preferring the holistic and more personalized placement approach.

Acknowledgments

We thank Dr. Eric Brooks, Angela Garcia, Travis Ambrose, Renee Rhodehamel, Karen Emmer, and Cochise College advisors for their contributions researching, developing, and implementing the English and reading directed self-placements at Cochise College. Additionally, we thank Dr. Eric Brooks, Rebecca Dorman, Mark Boggie, and Dr. Jeroen Gevers for their comments on manuscript drafts.

References

Bickerstaff, S., Kopko, E., Lewy, E. B., Raufman, J. & Rutschow, E. Z. (2021). *Implementing and scaling multiple measures assessment in the context of COVID-19*. Center for the Analysis of Postsecondary Readiness. https://ccrc.tc.columbia.edu/publications/implementing-scaling-multiple-measures-covid.html .

Gevers, J. & Whittig, E. (2019). *"I loved it because it is truly up to you": Student perspectives on choice and agency in Directed Self-Placement* [Paper presentation]. Council of Writing Program Administrators, Baltimore, MD, United States.

Glatter, H. (2020, April 7). Emerging challenges the coronavirus poses for community colleges. *The Mixed Methods Blog, Community College Research Center*. https://ccrc.tc.columbia.edu/easyblog/challenges-coronavirus-community-colleges.html.

Hanover Research. (2016). *Best practices in community college developmental English: Prepared for Cochise College*. https://drive.google.com/file/d/1cvw5tZUxpTEaTVdbHuJXHNEsE921KHgn/view?usp=sharing.

Inoue, A. B. (2009). Self-assessment as programmatic center: The first year writing program and its assessment at California State University, Fresno. *Composition Forum, 20*. http://compositionforum.com/issue/20/calstate-fresno.php.

Inoue, A. B., Fernandez, M., Gary, L., Gomes, M., Harriger, D., Johnson, K., Maddox, S., Nakamura, B., Richmond, T., Sinha, A. & Speechly, D. (2011). Directed self-placement. *WPA-CompPile Research Bibliographies, 16*, 1–17. http://comppile.org/wpa/bibliographies/Bib16/DSP.pdf.

Kelly-Riley, D. & Whithaus, C. (2019). Editor's introduction: Special issue on two-year college writing placement. *Journal of Writing Assessment, 12*(1), 1–4. http://journalofwritingassessment.org/archives.php?issue=23.

Kenner, K. (2016). Student rationale for self-placement into first-year composition: Decision making and directed self-placement. *Teaching English in the Two-Year College, 43*(3), 274–289.

Klausman, J., Toth, C., Swyt, W., Griffiths, B., Sullivan, P., Warnke, A., Williams, A. L., Giordano, J. & Roberts, L. (2016). TYCA white paper on placement reform. *Teaching English in the Two-Year College, 44*(2), 135–157.

Lopez, A., Pellegrino, L. & Leasor, L. (2020). How colleges adapted advising and other supports during COVID-19 shutdowns. *The Mixed Methods Blog, Community College Research Center.* https://ccrc.tc.columbia.edu/easyblog/colleges-adapted-advising-covid-supports.html.

Moos, A. & Van Zanen, K. (2019). Directed self-placement as a tool to foreground student agency. *Assessing Writing, 41,* 68–71. https://doi.org/10.1016/j.asw.2019.06.001

Ockey, G. (2021). An overview of COVID-19's impact on English language university admissions and placement tests. *Language Assessment Quarterly, 18*(1), 1–5. https://doi.org/10.1080/15434303.2020.1866576.

Poe, M. & Inoue, A. (2016). Toward writing as social justice: An idea whose time has come. *College English, 79*(2), 119–126.

Rottweiler, J. D. (2015). *2014–2015 annual report to the governor.* Cochise College. https://www.cochise.edu/cfiles/files/36/Annual-Report-to-the-Governor-2014-15.pdf.

Saenkhum, T. (2016). *Decisions, agency, and advising: Key issues in the placement of multilingual writers into first-year composition courses.* Utah State University Press.

Toth, C. (2019). Directed self-placement in two-year colleges: A kairotic moment. *Journal of Writing Assessment, 12*(1). http://journalofwritingassessment.org/article.php?article=134.

Appendix A: Transfer Data

Table 10.A1. Transfer-Out Data for First-Time English or Reading Developmental Education Students

Year	Head Count	1 Year	2 Years	3 Years	4 Years	5 Years	6 Years
2014	358	0.3%	1.4%	5.6%	10.6%	13.7%	15.4%
2015	357	0.0%	1.7%	8.1%	14.3%	18.5%	
2016	334	0.3%	2.1%	9.0%	15.6%		
2017	299	0.7%	4.4%	14.4%			
2018	283	0.4%	2.1%				
2019	226	0.9%					

Table 10.A2. Transfer-Out Data for First-Time Non Developmental Education Students

Year	Head Count	1 Year	2 Years	3 Years	4 Years	5 Years	6 Years
2014	585	0.2%	3.6%	9.7%	14.9%	18.6%	22.2%
2015	500	0.6%	3.2%	9.8%	15.2%	18.6%	
2016	450	1.1%	5.3%	12.7%	18.0%		
2017	359	0.3%	2.8%	13.1%			
2018	437	0.2%	6.0%				
2019	521	1.0%					

Appendix B: DSP Self-Assessment Questions

1. I have a strong grasp of the conventions of academic writing, such as grammar, spelling, and punctuation.
    A) Not really
    B) Kind of
    C) Mostly
    D) Absolutely

2. When I have a writing assignment, I know exactly what I need to do to get it done.
    A) Not really
    B) Kind of
    C) Mostly
    D) Absolutely

3. I prefer to read and analyze multi-page academic texts . . .
    A) with a lot of assistance and guidance from my peers and instructor.
    B) with some assistance and guidance from my peers and instructor.
    C) with little to no assistance and guidance from peers and instructor.
    D) more independently, with very little support from my peers and instructor.

4. I prefer to work on major assignments for the course . . .
    A) mostly during class time.
    B) during class time and on my own as homework.
    C) mostly on my own as homework, with limited in-class writing time.
    D) on my own, without in-class writing time.

5. I prefer to decide what I write about for my major projects . . .
    A) with a lot of assistance and guidance from my peers and instructor.
    B) with some assistance and guidance from my peers and instructor.
    C) with limited amount of assistance and guidance from my peers and instructor.
    D) with little to no assistance and guidance from my peers and instructor.

6. I prefer to engage in the writing process (brainstorming, prewriting, outlining, drafting, revising) . . .
   A) With a lot of support from my peers and instructor.
   B) With some support from my peers and instructor.
   C) Somewhat independently, with limited support from my peers and instructor.
   D) More independently, with very little support from my peers and instructor.
7. I can read and annotate (take notes on) 15 or more pages for weekly homework.
   A) Not really
   B) Kind of
   C) Mostly
   D) Absolutely
8. I can discuss a text with an instructor and/or peers.
   A) Not really
   B) Kind of
   C) Mostly
   D) Absolutely
9. When I read something (a book, an essay, an article), I always have a lot of ideas for how to respond to it.
   A) Not really
   B) Kind of
   C) Mostly
   D) Absolutely
10. I know how to clearly summarize key arguments in others' writing.
    A) Not really
    B) Kind of
    C) Mostly
    D) Absolutely
11. I have written many (5+) academic texts that are longer than five pages.
    A) Not really
    B) Kind of
    C) Mostly
    D) Absolutely
12. I have regularly written for an audience other than a teacher.
    A) Not really
    B) Kind of
    C) Mostly
    D) Absolutely
13. I have a lot of experience locating, selecting, and evaluating sources for researched academic writing.
    A) Not really
    B) Kind of
    C) Mostly
    D) Absolutely

14. I seek other writers' advice on my writing while I am drafting.
    A) Not really
    B) Kind of
    C) Mostly
    D) Absolutely
15. I have a lot of experience citing others' ideas in my writing to avoid plagiarism or academic dishonesty.
    A) Not really
    B) Kind of
    C) Mostly
    D) Absolutely
16. I have completed many writing assignments integrating multiple sources.
    A) Not really
    B) Kind of
    C) Mostly
    D) Absolutely
17. I have strategies to overcome the challenges I confront in a writing project.
    A) Not really
    B) Kind of
    C) Mostly
    D) Absolutely

Appendix C: DSP Placement Recommendations

Placement Score	Course Recommendation
425–849	ENG 095—Many of your answers in the self-assessment indicate that you may desire or benefit from additional writing support and time with your instructor that ENG 095 provides.
850–1274	ENG 096—Many of your answers in the self-assessment indicate that you may desire or benefit from additional research and academic reading and writing practice that ENG 096 provides. OR ENG 101 with Corequisite Support—Many of your answers in the self-assessment indicate that you may desire or benefit from taking college-level ENG 101 coupled with a support lab in which you receive more individualized support as you work to complete a college-level writing course. Note: Once you successfully complete ENG 101 with Corequisite Support, you will receive credit for ENG 101. *Note: The ENG 101 with Corequisite Support option was added to the course recommendations in DSP Pilot Phase II.
1275–1700	ENG 101—Many of your answers in the self-assessment indicate that you may desire or benefit from the challenge and the rigor of a college-level writing experience that ENG 101 provides.

Chapter 11. Community College Online Directed Self-Placement During the COVID-19 Pandemic

Sarah Elizabeth Snyder, Sara Amani, and Kevin Kato
Arizona Western College

Abstract: Recent research at several colleges and universities around the US has suggested directed self-placement (DSP) programs are better predictive indicators of students' actual performance in their first-year writing courses than single-score placement tests (Conference on College Composition and Communication, 2014; Ferris et al., 2016). Students deserve to exercise some agency in their placement (Crusan, 2011) and are encouraged to take responsibility for their own education through DSP (Royer & Gilles, 1998; Toth & Aull, 2014). In our chapter, we share a pared-down, emergency/COVID-19 online DSP (ODSP) tool and the effect that it had on placement of students during the COVID-19 pandemic starting in Spring 2020. We also present the data of students' choices and their outcomes as well as implications as an interrogation of placement effectiveness and equity (e.g., Poe et al., 2018). We hope that this detailed presentation of this ODSP will help other institutions that seek to explore implementing DSP or ODSP.

Genesis of the ODSP

Our community college in southwestern Arizona has long used the ACCU-PLACER exam to place incoming students into the first-year composition (FYC) courses. Because of the large number of multilingual students who enroll at our college, particularly at the campuses closer to the U.S.-Mexico border, we believe it is crucial that writing instruction and pedagogical practices be adapted to better serve these linguistically diverse students. In order to address vast differences in their linguistic backgrounds, writing experiences, and unique needs, we originally designed an online directed self-placement (ODSP) survey to help students determine their placement in mainstream or multilingual FYC classes. The questions in this ODSP were aimed at asking students to reflect on their prior writing and reading experiences in relation to the new writing context they were about to enter in order to encourage identification as multilingual writers. Ultimately, the ODSP was designed for the students to make the final decision, but it was hoped that students positively identified as multilingual writers, thus shedding a stigma that has been placed on students in "ESL" classes (e.g., Ortmeier-Hooper, 2008).

DOI: https://doi.org/10.37514/PRA-B.2022.1565.2.11

When we proposed this multilingually sensitive placement tool to the college in the spring of 2020, COVID-19 had just begun to wreak havoc on higher education, including the ACCUPLACER exam, which was rendered unusable due to the need for in-person proctoring. We were asked by administration to quickly repurpose the survey to place students into transfer- or below-transfer-level FYC classes without sensitivity to multilingual students or classes. Administration further requested that the original 17-question survey be cut to five questions so as to reduce or eliminate as many barriers to enrollment as possible. In this chapter, we share the pared-down, emergency/COVID-19 ODSP and the effect that it had on placement of students. We also present the data of students' choices and their outcomes as well as implications as an interrogation of placement effectiveness and equity (e.g., Poe et al., 2018). We hope that this detailed presentation of the emergency ODSP will help other institutions that seek to explore implementing DSP or ODSP.

Literature Review

Writing Placement Overview

At many institutions, before taking college-level composition courses, incoming students are required to demonstrate specific levels of literacy and readiness. The widely used tests at many postsecondary institutions, particularly in community colleges in Arizona, are ACCUPLACER, SAT, and ACT. Students who have proven ready based on their placement test scores are allowed to enroll into the appropriate transfer-level FYC course, while those whose placement results have shown that they are academically underprepared are referred to take below-transfer-level, developmental coursework before beginning FYC. Many of these tests cost students and institutions money to take and administer. EdReady is another example of a standardized placement test, much like ACCUPLACER; however, it is different as it allows the student to take developmental coursework and retake the placement test recursively until the student has successfully "passed" the placement test or has earned the placement score that is acceptable to the student. EdReady is also free to the student.

Furthermore, instead of using single measures for placement, there has been an increasing interest among institutions to seek ways beyond the commonly available placement tests to improve college-entry assessments (Klausman et al., 2016). These options include using alternative measures; for example, Virginia and North Carolina have developed assessment systems that place students into specific developmental modules (e.g., Hodara et al., 2012) and "multiple measures" as a system to combine two or more (typically existing) measures for placement purposes. "Multiple measures" can include high school grade point average (GPA) and other items from the high school transcript, and SAT/ACT scores that are less than ten years old. Course grades in high school writing have also been used for placement decisions.

Some colleges have incorporated the use of noncognitive assessments to measure students' psychosocial characteristics, such as motivation, learning strategies, academic tenacity (grit), or sense of belonging (Lipnevich et al., 2013). SuccessNavigator (offered by Educational Testing Service), Engage (offered by ACT), the Learning and Study Strategies Inventory (offered by H&H publishing), and the College Student Inventory (offered by Noel Levitz) are some examples of noncognitive tests.

In some institutions, such as Wright State University and the University of Wisconsin, students both take a standardized placement test and write an essay which then gets scored by faculty based on the FYC learning outcomes (e.g., Crusan, 2011). While such performance assessments can provide information helpful to placement, they require added faculty time to score large numbers of incoming students within a short period of time (Rodríguez et al., 2015). Critiques of this measure include that relying upon a one-shot essay as the sole means of placing incoming students lacks interrater reliability and predictive ability, and places too much emphasis on one rhetorical mode (Haswell, 2004).

Directed Self-Placement

Alternatively, colleges may ask incoming students to take a survey about their prior writing experiences and their readiness and confidence about future college courses (Venezia et al., 2010). Overall, many writing assessment scholars are calling for a revolution in placement procedures. In particular, they are pointing to the complexity and value of directed self-placement (DSP), which emphasizes student agency, or the ability of the incoming students to choose their appropriate class (Conference on College Composition and Communication, 2014; Crusan, 2011; Klausman et al., 2016; Nastal, 2019; Royer & Gilles, 1998; Ruecker, 2011; Toth, 2018; Toth et al., 2019).

Recent research at several colleges and universities around the US has suggested DSP and online DSP (ODSP) programs are better predictive indicators of students' actual performance in their first-year writing courses than single-score placement tests. Researchers argue that much of this success is due to students exercising agency in their placement (Crusan, 2011) and being encouraged to take responsibility for their own education (Royer & Gilles, 1998; Toth & Aull, 2014).

With ODSP, students are integrated into the important process of decision-making and are guided to place themselves into the course level of choice. This decision is usually informed by the information provided to students about college-level expectations in FYC, results of placement scores, review of high school GPA and other transcript data, and/or consultations with college advisors and faculty who have knowledge about and experience with the curriculum and its demands. For instance, all colleges in Florida have been administering self-placement since Florida's 2013 legislation ending mandatory placement testing. Shouping Hu et al. (2016) have reported that the use of DSP in Florida has led to higher enrollment rates in first-year courses (FYC) in English as well as math, and higher pass rates for cohort analysis, especially for Hispanic and Black populations. Additionally, students in corequisite courses (also known as ALP or Accelerated Learning Program by Adams et al., 2009) had the highest rates of passing in comparison to others (Hu et al., 2016).

More research is coming concerning DSP in multilingual writing programs—an important factor in determining the appropriateness of ODSP for our highly multilingual student population described in the next section. In some initial versions of DSP, multilingual writers were even excluded from any form of self-placement. The main objections to administering DSP to multilingual writers were that the students would make unrealistic evaluations of their proficiency and would choose a higher level in order to save time and money (Crusan, 2002, 2006; Reynolds, 2003). However, the findings in some more recent DSP research studies suggest that multilingual students are capable of exercising agency and choice in their educational decisions in responsible ways (Ferris & Lombardi, 2020; Inoue, 2015; Sinha, 2014). Furthermore, the inclusion of multilingual writers in well-designed DSP can afford them a sense of belonging and can convey a powerful message to them by affording them not only some agency and autonomy in their self-evaluations, but also fairness and social justice (Crusan, 2006, 2011; Toth, 2018). Tanita Saenkhum (2016) and Dana Ferris and Amy Lombardi (2020) argued that giving multilingual students a voice in their placement contributes to their overall satisfaction with the placement process, and affects their attitudes, motivation, and self-efficacy levels. The research conducted in the field of L2 writing on the issues concerning multilingual writers in mainstream composition classrooms continues to address considerable linguistic, cultural, and rhetorical challenges of these students (Ferris, 2014; Matsuda, 2006, 2012; Zamora, 2020).

Context

Setting

Arizona Western College (AWC) almost exclusively serves the counties of Yuma and La Paz, which cover almost the entire southwest quadrant of the state of Arizona. According to the 2018–2019 AWC Fact Book, AWC served 11,521 students (unduplicated headcount) of which the population is roughly 55 percent female, 45 percent male, and 68 percent Latinx, 19 percent White, and 13 percent all additional race/ethnicities combined (Lopez et al., 2019, pp. 6–7). The largest population of students is between the ages of 20 and 24 (34%), but the fastest-growing age demographic is 18 and under at 30 percent. Thirteen percent of the students are in the age category of 25–29 and another 13 percent are 30–39 years old (Lopez et al., 2019, p. 8).

AWC was using the ACCUPLACER test to place students into reading, writing, and mathematics classes. For writing, the cutoff score into transfer-level FYC classes (e.g., ENG 101) was 80, and a score below 40 would indicate an ESL placement ("ACCUPLACER," n.d.). This was the only method of placement before the

COVID-19 pandemic. The ODSP survey was created in the hopes of affecting change to the multilingual placement practices, but was quickly repurposed to differentiation between transfer- and below-transfer-level student placement and replaced ACCUPLACER in response to the pandemic.

Description of Emergency/COVID-19 ODSP Tool

As described in the "Genesis of the ODSP" section, the focus of the Multilingual ODSP changed abruptly because of the COVID-19 pandemic, from multilingual to mainstream placement, differentiating between transfer-level and below-transfer-level placement. With heavy emphasis on removing barriers to enrollment, we were forced by administration to pare the original 17-question Multilingual ODSP survey down to five questions without a multilingual emphasis (Figure 11.1).

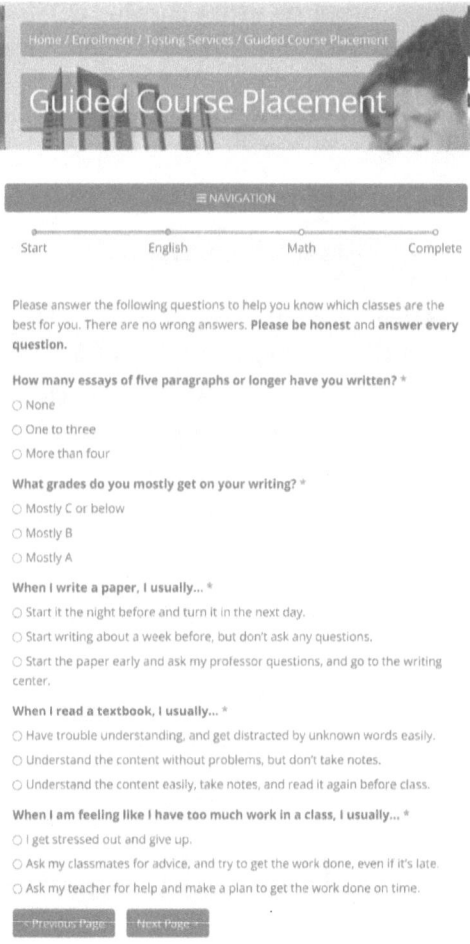

Figure 11.1. Multilingual ODSP survey.

We asked questions that we thought could help students critically reflect on the following criteria: the amount and quality of their previous writing experiences (questions 1 and 2), their knowledge and practice of the writing process (question 3), their reading abilities (question 4), and their grit/independence (question 5). Although it was not our intention, the pattern of answers was limited by the complexity of the webpage coding, and therefore was kept in a predictable pattern of low to high score (or developmental/non-transfer to mainstream/transfer-level recommendation). The options that each pattern of scores and their cutoffs were to be placed into included the following:

1. ENG 090: prematriculation/below-transfer-level/developmental*
2. ENG 100+101 (ALP) or ENG 100 standalone
3. ENG 101 transfer-level graduation coursework (Composition I)

Students also took separate three- to five-question ODSP surveys for ESL and mathematics, and received their results at the end of the web form. Students were given recommended class descriptions on the final page based on their ODSP answers, and chose accordingly either by themselves or with the help of an advisor.

Research Design

Research Questions

The research questions that this study aimed to answer were:

1. What differences (if any) exist between placement tool and placement level?
2. What differences (if any) exist between placement tool and enrollment level?

For analysis purposes, we considered two tiers of placement: transfer and below-transfer level. Students who were placed into the ENG 100+101 corequisite model (or what is otherwise known as the ALP [e.g., Adams et al., 2009]) were considered transfer level because students were simultaneously earning transfer- and non-transfer-level credits.

Data

Student data for English placement and enrollment were applied for and collected through the office of Institutional Effectiveness, Research, and Grants (IERG). The roughly 2,500 administrative records span four semesters between the spring of 2019 and the fall of 2020. Linked to these data are each student's demographic information, placement, enrollment, success, and placement tool. This data structure allowed for tracking of individual students' patterns (i.e., placement, enrollment, and success) from semester to semester. As the analysis focuses on exploring any differences between placement tools, the IERG data was sorted into two major groups by placement tool. The ACCUPLACER group consisted of 2,240 student records, while the ODSP group contained 203 student records.

Method

Student data were analyzed primarily through the use of frequency and descriptive statistics. The crosstab and select cases features of SPSS were extensively used to calculate frequencies and generate tables for analysis. The chi-square statistic was also calculated to provide insights into answering the research questions, with placement tool as an independent variable. Chi-square was selected as a non-parametric (distribution free) test and for its ability to handle diverse data and unequal study group sizes. Individual cell chi-square values were calculated to enhance the interpretation. Cramer's V, a statistical strength test measuring correlation, was also calculated to provide better insights into any differences emerging from the chi-square statistic. Student success was considered a grade of A, B, or C, and a designation of unsuccessful was all other labels, including grades of D and F, or W (withdrawal) and I (incomplete).

Results and Discussion

As can be seen in Table 11.1, the chi-square test revealed a statistically significant p-value ($p=.001$), which resulted in rejecting the null hypothesis for research question 1 (i.e., there is no difference between placement tool and placement level) and accepting the alternative hypothesis (i.e., there is a difference between placement tool and placement level). This result was primarily due to the much larger observed count (vs. the expected count) of the ODSP student group being placed into ENG 101 (χ^2 cell value=128.98).

The result from the chi-square statistic can also be observed descriptively in Table 11.1 through the variance in placement distributions between ACCUPLACER to ODSP. Whereas ACCUPLACER has an overwhelming pattern of placing students into below-transfer-level courses (84.64%, $n=1,896$), the ODSP has a pattern of placing students into transfer-level courses more often (52.71%, $n=107$).

The chi-square test revealed a statistically significant ($p=.001$) change in enrollment distributions across writing courses. Regarding research question 2, the second null hypothesis (there is no difference between enrollment level and placement tool) was rejected, and the alternative hypothesis (there is a difference between enrollment level and placement tool) was accepted. Students who enrolled in ENG 101 and were placed by ODSP had a higher observed count versus expected count (176 vs. 130.1), which contributed to the distribution differences between the placement tools as evidenced by the cell chi-square value ($\chi^2=16.17$). Additionally, there were lower observed counts versus expected counts for ENG 90 (0 vs. 24.6, $\chi^2=24.60$) and ENG 100 (27 vs. 45.8, $\chi^2=7.71$).

Table 11.1. Overall Student Placement Results in English Courses by Placement Tool and Course Level

		Placement Tool				Total	
		ACCUPLACER		ODSP			
		N	%	N	%	N	%
Course Level	Placement Course						
Transfer level	ENG 101	344	15.36%	107	52.71%	451	18.46%
Transfer Level Total		344	15.36%	107	52.71%	451	18.46%
One level below transfer level	ENG 100	1,531	68.35%	91	44.83%	1,622	66.39%
Two levels below transfer level	ENG 090	315	14.06%	5	2.46%	320	13.10%
Three levels below transfer level	ENG 080	50	2.23%	—	—	50	2.05%
Below Transfer Level Total		1,896	84.64%	96	47.29%	1,992	81.54%
Total		2,240	100.00%	203	100.00%	2,443	100.00%

Note. Includes successful and unsuccessful students. A significant difference was found between placement tool and level of course placement, chi-square (df=3) = 179.829, p <.001, Cramer's V=.271

Table 11.2 shows that 86.70% (n=176) of ODSP students began their journeys in a transfer-level course compared to 62.05% (n=1,390) of traditionally test-placed enrollees. This discrepancy in enrollment behaviors was drastically different from the placement recommendations from ACCUPLACER and ODSP although at different rates. ACCUPLACER only placed 15.36% (n=344) of students into ENG 101, but 1,390 students enrolled into ENG 101. In comparison, ODSP placed 52.71% (n=107) of students into ENG 101, while a total of 176 students in this group enrolled into ENG 101.

Cross Sectional Ad Hoc Analysis

As for overall success rate by placement tool, results of an ad hoc analysis, shown in Table 11.3, indicate that ACCUPLACER has a higher success rate (68.84%) than ODSP (55.67%), but when the data is further disaggregated, as shown in Table 11.4, students placed by ODSP are successful more often in transfer-level classes (57.52%). Conversely, Table 11.4 shows that none of the students who were placed in ENG 101 (the transfer-level course) by ACCUPLACER were successful, regardless of course enrollment. ACCUPLACER students were instead successful in below-transfer-level classes.

Table 11.2. Overall Students Enrolled in English Courses by Placement Tool and Course Level

		Placement Tool				Total	
		ACCUPLACER		ODSP			
		N	%	N	%	N	%
Course Level	Enrolled Course						
Transfer level	ENG 101	1,390	62.05%	176	86.70%	1,566	64.10%
Transfer Level Total		1,390	62.05%	176	86.70%	1,566	64.10%
One level below transfer level	ENG 100	524	23.39%	27	13.30%	551	26.70%
Two levels below transfer level	ENG 090	296	13.21%	0	0.00%	296	11.47%
Three levels below transfer level	ENG 080	30	1.34%	0	0.00%	30	1.16%
Below Transfer Level Total		850	37.95%	27	13.30%	877	35.90%
Total		2,240	100.00%	203	100.00%	2,443	100.00%

Note. Includes successful and unsuccessful students. A significant difference was found between placement tool and level of course placement, chi-square (df=3) = 55.587, p <.001, Cramer's V=.151

Table 11.3. Overall Student Success in English Courses by Placement Tool

	Placement Tool				Total	
	ACCUPLACER		ODSP			
	N	%	N	%	N	%
Successful	1,542	68.84%	113	55.67%	1,655	67.74%
Unsuccessful	698	31.16%	90	44.33%	788	32.26%
Total	2,240	100.00%	203	100.00%	2,443	100.00%

Table 11.5 shows the course enrollment distribution of successful students who were placed by ACCUPLACER and ODSP. While 64.85 percent (n=1,000) of all successful ACCUPLACER students were successful in transfer-level courses, 88.50% (n=100) of all successful ODSP students were successful in transfer-level courses. As previously mentioned, there were variances in the distribution of recommended and enrolled courses by both placement tools. The largest deviations occurred between the number of students ACCUPLACER placed into ENG 101 and the number of students who enrolled in ENG 101. This was also observed to a lesser degree with the ODSP placement tool.

Table 11.4. Successful Students Placed in English Courses by Placement Tool and Course Level

Course Level	Placement Course	Placement Tool				Total	
		ACCUPLACER		ODSP			
		N	%	N	%	N	%
Transfer level	ENG 101	0	0.00%	65	57.52%	65	3.93%
Transfer Level Total		0	0.00%	65	57.52%	65	3.93%
One level below transfer level	ENG 100	1,314	85.21%	46	40.71%	1,360	82.18%
Two levels below transfer level	ENG 090	207	13.42%	2	1.77%	209	12.63%
Three levels below transfer level	ENG 080	21	1.36%	—	—	21	1.27%
Below Transfer Level Total		1,542	100.00%	48	42.48%	1,590	96.07%
Total		1,542	100.00%	113	100.00%	1,655	100.00%

Table 11.5. Successful Students Enrolled in English Courses by Placement Tool and Course Level

Course Level	Enrolled Course	Placement Tool				Total	
		ACCUPLACER		ODSP			
		N	%	N	%	N	%
Transfer level	ENG 101	1,000	64.85%	100	88.50%	1,100	66.47%
Transfer Level Total		1,000	64.85%	100	88.50%	1,100	66.47%
One level below transfer level	ENG 100	339	21.98%	13	11.50%	352	21.27%
Two levels below transfer level	ENG 090	191	12.39%	0	0.00%	191	11.54%
Three levels below transfer level	ENG 080	12	0.78%	—	—	12	0.73%
Below Transfer Level Total		542	35.15%	13	11.50%	555	33.53%
Total		1,542	100.00%	113	100.00%	1,655	100.00%

Although Table 11.1 shows only 15.36 percent (n=344) of ACCUPLACER students were placed into ENG 101, Table 11.5 reveals a total of 1,390 ACCUPLACER students enrolled in ENG 101. A cross-sectional view of the ACCUPLACER data revealed 74.39 percent (n=1,034) of students who enrolled in ENG 101 were originally placed into ENG 100—that is, these students opted to enroll in a higher course than they were placed into. Interestingly, 95.45 percent (n=987) of ACCUPLACER students who were placed in ENG 100 but who enrolled in ENG 101 were successful.

Variance between the recommended and enrolled courses was also observed in the ODSP student group. As noted earlier, the ODSP placement tool more often placed students in transfer-level courses (52.71%, n=107), but a total of 176 ODSP students enrolled in ENG 101. Similar to the ACCUPLACER student group, many ODSP students were originally placed in ENG 100 and elected to enroll in ENG 101. Of the 176 students who enrolled in ENG 101, 40.34% (n= 71) were originally placed into ENG 100 by ODSP. The success rate for these students was 52.11 percent (n=37). However, nearly 94 percent (n=61) of successful ODSP students placed into ENG 101 also enrolled in ENG 101. Moreover, these students comprised 61 percent (n=61) of all ODSP students successful in transfer-level courses.

One of the most interesting ACCUPLACER findings was a significant misalignment between ENG 101 placement result and course enrollment. In the data set, ACCUPLACER placed only 344 students into ENG 101, but nearly four times the number of students enrolled in ENG 101. Concerning enrollment practices, of the 344 students placed into ENG 101 by ACCUPLACER, 338 students enrolled in ENG 101, while six enrolled in ENG 100, and interestingly, none were successful in either of the composition courses.

ACCUPLACER also placed 1,531 students into ENG 100. Only 31.38 percent (n=487) of these students placed in ENG 100 followed their ACCUPLACER results and enrolled in the course they were placed in. Regardless of their ACCUPLACER placement, 67.53 percent of these students (n=1,034) chose to enroll one level higher into ENG 101. Placement data show that of the 1,034 ENG 101 students, 910 students enrolled into the mainstream ENG 101, and 121 students enrolled into the corequisite (three students enrolled for only the 101 portion of the corequisite class). However, of the total 1,390 students enrolled in the ENG 101 course, 1,000 students were successful, which is around a 70 percent success rate.

From this data set, we cannot speculate how these students were enrolled, although the pre-COVID policy required students to abide by the ACCUPLACER placement. One possible hypothesis for why this anomaly exists in the data is the lifting of placement algorithms within the student enrollment software. When ACCUPLACER was no longer tenable, the holds that normally would have prevented students from enrolling in classes that they did not place into were lifted. This finding requires further exploration.

Conclusion

Findings are consistent with many of the previous studies about DSP and ODSP. ACCUPLACER consistently underestimates students for placement (Bahr et al., 2019; Scott-Clayton, 2012). Also, students, when given the information to enroll in classes via ODSP recommendations and their own agency, can be successful in the class that they choose. The main finding of this study, however, is that even a five-question survey created and deployed quickly and under pressure can be a useful tool for students.

So the question that becomes is: Which is better: ACCUPLACER or ODSP? This data set did not allow for a direct success comparison between the ACCUPLACER and ODSP because ACCUPLACER rarely placed students into the transfer-level courses, but ODSP did, and students were passing the transfer-level course after being placed (or deviating from the test/survey placement and placing themselves). These findings reiterate the importance of redistribution in placement scores for equity and ethical impact, as the placement of our largely Hispanic and multilingual student population was essentially redistributed by the ODSP, as other studies have also shown (e.g., Poe et al., 2018). The nature of the question is complicated, and the interpretation of it relies on the values of the interpreter.

We came to the conclusion that, as an open-access institution, and in terms of time and resources, the ODSP was more advantageous. It was a brief five-question survey (not a test), which helped students understand the behaviors that were required of them in the transfer-level course of ENG 101. Furthermore, the ODSP was free to the institution (save the wages of the people who created and administered it) and did not need to be proctored. Perhaps most importantly, it was also beneficial for students to have the flexibility, or what Saenkhum (2016) calls agency, to reject the recommended placement, especially from the ACCUPLACER, but also from the ODSP. This could focus on student empowerment in meaningful ways. Students were allowed to make decisions based on available information and choose the FYC course that they thought would best serve them. By fostering choice, the college trusted students with their perceptions of their writing abilities, their preparedness level, and FYC expectations.

ACCUPLACER's tendency to place students into below-transfer-level courses supports the concern by multiple scholars that students who are required to take courses before their transfer-level courses will be delayed in their studies through higher education (Adams et al., 2009; Caouette, 2019; Snyder, 2017, 2018). In our experience, it is advantageous for a placement tool like the ODSP to place higher than previous tools, and for students to have the option to place themselves into higher courses because, according to the data—and Wayne Gretzky—students miss 100 percent of the shots they do not take. When the placement rate of the ACCUPLACER into the transfer-level course is just over one-third that of the ODSP, but the ACCUPLACER success rate in the same class is zero, something is wrong, and students are paying for that in multiple ways.

Limitations

This data set represents a year of anomalies as the COVID-19 pandemic raged through the United States, and we hope to continue this research as higher education recovers from the pandemic to make sure that this data is consistent longitudinally. Also, at the onset of the COVID-19 pandemic, our institution took an important step to invite students to participate in ODSP as a means to locate their FYC courses. However, we acknowledge that students were experiencing an immense amount of stress and the emergency implementation was not perfect. The data should be acknowledged and interpreted in this light as an anomalous year, and not representative or generalizable to future years.

Future Implications

The in-house ODSP process is continuing to be refined as it should be revised continuously to fit our student population. Incorporation of the multilingual factor into the ODSP is also important moving forward, as we feel that the lack of placement options for multilingual students signals a lack of equity. We want ODSP to empower students to positively identify and choose through their own agency multilingual-specific courses in the future. Because the multilingual FYC courses were put on hold during the pandemic, and the multilingual ODSP was not actually used, we hope to reconstruct the multilingual ODSP survey in order to help students with lateral transfer into a multilingual section.

References

ACCUPLACER course placement. (n.d.). Arizona Western College. https://www.azwestern.edu/sites/default/files/awc/dual-enrollment/ACCUPLACER_Course_Placement.pdf.

Adams, P., Gearhart, S., Miller, R. & Roberts, A. (2009). The Accelerated Learning Program: Throwing open the gates. *Journal of Basic Writing*, 28(2) 50–69. https://doi.org/10.37514/JBW-J.2009.28.2.04.

Bahr, P. R., Fagioli, L. P., Hetts, J., Hayward, C., Willett, T., Lamoree, D., Newell, M. A., Sorey, K. & Baker, R. B. (2019). Improving placement accuracy in California's community colleges using multiple measures of high school achievement. *Community College Review*, 47(2), 178–211. https://doi.org/10.1177/0091552119840705.

Caouette, B. L. (2019). Directed self-placement, corequisite models, and curricular choice. *Journal of Basic Writing*, 38(1), 56–77. https://doi.org/10.37514/JBW-J.2019.38.1.04.

Conference on College Composition and Communication. (2020). *Statement on second-language writing and multilingual writers.* National Council of Teachers of English. http://www.ncte.org/cccc/resources/positions/secondlangwriting.

Crusan, D. (2002). An assessment of ESL writing placement assessment. *Assessing Writing*, 8(1), 17–30. https://citeseerx.ist.psu.edu/viewdoc/download?doi=10.1.1.620.7610&rep=rep1&type=pdf.

Crusan, D. (2006). The politics of implementing online directed self-placement for second language writers. In P. K. Matsuda, C. Ortmeier-Hooper & X. You (Eds.), *The politics of second language writing* (pp. 205–221). Parlor Press.

Crusan, D. (2011). The promise of directed self-placement for second language writers. *TESOL Quarterly*, 45(4), 774–780. https://www.jstor.org/stable/41307667.

Ferris, D. R. (2014). Review: "English only" and multilingualism in composition studies: Policy, philosophy, and practice. *College English*, 77, 75–85. https://secure.ncte.org/library/NCTEFiles/Resources/Journals/CE/0771-sep2014/CE0771Review.pdf.

Ferris, D. R., Evans, K. & Kurzer, K. (2016). Placement of multilingual writers: Is there a role for student voices? *Assessing Writing*, 32, 1–11. https://www.sciencedirect.com/science/article/abs/pii/S1075293516300691.

Ferris, D. R. & Lombardi, A. (2020). Collaborative placement of multilingual writers: Combining formal assessment and self-evaluation. *The Journal of Writing Assessment*, 13(1). http://journalofwritingassessment.org/article.php?article=149.

Haswell, R. H. (2005, March 1). Post-secondary entry writing placement. *CompPile*. https://wac.colostate.edu/docs/comppile/pd/placement.htm.

Hodara, M., Jaggars, S. S. & Karp, M. M. (2012). *Improving developmental education assessment and placement: Lessons from community colleges across the country*. Community College Research Center, Teachers College, Columbia University. https://doi.org/10.7916/D8SB4F49.

Hu, S., Park, T., Woods, C. S., Richard, K., Tandberg, D. & Bertrand Jones, T. (2016). *Probability of success: Evaluation of Florida's developmental education redesign based on cohorts of first-time-in-college students from 2009–10 to 2014–15*. Center for Postsecondary Success, Florida State University. https://diginole.lib.fsu.edu/islandora/object/fsu%3A388909/datastream/PDF/view.

Inoue, A. B. (2015). *Antiracist writing assessment ecologies: Teaching and assessing writing for a socially just future*. The WAC Clearinghouse; Parlor Press. https://doi.org/10.37514/PER-B.2015.0698.

Klausman, J., Toth, C., Swyt, W., Griffiths, B., Sullivan, P., Warnke, A., Williams, A. L., Giordano, J. & Roberts, L. (2016). TYCA white paper on placement reform. *Teaching English in the Two-Year College*, 44(2), 135–157.

Lipnevich, A. A., MacCann, C. & Roberts, R. D. (2013). Assessing non-cognitive constructs in education: A review of traditional and innovative approaches. In D. Saklofske & V. Schwean (Eds.), *Oxford handbook of psychological assessment of children and adolescents*. Oxford University Press. https://doi.org/10.1093/oxfordhb/9780199796304.013.0033.

Lopez, B., Magaña, A. & Dickman, M. (2019). *2018–2019 Arizona Western College Factbook*. Arizona Western College. https://www.azwestern.edu/sites/default/files/awc/institutional-research/2018-2019%20Fact%20Book-Final%20Complete.pdf.

Matsuda, P. K. (2006). The myth of linguistic homogeneity in US college composition. *College English*, 68(6), 637–651. http://www.bu.edu/wpnet/files/2015/08/The-Myth-of-Linguistic-Homogeneity-in-U.S.-College-Composition.pdf.

Matsuda, P. K. (2012). Teaching composition in the multilingual world: Second language writing in composition studies. In K. Ritter & P. K. Matsuda (Eds.),

Exploring composition studies: Sites, issues, perspectives (pp. 36–51). Utah State University Press.

Nastal, J. (2019). Beyond tradition: Writing placement, fairness, and success at a two-year college. *The Journal of Writing Assessment*, 12(1), 1–16. https://escholar ship.org/uc/item/4wg8wong.

Ortmeier-Hooper, C. (2008). "English may be my second language, but I'm not 'ESL'". *College Composition and Communication*, 59(3) 389–419. http://academic .brooklyn.cuny.edu/english/moser/eng%207506/English%20may%20be%20my %20second%20language.pdf.

Poe, M., Inoue, A. B. & Elliot, N. (Eds.). (2018). *Writing assessment, social justice, and the advancement of opportunity*. The WAC Clearinghouse; University Press of Colorado. https://doi.org/10.37514/PER-B.2018.0155.

Reynolds, E. (2003). The role of self-efficacy in writing and directed self-placement. In D. Royer & R. Gilles (Eds.), *Directed self-placement: Principles and practices* (pp. 73–103). Hampton Press.

Rodríguez, O., Bowden, B., Belfield, C. & Scott-Clayton, J. (2015). Calculating the costs of remedial placement testing. *CCRC Analytics*. Community College Research Center, Teachers College, Columbia University. https://files.eric.ed.gov /fulltext/ED562055.pdf.

Royer, D. J. & Gilles, R. (1998). Directed self-placement: An attitude of orientation. *College Composition and Communication*, 50(1), 54–70. http://www.jstor.org /stable/358352.

Ruecker, T. (2011). Improving the placement of L2 writers: The students' perspective. *WPA: Writing Program Administration*, 35(1), 91–117. http://associationdatabase .co/archives/35n1/35n1all.pdf#page=92.

Saenkhum, T. (2016). *Decisions, agency, and advising: Key issues in the placement of multilingual writers into first-year composition courses*. Utah State University Press.

Scott-Clayton, J. (2012). *Do high-stakes placement exams predict college success?* (CCRC Working Paper No. 41). Community College Research Center, Teachers College, Columbia University. https://ccrc.tc.columbia.edu/publications/high -stakes-placement-exams-predict.html.

Sinha, A. (2014). *Exploring directed self placement as a placement alternative for first year college students in writing classes* [Doctoral dissertation, University of California, Davis]. UC Davis Electronic Theses and Dissertations (ProQuest).

Snyder, S. E. (2017). Retention rates of second language writers and basic writers: A comparison within the Stretch Program model. In T. Ruecker, D. Shepherd, H. Estrem & B. Brunk-Chavez (Eds.), *Retention, persistence, and writing programs* (pp. 185–203). Utah State University Press.

Snyder, S. E. (2018). *The Stretch Model: Including L2 student voices*. (Publication No. 156480) [Doctoral dissertation, Arizona State University]. ProQuest Dissertations and Theses Global. https://arizona-asu-primo.hosted.exlibrisgroup.com/perma link/f/ch16tq/01ASU_ALMA511068289870003841.

Toth, C. (2018). Directed self-placement at "democracy's open door": Writing placement and social justice in community colleges. In A. B. Inoue, M. Poe & N. Elliot

(Eds.), *Writing assessment, social justice, and the advancement of opportunity* (pp. 139–172). The WAC Clearinghouse; University Press of Colorado. https://doi.org/10.37514/PER-B.2018.0155.2.04.

Toth, C. & Aull, L. (2014). Directed self-placement questionnaire design: Practices, problems, possibilities. *Assessing Writing, 20*, 1–18. https://doi.org/10.1016/j.asw.2013.11.006.

Toth, C., Nastal, J., Hassel, H. & Giordano, J. B. (2019). Introduction: Writing Assessment, Placement, and the Two-Year College. *Journal of Writing Assessment, 12*(1). https://escholarship.org/uc/item/8393560s.

Venezia, A., Bracco, K. R. & Nodine, T. (2010). *One-shot deal? Students' perceptions of assessment and course placement in California's community colleges.* WestEd. https://files.eric.ed.gov/fulltext/ED566386.pdf.

Zamora, F. E. (2020). *Digital native tongue: Bringing multilingual, multimodal curriculum to college composition for beginning Latinx writers* [Master dissertation, Texas A&M International University]. Research Information Online. https://rio.tamiu.edu/cgi/viewcontent.cgi?article=1027&context=etds .

Afterword. Placement, Equity, and the Promise of Democratic Open-Access Education

Darin L. Jensen and Joanne Baird Giordano
SALT LAKE COMMUNITY COLLEGE

For many two-year college faculty, the central ethos of the community college is its promise of open-access education. The concept of local public open-access education centers on the assurance of free and unrestricted entrance to opportunities for learning and literacy development for an entire local population. This type of education is a community good and an essential ingredient in a democratic society that values its citizens. The possibilities that effective community college programs provide to students individually and collectively are predicated on the notion that more access to education is better and fairer in comparison to the restrictive gateways that limit who can participate in learning at other types of institutions.

We have been teaching at community colleges for many years. We self-identify as scholars who are expert practitioners. Both of us have been immersed in developmental education reform, placement, and program (re)design. We intentionally use the term literacy programs here instead of writing programs. Literacy programs take up the entire breadth of literacy work at two-year colleges, including reading, integrated reading and writing, English for speakers of other languages, corequisite support, writing and learning centers, and writing studies courses. Placement affects all of these areas, and curriculum, assessment, and teaching in these spaces largely determines student success. Moreover, as noted in the Conference on College Composition and Communication's 2021 position statement on reading and in Patrick Sullivan et al.'s 2017 book *Deep Reading*, reading has become more of a central feature in composition classrooms over the last decade. Therefore, literacy programs are central to the literacy ecology of an institution and community. English placement is an essential component of that ecology.

This volume, with its attention to the equity of placement in two-year college writing, is at the heart of that democratic work. As is made clear in chapter after chapter, equity in placement can help achieve the central goal of democracy and open-access literacy education. What is equity? The term is often placed with diversity and inclusion or in some combination reduced to initialisms like DEI or JEDI. However, considering what equity means in higher education is essential for both two-year college program change work (including placement reforms) and the mission of community colleges. We define equity in postsecondary education as equal opportunities, fair treatment, equal access to resources, and fair processes within our institutions. Equity efforts in higher education must acknowledge that some students have been structurally disadvantaged by inequities in society. Many community college students have experienced unequal access to educational resources and social power before enrolling in college, and many continue to experience those inequities. As this collection and other recent research (Gilman et al., 2019) have pointed out, placement is a site where two-year colleges' pursuit of equity has fallen short. Some methods of placement (especially high-stakes standardized tests used without other measures), which concentrate on nebulous ideas of "college-readiness," can create levels of unnecessary coursework and serve as gatekeepers that often steadily reduce access for students. In this volume, Jeffrey Klausman and Signee Lynch tellingly examine such a program that illustrates how placement processes can reduce access to higher education and limit students' progress toward a postsecondary credential:

> So of 100 students placed into English 92: Developmental Reading, only about 78 would finish the course; of those 78, only about 62 would start the next class, English 95; of those, only about 48 would finish that class. . . . Ultimately, only around 22 percent of students who began in English 92 completed English 101 within three years (and likely forever).

The authors of this collection address placement mechanisms that sort students as a way of intervening in policies where they are decontextualized into a score on a placement test rather than their lived experiences. As community colleges and literacy practitioners move away from arbitrary placement measures, we will hopefully create conditions where students can be educated in accordance with principles of justice. But from where will these principles come? The teacher-scholar-activists of this volume offer answers and an auspicious beginning to moving two-year colleges toward their mission of achieving equity for the communities they serve. For example, Charissa Che's examination of the "monolithic assumptions of what makes an 'ESL student'" as a heuristic for reexamining placement practices which track multilingual students or Carolyn Calhoon-Dillahunt and Travis Margoni's work to see placement reform as a beginning to systemic reform which might lead to an antiracist local writing ecology. Both point to direct application of theory to enact a more just approach to writing studies (see Griffiths, 2022).

As most readers of this volume probably know, the struggle for open-access education can be traced back to the civil rights movement. For decades, community, junior, technical, and two-year colleges have been attempting to provide increased access to more people in a wider selection of technical and transfer coursework. Most of the public dialogue around community colleges aims squarely at defining our institutions as places for students to receive training for employment so that they can enter the economy. Community colleges are judged by their completion and success rates, although as pointed out in the introduction to this volume, such measures are dubious and problematic at best. An emphasis on job training is not necessarily open access. Further, access is not the same as equity. Mere job training and access do not create equity or a more democratic society.

Similarly, students' mere presence in a credit-bearing first-year writing course does not mean that a placement process is equitable and inclusive. Equity in a literacy program means that students have equal access to educational opportunities and resources to support their development as readers and writers regardless of their educational, cultural, social, linguistic, racial, or economic backgrounds—and regardless of their mental and physical (dis)abilities. Successful efforts to address inequities in writing courses and the other types of literacy programs offered at community colleges must acknowledge that some students experience structural inequities, bias, and discrimination that create barriers to learning. Disproportionate numbers of students who experience intersectional inequalities access higher education through community colleges. To create an equitable postsecondary literacy program and placement process, faculty and administrators at open-access institutions must actively seek to make it possible for students to achieve their individual educational goals, complete degree requirements, stay in college, maintain academic standing and access to financial aid, and receive an associate degree (or other credential) or successfully transfer to a four-year institution. Kris Messer, Jamey Gallagher, and Elizabeth Hart illustrate this point as they examine their self-directed placement program, noting that collaboration across the college must continue so that the program "is given a chance to be studied, shaped, and institutionalized." The authors realize their own limited faculty agency and that a local literacy ecosystem's success is predicated on comprehensive involvement across the college.

Beyond quantifiable measures of success that focus on grades and retention, equitable placement processes and the literacy courses in which students are placed must create conditions for learning that support students' development as readers and writers both collectively and individually. Inclusive placement processes don't just merely allow a student to enroll in a particular course and occupy a seat in a room or space in an online course. For most community college students, placement processes must provide access to carefully designed courses, learning activities, feedback, and effective resources that meet their individual needs and allow them to do their best learning in classrooms or online course communities in which they feel welcomed, valued, and supported. For students who would be excluded from higher education at most institutions, inclusive open-access literacy programs help develop the sense that they belong in college and that they are capable of growth as readers, writers, and learners. The experiences in the classroom which follow placement help create an academic identity. The realities of teaching and learning at a community college mean that the promise of equitable and inclusive open-access literacy education can't be met through changes to placement processes without labor-intensive, challenging work to transform curriculum, instruction, and assessment practices and align them with the changing needs of students in courses that accompany adjustments to placement.

The work of developing, piloting, implementing, and assessing placement changes can also create inequities for faculty and program coordinators, especially when changes are imposed on a program without funding. Effective placement changes require ongoing work that can result in an unfair workload for English faculty in comparison to their peers in other disciplines if they aren't compensated for their time through stipends, dedicated and funded coordinator positions, or reassigned time. Similarly, new placement processes require instructors both on and off the tenure track to engage in time-consuming work to create equitable and inclusive conditions for learning to support students whose placements are changed while also revising courses and programs to reflect new realities and populations in their local communities. A placement process that creates more equitable access to first-year writing courses for students is still inherently inequitable if it places an unfair and uncompensated workload on faculty, especially adjunct instructors who are already underpaid for their work. Locally situated conditions for teaching and learning always determine the extent to which placement changes and accompanying transformative program work are equitable.

Throughout this volume, the editors and contributors make clear that the work of placement is part of the ecology of writing—that is, writing placement and students exist in a relationship with the school and society around them. A local placement context is more than the structure of programs; it is the all-encompassing environment in which students, placement, writing courses, and faculty exist. As others in this book have pointed out, this ecology is frequently racist and classist—and as we pay more attention and learn more, we know it is ableist, too. The principles equity-minded literacy educators and program administrators seek are ones that challenge the racist, classist, and ableist ecologies in which our students, faculty, writing courses, placement instruments, and institutions exist. Moreover, the principles we seek must resist deficit ideologies that have plagued education and manifest themselves in academic and literacy crises.

The solutions—that is, the methods and processes to deal with inequitable placement—presented in this volume are case studies. What's compelling about these studies is not that they each provide a road map—although they do—but rather that they are examples of located agency in a local literacy ecology. Located agency is "action or intervention within a particular place or context meant to produce a particular effect" (Jensen & Suh, 2020). The discussion of writing ecologies is, for us, best understood as a local context within the lived environment of a literacy program, the college within which the program is situated, and the community within which both are situated. There is no one writing ecology writ large in theory; rather, there are micro ecologies which have specific contexts and which evolve over time in practice. Calhoon-Dillahunt and Margoni's essay in this volume is an excellent example, as it looks at the evolving local demographics of their college.

Demographics, legislative fiats, administrative whims, shared governance, and more affect local conditions, thus shaping local ecologies. The case studies in this book locate their agency in interventions and reforms of placement practices in order to affect greater equity for students. We laud the work in these local contexts; at the same time, we want to frame the strategies the chapters provide for other teacher-scholar-practitioners working in both similar or widely different contexts. We must consider questions about how to adapt practices and models from this book to other programs. As seen in this volume, two-year college faculty and program administrators need to look at the constellation of ingredients that make up a literacy education ecology as they address placement as a local intervention.

As faculty and program administrators consider the strategies in this book and plan for their local implementation, it will be useful to consider the following questions:

- What measures are used to place students into English literacy courses and programs? How were existing placement processes developed? What are the reasons for using those measures?
- Which literacy courses and programs need to be included in assessing the effectiveness and equity of existing placement process(es)? What are the purposes of those local programs in relation to the literacy and learning needs of the student communities that the institution serves?
- To what extent are placement measures consistently used across all English literacy programs (first-year writing, developmental writing, reading, ESOL, corequisite support, dual-credit high school programs, bridge programs, adult basic education, etc.)?
- What systematically collected evidence is available for assessing the effectiveness of existing placement measures in supporting college success for the student communities the institution serves?
- What systematically collected evidence is available for assessing students' experiences, outcomes, and literacy development in existing programs?
- When available placement and assessment data is disaggregated by student communities, what do they reveal about inequities in how students are placed into writing courses and available literacy programs?
- What do systematically collected data show about the need for change in placement processes?
- What do data show about why and how available courses and programs might change to support the literacy development and college success of the student communities those programs serve?

The authors of these chapters have done much of this work in their local contexts. As we consider next-generation writing placement reform, we want to emphasize that writing programs are only part of the overall literacy effort at colleges. Literacy programs are transdisciplinary—that is, they take up work in multiple disciplines like writing studies, reading, linguistics, TESOL, and developmental education—and involve faculty and support staff from across disciplines (Suh & Jensen, 2020). Placement reform efforts at open-access institutions are part of literacy efforts that require multiple types of disciplinary expertise in a locally situated context.

Over the last two decades, many externally driven developmental education reforms have negatively impacted student success and have devastated developmental education, reading programs, and basic writing programs. It isn't enough to flatten placement or get rid of developmental education. Placement into first-year writing itself is not equity. Many community college students need appropriate academic and personal support, instructional scaffolding, and a well-conceived institution-wide literacy program. We do not wish to engage in deficit language or thinking. We believe in the potential of our students, but it is a fair assessment that many community college students need more support than they receive in a traditional first-year writing course. As placement has been reimagined and reformed at open-access institutions, that reform work does not diminish the need for intensive and sustained academic support structures across students' educational experiences. Vincent Tinto (2008) argued,

> it is clear that our nation will not be able to close the achievement gap unless we are able to effectively address student needs for academic support in ways that are consistent with their participation in higher education and do so in the community colleges.

He pointed to solutions like basic skills communities and supplemental instruction. We would add to that writing studies corequisite support programs, including the studio model and the well-documented work being done with Accelerated Learning Programs (ALP). This collection, with its emphasis on equity in writing placement, cannot be disentangled from larger postsecondary education reform efforts—many of which are informed by neoliberal ideologies and are driven by austerity.

To ensure that placement reforms at community colleges achieve the goals of equity, inclusion, and social justice, they must be part of a movement for justice-informed literacy work and teacher-scholar-activism aimed at achieving the democratic promise of open-access education. Importantly, for the context of our work, achieving equity through changes to placement processes requires writing program reform work—how we enact curriculum, program assessment and redesign work, and pedagogy as well as a reimagining of what it means to be a literacy educator in a two-year college. Placement reform is one part of evidence-based linguistically just writing program change work and one facet of creating an effective and just locally situated literacy ecology (Baker-Bell, 2020; Schreiber et al., 2022).

The placement case studies explored in this book offer hope to community colleges in meeting their democratic and open-access goals—and frankly, the goals of creating citizens with agency and access to powerful literacy. As the editors of this collection point out,

> placement into composition courses is still viewed *not* as a pivotal educational moment for introducing students to local pedagogical orientations and the valued construct of writing, but rather a mechanism for putting students in their "proper" seats quickly, easily, and inexpensively.

Moreover, the literacy ecology of each college and community needs holistic reforms to meet the equity goals sought in placement changes. Placement itself does not eliminate racist, classist, ableist moments in other parts of the curriculum, in the college, or from individual instructors.

As we read all the chapters in this book, we were heartened at the work groups of faculty undertook in changing the machinery of their institutions to better serve students in their particular local contexts. This volume sets the stage for the next steps. We know community colleges will need wide-scale long-term data collected at multiple institutions that systematically studies the literacy development and college success outcomes for large numbers of students. Writing studies and related literacy disciplines need research on placement methods from widely diverse communities, especially those who have been historically excluded from higher education and who continue to be excluded from writing programs outside of open-access institutions. We look forward to readers of this book who will engage in placement work and then systematically collect and analyze data on how reforms work in diverse local contexts. To achieve the promise of community colleges, we need a reimagining of literacy education.

References

Baker-Bell, A. (2020). *Linguistic justice: Black language, literacy, identity, and pedagogy*. Routledge.

Conference on College Composition and Communication. (2021). CCCC *position statement on the role of reading in college writing classrooms*. Conference on College Composition and Communication. https://cccc.ncte.org/cccc/the-role-of-reading.

Gilman, H., Giordano, J., Hancock, N., Hassel, H., Henson, L., Hern, K., Nastal, J., Toth, C. (2019). Two-year college writing placement as fairness. *Journal of Writing Assessment*, *12*(1). https://escholarship.org/uc/item/4zvor9b2.

Griffiths, B. (2022, March 9–12). *A just writing studies* [Conference presentation]. Conference on College Composition and Communication 2022 Conference, online.

Jensen, D. & Suh, E. (2020). Introducing lived interventions: Located agency and teacher-scholar-activism as responses to neoliberalism. *Basic Writing e-Journal*, *16*(1), 1-11. https://bwe.ccny.cuny.edu/Introduction%20Jensen%20and%20Suh.pdf.

Schreiber, B. R., Lee, E., Johnson, J. T. & Fahim, N. (Eds.). (2022). *Linguistic justice on campus: Pedagogy and advocacy for multilingual students.* Multilingual Matters.

Suh, E. & Jensen, D. (2020). Examining communities of practice: Transdisciplinarity, resilience, and professional identity. *Journal of Basic Writing, 39*(2), 33–59. https://doi.org/10.37514/JBW-J.2020.39.2.03.

Sullivan, P., Tinberg, H. & Blau, S. (Eds.). (2017). *Deep reading: Teaching reading in the writing classroom.* National Council of Teachers of English.

Tinto, V. (2008, June 9). Access without support is not opportunity. *Inside Higher Ed.* https://www.insidehighered.com/views/2008/06/09/access-without-support-not-opportunity.

Contributors

Sara Amani is Professor of Multilingual Composition (NTT) at Arizona Western College, where she serves as the multilingual specialist. Her doctoral thesis won ALANZ (Applied Linguistics Association of New Zealand) Best Doctoral Thesis Award. Her essays have been published by John Benjamins.

Ashlee Brand is Associate Professor of English & Women's Studies at Cuyahoga Community College (Tri-C), where she serves as the English & Women's Studies Coordinator for the Westshore Campus. She is a recipient of the Ralph M. Besse Award for Excellence in Teaching, the National Institute for Staff and Organizational Development (NISOD) Award for Teaching Excellence, and has been a community college faculty member for almost 20 years. She has presented at numerous conferences, including Ohio Association of Two-Year Colleges, the League of Innovation, and the Conference on College Composition and Communication (CCCC).

Lesley Broder is Associate Professor of English at Kingsborough Community College, in the City University of New York, where she coordinated the Accelerated Learning Program (ALP) until 2022. Her scholarship centers on popular New York City theater trends and has recently appeared in *Modern Drama* and *New Perspectives in Edward Albee Studies.*

Carolyn Calhoon-Dillahunt teaches English at Yakima Valley College. She has published in *College English, CCCC, New Directions for Community Colleges, WPA Journal,* and *Teaching English in the Two-Year College (TETYC)*, where her co-authored article with Dodie Forrest, "Conversing in Marginal Spaces: Developmental Writers' Responses to Teacher Comments," received the 2014 Mark Reynolds *TETYC* Best Article Award.

Denisse Cañez has been teaching Developmental Reading full-time at Cochise College since 2011, serving as adjunct faculty at Cochise College and University of Arizona before then.

Charissa Che is Assistant Professor of English at Queensborough Community College (City University of New York). Her writing has appeared in *Teaching English in the Two-Year College (TETYC)* and *Writing on the Edge (WOE)*, and she currently serves as the program chair of the 2022 Two-Year College Association (TYCA) National Conference and the Book Review Editor of *TETYC*. She was the recipient of the 2019 CCCC Chairs' Memorial Scholarship and the 2018 CCCC Scholars for the Dream Award.

Annie Del Principe is Professor of English at Kingsborough Community College, in the City University of New York, where she served as the writing program administrator until 2022. Her scholarship has appeared in *Teaching English in the Two-Year College (TETYC), WPA, Across the Disciplines,* and the *Journal of Basic Writing (JBW)* She received the 2011 Mark Reynolds Award for her article

"Variations in Assessment, Variations in Philosophy: Unintended Consequences of Heterogeneous Portfolios."

Jane Denison-Furness is Assistant Professor of English at Central Oregon Community College, where she also serves as Developmental Literacy Coordinator. She and Stacey Lee Donohue were awarded the 2021 Diana Hacker TYCA Outstanding Programs in English Award in Fostering Student Success for their work redesigning placement.

Stacey Lee Donohue is Professor of English at Central Oregon Community College, where she serves as Interim Chair of Humanities. She is the recipient of the Francis Andrew March Award for Service to the Humanities, from the Association of Departments of English (part of the Modern Language Association) in 2020, and the Carolyn DesJardin's Leadership Award, from the American Association of Women in Community Colleges, in 2018.

Jason C. Evans is Professor of Developmental Writing and English at Prairie State College in Chicago Heights, Illinois. His work has appeared in the Basic Writing e-journal (*BWe*), *Open Words*, and *Teaching English in the Two-Year College*, and his research examines the relationships between composition, racial identity, and social class in community college writing programs.

Jamey Gallagher is Associate Professor of English at the Community College of Baltimore County. His writing has appeared online in *Hybrid Pedagogy*, in the *Journal of College Reading and Learning*, *Teaching English in the Two-Year College*, and elsewhere.

Joanne Baird Giordano is Associate Professor of English, Linguistics, and Writing Studies at Salt Lake Community College. Her collaborative research focuses on placement, the experiences of two-year college literacy educators, and students' transitions to college reading and writing at open-access institutions. She is Associate Chair of the Two-Year College English Association.

Jessica Gravely is Associate Professor of English at Prairie State College, where she serves as departmental coordinator for the writing program sequence. Previously, she worked as a developmental editor and writer in the educational publishing industry.

Elizabeth Hart is Assistant Professor of English and teaches English and Academic Literacy at the Community College of Baltimore County. She also taught for the Goucher Prison Education Partnership. Her research interests include retention efforts to improve completion and the concept of "belonging" in higher education.

Annemarie Hamlin is Instructional Dean at Central Oregon Community College. She is a former faculty member and department chair of humanities.

Darin Jensen is Assistant Professor of English, Linguistics and Writing Studies at Salt Lake Community College. He is the editor of *Teaching English in the Two-Year College* and the Teacher-Scholar-Activist blog. His research focuses on two-year college professional issues, basic writing, and graduate preparation.

Kevin Kato is Professor of English (NTT) at Arizona Western College, where he teaches first-year writing courses. Kevin specializes in second language writing and writing program administration. His essays have been published by the Japan Association of Language Teaching (JALT).

Jeffrey Klausman is Senior Professor of English, Writing Program Administrator (WPA), and Writing Across the Curriculum (WAC) coordinator at Whatcom Community College. He has written numerous articles and book chapters on two-year college writing programs and was a lead author of the *TYCA White Paper on Placement Reform* and *TYCA White Paper on Developmental Education Reform*.

Bridget Kriner is Associate Professor of English & Women's Studies at Cuyahoga Community College (Tri-C). She was recently nominated for Teacher of the Year by Ohio Association of Community Colleges. She is currently serving as the Community College Caucus Chair at the National Women's Studies Association. Her scholarship has appeared in *Adult Learning* and *The International Journal of Teaching and Learning*; she published a book of poems, *Autoethnography*, through Guide to Kulchur-Green Panda Press.

Jessica M. Kubiak is Associate Professor of Reading and Composition at the State University of New York's Jamestown Community College, where she has served as program director and interim dean. A Ph.D. candidate in English at Old Dominion University, Kubiak won a 2020 SUNY Chancellor's Award for Excellence in Teaching and the 2021 Conference on College Composition and Communication's Outstanding Teaching Award.

Lauren Levesque is Director of Institutional Research at Kingsborough Community College, in the City University of New York.

Signee Lynch is Senior Professor of English at Whatcom Community College, where she has served several terms as English department chair. She collaborated with Jeffrey Klausman on the design and implementation of the Informed Self-Placement Program at Whatcom Community College, which was awarded the 2020 Diana Hacker TYCA Outstanding Program in English Award in the category of Fostering Student Success.

Travis Margoni teaches English at Yakima Valley College, where he coordinates writing across the curriculum initiatives and serves as an instructional coach for faculty at Hispanic-Serving Institutions. He has co-authored *Sensing, Moving, Thinking, and Writing: Embodied Practices for College Writers* and served as the Two-Year College English Association of the Pacific Northwest (TYCA-PNW) regional contributor for *TETYC*.

Kris Messer is Assistant Professor of English at the Community College of Baltimore County (CCBC), where she co-coordinates service-learning and leads CCBC's self-directed placement efforts. She has published on community-based pedagogy and political performance. She serves on the Editorial Board of *Teaching English in the Two-Year College*.

Ella Melito is Department Chair for English and Reading at Cochise College. She is also a co-creator of the college's English directed self-placement.

Jessica Nastal is Interim Dean for Learning Resources and Assessment and Associate Professor of English at Prairie State College (PSC), where she has led assessment justice efforts since 2015. She is the first woman in her family to have earned a bachelor's degree. Jessica launched the PSC Learning Environment Faculty Award in 2022. Her undergraduate students' work has appeared in *Composition Studies* and *Queen City Writers*.

Mya Poe is Associate Professor of English at Northeastern University. Her research focuses on writing assessment and writing development, with particular attention to justice and fairness. Her books include *Learning to Communicate in Science and Engineering, Race and Writing Assessment,* and *Writing Assessment, Social Justice, and the Advancement of Opportunity*.

Tony Russell is Instructional Dean at Central Oregon Community College. Formerly, he was an Associate Professor and Chair of Humanities. He currently serves as a two-year college representative on the executive committee of the Association of Departments of English.

Cathy Sander Matthesen is a Developmental Reading Instructor at Cochise College. She is also a co-creator of the college's reading directed self-placement and a doctoral candidate at Arizona State University.

Sarah Elizabeth Snyder is Professor of English (NTT) at Arizona Western College, where she serves as the writing program administrator and Writing Across the Curriculum/Writing in the Disciplines (WAC/WID) coordinator. Her essays have appeared in *WPA: Writing Program Administration* and various edited collections.

Christie Toth is Associate Professor in the Department of Writing and Rhetoric Studies at the University of Utah. In collaboration with colleagues at Salt Lake Community College, she coordinates her department's initiatives to support transfer student writers. She has been involved in writing placement reform at community colleges since 2010.

Erin Whittig is Assistant Director for Placement and Assessment in the University of Arizona Foundations Writing Program. She's written about international student placement for *TESOL Quarterly* and directed self-placement in the context of dual enrollment for *The Journal of Writing Assessment*.

www.ingramcontent.com/pod-product-compliance
Lightning Source LLC
Chambersburg PA
CBHW020519080526
44583CB00013B/656